Agrippina Tragödi:

Die Belagerung zu Antwerpen.
Marbach.

Die Polizey ein Schauspiel.

1803. ~~Die feindlichen Brüder zu Messina.
Tragödie.~~

Themistocles. Tragödi:

Gräfinn von Flandern. Schauspiel.

1804. Wilhelm Tell. Tragödie.

Gräfin v. P. Geran.

Die Kindsmord. Schauspiel.

Blutshochzeit zu Moskau.

Das Schiff.

Schiller's Drama

*Talent and
Integrity*

Schiller's Drama

Talent and Integrity

Ilse Graham

BOOKS
10 East 53d St., New York 10022
(a division of Harper & Row Publishers. Inc.)

Published in the U.S.A. 1974 by
HARPER & ROW PUBLISHERS, INC.
BARNES & NOBLE IMPORT DIVISION
© *1974 by Ilse Graham*
Printed in Great Britain
by W & J Mackay Limited, Chatham

ISBN 06 492510 2

Endpapers: Schiller's work plan

in memory of
Inna Arian Baykov
11 October 1913 - 11 August 1970

—————————⊰⟪⟫⊱—————————

Auch ein Klaglied zu sein im Mund der Geliebten, ist herrlich,
Denn das Gemeine geht klanglos zum Orkus hinab.

Siehe, voll Hoffnung vertraust du der Erde den göttlichen Samen
Und erwartest im Lenz fröhlich die keimende Saat.
Nur in die Furche der Zeit bedenkst du dich Taten zu streuen,
Die, von der Weisheit gesät, still für die Ewigkeit blühn?

(*Schiller*)

L'homme n'est rien d'autre que ce qu'il se fait.

(*Sartre*)

Der große Dichter ist aber ein großer Realist, sehr nahe
allen Wirklichkeiten—er belädt sich mit Wirklichkeiten. . . .
Er wird das Esoterische und Seraphische ungeheuer
vorsichtig auf harte realistische Grundlagen verteilen.

(*G. Benn*)

But what will it be . . . when the springs of our nature
will not be thinner and cooler, but warmer and more copious
than they now are, yet running without reluctance in the
channels our mind opens to them?

(*A. Farrer*)

The whole man must move at once.

(*Addison*)

Contents

Author's Note

The following pages contain readings of Schiller's dramas one by one as well as some chapters on special issues raised by the plays as a whole. I have decided not to arrange them in chronological order but rather to group them in such a fashion that the most characteristic aspects of Schiller's work — those thematic, artistic and aesthetic idiosyncrasies which constitute the poet's signature — stand out clearly and distinctly. In my approach to any given play I have endeavoured to concentrate on the feature, or features, that I consider central to it. At the same time I have not hesitated to adopt a specific slant when this promised to shed light upon any abiding characteristic of Schiller's art. Such an integrative approach has its dangers. It involves selectivity in one place and repetition in another. These shortcomings are, I think, unavoidable. They are the price the critic with a unifying conception must be prepared to pay for not being a poet. I do not regret them. Emphasis where it is due provides an illuminating framework for the reader's perception. And as for those facets of a given play I was forced to neglect in the chapter devoted to it, I have endeavoured to develop them in other sections, some of which range widely over Schiller's dramatic and theoretical writings, and have frequently followed them up in notes. Thus I hope that I have succeeded in giving a reasonably rounded picture of each single play and of Schiller's entire dramatic *opus*, viewed in the context of his theory.

Full account has been taken of the work of fellow scholars, past and present. I have sought to indicate my debt to them and to define my position in regard to them. Here again, the prohibitive flood of material which has

accumulated over the hundred and sixty-five years or so since the poet's
death has required selection. I have preferred to conduct most of the 'conversation' with my colleagues in the notes at the end of this book. Critical
controversy has a way of intruding between the reader and the work of
art; and to let this great body of dramatic poetry speak to my readers as
directly and forcefully as possible has been the most cherished aim of this
study.

References to and quotations from Schiller's works are based on the text
of the Säkular-Ausgabe, abbreviated as *SA*. Writings which are not included in that edition are cited according to the Bibliographisches Institut,
abbreviated *BI*. Goethe's works are referred to according to the
Artemis Gedenkausgabe, abbreviated as *AGA*. Those that do not
appear there are referred to according to the Weimar Ausgabe, abbreviated *WA*.

Letters to and from Goethe are cited according to *Der Briefwechsel
zwischen Schiller und Goethe*, ed. E. Staiger (Frankfurt, 1966).

Where there are several monographs on Schiller by the same author,
they are identified by numbers: Benno v. Wiese, *Die Dramen Schillers.
Politik und Tragödie* (Leipzig, 1957) = v. Wiese, I.

Benno v. Wiese, *Schiller* (Stuttgart, 1959–63) = v. Wiese, II.

Benno v. Wiese, *Die Deutsche Tragödie von Lessing bis Hebbel* (Hamburg,
1948) = v. Wiese, III.

H. B. Garland, *Schiller* (London, 1949) = Garland, I.

H. B. Garland, *Schiller The Dramatic Writer. A Study of Style in the
Plays* (Oxford, 1969) = Garland, II.

Other abbreviations are:

Schillers Werke: Nationalausgabe	= *NA*
Der Deutschunterricht	= *DDu*
Dichtung und Volkstum	= *DuV*
Études Germaniques	= *EG*
German Life and Letters	= *GLL*
German Quarterly	= *GQ*
Jahrbuch der Deutschen Goethegesellschaft	= *JbdDGG*
Jahrbuch der Deutschen Schillergesellschaft	= *JbdDSG*
Jahrbuch des Freien Deutschen Hochstifts	= *JFDH*
Modern Language Review	= *MLR*
Modern Quarterly	= *MQ*
Proceedings of the English Goethe Society	= *PEGS*

Acknowledgements

I am grateful for permission to use material in this book which has been previously published in the following journals:

> *Proceedings of the English Goethe Society* (Chapter 2)
> *Deutsche Beiträge zur Geistigen Überlieferung* (Chapter 3)
> *German Life and Letters* (Chapter 5)
> *Modern Language Review* (Chapter 10).

My indebtedness to fellow critics, past and present, is too manifold to permit of adequate let alone exhaustive acknowledgement. Special thanks are due to the inspired work of Thomas Mann, Max Kommerell and Oskar Seidlin; and to E. M. Wilkinson and L. A. Willoughby for their commentated edition of Schiller's *Ästhetische Briefe*.

For the rest, my gratitude goes out to Ann Shotts, who transformed a smudgy manuscript and blurred tapes into immaculate type, and, most of all, to my friend Mary E. Gilbert, who gave me all the time and energy I needed to claim from her.

Introduction

It has often been said, and with much justification, that the distinctive mark of Schiller's genius is the vigour of his moral drive. He was moral from tip to toe, and there was no area of experience he did not as a matter of course approach, explore and assess in this all-encompassing context.

It has also been said, with equal justification though less often, that Schiller was an out-and-out artist and that, as he grew older, he practised art for art's sake in ever increasing measure. The lavish poetic output of his maturity and the unremitting stream of reflection on artistic problems which accompanied his creative work leave no doubt of the fact that here was an artist as hard pressed by visions and forms as any we might choose to think of.

In my opinion it still needs saying that Schiller's uniqueness lay in the coalescence of his moral and his artistic drives in a rare combination of talent and integrity shared, in German letters, only by Lessing and Goethe.

Schiller was a denizen of two worlds. Temperamentally and by cultural heritage, he was a dualist – his affinity to the spirit of the baroque has often enough been stressed. He passionately aspired to spiritual values and was ready to exercise an unbending rule over his sensual and physical nature in order to be loyal to their exacting demands. Perhaps his history of illness is a legacy of this ascetic streak – Goethe was not just being naïve when he remarked, in conversation with Eckermann, that the Categorical Imperative had killed him.

But he was also a born artist. And as an artist new depths of experience became available to him: the awareness of the indivisible oneness of body and soul, of mind and matter, in the creative act. When an artist is impressing the clay in his hands with the power of his vision and that vision, in turn, is spelt out to him by the feel and touch of his clay; when a poet patterns words to express his mind's intent and that intent, in turn, is modified, magnified and transformed by the life residing in the words themselves, their 'sound-shape' and their associations; when a dancer informs his body of the theme it is to convey, and the muscles of his body and the very space into which he projects it tell him what it is he is expressing: then the dichotomy between the mental and the material poles of awareness, between psyche and soma, ceases to exist and an underlying oneness is revealed.

This is what happened to Schiller as it is bound to happen to any true artist. It must have been the happiest moment of his life when he could write from innermost conviction, as he did in the *Ästhetische Briefe*:

> Da nun aber bei dem Genuß der Schönheit oder der ästhetischen Einheit eine wirkliche Vereinigung und Auswechselung der Materie mit der Form und des Leidens mit der Tätigkeit vor sich geht, so ist eben dadurch die *Vereinbarkeit* beider Naturen, die Ausführbarkeit des Unendlichen in der Endlichkeit, mithin die Möglichkeit der erhabensten Menschheit bewiesen.

Here is the confluence of the two main streams, the point of intersection between the two overriding themes of Schiller's life. The question posed by his moral self – the relation and reconciliation of our two natures – found its desired answer in his experience as an artist. Through the offices of art, the divided self is capable of being united, and in its unison testifies to the possibility of the sublimest humanity, to our joint moral and aesthetic perfection.

It is impossible to exaggerate what the discovery of the central moral significance of art and art-making must have meant to a man of Schiller's make-up. So powerful was his drive to create spiritual values and to achieve the ideal in reality that he could never have given all of himself to an activity, had he felt it to be unrelated or even only peripherally connected with his besetting aim. He would, at best, have been an artist with a bad conscience, and the way he was made, a bad conscience would have crippled his creativity. As it was, he found out that what he had to do was what he ought to do. His artistic passion received the full and solemn sanction of his moral self. This is the absolutely central event of his life, a process no doubt in time, begun when poetry first began to take shape in his hands and culminating in his alliance with Goethe. It is to this inner event that we owe the unimpeded outpouring of poetry, especially after he had consolidated his position *vis-à-vis* art during the years he devoted to the study of Kant. An outpouring overwhelming both in its actual quantity and in the quality of its engagement, and at the same time quite uncompulsive and serene. However passionately engrossed in creation, he was at all times free to *perceive* what he was doing and how he was doing it, to reflect with the best powers of his mind on the processes and products of his artistic imagination.

It is this characteristic interplay between creation and reflection, between intuition and critical intelligence, which is the ultimate token of his all-out engagement with art. The whole man was liberated to respond to its challenge. And it is surely no accident that Schiller, who has so often been regarded as a born preacher or man of action who missed his true vocation, should so serenely have claimed the title of a 'maker' in his capacity as – a poet. His poetic dreaming *was* a doing; and he had no need to cast guilty and nostalgic glances in the direction of 'real' life, as did Kleist and Hofmannsthal after him.

II

But to stress the wholeheartedness of his engagement with art is to tell only one half of the story. The liberating discovery that to make art is to do the morally right thing resulted not only in the impassioned pursuit of poetry, and in the fullest opening of the sluice-gates of his creativeness. It led to the assimilation, by the whole man, of the insights gained from his artistic activity. Schiller did not permit that knowledge of psycho-physical oneness which had come to him through the creative act to remain a compartmental insight, any more than he suffered his art to remain a compartmental activity. As art took possession of its man, so the man took possession of his art and all it had to teach him. He let the experience of oneness it afforded him pervade his whole being. He assimilated it on every level, emotionally, intellectually, morally and metaphysically.

Thus gradually the dualist came to experience life as an indivisible whole and this experience, in turn, enabled his poetic genius to explore new avenues and to flourish more profusely. As he matured, he felt his way towards a monistic view of the world, in which the spiritual and the

material, the inner and the outer were recognized to be adequate equiva-
lents of one another. It is such a universe of discourse that poetry most
requires. For only a world thus sacramentally envisaged will yield public
and objective symbols for inner experience.

Schiller was the last great German dramatist to succeed in fashioning
for himself out of the shambles of our crumbling spiritual heritage a
world view that is germane to poetry in that it offered adequate objective
correlatives to inner imports. This might seem a strange statement, more
appropriate to Goethe and to the natural affinity between subject and object, between self and world we associate with the latter. Yet it is true of
Schiller too. What in Goethe was an inborn endowment of incredible
felicity, in Schiller was the result of an interaction of talent and integrity
sprung from deepest moral conviction. He discovered through art that life
is one and whole. He used this discovery, and conceived a poetic world, a
multiplicity of worlds, indeed, in which the outer answers to the inner, the
movement of objective events to the inner movements of the spirit. He
envisaged the historical world of *Fiesco*, *Wallenstein* and *Demetrius* in
which Nemesis reigns supreme, the contemporary world of *Kabale und
Liebe* in which character and class are insolubly intertwined, the legen-
dary and mythical world of *Die Jungfrau von Orleans*, *Die Braut von
Messina* or *Wilhelm Tell* where claps of thunder betoken inner failure,
tempests defeat the wicked, and character is revealed through fate, the
religious world of *Maria Stuart* in which the outward and the visible are
the sacramental signs of the inward and the spiritual: worlds, all of these,
in which psychological laws and the laws of physical nature mysteriously
coincide, and all of them worlds teeming with possibilities of new dramatic forms clamouring to be explored. Most of all, the discovery of a unitary
view of life empowered him to forge his principal dramatic tool, the technique of externalizing, and objectivating, the buried aspect of one person
in the dominant aspect of his antagonist, and thereby to achieve that perfect dynamic balance between dissociative and integrative drives which is
the mark of the man and the dramatist alike.

In this willing feedback from art to life and from life back to art, in this
capacity, hard-won and cultivated as the tiller cultivates his soil, to see
things steady and to see them whole, lies the secret of his sanity, of an un-
swervingness of aim which always remained coupled with flexibility and,
last but not least, the grandiose simplicity of his 'große Stil'. Let no one
think that *Die Glocke* and *Wilhelm Tell* are the naïve products of an optimistic idealist who dealt in outworn popular clichés. This popularity, this

simplicity are the crowning achievements of a man acquainted with all the dangers of fragmentation and alienation, who, made whole by the healing power of art, emerged at the far end of complexity and learnt to speak clearly, objectively and publicly of ultimate human concerns.

III

The four most influential recent studies of Schiller – a seminal article by Gerhard Fricke, and the impressive monographs by Benno von Wiese, Gerhard Storz and Emil Staiger – begin from different starting-points and arrive at conclusions which are in many respects diametrically opposed to one another. From their various angles, all illuminate different, and important, facets of the man and the poet. But all unintentionally concur in lending support to the image of a man committed to nothing objective outside his gigantic self. Fricke, by his emphasis on the idealist who could at all times evade the real by seeking refuge in the unassailable autonomy of the spirit; Storz, by stressing Schiller's increasing tendency towards adopting the stance of *l'art pour l'art*, in which the message became an ever more interchangeable counter in the search for ever purer forms; von Wiese, by suggesting that the later poet arrogated to poetry the cultic function of religion and to himself that of saviour; and Staiger, finally, by arguing that Schiller was a demagogic virtuoso whose aim lay in manipulating his readers so as to project on to them an image of his own Promethean self.

Such modern readings – and they are the most fascinating by far – have their roots in the nineteenth century; in the view of the poet propagated by the brothers Schlegel, by Jean Paul, by Ludwig Tieck and by Otto Ludwig, all of whom harped tirelessly on Schiller's reflective subjectivism and lack of 'world'. Ultimately, it must be said, this view derives from Humboldt and Goethe, with their stress on Schiller's excess of mental activity and that high-handed fashion of dealing with objective reality which the older Goethe never ceased to regret.

This is unfortunate; and it is just possible that Schiller's best friends, the two last named, became his worst enemies in that they saddled him with that label of wilful subjectivism which has stuck to him ever since and which has become most damaging in the hands of those who mentally measure him against the yardstick of his great and so very different friend. The man and the poet, in those recent accounts – and in none more so than Staiger's – have become tainted with a tinge of demoniacal irresponsibility accountable to nothing beyond its own will to unbounded freedom and to unalloyed form. He has come to appear as a footloose if majestic stranger in our homely world. An existentialist in that, thrown into 'die Fremde des Lebens', he arbitrarily posits his very self and his very character and decrees what its value shall be.

Schiller *was* an existentialist, but of a different order. An existentialist in that he never evaded the grave reality of life and of action in the stream of time, and accepted the consequences of action as the final arbiters of their author's true intent; an existentialist, moreover, in that he humbly acknowledged the fact that the nature of nobility is founded in some ultimate and inexplicable nobility of nature. Some have it, others don't. To this poet, a man is what he is; and what he is, he does: a hard knowledge which stamps every figure and every fate in his dramatic world.

To demonstrate this human substance, this objectivating power, and this remorseless commitment to the real is the aim of this book. Such greatness was vouchsafed to Schiller by the transcending grace of his life; the courageous interlacing of artistic and moral concern, of talent and integrity in the pursuit of an ideal first sighted by the poet – the renewed wholeness of humanity.

1
Possibility

. . . der Mensch soll mit der Schönheit *nur spielen*, und er soll *nur mit der Schönheit* spielen.

(*Ästhetische Briefe*)

1

Die Verschwörung des Fiesco : a time for playing

———————⟐⟐⟐———————

I

Schiller's *Fiesco* has commonly been criticized on the ground that the main action is cluttered up, to the point of confusion, by a mass of theatrically effective but dramatically unnecessary incidents.[1] And indeed, if *Fiesco* is taken to be a political play, as it virtually always is, there would seem to be a surplus of incident beyond that required for the management of the plot. The bewildering complexity of the first act, with its masked ball, its criss-cross of intrigues and, most of all, the elusive role played by the central figure in all this confusion, has often been commented upon. It may be argued that most, if not all, of this maze of incidents is necessary for the purposes of exposition: it is part of Fiesco's political genius to mask his conspiratorial schemes from both camps alike, the Republicans as well as the tyrants, so as not to endanger them. But neither the elaborate pretence enacted in front of Verrina's tableau, nor indeed the theatrical staging of the conspiracy itself in Act IV, can be similarly explained. The latter in particular seems to run counter to the direction of the plot. The cluster of incidents necessitated by it seems dramatically redundant.[2] Most striking among these is the confusion among the nobles who had been invited to Fiesco's entertainment and now uncertainly await admission. The purpose of this retarding incident, which takes up the six opening scenes of Act IV, is difficult to see. The plot at this point requires the dénouement of the action, not further procrastination. Again, the treachery of the Moor would seem dramatically significant if it either served to foil Fiesco's conspiracy or else showed him retrieving the situation, thus demonstrating his powers of leadership. In fact, it does neither. It no more leaves a proper impress on the plot than do the extraordinary actions of Fiesco to which it gives rise. Fiesco's reassurance of the frightened Republicans is offset by his resolve to give up the conspiracy and by his liberation of the traitor. On the other hand, this liberation and the additional information the traitor discloses to the departing messenger of the Duke are nullified by the barrenness of their effect upon the further course of the action. True, Fiesco seems to follow up the trend begun in the fourth act by the warning he gives to his opponent in the opening scene of the fifth act, in the midst of the conspiracy: but like the events leading up to it, this crowning incident, whilst running counter to the overall direction of the plot, at the same time fails to modify it: Andreas does not heed the warning extended to him and all continues as before. Here is perhaps the most blatantly redundant incident of all. There is no doubt that, were Fiesco's quixotic warning to the Duke to be cut out of the plot, we should feel a sense of loss. But it would be difficult to defend this intuition. It is scarcely sufficient to insist that this and the other inconsequential acts are 'somehow' in keeping with Fiesco's character. For if they did fit into the customary picture we have of him, we should not call them redundant; we should prefer to describe the surplus of activity in terms which would show it to be not an accident, but an essential quality inherent in Fiesco's make-up.

Is there such a way of defining this disturbing but distinctive quality? To answer this question, an examination of the situations in which Fiesco displays it is necessary.

Seen from the point of view of Julia, each one of her three encounters with Fiesco bears a more urgent, a more passionate character than its predecessor. She starts by calling him her slave (I. iv) and ends up by confessing herself to be his. (IV. xii) By contrast with this movement, the unchanging character of Fiesco's own response is all the more striking.[3] And as we watch him statically sustaining the note of passion he had struck at the beginning, we begin to doubt its spontaneity. Eventually Fiesco himself tells us that he has been playing throughout. The sententiousness of his words in the first encounter and the exaggerated aptness of his gestures at once draw the reproof from Julia that he is performing a 'Schauspiel' (I. iv); and the impression that he is performing a deliberate 'act' is strengthened by all that ensues. The silhouette, at first demanded from Julia with every show of passion, is duly returned to her at the end and contemptuously called a 'Theaterschmuck'. Julia's sardonic request that Fiesco's wife be called to the scene, far from being forgotten as a casual remark would be, is literally fulfilled by Fiesco. Leonore is made to watch the final humiliation of her rival behind the scenes of the concert hall, an arrangement of which the reader is aware, and which serves to heighten the sense of the theatrical. Julia's hair-style, the topic of an amorous conversation in her rooms, is once more pointedly alluded to as she is being led to prison. Not a thread that is not gathered in, not a reaction that is not to the point in the extreme – as when Fiesco describes the spectacle he has prepared for Julia as being 'zum Totlachen' (III. xi) or as when, taking his cue from Julia's 'wenn du mich kalt würgtest, Fiesco?' (IV. xii), he plays on the word until he has found a pretext for ending an embarrassing scene. Thus, there is every indication of a conscious pattern both in what he does and what he says – he calls his amorous affair a *Roman* as early as II. iv and again in IV. xiii and a *Komödie* (IV. x). And it is the pattern itself, not Julia, that commands his passionate interest.[4]

II

The possibility begins to suggest itself that the superfluity of Fiesco's actions here and his playful detachment may perhaps both have to be included as an essential part of his character.[5] At a first glance, we do find Fiesco persisting in the same playful response in a variety of widely different situations, just as he was found to maintain the same response in the face of Julia's rapidly changing reactions. In the first act, he plays with Gianettino's vanity, with Verrina's earnestness and Bourgognino's indignation as he plays with Julia's sensuality; in the second, with the outraged aristocrats, the seething crowds in the street and the artisans in his palace, with his fellow Republicans, and finally always with the Moor, who alone responds to his mood and plays back.

With his henchman Fiesco is under no constraint to pretend: with him he is perfectly candid. In this figure and in this relationship, conceived in full freedom from historical sources, lay Schiller's opportunity to reveal, from the beginning, the 'real' Fiesco behind his mask: and he used it to show us a Fiesco delighting in play! In this connection the scene between Julia and Leonore, so frequently singled out for attack on the ground of its redundance, assumes an unsuspected significance; for the topic of conversation in this scene, totally independent as it is of Fiesco and his plots and plans, is none other than genuinely felt love versus love playfully handled as an art. A coincidence indeed, if this tragedy is not concerned

with the problem of playfulness except temporarily and incidentally on its
upper levels.

Thus a certain amount of evidence, and evidence of different kinds,
would seem to point in the direction of the hypothesis we are examining.
Yet as long as there remain two motives for Fiesco's behaviour it is impossible to discover with certainty which of them is the determining one.
It is only when the external constraint to pretend is obviated, and re-
placed by an opposing necessity for straightforward action, that it is possible to know unambiguously whether Fiesco's playfulness is more than a
passing accident of his behaviour: whether in fact it is its underlying
cause. What then is the nature of his actions once his pretence is shed, his
purpose declared and his course set? If Fiesco were the man of action he is
commonly deemed to be,[6] his actions now would be practical, purposive
and pressing in the measure in which they lacked these qualities before.

But what, in the light of such expectations, are we to make of Fiesco's
monologue at the opening of Act III? This monologue inaugurates the
active phase of his political career. Here, the full range of Fiesco's aims and
ambitions is disclosed, with the frankness of which soliloquy permits and
in the final form in which they will henceforth govern his actions. Is it not
paradoxical that Schiller should have prescribed in the stage directions that
these revelations be accompanied 'mit erhabenem Spiel'? Again, what are
we to make of Fiesco's sudden dropping of his avowed purpose when, on
receiving the message from Andreas, he unconditionally discharges the
Moor who has just proved the danger he represents to Fiesco's cause by
betraying the conspiracy to the tyrant? And of the warning which Fiesco
himself, at the crucial moment of the battle, extends to Andreas, whom
he had previously recognized to be the real head of the opposition? A clue
to the nature of these actions may be found in the reactions of others. Concerning the first incident, Verrina exclaims: 'Bist du wahnsinnig, Mensch?
War es denn irgend ein Bubenstreich, den wir vorhatten? . . . Oder
war's nicht Sache des Vaterlands?' (IV. ix). Similarly, Calcagno comments
on the release of the Moor: 'Was? was? Leben soll der Heide, leben und
uns alle verraten haben?' (IV. ix) whilst Andreas retorts, laughing, as did
also the departing Moor, 'Du bist bei Laune, Freund! Bring' deine
Schwänke bei Tag. Mitternacht ist eine ungewöhnliche Stunde.' (V. i.)
The incredulousness of each one of the speakers is the measure of the utter
lack of purpose which friend and foe alike discern in Fiesco's actions. But
their consent about the nature of these actions goes further. A *Bubenstreich*
Verrina calls Fiesco's plan, and Andreas uses words evoking similar associa-

tions: *Laune, Schwänke*; and both he and the Moor are moved to laughter. Are not these sufficient indications that Fiesco is here playing, playing at rebellion, as Verrina hints, and playing at chivalry, as he had before played at plotting and pretending?

Thus playfulness remains dominant in a situation in which every motive for such a response has been removed and the strongest motives for an opposite mode of response are at hand. Does Schiller, by means of indirect characterization, support and throw further light on this trait which is so powerfully suggested by the plot?

When, at the opening ball, Fiesco recognizes Verrina in one of the three black masks that seek him out, the latter observes: 'Fiesco findet seine Freunde geschwinder in ihren Masken, als sie ihn in der seinigen.' (I. vii.) This might seem to mean no more than that Fiesco disguises his real intentions more cunningly and thoroughly than the Republicans. But the interesting thing is that Fiesco is not actually wearing a mask, whilst the Republicans are. Thus, with regard to Fiesco, Verrina uses the word mask in a purely metaphorical sense, to draw attention to a trait of his character. And this more intimate association of the mask with Fiesco's person is underlined by the comparison with himself, to whom the mask is a physical, and in that sense extraneous property. Fiesco's mask of playfulness then, he seems to suggest, is of an altogether different kind from his own; not an accessory to be used or discarded but something more closely connected with his real nature: for with him, mask and real face are one and the same.[7]

A variety of comments reveals a Fiesco playing with other human beings, even as he plays with life and fortune. When asked to invite certain nobles 'zu einer Komödie auf die Nacht', which is to see the rebellion, the Moor comments adroitly: 'Mitzuspielen vermutlich' (III. vi). And one of these nobles, waiting for Fiesco to receive his guests, remarks: 'Mich deucht, es [das Lustspiel] fing schon an, und wir spielten die Narren drin.' (IV. iv.) When Fiesco discloses his project to his wife, Leonore likens it to a *Spiel*; she tries to shake his confidence by reminding him of the dangers, saying: 'Sagst du das – und standest bei jenem geisterverzerrenden Spiele – ihr nennt es Zeitvertreib, sahst zu, der Betrügerin, wie sie ihren Günstling mit kleinen Glückskarten lockte, bis er warm ward, aufstand, die Bank foderte – und ihn itzt im Wurf der Verzweiflung verließ – ' (IV. xiv). The same image is once more taken up in Verrina's judgement of Fiesco, shortly before he sends him to his death: 'der verschlagene Spieler hat's nur in einer Karte versehen', he says to Fiesco. 'Er kalkulierte das ganze Spiel des *Neides*, aber der raffinierte Witzling ließ zum Unglück die *Patrioten* aus.' (V. xvi.)[8] These last two views assume a special significance; for not only does Schiller assign them to the two characters most intimately acquainted with Fiesco; they are also stated well after the turning-point in Fiesco's career when his true intentions are known to both Leonore and Verrina: yet the metaphors of playing persist. And though in some instances *Spiel* means gambling rather than playing, and *Kunst* means intrigue or artificiality rather than art, the salient point is surely that the poet *does* use the identical words, delineating the variants of *one* overall attitude to life and thus builds up an image pattern which consistently points in one and the same direction. Julia uses words reminiscent of Verrina, again after the supposed turning-point: 'Über den verschlagenen Kopf! Wie künstlich er's anlegte, mich in seinen Willen hineinzulügen!' (III. x), just as earlier on she had said 'Schön! Schön! Sehenswürdig! Rufte doch jemand die Gräfin von Lavagna zu diesem reizenden Schauspiel!' (I. iv.) Julia's words add a new facet to his characterization: she sees playfulness as being connected with art. And this association gains in importance as it is corroborated independently by other characters. Verrina calls Fiesco 'ein Anbeter der Kunst', who 'erhitzt sich gern an erhabenen Szenen'; and indeed he bases his plan to test Fiesco on this very trait (I. xiii). In the eyes of his wife, Fiesco is more than 'art-ful', more even than a lover of art. When Leonore calls him a 'blühender Apoll' (I. i), a yet closer connection is hinted at, and this is borne out later in the same scene, when she says of him: '*Mein* Genuas größten Mann! . . . der vollendet sprang aus dem Meißel der unerschöpflichen Künstlerin, alle Größen seines Geschlechts im lieblichsten Schmelze verband . . .' She sees in him a perfect work of art sprung from the chisel of the divine artist: a common enough metaphor in the heyday of Shaftesbury's influence, and frequently recurring in the work of the young Schiller,[9] it is true, but not without special import here. This is brought out by a very revealing simile. Recalling the scene between Fiesco and the Countess which she had witnessed, Leonore describes 'die starre, tiefe Betäubung, worein er, gleich dem *gemalten Entzücken*, versunken saß, als wär' um ihn her die Welt weggeblasen und er *allein mit dieser Julia* im ewigen Leeren' (I. i). Fiesco's transport – the 'heißen Wallungen seines Herzens', as a critic has called it – in truth is an artistic transport, a 'gemaltes Entzücken'. No doubt Fiesco has a design on the Countess: but in the act of carrying it out, passion – not for the woman, but for the design itself – overtakes him; it becomes its own end. The designer, interweaving himself in the human pattern he is creating, himself becomes part of the design and all purposes that point beyond it lapse into abeyance: 'als wär' um ihn her die Welt weggeblasen und er *allein mit dieser Julia im ewigen Leeren*'. Leonore, through her simile, tells the reader more than she herself consciously knows; for she believes Fiesco to be passionately in love with Julia. But that she is here the mouthpiece of the poet is evident from the fact that her description is independently borne out, on the dramatic level, by Fiesco's behaviour with the Countess, which has already been discussed.

This description illuminates other incidents as well, which convey the impression at once of aimlessness and yet purposiveness, of playfulness and yet absorption, of coldness and yet of passion. We need only think of the scene in which the *Malerei*, here alluded to in a purely metaphorical sense, is introduced into the actual plot; or of the nocturnal warning of Andreas. Thus a variety of widely different characters, placed in widely different relationships with Fiesco, all concur in attributing to Fiesco a set of characteristics ranging from gambling via 'art-fulness' and love of art to pure 'playfulness': and these characteristics, notwithstanding their difference, are bound together by the recurrent use of the words *Spiel* and *Kunst*.

Does what Fiesco says of himself, by its matter and style, bear out this indirect characterization?

Perhaps the most immediately striking statements from Fiesco's own lips are those he makes when the Republicans come to him to test his true intentions. On being introduced to the painter Romano, Fiesco greets him with the words: 'Ihre Hand, Romano. Ihre Meisterin ist eine Verwandte meines Hauses. Ich liebe sie brüderlich. *Kunst ist die rechte Hand der Natur*. Diese hat nur *Geschöpfe*, jene hat *Menschen* gemacht.' (II. xvii.) And he welcomes the painter's offer to show his latest work, saying: 'Ich bin heute ganz ungewöhnlich heiter, mein ganzes Wesen feiert eine gewisse heroische Ruhe, ganz offen für die schöne Natur.' (II. xvii.) What manner of state is this, in which the whole person relaxes, freed from all constraints, and responds with a receptivity which is at the same time active, 'heroisch' – what state is this but the aesthetic state as Schiller was to define it later, in the letters *Über die ästhetische Erziehung des Menschen?*[10] And indeed, Fiesco's greeting to the painter, with its proud dictum that art alone makes men, adumbrates the crucial challenge of the letters on aesthetic education: 'Der Mensch spielt nur, wo er in voller Bedeutung des Worts Mensch ist, und *er ist nur da ganz Mensch, wo er spielt.*' These then are weighty words on the lips of any Schillerian hero; and the present context contains nothing to gainsay the fact that they are a sincere expression of Fiesco's personality and convictions.

Another important piece of self-characterization we actually hear from Leonore: 'Ich hörte dich wohl einst schwören, meine Schönheit habe alle deine Entwürfe gestürzt' – she reminds him as he is about to head the rebellion (IV. xiv). In the light of the earlier statements about himself, the word 'Schönheit' claims our attention. Yet, as she herself realizes in the following words, this assessment of his own motives is not quite correct: for her beauty cannot now keep him from pursuing his ambitious plans. What is it, then, that does in fact induce Fiesco to overthrow his projects? On receiving Andreas's letter, Fiesco exclaims, 'in heftiger Bewegung': 'Bei Gott! Auf die ganze Kriegsmacht der Republik – auf das war ich nicht gefaßt. Der alte schwächliche Mann schlägt mit vier Zeilen dritthalbtausend Mann. (Läßt kraftlos die Hände sinken.) Doria schlägt den Fiesco.' (IV. ix.) Four lines on a scrap of paper versus an army of men: this suggests the victory of a light and spiritual thing – or is it a thing at all? – over something heavy and material; and the epithet 'schwächlich' adds the suggestion of frailness. The qualities suggested by Fiesco's words are reinforced by the content of the letter. It reflects not merely a good deed, but a good deed done lightly, naturally, with effortless grace – a deed such as that of the Samaritan, which Schiller was later to describe as the prototype of the beautiful deed, and which is superior to the 'merely' dutiful or good deed in virtue of just this quality of grace.[11] Is it too much to suggest that the lightness here alluded to, which by its very lightness rises superior to a thing both weighty and good, should be the lightness induced by form?[12] Having read Andreas's letter, Fiesco resolves (and the stage direction reads 'mit Adel'): 'Ein Doria soll mich an Großmut besiegt haben? *Eine* Tugend fehlte im Stamm der Fiesker? – Nein! So wahr ich ich selber bin . . . Ich werde hingehen – und alles bekennen.' (IV. ix.) In discussions of Fiesco's character, much has been made of his magnanimity, which has been regarded as the chief impulse running counter to and foiling his ambition. But such an interpretation fails to account for the second question Fiesco asks here, which adds an important qualification to the first one. It is not so much the thought of magnanimity, as the thought of any quality whatsoever missing from his make-up, which prompts Fiesco's decision to throw up his project. Is not this ideal of the fully developed personality, affirmed by the words 'so wahr ich ich selber bin', an aesthetic ideal? Already the Schiller of the

Schaubühne had seen the function of theatrical art in that it 'jeder Seelenkraft Nahrung gibt, ohne eine einzige zu überspannen', and the mature Schiller was to insist that only aesthetic culture can restore to man 'die höchste aller Schenkungen . . . die Schenkung der Menschheit'. (Letter XXI.) He called 'die Schönheit "unsre zweite Schöpferin"', words which do indeed echo those which Fiesco speaks to Romano. Thus, taking all his utterances together, it seems as if Fiesco is moved to respond absolutely, not to the beauty of Leonore, but to beauty as such, and that for the sake of beauty he overthrows all specific aims and projects, however cherished.

The matter of Fiesco's revelations about himself is borne out by his manner. At the opening of the monologue that marks the turning-point, he says 'wilde Phantasien haben . . . mein ganzes Wesen krampfig um *eine* Empfindung gewälzt. – Ich muß mich im Offenen dehnen.' (III. ii.) These words follow closely upon the shortlived subordination of his own ambitions to the happiness of Genoa. The image underlying this statement is not immediately evident. It is, however, brought out by juxtaposition with another statement, made by Sacco about Verrina: '*Genua* . . . ist die Spindel, um welche sich alle seine Gedanken mit einer eisernen Treue drehen.' (I. iii.) Clearly, the two statements require to be read together. It is Genoa round which all Verrina's thoughts revolve, and on which Fiesco had likewise sought to centre his whole being. But this concentration of the whole personality on any *one* object or overriding emotion in the case of Fiesco is expressed in an image connoting extreme constraint and revulsion. 'Krampfig' and 'wälzen' represent a significant intensification of 'mit einer eisernen Treue' and 'drehen'. And the right of the whole person is at once affirmed in the words that follow – words that evoke a sense of unlimited freedom and expansion.

By the choice of his words here, Fiesco adumbrates the choice he will later make on the level of the plot, when he rejects a course of action which, though good, fails to bring into play the whole of his personality. The full development of his personality and comprehensiveness of experience – this indeed is the keynote of the soliloquy that follows. At first sight, it reads like an ebullition of a 'großer Kerl' in the typical manner of the *Sturm und Drang*. Yet do the images he uses bear out such an impression? 'Drüber zu *brüten** mit Monarchenkraft', 'Zu *stehen** in jener schröcklich erhabenen Höhe – *niederzuschmollen** in der Menschlichkeit reißenden Strudel', 'den ersten Mund am Becher der Freude', 'schlagen

* My italics.

zu *sehen* * unvergoltene Wunden' – none of these connotes active participation in the rough and tumble of life, but its contemplation from a distant
and elevated vantage point. The verbs especially are devoid of any active
meaning; furthermore their grammatical form – they are all infinitives –
helps divest them of what active force they would carry if used in a finite
form; and finally, their initial position helps further to reduce the tension
of the periods that follow. When finally Fiesco uses the ancient symbol of
mastery over life, the symbol of the charioteer, play significantly pre-
dominates over passion. 'Die unbändigen Leidenschaften des Volks, gleich
soviel strampfenden Rossen, mit dem weichen Spiele des Zügels zu
zwingen . . .'

Thus, a variety of indications on the levels of plot, character and language, independently and consistently all point in one direction: the playfulness of his response is not an extraneous accident of Fiesco's behaviour,
but a constituent inherent in his very nature. And a mass of references to
art in general and to the theatre in particular indicate the more specific
character of Fiesco's mode of response. Is Fiesco then an actor? This hypothesis must now be more closely examined.[13]

IV

Jakob Minor criticizes Schiller for having bestowed an inordinate amount
of attention upon the figure of Julia and Fiesco's relationship with her.
'Denn die bloß geheuchelte Liebe hat er mit dem ganzen Feuer einer
wahren Leidenschaft geschildert und nicht ohne eine gewisse Selbst-
zufriedenheit den Zuschauer irregeführt, welcher seinem Helden die
erlogene Liebe eher als die wahre zu seiner Gattin glaubt.'[14] There is un-
deniably some truth in this observation. In the two scenes in which
Fiesco is shown with his wife, he appears unsure of himself, faltering,
torn. With Julia he is reckless and fiery. Leonore doubts his love. Julia
believes in it, and in their last encounter which, what with Leonore
watching behind the scenes and the nobles appearing at a prearranged
sign, is staged in the literal sense of the word (he himself calls it a 'Schauspiel'), she is ready to surrender to him, and abjures all the 'Künste' by
which she has hitherto kept him at bay. There does indeed appear to be an
inverse ratio between the artificiality of Fiesco's behaviour and the
naturalness of its effect. Nor is the instance Minor notes the only one in
the play. Consider for instance Fiesco's relationship to his wife. His feelings

* My italics.

carry the mark of conviction only when he displays them in public: as
when, on being made a duke, he thinks of his duchess first; or when,
having murdered her, he recalls the triumph he would have enjoyed at
her side; or when he blows her kisses on horseback after the faked attempt
on his life. This whole incident is worth examining more closely. Up to
this point Leonore has doubted her husband's affections: 'Hätte Fiesco
mich lieben können,' she muses, 'nie hätte Fiesco sich in die Welt
gestürzt.' (II. x.) Yet when his gallantry is reported to her, she at once
blushes 'in Entzückung' (II. xi). Not that she is under any illusion that
Fiesco shares the emotion he has inspired. 'Sein Herz wirft er den Dirnen
nach,' she says, 'und ich jage nach einem Blick' (ibid.). This comment betrays a strange double-consciousness: he prostitutes his feelings as she well
knows, and yet they compel her assent. This is what might be said of the
performance of an actor, or, for that matter, of any artist. Again, there
are the two attempts on Fiesco's life, one real, the other faked. The actual
attempt on Fiesco's life is perhaps not very impressive. There is next to no
action – the Moor's move to stab Fiesco being foiled by the latter – and,
instead, an uninterrupted patter of conversation. Fiesco's immediate
reaction to the Moor's attempt in particular strikes a very prosaic note.
'Sachte, Kanaille!' he says (and there is no stage direction even to hint
that he is raising his voice), and, a moment later: 'Du hast schlechte
Arbeit gemacht' (I. ix). A dispassionate observation such as this divests the
situation of any emotional appeal it might otherwise have had. Now compare with this the fake: the very fact that the incident is staged excludes
the possibility of any emotions on the part of Fiesco. His preparations are
precise, technical and workmanlike – yet oddly, the ensuing scene differs
from its model in that it is charged with emotion.

> Die ganze Versammlung hing ihm odemlos in starren schröcklichen
> Gruppen entgegen; er sprach wenig, aber streifte den blutenden Arm
> auf, das Volk schlug sich um die fallende Tropfen, wie um Reliquien.
> Der Mohr wurde seiner Willkür übergeben, und Fiesco . . .
> Fiesco begnadigte ihn. Itzt raste die Stille des Volks in einen
> brüllenden Laut aus, jeder Odem zernichtete einen Doria, Fiesco
> wurde auf tausendstimmigem Vivat nach Hause getragen. (II. xiv)

Formerly there had been next to no action; here there is next to no talk,
but pure pantomime addressing itself through the eye to the emotions.
The few drops of blood are a palpable example of the extraordinary
economy of means employed to bring out the essentials of the situation,

whilst the impression they make on the crowd testifies to the extraordinary effect engendered by such economy. Here indeed, as the effect proves, is an evocation of a perfect situation of its kind. Once again we are inclined to regard the imitation as more real than the real thing.[15]

This impression is confirmed as we compare the two conspiracies of Fiesco and Gianettino running side by side; one conducted with blustering violence on the principle that 'Gewalt ist die beste Beredsamkeit' (I. v); the other staged as a *Komödie*; and at least two incidents are so similar as to provoke comparison. German soldiers figure in both; and by this fact alone the poet binds the two incidents together. For these characters, so out of keeping with the rest, make their appearance in no more than three situations in all, once with each tyrant; thus they serve as a connecting link between them. In the first incident German soldiers inform Gianettino in the presence of Fiesco of the appearance of a suspicious throng in town and harbour. These are in fact Fiesco's soldiers. In the second instance they inform Fiesco, in the presence of his shaken fellow conspirators, that the conspiracy is known to the enemy. Gianettino responds sincerely to a piece of news which might well be his salvation; Fiesco's reaction to a piece of news which might be his undoing is, in the literal sense of the word, staged: for when the news first transpires he alleges it to be his 'Veranstaltung' and forces the messenger to carry through his 'Rolle' in the ostensible fake. And again the superiority of the artificial response is brought home; Fiesco masters a situation fraught with danger, while Gianettino allows his chance to slip by. We have thus no less than four instances in which Fiesco's highly stylized response to a given situation is contrasted with his own or someone else's spontaneous response to the same or similar circumstances. The circumstances, in each case, are such as to call for a straightforward emotional rather than an artificial reaction. Yet, paradoxically, the contrived response is each time shown to be the more compelling of the two. Fiesco, the poet tells us, responds to situations of life as if life were a great stage.

Nor indeed are these the only instances where Fiesco responds primarily not as a man but as a showman. One need only think of his handling of the patricians and the journeymen that storm his palace in noisy indignation: smiling, aloof, turning their excited confusion into consternation at their own helplessness and into adoring faith in his power and wisdom; or of his dealing with the Republican leaders and the painter, fanning their sense of superiority and then shattering it as he shatters the *tableau* before him, and putting up his own image instead; or of his cal-

culated entry into the courtyard, which by the modesty of his bearing de-
flates the passions his delay had previously aroused; or, finally, of his nocturnal visit to Andreas, dreamlike and dazzling like a visitation.[16] Are
these scenes, each one of which leaves a profound impression on those that
witness them, spontaneous effusions of his personality, or are they not on
the contrary so effective because a virtuoso here carefully impersonates a
role? This virtuosity is particularly striking in an emergency situation in
which Fiesco visibly works his way back from initial consternation to self-
control. The Republican conspiracy has been betrayed by the Moor, and
Fiesco at once responds to the unforeseen news by pretending that it was a
put-up show – in fact by staging the situation and assuming a part. But he
is as yet shaken and Verrina, for one, suspects that he is pretending. The
interesting thing is that, from this point onwards, Fiesco begins to conduct
two conversations, a whispered one with Calcagno and a public one with
the conspirators, the change-over being marked by stage directions pres-
cribing *laut* or *leise* respectively. Not all this switching over is necessary.
At one point at least, he repeats himself literally: '(*Laut*) He! Man soll
Wein bringen. (*Leise*) Und sahn Sie den Herzog erblassen? (*Laut*)
Frisch, Brüder! Wir wollen noch eins Bescheid tun auf den Tanz dieser
Nacht! (*Leise*) Und sahn Sie den Herzog erblassen?' (IV. vii.) Six times
in all he breaks into the part he has assumed to discuss the truth with Calcagno and six times he returns to it again. Oddly enough, this procedure
seems to steady him. For when at the end of the scene the arrival of the
Duke's men causes the situation to deteriorate, he not only calms the despairing conspirators but successfully plays the role of indifferent innocence
towards the soldiers. Does it not seem as if Fiesco posed himself a technical
problem here because the exercise of his virtuosity is instrumental in restoring his mastery over the situation? In the measure in which his interest is switched to the handling of his part, the urgency of the situation
itself recedes, and its emotional grip on him relaxes.[17]

V

Does not the presence of all these features in combination point to the conclusion that Fiesco's dominant response to all manner of situations is an
aesthetic one? And if so, in what relation does this mode of response stand
to the practical side of his being? To answer this question, Fiesco's behaviour had best be examined in that part of the play in which the practical side should, by rights, be uppermost. This situation arises when he has

revealed his intentions and must implement them in action. It arises more acutely when the conspiracy is prematurely betrayed to the enemy. To appreciate the significance of Fiesco's reactions, the external situation must be visualized as concretely as possible.

Fiesco's party is ready to strike at the tyrant, all roles are distributed, the last orders given. It is vital to strike at this very moment; for the tyrant has prepared his own *coup*, and the only way to avoid the death of the Republican leaders and ruin of the cause is to forestall him at once. Moreover the Republicans' plan has been betrayed to the enemy and their only remaining chance lies in immediate action, before the tyrant has had time to exploit his tactical superiority. It is at this moment that Fiesco, moved by the beauty of Andreas's response, elects to call off the conspiracy. Schiller could hardly have conceived a situation of more unambiguous urgency: if Fiesco had it in him to respond to practical and moral needs, he would do so now.[18] Yet he responds as the 'artist' he is. Schiller, however, has not left it at this one test: he has repeated it under more stringent conditions. At the very moment when the Moor, having already betrayed the conspiracy in the first instance, wantonly divulges further information concerning Fiesco's movements to the Duke's messengers, Fiesco releases him with the words 'Du hast das Verdienst, *eine große Tat zu veranlassen* – Entfliehe!' (IV. ix).

When eventually Fiesco goes to warn his enemy Andreas, the situation has become aggravated. Fiesco has meanwhile inflicted mortal insult upon Gianettino's sister and has imprisoned her as a hostage. His own words show that he is aware of the fact that he cannot now retract his steps but must go on, to the end. 'Die Brücke ist hinter mir abgehoben' (IV. xiv), he says to his wife as she endeavours to stop him. Thus he is in no doubt about the inevitability of his step. Nor are its implications allowed to escape him. For in the conversation with his wife he is made to realize that her life as well as his own and that of the Republicans depends upon the issue of the fight.

He leaves her in a frenzy of anguish hovering between life and death. It is in this situation that Fiesco befriends his enemy, and cautions him, in an assumed voice and in language rich with metaphor.

Each one of these three actions argues, more cogently than the one before it, the purposefulness of Fiesco's response: their cumulative effect is overwhelming. In the last one, the essential disconnectedness of Fiesco's specific mode of activity from other modes of activity is fully apparent. It is neither caused by the projects of his active life – indeed it cuts right across them – nor is it designed to affect these activities: Fiesco goes to fight for the cause he has first championed and then so utterly disregarded, as if the interruption did not exist. His isolated act achieves nothing, modifies nothing, and is modified by nothing outside itself. And this unrelatedness of Fiesco's response to anything outside it is the final token of its aesthetic quality. Disconnectedness with the world of purposes has been regarded as the hallmark of the aesthetic mode, by Kant as well as Schiller. Kant defined the aesthetic judgement as the perception of *Zweckmäßigkeit ohne Zweck*, and Schiller's own statement runs as follows:

> In dem ästhetischen Zustande ist der Mensch also *Null*, insofern man auf ein einzelnes Resultat . . . achtet und den Mangel jeder besondern Determination in ihm in Betrachtung zieht. . . . die Schönheit gibt schlechterdings kein einzelnes Resultat weder für den Verstand noch für den Willen, sie führt keinen einzelnen . . . Zweck aus, . . . hilft uns keine einzige Pflicht erfüllen . . .[19]

This position has been consolidated by modern aesthetic thought. Samuel Alexander, for instance, considers the beautiful as being 'the object of the constructive impulse when that impulse has become contemplative instead of practical'.[20] And Edward Bullough insists that a fundamental characteristic of aesthetic and artistic experience is the 'putting of the phenomenon . . . out of gear with our practical, actual self; . . . allowing' it to stand outside the context of our personal needs and ends . . .'[21] This describes precisely the relation in which Fiesco's action has been seen to stand to his personal needs and ends and to those implied in the general situation. His action exists outside the world of purposes, outside the requirements of cause and effect; what purpose and justification it has it carries within itself; they lie in its own perfection. Its autonomy is the autonomy of art.

Schiller's second tragedy then is a play about art; a peculiar kind of art, that is, practised not in the special medium of the poet, or the sculptor or the painter, but in the vast and intangible medium of life itself, and not at certain times nor in a place set off from the everyday scene like the stage or studio, but always and everywhere; wherefore it is difficult to apprehend the distinct character of the activity. Edward Bullough, who like Schiller insists that the aesthetic mode is not compartmental, operative in certain specifiable situations, but an attitude to life, capable of pervading it in its entirety, gives a description of the 'artist in life' which is noteworthy because of the closeness of its bearing on our theme. He says:

There are many who are 'actors', not in the sense that they *pretend* to do and think before others what they would neither do nor think in the privacy of their own chamber . . . , but in the sense that they perform perfectly natural and spontaneous acts with so clear a perception of their nature, their value and their sensuous, concrete effectiveness that these acts assume for them an intrinsic importance (quite apart from ultimate aims or results). . . . In the doing of them they experience a kind of separation within themselves, a doubling of consciousness, as if they were two individuals, of which one acts while the other looks on, criticizes and enjoys, with the free and impartial interest and the satisfaction which the artist feels in the production of his own handiwork. Thus they combine in themselves the threefold aspect of artist, work of art and spectator, an exceedingly complex mental state, common enough in the actor, but realized in actual life, too, more often than we are inclined to think. The result is a curious enhancement of the acts. . . . They are invested with a value as ends in themselves, done for their own sake . . .[22]

Fiesco, too, by that strange switch of the attention from the practical and emotional aspects of any given situation to its formal qualities – a switch for which Bullough has coined the term 'aesthetic distance' – invests his actions, and the situation in which he acts, with a value by which they become an end in themselves. This quality is present in his actions, no matter whether he seems to be pretending or emerging from pretence; for even where he would seem to throw off his mask, as when he knocks over the painter's *tableau*, saying 'der Schein weiche der Tat', he is not relinquishing art; rather, he composes a *tableau* of the living group before him frozen in awed amazement. He enters into life, not to be bound by it, but to subjugate life itself in its entirety, spellbinding it into the motionless perfection of form.

Not, of course, that Fiesco has no ends and purposes outside his art. He has. He is the practical intriguer that critics have taken him to be, busy with designs on friend and foe alike. But what starts by being a design with an object, in the end becomes a design for its own sake, whose end lies in its internal coherence. This reading of the play as a whole would seem to be finally borne out by Schiller's statement of his theme in the foreword to the play. 'Ich habe in den "Räubern" das Opfer einer ausschweifenden Empfindung zum Vorwurf genommen,' he says. 'Hier versuche ich das Gegenteil, ein Opfer der Kunst und Kabale.' *Kabale*, the design with an ulterior end becoming *Kunst*, a design which is its own end; a process which inevitably leads to tragedy in the world of purposes: this is the tragic theme of the play.[23] But before pursuing its tragic implications we must indicate something more of the total statement of the theme throughout the play, of which it is indeed the organizing principle.

VI

'The style in *Fiesco* is extremely uneven', Mr Garland observes;[24] and in this judgement critical opinion has generally concurred. Time and again, exception has been taken to the tendency in some scenes towards bombast and hyperbole, and regret has been expressed that the new urbanity of dialogue which Schiller achieved in his second drama should have been confined to a few scenes only, notably those with the Moor.[25] If, for the moment, we disregard the much-criticized scene showing Fiesco by the dead body of his wife, the drama, from the point of view of language and style, seems to be divided into two sharply contrasting halves: the one dominated by Fiesco and, to a lesser degree, the Moor, Julia and Gianettino, the other dominated by Verrina, Berta, Leonore and the lesser Republican figures. Is this division haphazard, indicative of the poet's intermittent command of his new idiom? Or does it rather reflect his intention?

The style in the Fiesco half of the play, on the whole, is conversational, ironical, and of a certain elegance. This impression is created by various means, such as the use of an ironic form of address suggesting a superior intellectuality – a device the effect of which is strengthened by the fact that it is a literary echo: Lessing makes frequent use of it.[26] Julia addresses her rival variously as 'gutes Tierchen' (II. ii), 'mein Schatz' (II. ii), 'Würmchen' (II. ii); she refers to her as 'die Fratze' (I. iv) and asks of her 'was will denn das Köpfchen' (I. iv), whilst to Fiesco she says 'über den verschlagenen Kopf' (III. x). Fiesco himself calls the Moor 'Kanaille', 'Bestie' and 'höfliche Bestie' (all I. ix), the last denomination bringing out the humorous quality in his earlier contemptuous references. The sudden change from 'Sie' to 'Du' in Fiesco's address to Romano, 'Tritt her, Maler' (II. xvii), produces a similar effect. Similarly, Gianettino calls his Councillor Lomellino 'Närrchen' (II. xiv), his sister, with patent irony, 'Schwesterchen' (III. viii); he refers to Fiesco as an 'armer Wicht' (III. x). Then there is a striking use of foreign, chiefly French, words which helps to build up the same impression. They abound in the speech of Julia, who speaks of 'Delikatesse' (I. iv), of the 'delikatesten Zirkel' (II. ii), 'Assembleen' (II. ii), 'Connaissancen', 'Galanterien', 'Impertinenzen' (I. iv), 'Garnierung' (I. iv) and 'Karessen' (II. ii). A sentence such as 'Scharmant, Madam! Ihre Gäste durch Domestiken bekomplimentieren zu lassen' (II. ii) is by no means an isolated occurrence. Fiesco, too, speaks of 'Kavalier' (I. viii), of his 'delikate Ohren' (II. i), of 'Sottise' (III. x), of a 'Rakette' (II. v); and when, by the body of his wife, he ends by promising Genoa a 'Fürsten . . . wie ihn noch kein Europäer sah' (V. xiii), the word *Europäer*, in an ostensibly emotional context, has a suggestive force far exceeding the conscious intention of the statement and alien to it, a force derived from the cumulative effect of foreign words throughout the play. The Moor's speech, in particular, is permeated with foreign elements; such as 'Exerzitium', 'Testimonium', 'mein Genie' (all I. vi), 'Kavalier' (II. iv), 'Kreaturen', 'pardonnieren' (III. iv), 'karessieren' (II. xv), 'Entree' (III. xvi), and many others. His last words, by the introduction of a foreign word, achieve an effect comparable to that of Fiesco's 'Europäer' speech. Condemned to hang, he says 'so mag's sein, – und der Teufel kann sich auf den Extrafall rüsten' (V. x) – and the choice of 'Extrafall', by the sense of civilized aloofness with which such words – admittedly a feature of contemporary polite usage – have been invested, during the course of the play, through their consistent association with Fiesco, fully bears out the stage direction 'resigniert'.

The remarkable thing is that these stylistic devices on the one hand virtually do not occur in relation to the Verrina group, and that, on the other, they extend to the whole Fiesco group, regardless of the differences of character it encompasses, creating a stylistically homogeneous block. It is the same with the images used by these various characters. The same images drawn from the sphere of play, and craft and art, which have been found associated with Fiesco,[27] recur in the cases of these subordinate characters, welding them even more firmly together into a group with Fiesco than the use of a common vocabulary alone could have done. Julia uses, in metaphorical contexts, relating to love and the passions, words such as 'Schauspiel' (I. iv), 'Kunst' and 'Künste' (IV. xii), 'Geschmack' (I. iv and II. ii) and 'Gewerbe' (II. ii). She likens love to a game of chess and makes the metaphor that is involved explicit by concluding: 'Ach! schon zu unglücklich hab' ich gespielt, daß ich nicht auch mein Letztes noch setzen sollte' (IV. xii). The Moor makes free and unsolicited use of words like 'Geschmack' (I. iv, I. vi), 'Komödie' (IV. ix) or 'Spektakel' (III. vii). He considers his profession as a 'Gewerbe', a 'Zunft' (I. iv), considers himself a 'Stümper' or 'Genie' alternatively; and he is echoed by Fiesco himself in his use of 'Meisterstück' (I. iv and V. xiii). He echoes the gambling images used by and of Fiesco, when he says to the latter: 'um Köpfe werden sie karten, und der Eure ist Tarock' (III. iv). Even Gianettino is brought within the orbit of this imagery by his insistent use of 'Possen' (II. xii) and especially by a simile which stands out because of its notorious associations: 'So steh' ich wie Nero auf dem Berg und sehe dem possierlichen Brande zu' (II. xii); and not only the association of Nero fiddling, but also that of Fiesco standing on 'jener schröcklich erhabenen Höhe' (III. ii) and gazing down in aesthetic enjoyment upon the human vicissitudes below, comes to mind; and indeed the latter image receives some of its tone and colour from its conjunction with the first.

Furthermore, the Fiesco group is united by means of direct characterization. This comes out very clearly in the stage directions. It is Fiesco, Julia, Gianettino and the Moor who laugh in this play; and it is they who are constantly characterized by directions such as 'spöttisch', 'hämisch', 'boshaft' – traits that are fully borne out by their actual behaviour.

The same cohesion between the individual figures of this group exists on the plane of action. There is the parallelism of the two conspiracies, of Fiesco and Gianettino, one of whom misuses the woman whose fate is so persistently identified with that of Genoa (cf. I. xii), whilst Fiesco is charged with the same crime against Genoa herself: 'Du hast eine Schande begangen an der Majestät des wahrhaftigen Gottes, daß du dir die Tugend die Hände zu diesem Bubenstück führen und Genuas Patrioten mit Genua Unzucht treiben ließest' (V. xvi). And both would-be tyrants die by violence. Again there is the parallelism between the execution of the Moor and Fiesco's own end, a parallelism which Verrina makes plain, when he uses the word 'Galgen' – which we associate with the Moor's end – with reference to Fiesco's crime, asking 'Aber doch die Gesetze ließ *die* Kanaille noch ganz?' (V. xvi). And then there is, finally, the connection between Fiesco's and Julia's fates,[28] of which the reader grows aware when Fiesco – perhaps himself conscious of the echo, picks up, in a sudden realization of his helplessness, the very word which Julia had used before, when she was about to surrender to him: 'Das Bekenntnis willst du noch haben,' she had owned to him '. . . daß alle unsre weiblichen Künste einzig für dieses wehrlose Stichblatt fechten, wie auf dem Schach alle Offiziere den wehrlosen König bedecken?' (IV. xii.) And he echoes: 'Wahr ist's – Wahr – und ich das Stichblatt des unendlichen Bubenstücks.' (V. xiii.)

It seems, then, that there is a homogeneity of treatment extending over that area of the play which is dominated by the figure of Fiesco. This homogeneity encompasses not only the planes of action and language but that of character as well. It points to the operation of an organizing principle more potent than any one of these, namely the controlling poetic theme.

VII

The area of the play that is dominated by Verrina presents a similarly unified aspect. The high emotional pitch of the language has frequently been commented upon, in general adversely. It is caused partly by the persistent use of words denoting basic human facts, passions and experiences – words, moreover, permeating a vocabulary which in contrast to that used by the Fiesco group is almost wholly German. The perpetual reiteration of words such as 'Herz', 'Blut', 'Seele', 'Vaterland', 'Tränen', 'Himmel' or 'Schwert',[29] by every figure connected with this group, keeps up the tension, and serves to embed such varied figures as Leonore, Calcagno and Sacco, Verrina, Berta and Bourgognino in a homogeneous verbal texture. We may pick out almost at random phrases such as the following, spoken independently by different characters in various contexts: 'Ein Schwert liegt im Saal. Verrina schaut wild. Berta hat rote Augen,' says Sacco (I. xi). A little later, Verrina echoes: 'Diese Männer sind tapfer und gut. Beweinen dich diese, wird's irgendwo bluten.' (I. xi.) And Bourgognino, earlier on in the play, had challenged Fiesco to a duel in words recalling Leonore's grief, not Berta's: 'Man wird Ihnen auf eine gewisse Träne eine blutige Antwort abfodern.' (I. viii.) These statements, alike in their succinctness as well as in the images that nourish them, not only point to a connection between the characters referred to – Berta and Leonore – but also establish an overriding link between the diverse characters of the speakers. Furthermore, we may assume that the connection between tears, i.e. suffering, and action, stressed as it is so explicitly and consistently, will bear on the theme that is being developed.

Throughout the area of the play with which we are concerned, yet another curious and recurrent opposition is noticeable. It is perceptible in the vocabulary itself; for side by side with words expressive of a state of being deeply moved which have been noted above, there is to be found a steady stream of words denoting obstruction, impediment, disease and death. References abound on all sides to physical conditions such as convulsions, goitre and sickness in general, and mental conditions such as paralysing grief, rigidity – all culminating in death.

If we turn to characterization, it becomes evident that just as the Fiesco group is characterized by laughter and malignity, the group centred in Verrina forms a homogeneous whole in virtue of the earnestness, the sincerity and violence of the emotions depicted. This common trait is quite evident from the stage directions, and is borne out by the content of the speeches and character's references to one another.

On the plane of action the same unified picture emerges, in this area of the play as much as in that governed by Fiesco. Take, for instance, Leonore's appearance on the field of battle, in disguise. That this action is not solely dictated by her individual make-up is indicated by the fact that it has its exact parallel in the action of a different character: Berta, too, joins in the battle, also in disguise. In both scenes the sword plays an important role. But whereas Berta, despite her disguise, is recognized by Bourgognino, Leonore fails to be recognized by her husband. The words 'Ich kenne die Stimme', and 'Ich bin hier sehr bekannt' (V. viii) are ironically echoed, a very little later, in Fiesco's: 'Kenn' ich nicht diesen Busch und Mantel? Ich kenne den Busch und Mantel!' (V. xi.) Both actions then serve to state one theme; and both would seem to be related to Fiesco, the chief carrier of the theme of the play, and have the function of elucidating the theme centred in him. Indeed the conclusion suggests itself that the whole Berta complex – her rape and her relation to Bourgognino, which have very frequently been denied any significance in the plot and structure of the play[30] – has the function of elaborating the main theme, by means of parallel and contrast. This possibility is further confirmed by another part of the action. Verrina orders Berta and Bourgognino to flee even though it is their wedding night, and takes a heavy-hearted leave of them, the thought of Fiesco's impending death uppermost in his mind. Why this intrusion of an irrelevant incident which, coming so near the main catastrophe, cannot command the reader's interest? The answer lies in the fact that this situation again parallels one in which Fiesco has been shown just before: Fiesco, by his wife's dead body, swears that he will 'dieser unglücklichen Fürstin . . . eine Totenfeier halten, daß das Leben seine Anbeter verlieren und die Verwesung wie eine Braut glänzen soll.' (V. xiii.) There is the same clash between the notions of a bridal feast and death in both incidents. Only whereas Verrina makes a grim and deadly business even out of a 'Brautnacht', Fiesco makes a feast and a thing of beauty even out of death and decomposition. He transforms it into art.[31] The function of this incident then – like the rest of the complex to which it belongs – is to help towards the realization of a general theme concerning itself with a mode of action; and the function of this theme, in turn, is to throw light upon the central theme of the play.

But what is this theme which language, characters and action of the Verrina complex combine in stating, and how is it related to the central theme of the play? Here the examination of a speech by Verrina may be useful. In it he describes to Bourgognino the state of mind and soul appropriate to the deed on which he has resolved – the murder of Fiesco. It runs as follows:

> Jüngling! ich fürchte – Jüngling, dein Blut ist rosenrot, dein Fleisch ist milde geschmeidig; *dergleichen* Naturelle fühlen menschlich weich; an dieser empfindenden Flamme schmilzt meine grausame Weisheit. Hätte der Frost des Alters oder der bleierne Gram den fröhlichen Sprung deiner Geister gestellt – hätte schwarzes klumpigtes Blut der leidenden Natur den Weg zum Herzen gesperret, dann wärst du geschickt, die Sprache meines Grams zu verstehen und meinen Entschluß anzustaunen. (III. i.)

This passage, and the scene of which it is part, are central. They are central to the plot because Fiesco's downfall is here decided; and they are central to the theme because it receives its fullest imaginative statement here, in the characterization of the general attitude and specific deed which Verrina opposes to Fiesco's mode of being. These lines mark the point of intersection between the two main groups of images that recur throughout this area of the tragedy. On the one hand, we have 'Blut', 'Fleisch', 'Natur', 'Herz', 'menschlich', 'empfindend'; on the other, 'grausam', 'Gram', 'Frost', 'bleiern', 'schwarz' and 'klumpigt', 'gestellt' and 'gesperret', with their logical opposites 'weich', 'geschmeidig' and 'schmelzen', words indicative of states which preclude an action such as is demanded now. The connection between these two sets of images, hinted before, here becomes patent. By piling them up together in this short passage, the poet tells us, more surely than through the content of Verrina's words, what Julia, speaking of 'mißfärbige Leidenschaft', 'grämliche Empfindsamkeit' and 'frostiger Kuß', has already indicated: ugliness and distortion are inherent in a passionate and single-minded response to a given situation. To be fitted for Verrina's one-track-minded deed, the psychic organism cannot be vibrantly alive. There is no supple interplay of its functions, they do not feed and vitalize each other. Instead, it is in a process of hardening, congealing, stagnating, with intercommunication all but brought to a standstill. Such is the state of mind of

Verrina, who, like Leonore, Berta and Bourgognino, is devoted to one overruling emotion, be it love of a person, love of a country, or love of freedom, and who subordinates to that emotion the rest of his being. His organism is no longer the sentient living whole it should be. It is not only the horrifying nature of the deed on which Verrina has resolved that reduces a man to this state. Rather, as Verrina points out to Bourgognino, the state is the condition of the deed. And, indeed, the characterization of Verrina throughout the play, both by himself and others, puts the emphasis on that rigidity which reaches its culmination here. He is referred to variously as being the 'starrköpfigste Republikaner' (I. v), 'hart wie Stahl' (I. vii) and possessed of an 'eiserne Treue' (I. iii). He compares himself to the 'eisgraue Römer' (I. x), calls himself 'eisgrauer Vater' (II. xvii), speaks of his 'frozen' heart (I. x) and says to Bourgognino – 'ich werde zu Eis, wenn ich mir etwas denke' (IV. v). The life to which he condemns Berta he likens to 'das gichterische Wälzen des sterbenden Wurms' (I. xii). His 'Zorn' is 'totenfarben' (I. x).

The human personality governed by one dominant emotion: this then is the theme developed through the Verrina complex and crystallized in the passage we have examined. Its full importance, however, and the bearing it has on the main theme of the play is brought home by the formal arrangement of the play. The poet has placed this key passage next to the great monologue in which Fiesco gives the fullest expression to the aesthetic mode of experiencing and finally decides in its favour. A close connection between the two scenes is thus established. It is reinforced by the echo of a crucial phrase: 'es ist eine Qual, der *einzige große Mann* zu sein' (III. i), says Verrina, and Fiesco reiterates: 'Daß ich der größte Mann bin im ganzen Genua' (III. ii). Thus the poet invites us to compare the two modes of being represented by Verrina and Fiesco respectively, each with a claim to human greatness. Verrina's life turns on *one* passion, the freedom of Genoa; and never more than at the moment when he sacrifices Fiesco for the sake of it. This is precisely what a moment later Fiesco rejects: 'Wilde Phantasien haben . . . mein ganzes Wesen um *eine* Empfindung gewälzt. – Ich muß mich im Offenen dehnen.' It is significant that the emotion is not specified: the opposition is between any *one* emotion and wholeness of his being. Wholeness of being and experience, the supple interplay of all his faculties, sensitive responsiveness to every impression – these indeed are the marks of the aesthetic mode of life as Fiesco develops it in this scene: a mode in every characteristic diametrically opposed to the one realized by Verrina, which is summed up in the words

that precede the solemn announcement of his intentions, 'Ich . . .
[will] zu dir durch Verzerrungen sprechen . . .' (III. i).[32]

It is not easy to find a description for the mode of being which the poet
contrasts with that of Fiesco. For the figures through which it is gradually
defined are moved in different ways and by different objects: Sacco and
Calcagno are motivated by selfish and ignoble ends, the one by need for
money, the other by his passion for Leonore; Leonore by love of Fiesco;
Bourgognino by love of Berta – as she by love of him – and by patriotism;
and Verrina, finally, by the pure idea of freedom. But different as the
objects they strive for may be, they all do strive for some object, and it is
this object and the emotions aroused by it, which is the motive of their
actions.[33] This response is diametrically opposed to Fiesco's. It has been
seen that he responds disinterestedly to a given situation; and even where
the situation has an urgent practical or emotional appeal for him, he proceeds to cut out this side of it altogether and instead concentrates on its
formal aspects. Fiesco then seeks to maintain aesthetic distance in all his
actions; Verrina and the group that he dominates seek to reduce distance
altogether. Fiesco keeps aesthetic distance even when in danger of his
life. Verrina lets a practical interest intervene even when looking at a picture. Fiesco treats even actions that serve a purpose beyond themselves as
though they were an end in themselves. Verrina, by the curse he lays on
Berta, imposes a super-end over all the single ends – *deine, meine, eure
Pflichten* – that motivates the different characters. Fiesco's actions, being
an end in themselves, are ultimately ineffectual – he neither kills the
tyrant nor does he gain his object. But by the same token they are also
beautiful. The actions of Verrina and his group do lead to their objective:
the tyrant is killed by Bourgognino. But, being merely means to an end
beyond them, they are also ugly. Some are morally ugly, such as those of
Sacco and Calcagno – this is brought out even in the way in which they
propose to do away with the tyrant (III. v); other actions, especially those
of Leonore and Verrina, are aesthetically repulsive. It is not for nothing
that the deed of Verrina on which he bases his melancholy claim to greatness should be the murder of a friend, executed in an aesthetically dis-
tasteful fashion. Verrina himself stresses the essential ugliness of it when
he corrects his first formulation '*ertrunken*' to '*Ertränkt, wenn das hüb-
scher lautet*' (V. xvii). And indeed there is scarcely an action or reaction of
Verrina's which does not reflect the ugliness inherent in what may be
called, in a very wide sense, the interested or practical mode which he
represents. Critics have often enough noted the fact; but they have not

seen the necessity of its being so, a necessity founded in the exigencies of the theme of the play itself. This theme may now be more fully stated as the basic polarity between the aesthetic mode of being which is disinterested and impractical, and the interested and practical mode of being, be the interest moral or pragmatic.

VIII

But, it will be objected, this whole analysis falls to the ground; it rests on an artificial and untenable division. For Fiesco's reaction by the dead body of his wife is just as ugly as any reaction of Verrina's, probably more so. Indeed critics have usually cited this scene as the most offensive of all. In it, Fiesco behaves scarcely like a human being. The stage directions describe him as 'viehisch um sich hauend', 'mit frechem Zähnblöken gen Himmel', and additional force is lent to such suggestions of bestiality by his own words: 'Tretet zurück, ihr *menschlichen Gesichter*!* – Ah, hätt' ich nur *Seinen* Weltbau zwischen diesen *Zähnen**' etc. (V. xiii). These are excessive words and gestures, even for a *Sturm und Drang* hero; and they are all the more striking because of their contrast to the perfect poise and control usually evinced by Fiesco. He is depicted as the most civilized of human beings, formed, playfully superior; and then, when he sees himself confronted with the human lot, he is reduced to a response that altogether falls below the human. The unusual aesthetic distance which we have come to associate with him gives way to an equally striking lack of any distance at all.[34] Nor is this the only instance there is of the limits to Fiesco's composure. Three times in the play allusion is made, in front of Fiesco, to death by poisoning; and each time the mention elicits a similarly uncontrolled response from him.[35] The peculiar quality of death by poisoning, which distinguishes it from death in open battle, is its insidiousness. The victim is doomed before he knows it. Death is under his skin; he was as incapable of foreseeing it as he is now unable to evict it. It is a very similar quality in the later situation, Fiesco's murder of Leonore, which enrages him in special measure. Here, too, what happened could not be guarded against. It is the result of a configuration of accidents which eludes human calculation. In the later, as in the earlier incidents, then, it is the experience of the incalculability of life and of the helplessness of human beings which causes Fiesco's composure to break down in such a startling fashion. His aesthetic distance, then, one must conclude, is not

* My italics.

based upon an acceptance of the human condition, its uncertainty of all but death. Rather does it seem designed as a bulwark against this precarious condition; for when fate overtakes him, it does so destructively, inimically, sweeping all aesthetic distance before it. That this conjecture is not far off the mark becomes clear from Fiesco's great monologue which represents the most concentrated and explicit statement of the aesthetic attitude. There he says, in what the stage direction 'mit erhabenem Spiel' indicates as being the most directly revelatory passage:

> Zu stehen in jener schröcklich erhabenen Höhe – niederzuschmollen in der Menschlichkeit reißenden Strudel, wo das Rad der blinden Betrügerin Schicksale schelmisch wälzt . . . tief unten den geharnischten Riesen *Gesetz* am Gängelbande zu lenken – schlagen zu sehen unvergoltene Wunden, wenn sein kurzarmiger Grimm an das Geländer der Majestät ohnmächtig poltert, etc. (III. ii)

The deepest spring of the aesthetic attitude which would treat life as sublime play is the wish to remain above it, out of reach of its treacherousness and inaccessible to the wounds it would inflict. It springs from the resolute refusal to close with fate, and with life altogether.

That Fiesco's attitude is a defensive mechanism inspired by fear, and designed to ward off the object of his fear, also becomes clear from the rigidity with which that attitude is maintained.[36] It has already been shown that he persists in an emotionally distanced aesthetic response in at least four situations demanding a straightforward response of feeling, and in fact eliciting it from other characters. It is not that feeling and instinctual reactions do not enter into his response at all. It is only because they are present too that his response can be legitimately called an aesthetic one; for the hallmark of the aesthetic state is the presence and harmonious interaction of all human faculties. But if feeling and instinct enter into his response, they do so in a subordinate fashion, strictly controlled by the overall aesthetic intention. Never is feeling allowed to endanger form, let alone to disrupt it.

This permanent subordination of feelings and instincts is manifest in Fiesco's relations to other characters of the drama, not only, however, in the sense that from his end the relationship is characterized by lack of warmth and spontaneity: over and above this, the character at the receiving end of the relationship has come to embody in his being some aspect of Fiesco's own emotional make-up. Some submerged trait of his is externalized and embodied in another character as well as in the outward situation of that character. In various fashions, the Moor, Leonore, Berta and Julia, through their very being, their situation, as well as through Fiesco's relation to them, tell us something about the inner drama that is enacted in the hero's soul.

IX

This device of externalizing inner states and conflicts in the manner described is so characteristic of Schiller's dramatic technique, and becomes so absolutely fundamental to the structure of his dramas, that it may be as well to show its working in some detail here, using the figure of the Moor as an illustration.

On the face of it, there is no unequivocal suggestion of any close relationship between Fiesco and the Moor. The Moor, it is true, has an important part in putting the schemes hatched in Fiesco's brain into practice. Even Fiesco must grudgingly admit the value of his complicity. Furthermore there is Verrina's insistence on the similarity of the crimes perpetrated by slave and master, and of the punishment due to both. Against these indications of a link must be set the Moor's double treachery towards his master, and Fiesco's no less callous dismissal of his servant the moment he has done his work.[37] These argue the most casual of connections. Nor could their respective situations put them more widely apart. The one, an aristocrat, an Apollo clad in white, a knight and a Christian gentleman. The other, a slave, ugly, black, a scoundrel and a pagan. Or does perhaps the very nicety of this opposition suggest an inner link between the two?

Fiesco explains to Julia the place and function of the senses and instincts in the following metaphors: 'Die Sinne müssen immer nur blinde Briefträger sein . . .'; and 'Unsere Sinne sind nur die Grundsuppe unsrer innern Republik. Der Adel lebt von ihnen, aber erhebt sich über ihren platten Geschmack.' (III. x.) Three things are striking in these words: firstly the Platonic analogy between individual and State, between the inner psychological and the outer social organism which is implicit in the first metaphor and expressly stated in the second. This analogy suggests that the outer action of the 'Republikanische Trauerspiel' may itself be a metaphor for an inner, psychological meaning. Nor is this analogy isolated. It is supported by a great deal of the imagery of the play, as when Fiesco speaks of the 'aufgewiegelten Sinne' as slaves, and Julia addresses them as 'gärende Rebellen'.[38]

Secondly, the position assigned to the senses in this inner republic is worthy of note: they are serving members, vitally useful and exploited, but despised. Thirdly, the image of the *Grundsuppe* in itself is striking because of its unusualness. When in the fifth act we meet the dismissed Moor again, looting and burning, he introduces himself with the words: '*Ich* war der Mann, der diese Suppe einbrockte – *mir* gibt man keinen Löffel.' (V. vii.) The figure of speech he uses takes us back to Fiesco's words. And we see that Fiesco's servant has experienced that same exploitation at the hands of his master which the latter had laid down as the proper treatment for the senses; senses, moreover, which had been called servants and slaves. In the light of this link, the very first words of the Moor, in which he reveals his identity to Fiesco, take on a new significance in retrospect: 'Ein Sklave der Republik' he calls himself (I. ix). A cheated slave of the 'inner republic' as well as of the outer one, we ask ourselves? A host of other verbal links, both direct and indirect, confirm the suggestion that the Moor is an externalization of the sensual, instinctual side of human nature in general, and of that side of Fiesco's personality in perticular. Time and again, the senses are metaphorically associated with treacherous desertion, with darkness, and with fire. Julia speaks of 'unsere tödliche Seite, . . . die . . . beim ersten Seitenblick der Tugend den Feind *verräterisch** empfängt.' Fiesco combines fire and desertion in one metaphor: 'Eben dann würde *meine* Empfindung die *Feuerfahne** der *deinigen* gewahr und *lief*'* desto mutiger *über*.'* Fire, night, treachery are all interwoven in her plea: 'Mensch, dein Gesicht *brennt** *fieberisch** wie dein Gespräch. Weh, auch aus dem meinigen . . . schlägt wildes, *frevelndes Feuer*.* Laß uns das *Licht** suchen. . . . Die *aufgewiegelten** Sinne könnten den gefährlichen Wink dieser *Finsternis** merken. Geh. Diese *gärenden Rebellen** könnten hinter dem Rücken des verschämten *Tags** ihre gottlosen Künste treiben.' (IV. xii.) Is it not odd that these associations, examples of which could be multiplied, crowd in thick and fast just after the Moor's treachery has become known, and just before he is finally presented to our imagination, a deserter at large, burning and looting under cover of darkness? The interconnection between large dramatic facts and imagery is too close and persistent to be overlooked. It is as if through the figure and fate of the Moor, the poet were offering a comment on the playing with fire that is at the same time going on between Fiesco and Julia. As Fiesco allows the Moor some measure of freedom in the conviction that he has him under absolute control, so he, and, in a similar fashion, Julia, allows his senses an appearance of liberty on the

* My italics.

assumption that they can be put in their place under all circumstances; a mistaken assumption as it turns out, for Julia's passions are soon inflamed, and Fiesco, beside himself with rage at the Moor's incendiarism, in the very next scene stabs his wife. And it is as if to point the connection between the Moor and Fiesco, when Julia, in her last words, calls him '*Schwarzer heimtückischer* Heuchler*' (IV. xiii).

Other image patterns help to build up a complex network of connections between Fiesco and the Moor. They show the one to embody in his being a part of the other's nature; notably animal-imagery and the associated imagery of anatomical organs.[39] It is striking that this imagery is wholly limited to the Moor and Fiesco, and to references made to them by others. It thus constitutes a special bond between these two characters; on official occasions, it is true, Fiesco likes to see himself as the lion or tiger, and this would seem to put him far apart from the Moor, whom on three occasions he calls a *Bestie*, and who, by his own descriptions as well as Fiesco's, emerges as of a lesser breed – a dog, a snake, a fox, etc. But when he speaks with the Moor, Fiesco refers to himself in exactly the same terms, and permits the Moor to refer to him likewise. He is a fox, a dog, a snake, and so on. And, more importantly, the conversation between him and the Moor is full of references to the lower senses and to direct sensory knowledge obtained through them. Fiesco asks the Moor to find out 'die Witterung des Staates' (I. ix), 'Ob du nicht irgendwo einen Meuchelmord witterst' (II. xv). Of the Jesuit who suspects him, he says '*Ein Fuchs riecht den andern*' (II. iv). The Moor tells him that he has 'vorausgewittert' his master's command to call together the conspirators. (III. iv.) He remarks, 'ich wittere den Fraß'; and their conversation abounds with mentions of animals: 'Mäuse', 'Ratten', 'Kater', 'Lastochsen', and of words such as 'Morast', 'Mistbeet', creating in the reader a strong awareness of the animal side of life. Together, the Moor and Fiesco have a common language, the language of sense and instinct. And who would doubt that the animals to which they are likened symbolize that side of human nature in which they are one? In the light of this image pattern, the extravagance of Fiesco's behaviour by the dead body of his wife assumes a new significance. Are Fiesco's words and gestures theatrical excesses of a young poet as yet unversed in matters of taste? Or do they not represent an attempt to show as directly as is possible the instinctual side of Fiesco, his night side as it were, of which we have so far only known indirectly, through his connection with the Moor? To show, as it were, the animal in the man?

* My italics.

The animal imagery forges, on the level of language, a bond between Fiesco and the Moor; the imagery centred in organs of the body makes the nature of the connection that holds between these two clearer still. For the single organ is not self-sufficient but part of an encompassing whole. The effect of the recurrent association of the Moor and Fiesco with single organs of the body therefore is to suggest that neither is complete in himself but that they form part of one organism.[40] Fiesco is repeatedly associated with the head of a body; in the case of the Moor references abound to feet, until we begin to see in him a personification of a busy and servile pair of feet; a character, incidentally, which connects him with the 'blinde Briefträger' to which Fiesco likens the senses, thus giving a specific application to that general definition. A few examples will make the point clear. In II. ix the Moor enters with the words, 'Meine Sohlen brennen noch', and he counters Fiesco's announcement that he will give him orders, with the words: 'Wohin lauf' ich zuerst? Wohin zuletzt?' He conveys his acceptance of Fiesco's proposal that he should let himself be caught and suffer torture in the first degree, with the remark, 'Sie werden mir das Gelenk auseinander treiben, das macht geläufiger' (II. ix), as if the procedure should be justified if only this one capacity were enhanced. Fiesco, in speaking to the Moor, does so in terms suggesting the physical speed of the latter. 'Woher so in Atem?'; 'Du eilst nunmehr, was du eilen kannst'; 'unsere flinke Nacht' (III. iv); and, as he frees him finally, 'Fort, Bursche! Sorge, daß du Genua auf den Rücken kriegst'. None of these references in itself is particularly remarkable, but by their cumulative force they build up a picture of this character which is finally consolidated by a very striking remark of the Moor's: 'Aber nun hell auf, Freund Hassan. . . . Meine Füße haben alle Hände voll zu tun – ich muß meinen Magen karessieren, daß er mir bei meinen Beinen das Wort redt.' (II. xv.) Here the humorous variation of the familiar idiom 'ich habe alle Hände voll zu tun' to 'Meine Füße haben alle Hände voll zu tun' forces us into awareness of the identification of this man with his feet; and the following sentence bears out the impression that he in his entirety consists only of the inferior organs, and that of these the most vital are the feet he uses to serve his master.

Only a small number of the links have been mentioned which constitute the connection between Fiesco and his servant. They are to be found on every level of the play: in the choice of character and circumstance, in the organization of the plot, in the related themes of discourse, and most of all on the poetic level of the play, within its verbal fabric. Dramatic characters, like the world in which they have their being, are a composite creation of words, words spoken by them and of them. It is the unusual degree of intercommunication between these word complexes – their likeness, the likeness of their associations, etc. – which in the last resort makes us ascribe to the characters that special relationship of a partial identity, which we express by saying that an aspect of one has become the whole being of the other.

Externalization of inner states is not merely achieved through other characters. It extends, in this play as in all other plays by Schiller, to the natural as well as to the political and social scene in which the characters are set. *Fiesco* is indeed a 'Republikanisches Trauerspiel', tracing the development of a social and political organism from a state of latent oppression through open rebellion to tyranny, and ending in the liquidation of the principal champion of freedom who has turned out to be more dangerous than the official tyrants. But for all that, this political and social development is *also* an extension of the inner, psychological development of the principal character, and unless these overtones of meaning are perceived, the full significance of the play is missed. Schiller himself has made the analogy between the outer and inner Republic explicit, and supported it by a vast amount of imagery which points in both directions: thus he has given us the cue for reading the inner in and through the outer. The state of suppression in which Fiesco seeks to keep feelings and instincts corresponds to the oppression which he tends to exercise in the body politic outside him. The poet has projected the inner state into the outer and it is the rebellion within Fiesco which is foreshadowed in the tumult of the battle without. The Moor and Leonore, both frustrated in their way, joining the battle and turning against him (Leonore dons the cloak of his enemy), are outer embodiments of his own impulses which, long frustrated, uncontrollably well up in the heat of battle and lead him to kill his wife. The symbolic significance of the outer action here becomes fully apparent. For Leonore is a part of Fiesco; and the outward act of murder is equally an inner act of self destruction.[41] And, finally, Fiesco's shortlived tyranny: what is it but the poetic metaphor for the absolute rule of the dominant impulse in him, when every other impulse has died off and atrophied? This inner tyranny is externalized not only in the political scene, but also in Fiesco's individual relationship with other characters apart from the Moor. Different as his attitude to his own wife is from that to Julia, and both these from that to the Moor, they are all alike in one respect: he thwarts every one of these characters. He will not go out fully to any one of them – not even Leonore – yielding himself up to his feelings and loyalties and allowing himself to be governed by them.

But there is yet another relationship. Languishing away in imprison-
ment, 'im untersten Gewölbe' (I. xii) of her father's house, is Berta, the
daughter of his friend and the cause and most powerful spring of the uprising of which Fiesco is the head. The closeness of the connection that
should exist between them is evident. Yet he knows nothing of her fate.
For Verrina's mention of his grief goes unheeded, and Fiesco's promise to
inquire into its causes is forgotten (II. xvii). From the point of view of
Fiesco, the two actions evolve quite separately. Has the poet forgotten to
forge an obvious link, or is Fiesco's ignorance a deliberate piece of characterization? That the poet has not been oblivious of the connection, has
already been seen. It became apparent when the connection was pointed
out between the rape of Berta by Gianettino and the rape of Genoa by
Fiesco. Through this parallel, supported by several other traits in the
characters of both tyrants, Fiesco is from the start associated with Berta's
fate. And this link, forged at the beginning of the play, is once again
brought before the reader at the end, by means, purely, of form; in the
penultimate scene the theme of guilt, suffering and redemption is taken
up by Verrina when he asks Fiesco to reprieve the most wretched victims of tyranny, the galley slaves. This motif had already received a full
statement in the first act in which Berta has been cursed by her father and
her redemption made contingent upon the fate of Genoa. Stripped of all
accidents peculiar to the particular situation, the similarity of the motifs
sounded at the beginning and end of the play is striking. In both cases
Fiesco's splendour is offset by the introduction of suffering creatures languishing in an underworld existence of which the world is oblivious,
harshly punished for an old or partial guilt, and vainly hoping for redemption. Verrina says that the ocean into which the galley slaves weep their
tears, knows nothing of their misery, and clearly this metaphor serves to
draw attention to Fiesco's complete ignorance of their plight. Similarly,
the carefree, gay Fiesco of the first act is totally unsuspecting of the tragic
events that take place in Verrina's house. The abrupt division of the first
act into two halves utterly opposed in mood suggests their lack of connection on the psychological, or at least on the conscious plane; at the same
time, however, the strictly contrapuntal arrangement of the two halves
suggests the awareness of a connection in the poet's mind. Clearly, then,
the incidents introduced at the beginning and at the end of the play must
be seen together. They are alike in themselves and connected moreover by
the fact that Fiesco reacts to them in a like fashion. Furthermore, they are

linked by the repeated use of the word *Erlösung*, and through the person
of Verrina who figures in both. Nevertheless, they are not mainly introduced to tell us something about Verrina. For the same motif is introduced
a third time in a totally different psychological context. The Moor, about
to be hanged, offers to redeem his crime as a galley slave. The association
of the Moor with this motif points its significance. For the Moor, as has
been shown, is an externalization of the animal side of Fiesco. It is Fiesco's
own instinctual self, its dark entanglements, its guilt, its suffering beyond
hope of redemption, which he denies in sending the Moor to his death.

But the full measure of his estrangement from these deepest levels of
his own humanity, the completeness of their repression, becomes apparent
in his ignorance of Berta's fate. He knows neither of the violence that has
been done to her, nor of her despairing hope of redemption. He is altogether shut off from that part of his humanity which to others is the
deepest spring of their suffering and strength and, paradoxically, of their
freedom. For it is Berta who fires the Republicans to overthrow the tyrant.
Motivated by fear of the human condition, he fails where, accepting it,
they succeed. Instead, he becomes a tyrant, in the inner as well as the
political significance of the word. This fact is once more brought home to
the reader in the conversation with Verrina which precedes Fiesco's
death. For when Verrina asks Fiesco to pardon the galley slaves, his words
are invested with a fuller meaning than any that Verrina himself is aware
of, by the verbal and thematic echoes they evoke in the reader. Verrina
murders Fiesco because he will not lay down the tyrant's cloak. The full
verdict of the poet is that Fiesco must die because he will not redeem the
violated deeps of his own humanity. That these are past redeeming the
reader knows. For by the dead body of his wife, Fiesco has for a moment
laid himself open and revealed depths which are no longer human. He has
all but turned into a dog.

X

But to say that Fiesco is repressing his emotions and vital impulses would
seem to be a contradiction to the main thesis advanced in this chapter. For
the aesthetic state is by definition a state in which all functions, the senses
as well as the intellect, are released in their totality, in which receptivity
and activity are harmoniously fused. How can such a state be associated
with repression of one part of the human personality by the other? The
apparent contradiction in the interpretation advanced here corresponds to

a contradiction within the play itself. It is implicit in the tragic irony of its final metaphor: that of the would-be champion of freedom who has become a tyrant *all unknown to himself*. The key to this contradiction is to be found in an observation made earlier on. There, Fiesco's unchanging playfulness had been contrasted with the rising tide of Julia's passion. Other characters too contrast similarly with Fiesco in this respect. As Julia is gradually and perceptibly dominated by a sensual passion, so Verrina in the course of the play subordinates all his responses to his will, so Leonore is gradually overruled by the strength of her emotions: everywhere Schiller has shown characters changing in response to the demands of the changing situation and yielding to a tendency towards imbalance common to all. Only Fiesco stands in their midst unmoved. However the outer situation may change, however the emotional constellations of those around him may change, his response evinces an unchanging inner balance, as if it were altogether removed from time and change. And the increasing inappropriateness of his reactions is reflected in the outer form he gives them. The whole of the fourth act, like the first, is dominated by one of Fiesco's entertainments. But while this framework for his intrigues strikes the reader as not altogether unnatural at first, the festivity of the fourth act is ludicrously out of keeping with the realities of the situation, and this impression is shared by every character. The same response in such a totally changed situation does not, in fact, remain the same. It is by reason of the static character of his balance that it becomes a spurious balance, and his wholeness a spurious wholeness, and thus becomes the cause of his undoing.[42] For to maintain it, he must arrest the ebb and flow of his inner being, he must avoid, by repression, that tendency towards imbalance to which everyone else in the drama is subject, and subject to their detriment. So far from allowing himself to be ruled, now by the intellect, and now by his emotions, as the situation demands, he meets every situation alike in the full harness of the aesthetic response.

Thus his response, still full and sensuous even while he muses over the beauty of Genoa, imperceptibly deteriorates as it becomes fixed. This change is reflected in the change of meaning that occurs within one of the principal symbols of the play. Seeing – e.g. seeing himself in a mirror – at first connotes a truly aesthetic response on Fiesco's part, sensuous yet distanced. By the end, it has come to connote a rigid control over senses and feelings: '*Herrschsucht* hat eherne Augen,' Leonore says to Fiesco, 'worin ewig nie die Empfindung perlt' (IV. xiv). The symbol of aesthetic activity is still used, but the quality of the activity has changed; for Fiesco, fearful of the incalculable, has excluded sense and feeling from his seeing, so that his control may be all the more complete. To describe this process of a shrinkage of perception, as it were, one might quote the words of a modern writer, who says: 'Superficial perception may be increasing, while the kernel of perception may be shrinking.'[43] This deterioration is confirmed from another side, again through the symbol of seeing; for the feelings which Fiesco fails to incorporate in his narrowing perception are now shown to be themselves unseeing or blind. 'Dann übereilen sich . . . zwei Augen, und . . . *ich – ermorde – mein Weib*' (V. xiii) – these are the terms in which Fiesco relates his impulsive rashness and its consequences. And the spiritual blindness by which he is overcome as he gives rein to his impulses finds expression in the plea for sight and distance which precedes the words just quoted: 'Ah daß ich stünde am Tor der Verdammnis, hinunterschauern dürfte mein Aug' auf die mancherlei Folterschrauben der sinnreichen Hölle . . . Könnt' ich sie sehen, meine Qual, wer weiß, ich trüge sie vielleicht.' (V. xiii.) The blindness and complete lack of aesthetic distance which he here evinces are the converse of the excess of distance that has increasingly marred his aesthetic response. Thus the latter in the end deteriorates into a pose which becomes apparent at the moment when Fiesco accepts the dukedom, the token of tyranny. He does so standing 'die ganze Zeit über, den Kopf auf die Brust gesunken, in einer denkenden Stellung' (V. xii). The inner significance of the act belies the contemplative appearance. The full measure of the debasement of the initial aesthetic response, however, becomes apparent when, after the death of his wife, he promises the Genoese 'eine Totenfeier . . . , daß das Leben seine Anbeter verlieren und die Verwesung wie eine Braut glänzen soll' (V. xiii). The aesthetic mode, which the 'Anbeter der Kunst' had chosen as the gateway to the fullest life, in the end comes to be associated with stagnation, decay and death. It is precisely this deterioration for which Oscar Wilde found the haunting symbol of the portrait in Dorian Gray which decays as surely as Dorian defies time in unchanging beauty. This failure to fix a contemplative response, its deterioration and the disintegration of the personality is not only Fiesco's tragedy. It is the central pillar in the architecture of every one of Schiller's tragedies, from *Die Räuber* to *Demetrius*. Sometimes we witness the tragic process from its inception, as with Marquis Posa, Don Manuel or Demetrius. At other times, as in the case of King Philip, or Elisabeth in *Maria Stuart*, the hero is presented in its final stages, his fuller and finer life already atrophied, his tyranny established, only his fearful persistence in total power telling us of that totality of being he once sought. In every case, however, the same paradox is voiced. Freedom and fullness of life can be gained only by being lost. The attempt to realize them by statically persisting in the freest and fullest of responses, the contemplative response, is inspired by fear, leads to repression and ends in the ultimate destruction of the personality.

2

Reflection as a function of form :
a reading of *Don Carlos*

———————————⇒≫◆≪⇐———————————

In a famous letter written to Goethe in August 1794, Schiller describes himself as a hybrid being hovering 'zwischen dem Begriff und der Anschauung, zwischen der Regel und der Empfindung, zwischen dem technischen Kopf und dem Genie,' and he concludes: 'Dies ist es, was mir, besonders in frühern Jahren, sowohl auf dem Felde der Spekulation als der Dichtkunst ein ziemlich linkisches Ansehen gegeben; denn gewöhnlich übereilte mich der Poet, wo ich philosophieren sollte, und der philosophische Geist, wo ich dichten wollte.'[1] Few statements made by poets about their own creative processes have had so disastrous an effect as this one by Schiller, in which he labels himself as a philosophical poet. For it has legitimized an all but universal, perilous and most regrettable shortcoming of artistic appreciation.[2] We find the greatest difficulty in responding *aesthetically* to a poetic subject-matter with a powerful intellectual, moral or emotional appeal. For far too long we have reacted intellectually to the Metaphysicals or T. S. Eliot, morally to Matthew Arnold, and emotionally to, say, D. H. Lawrence or Stefan George.

Nowhere is this problem more acute than in the case of Schiller. His art is fraught with philosophical matter. Its ideas loom large; they forcibly impinge on our minds; and so it is with our minds that we tend to respond to Schiller's art. We like it or we dislike it for its ideas, rather than because of the way its ideas, together with the rest of its materials – its emotions, its moral sentiments, its words – function in its total aesthetic organization.[3] This is a very real critical problem. Unhappily, Schiller's deprecatory assessment of himself has absolved us from facing it as such. For do we not have his own word that with him the creative act was not an autonomous process distinct from all other mental activities, involving intellectual and intuitive elements, it is true, but transcending both in a response which is qualitatively different? And does he not intimate that his artistic products, too, bear the marks of this heterogeneous origin?[4] With his self-criticism in mind, we scarcely expect a Schillerian poem or drama to be a unique and self-sufficient organism, sealed off from every other work of art, and from life, by the compactness of its aesthetic organization. Rather do we regard it as a conglomerate of matter and form, of discursive and poetic elements, of vision and technique, hanging together after a manner, it is true, but perpetually referring the reader to their point of origin, the philosopher-poet.

Thus it is that a difficult art and a diffident artist have set us on a perilous road, away from the work of art. We have waived the arduous task of surrendering to his poetry, unconditionally and completely, until we apprehend in every fibre of its meaning a function of its form, and in every fibre of its form a function of its meaning: until, that is, we have discovered that indivisible unity of meaning and form which *is* the poem. With the label 'Philosophical Poet' for our passport, we have grown accustomed to traffic to and fro between poetry and theory, paying lightning visits to the philosopher here in hopes that he may tell us what the poet might have meant, and looking to the poet there to elucidate for us the thinker's abstractions. What critic has not operated with the concepts of the *sinnliche* and *übersinnliche Wesen*, the *empirische* versus the *intelligible Charakter*, to shed light on the poet's notions of the tragic hero, tragic guilt and catharsis? Again, who has not resorted to such theoretical categories as the *schöne* or *erhabene Seele* to illuminate the dark intricacies of Johanna's or Maria Stuart's soul? Or the *Naive* versus the *Sentimentalische* to solve the riddle of *Demetrius*? Thus, crossing at will the sacred boundaries of the individual work of art, into the adjacent realms of prose, its contours have become blurred, its proportions distorted. We see it as a part of a larger whole: the system of Schiller's ideas in their totality.[5] We are not content to ask how these ideas enter into any given work of art, there to function as images and symbols. We want to know how the thought-content 'deposited' in a work of art hangs together with the ideas 'deposited' elsewhere by the poet-philosopher, in other works of art, in his theory, in his letters and in his conversations. We have, in fact, succumbed to the lure of the Master idea. However diverse the ideological premises underlying the

various studies of Schiller, and however contradictory the ultimate message extracted from the poet – the basic uniformity of the critical method
employed by the vast majority of critics is striking indeed. Whether we
consult the older works of Kühnemann or Petsch, or more recent studies
by Cysarz, Gumbel, Fricke, von Wiese, May or Gerhard, we read so many
treatises on ideas, as though the latter were disengaged from the verbal
structures in which they operate, and endowed with an absolute and
ultimate significance of their own. We have been told a great deal of
Schiller the apostle of duty;[6] of Schiller the votary of beauty;[7] of Schiller
the forerunner of a tragic culture such as Nietzsche was to proclaim half a
century later;[8] of Schiller the high priest of George's new Hellenism:[9] but
of Schiller the artist we have heard remarkably little, except in the studies
by Gerhard Storz and Emil Staiger.[10] It is true, the conventional nomenclature used by his critics tells us that they are treating of a poem or a
drama. But were it not for such extraneous reminders, we would sometimes be at a loss to know, from the inside, as it were, that these philosophical tracts deal with art and its formed meaning, rather than with – yet
another philosophical tract.

But ideas do not make a poet. Most of the world's great ideas were
thought of long ago. And even the profoundest ideas, in isolation, soon
wither, date and die. They become potent and enduring within the aesthetic organization that nourishes their life. The miracle of art lies in the
making. It resides, not in its matter, but in its manner. Its profound-
ness lies, not in the depth of its ideas, but in the density of their
design.[11] Having stripped Schiller's poetry of the magic of its form,
can we wonder that the residue of our findings should be shallow and
banal?[12]

It is indeed paradoxical that the hunt for ideas, for the intellectual content of his poetry, should have blighted our appreciation of an artist so
supremely disdainful of all mere content *per se*, of mere *Stoff*, as was
Schiller: Schiller who wrote 'daß dem Ästhetischen, so wenig es auch die
Leerheit vertragen kann, die Frivolität doch weit weniger widerspricht
als die Ernsthaftigkeit';[13] who calls the moral judgement about Wallenstein's crime 'eine . . . an sich triviale und unpoetische Materie', adding
that his work on that portion of the drama has made him feel 'wie leer das
eigentlich Moralische ist';[14] who speaks disparagingly of the heroic in
Corneille as 'dieses, an sich nicht sehr reichhaltige, Ingrediens';[15] and
who, once and for all, took the side of form against matter in that often
quoted and justly famous sentence from the *Ästhetische Briefe*:

Darin also besteht das eigentliche Kunstgeheimnis des Meisters, *daß er den Stoff durch die Form vertilgt*; und je imposanter, anmaßender, verführerischer der Stoff an sich selbst ist, je eigenmächtiger derselbe mit *seiner* Wirkung sich vordrängt, oder je mehr der Betrachter geneigt ist, sich unmittelbar mit dem Stoff einzulassen, desto triumphierender ist die Kunst, welche jenen zurückzwingt und über diesen die Herrschaft behauptet. (Letter XXII.)

Should Schiller the artist in truth have failed so utterly to master this problem of matter in general, and of intellectual matter in particular, which Schiller the aesthetician understood so perfectly?

I think that this is a very important question, maybe a decisive one: on our answer to it will largely depend any future assessment of Schiller's poetry. As a prolegomenon to a possible answer I propose to investigate Schiller's drama of transition, *Don Carlos*, a ravishing poetic product of youth, marred, it is widely felt, by an ungainliness of proportion which is due, at least in part, to the amount of philosophical matter which has accumulated without being fully assimilated into the poetic organism. Within this drama, I have chosen as a focal point one single scene. It is a scene in which, more than almost anywhere else in Schiller's entire dramatic work, the philosopher seems to have taken the pen from out of the poet's hand: I mean, of course, the *Audienzszene* between Posa and King Philip at the end of the third act, the centrepiece of the tragedy. A solid block of philosophizing disrupting the dramatic action and deflecting it from its course to no apparent purpose, this scene seems to illustrate to a nicety the flaw in his creative powers which the poet castigates so mercilessly in his letter to Goethe. No critic has doubted that this scene, for all its lofty beauty, represents a residue of intellectual matter which the poet has failed to assimilate into the organism of the play as a whole. Some see in it a typical expression of the political philosophy of the age of enlightenment;[16] others a reflection of the poet's unpolitical temper.[17] Yet another has recognized Posa's ideas as precursors of the notions to be developed later on in the *Ästhetische Briefe*,[18] but all alike have assumed that the ideas which Posa voices in this scene represent a direct incursion of the poet's own convictions into the body of the tragedy,[19] and they have accordingly interpreted these ideas within a biographical framework of reference rather than within the aesthetic context in which they are embedded.

Once the reflectiveness evinced by Posa is accounted for in this manner, that is to say as an extraneous adjunct to his character, a picture of him has crystallized as of an essentially and straightforwardly active personality. 'Ein glühender Künder und todbereiter Streiter einer besseren Zukunft', 'ein mutiger Künder', 'a man of daring action', 'a constructive reformer' – epithets such as these, drawn at random from various critical studies, could be almost indefinitely multiplied. Yet somehow this picture, temptingly simple though it seems, does not cover the facts. Instead, it points up the most tantalizing contradictions.[20] Naturally enough, the reflectiveness of the central scene which critics had discounted in forming their conception of Posa's character does not fit into this conception. Nor does his subsequent behaviour altogether fit the popular notion of 'the man of action'. For such a character he displays a remarkable lack of drive and clear objective. He neither seizes nor sacrifices the unique opportunity offered to him by the King. Irresolutely he vacillates between Don Philip and his son and the rival causes they represent which, as everyone in the play knows, are irreconcilable. And embracing both, he embraces neither. His activities in the one direction are perpetually nullified by the precautionary measures he is forced to take in the other. The King's confidant, he is yet constrained from exploiting his position by the need to keep it secret from his friend. Carlos's confidant, he is hampered in every step he takes on his behalf by his furtive alliance with the King. As the saying goes, he wants to have his cake and eat it, too. Yet in the last resort, what does he gain? His own life, the life of his friend, the cause he had championed, the better self of the king for which he had shown such solicitude – in the end they are all sacrificed.[21]

And again, do the expository acts of the tragedy preceding the great interview really support the popular assumption about Posa's character? We cannot conclude a great deal from his first reactions to Carlos's predicament. The situation is still in the making, his motives are veiled, he is as yet holding his hand. Two incidents, however, placed at important points of the drama, stand out from the flux of the present: both of them episodes from the past, finished and rounded-off bits of living as it were, they delineate Posa's character with the precision of a vignette. The one, related by Carlos at the beginning of the play, shows Posa as a boy in a strangely incongruous situation, passively evading punishment for an offence he had inadvertently committed whilst playing, and allowing his friend to suffer in his stead.[22] The second incident is related by Alba just before Posa's interview with the king. The Duke recalls the meteoric appearance of the youth before the beleaguered city of Valetta. The bastion lost, he, and he alone of all its defenders, escapes with his life and returns to Alcala, 'die angefangnen Studien zu enden'. These incidents suggest a good many things. The one thing they assuredly do not suggest is that Posa is a straightforwardly active, heroic character. On the contrary: taken together with his vacillating bearing in the latter part of the play, up to the catastrophe, these early scenes suggest a curious lack of dedication, a consistent reluctance to stick to a course of action once begun, for better or worse. (This is not just common sense on Posa's part. The Maltese Knights who perish for their cause, and Carlos who as boy and man suffers for his friend, certainly are no fools.)

It is remarkable that every one of the features I have mentioned, and many others besides, have at one time or another been singled out by critics who have felt them to be inconsistent with our generally accepted notion of Posa's character.[23] Indeed, were we to add up all the features that will not fit into the customary picture, precious little would be left of it. Had we not better abandon a conception which creates so many problems, and instead allow for the possibility that the strain of reflectiveness, so far from being an extraneous adjunct to Posa's character, may in fact be an intrinsic part of it, indispensable to its understanding? With this hypothesis in mind, let us review the problematic scene, to find out whether its themes of discourse, its actions and its imagery do not, after all, constitute a unity within themselves and with the main body of the tragedy.

II

It has been rightly pointed out that the notions Posa voices in his interview with the King bear a more than passing resemblance to the thoughts expounded some years later by the author of the *Ästhetische Briefe*.[24] And indeed, the Marquis's visionary words are pervaded, not only by the idea of freedom – to say this would be commonplace – but by that specific concept of total aesthetic freedom which forms the cornerstone of the 'Kallias-briefe' as well as of the mature poet's philosophical thought. The total freedom of which Schiller speaks permeates a given whole in such a fashion that it would appear to extend down to its minutest ramifications. Such freedom – 'Freiheit in der Erscheinung' as the author of the 'Kalliasbriefe' termed it – is the distinguishing mark of every aesthetic organization, and it is by virtue of this quality that we call a thing beautiful.[25] For what is beauty if not that configuration of a phenomenon in which every part seems free to declare its own essence and fulfil its own law whilst yet revealing the law and meaning of the whole? And what is the artist but the creator of such harmonies, he that causes the stone to shine and the words to sing that declare the vision of his spirit? Such total freedom then is the hallmark of Posa's thought, of his ideal vision of the individual, of society and of creation as a whole. For like a work of art the ideal personality harbours neither division nor strife. Spirit and nature are at one, moving together in mutual consent, in such a way that each fulfils the law of the other as it fulfils itself:[26]

> Und Freude wäre mir
> Und eigne Wahl, was mir nur Pflicht sein sollte . . .

Thus Posa describes the harmony within his self, a state he would destroy were he to sell himself to the despot. And the essentially aesthetic character of this state is revealed by the metaphor he uses a moment later:

> Ich aber soll zum Meißel mich erniedern,
> Wo ich der Künstler könnte sein?

By this metaphor and others like it, the Monarch, too, is designated as an artist. Already in one of Posa's opening sallies does this meaning become apparent:

> Ich bin gewiß, daß der erfahrne Kenner,
> In Menschenseelen, seinem Stoff, geübt,
> Beim ersten Blicke wird gelesen haben,
> Was ich ihm taugen kann, was nicht.

It emerges unmistakably when Posa goes on to describe the great error in calculation which the despot made

> Da Sie den Menschen aus des Schöpfers Hand
> in Ihrer Hände Werk verwandelten
> Und dieser neugegoßnen Kreatur
> Zum Gott sich gaben . . .
> . . . Da Sie den Menschen
> Zu Ihrem Saitenspiel herunterstürzten . . .

But by the ironic twist perceptible in every one of these images, the speaker is drawing our attention to a subtle distinction. Don Philip is an artist, undoubtedly; but an artist in an altogether different vein from the free personality that has created a harmonious whole out of the erstwhile warring elements of its nature. With the ruthlessness of the virtuoso, the

King has moulded his materials to his own purpose, as if it were dead
matter he was fashioning, rather than the living souls of beings like himself: 'In Menschenseelen, seinem Stoff, geübt', 'neugegoßne Kreatur',
'herunterstürzten' – every phrase, every word almost, bespeaks the despotic disregard for his material, the same contempt for its life and inner
law. Like the free individual, the sovereign of the future ought to be an
artist in an altogether higher sense.[27] Respecting his living medium, he
welds it into an organic whole, every one of whose parts participates in the
common weal in harmony and freedom. In formulation upon formulation,
the Marquis hammers out his conception of a body politic that is marked
by the freedom and, at the same time, the interdependence of all its
members with one another and with the whole whose life they share. In
such a society the will of ruler and ruled is one. No impulse of the people
but that finds expression in the ruler's will; and no prompting of the ruler
but that is carried out, freely and fully, by those he rules.[28] Each fulfils
his own law in fulfilling that of the other. It is this total interdependence
in total freedom that Posa designates when he calls the king of his future
society 'von Millionen Königen ein König' and addresses its people as 'der
Krone Zweck'. And it is by this token of total freedom that we recognize
Posa's conception of society for what it is – an aesthetic conception. So, too,
total freedom prevails in that greatest of all works of art, the universe. The
decrees of the Supreme Artist are but the natural laws themselves that
pervade his creation:

> . . . ihn,
> Den Künstler, wird man nicht gewahr, bescheiden
> Verhüllt er sich in ewige Gesetze . . .

Every being that has a place in divine creation is permitted to obey the
laws of its nature; and what it so does in perfect freedom mysteriously
helps to realize the design of the whole. Even evil is permitted to exist
unchecked:

> . . . der Freiheit
> Entzückende Erscheinung nicht zu stören . . .

'Der Freiheit entzückende Erscheinung' – do not these words call to mind
another, more famous formulation: 'Freiheit in der Erscheinung', that
magic formula in which the young aesthetician, at the outset of his
career, had impetuously sought to capture the essence of beauty? And can
we doubt but that in his threefold panegyric on freedom Marquis Posa

is giving expression to an aesthetic conception of the purest water? When he speaks of the 'traurige Verstümmlung' of a humanity that flees, in terror, 'vor dem Gespenste ihrer innern Größe,' having abjured its nobility and freedom; when he asks:

> . . . wenn die Freiheit,
> Die Sie vernichteten, das Einz'ge wäre,
> Das Ihre Wünsche reifen kann? . . .

when finally he pleads:

> Der Mensch ist mehr, als Sie von ihm gehalten . . .

and demands:

> Stellen Sie der Menschheit
> Verlornen Adel wieder her! Der Bürger
> Sei wiederum, was er zuvor gewesen,
> Der Krone Zweck! – ihn binde keine Pflicht
> Als seiner Brüder gleich ehrwürd'ge Rechte . . .

– he is surely lamenting that loss of aesthetic totality which the poet deplores in the sixth Aesthetic Letter, the letter in which, time and again, we read of 'unsrer verstümmelten Natur', of the 'Zerstückelung' of our being, and in which human beings are likened to 'verkrüppelten Gewächsen'. He is outlining that ideal of an aesthetic state of which we read, '*Freiheit zu geben durch Freiheit* ist das Grundgesetz dieses Reichs'; and again, 'In dem ästhetischen Staate ist alles – auch das dienende Werkzeug ein freier Bürger, der mit dem edelsten gleiche Rechte hat, und der Verstand, der die duldende Masse unter seine Zwecke gewalttätig beugt, muß sie hier um ihre Beistimmung fragen' (Letter XXVII).

The similarity between the ideas voiced by Posa and the notions expressed in Schiller's aesthetic writings is indeed striking, and many pages could be filled proving a correspondence that is vastly more far-reaching and detailed than has ever been suspected. But what would be the use of such an undertaking? Would not the proof of such a correspondence of ideas lend final support to the prevailing assumption that the tragic hero, in this climactic scene of the drama, is but a mouthpiece for the views of Schiller the philosopher? Not quite, at least not by itself. To warrant such a conclusion, we would have to show more than the mere compatibility, coherence or even identity of ideas within the drama with ideas outside it. In addition, we would have to prove the absence of internal coherence or indeed the positive incompatibility of those ideas with the total dramatic structure in which they are embedded. And here the most problematic feature of the great *Audienzszene* at once springs to mind: Posa's persistent refusal to swing into action. What manner of a hero is this, we feel inclined to ask, who, in the decisive hour of his life, expounds his ideals with dazzling eloquence and every semblance of sincerity only to spurn the chance to put them into practice?[29] The discrepancy between Posa's passionate protestations and his actual impassivity, between his words and his deeds, seems so glaring as to countenance the conclusion that his reflections, so far from springing from the depth of his being, have been put into his mouth by the philosophizing poet. This is a grave conclusion to draw, resulting, as we have already seen, in no end of ambiguities and contradictions. To deny Posa's reflectiveness as an integral part of his character is, in fact, tantamount to denying the drama any real unity as a whole. Before adopting such a position, therefore, we might do well to examine more closely Posa's strange refusal to act and to inquire whether his passivity is not perhaps, after all, rooted in the nature of the ideal he holds.

'Ich kann nicht Fürstendiener sein' declares the Marquis to the astonished King; and he goes on to explain his position as follows:

> . . . Wenn Sie
> Mich anzustellen würdigen, so wollen
> Sie nur die vorgewogne Tat. Sie wollen
> Nur meinen Arm und meinen Mut im Felde,
> Nur meinen Kopf im Rat. Nicht meine Taten,
> Der Beifall, den sie finden an dem Thron,
> Soll meiner Taten Endzweck sein.

These are difficult words. What exactly are we to understand by the *vorgewogne Tat* of which Posa speaks? And what by the kind of action he opposes to it later on, the kind that would flow from his own nature, freely? Two things clearly stand out in his description. The *vorgewogne Tat*, in the first place, is a kind of action in which this or that single capacity of the person is engaged rather than the whole person: only his physical strength and valour in one instance and only his mind in the other. In the second place, it is an activity which is cut to measure, weighed and packaged to an end beyond itself – for example, to the approval attending its success. Conversely, the mode of action envisaged by Posa involves the whole personality in the totality of its faculties; moreover, its purpose and justification lie in itself, in the very act of doing. What manner of activity can this be? Most of our actions, it would seem, are of the kind that Posa repudiates. For ordinarily, when we act, we are governed by some specific purpose or other, and to that purpose our faculties are forthwith geared. We exercise those powers that will promote its realization, and we suspend, or actively suppress, those that might stand in our way. The soldier about to give battle – not just Don Philip's soldier but any soldier anywhere – will use his *Arm* and his *Mut*, and will shut off his mind except in so far as it helps him gain his objective. The theorist – not just Don Philip's experts but the theorist or scientist of any age or place – will bring his mind to bear as closely as possible upon the problem before him, restraining any irrelevant emotion or premature impulse to action. Each is successful in the measure in which he pinpoints his response to meet the specific requirements of his purpose.[30] But there is one mode of activity which would seem to answer the Marquis Posa's description in that it is exempt from purpose and specialization: that is the activity of play and the aesthetic activity that is kindred to it. Schiller is at one with modern aestheticians in his belief that here alone, in play and in aesthetic experience, all our powers are quickened into a harmonious activity, and that this activity subserves no outward end, but rests in itself, complete and self-sufficient.[31] In play and in aesthetic contemplation alone are we not committed to achieve anything. We are not oriented towards a *telos*, an ultimate yardstick, as it were, against which we measure our performance until we have achieved the perfect *vorgewogne Tat*. We just are, not partially, but in our totality – 'Arm' *and* 'Mut' *and* 'Kopf' – and we experience ourselves, freely and uselessly, in the abundance of our untrammelled life. Can we doubt that this is the mode of activity of which Posa dreams and on account of which he rejects the King's service? When he says:

> Nicht meine Taten,
> Der Beifall, den sie finden an dem Thron,
> Soll meiner Taten Endzweck sein. Mir aber,
> Mir hat die Tugend eignen Wert . . .

he is not speaking of the contentment that attends the morally motivated deed, as a superficial reading through Kantian lenses might suggest; he is voicing that peculiar sense of self-containment and fulfilment that is the characteristic of the aesthetic mode. That this is so emerges beyond doubt from the metaphor in which he sums up his argument:

Ich aber soll zum Meißel mich erniedern,
Wo ich der Künstler könnte sein?

Thus Marquis Posa's failure to act cannot simply be written off as a
mark of the poet's failure properly to root his hero's thoughts in his
character. For Posa's refusal to take office, looked at more closely, does not
appear to be quite unrelated to the beliefs he has expressed. Indeed, it
springs from these beliefs in a more direct and fundamental fashion than
may readily be suspected. For Posa does not, as has so often been argued,
reject this or that course of action for this or that particular reason, e.g. the
specific duties enjoined on him by the tyrant because they might com-
promise his friend or the cause he himself champions. His words leave no
doubt, rather, that he rejects all purposive action *per se*, because of a
peculiar dilemma inherent in the aesthetic ideal. For aesthetic totality is
compromised by the imposition of any ulterior end whatever upon the
free play of the personality, be that end even its own realization. In purposive behaviour, totality of being inevitably gives way to partiality,
expansiveness to intensiveness and specialization. Inasmuch as to call a
thing an end presupposes that there must be means fitted for its realization, Marquis Posa's aesthetic ideal cannot be properly so called. To Posa it
signifies a changeless absolute, a state of grace in which his whole being has
come to rest.[32]

It is this paradoxical nature of Posa's ideal which accounts for his refusal to act on its behalf when the opportunity arises. More than that, it
explains the fitful and ultimately futile nature of the actions he does un-
dertake in the course of the tragedy.[33] The boy's refusal to pay the penalty
for his playful error, the tardiness of the youth to make the supreme
sacrifice for the Cross, the unwillingness of the man finally to throw in his
lot with his friend or with the King: do not all these acts betoken the same
deep-seated reluctance wholly to commit himself to any ulterior end and
to put its exigencies before the claims of his personality?[34] Seen in the
light of the central scene of the tragedy, and from the aesthetic viewpoint
established there, the pattern of Posa's actions becomes perfectly intelligible. He is ready enough to *lend* himself to a cause as long as its demands
do not encroach upon his freedom; as long, that is, as it permits the spontaneous and untrammelled activity of the whole person rejoicing in the
fullness of his powers and in the flawless grace of his performance;[35] as
long, in fact, as he is free to play, using the word in that grave and poignant sense given to it by the author of the *Ästhetische Briefe*. Directly,

however, that play becomes necessity enforcing its dictates regardless of the person or the cost, he shakes off its demands and, transcending all coercion and constraint, emerges unbound. Time and again, the desire for aesthetic totality of being overrides every other impulse, however powerful. Honour, valour, fidelity, the ambition even to better the world, strong though these promptings be in the virile character of the Maltese, they all terminate in the persistent pull towards that inclusive state of being in which every potentiality of the person – every power, every passion and every perception – is awakened and all are contained in the vibrant equilibrium of aesthetic awareness.

The desire for aesthetic totality – what a curious determinant of behaviour and how unlikely in the hero of a drama! Neither the inconclusiveness of Posa's actions nor yet the consistent tenor of his utterances would suffice, by themselves, to persuade us of the hidden presence of such a motivating force. To believe it, we have to see it enacted. We have to see the shift from action to contemplation, from outward-directed purposive behaviour to the self-containment of the aesthetic state taking place before our eyes and become a palpable dramatic reality. And see it we do, in the soliloquy that immediately precedes, and explains, the crucial encounter of the tragedy.

At the beginning of this scene, Posa seems to strike a utilitarian enough note. He resolves to heed the counsel given him by the Duke of Alba, most practical of men, and to use to the full the momentous opportunity that chance has played into his hands. His last words, too, convey the sense of one solemnly dedicated to his purpose: 'In diesem Glauben will ich handeln,' he vows as the scene ends. But no sooner have his words died away than something altogether unexpected happens. The hero's attention is arrested by – a picture on the wall. Presently he becomes oblivious of time and place, oblivious even of the entry of the King. This is how the stage direction runs: 'Er macht einige Gänge durch das Zimmer und bleibt endlich in ruhiger Betrachtung vor einem Gemälde stehen. Der König erscheint in dem angrenzenden Zimmer, wo er einige Befehle gibt. Alsdann tritt er herein, steht an der Türe still und sieht dem Marquis eine Zeitlang zu, ohne von ihm bemerkt zu werden.' On this quiet note ends the scene which had begun with a clarion call to action. On this note begins the climactic encounter of the tragedy. The fateful moment of his life finds a Posa tranquilly immersed in contemplation, that most self-sufficient and wholly useless of human states. All pressures have subsided, all purposes, so clearly envisaged but a moment before, have lapsed into abeyance. The

King's voice, heard in an adjoining room, breaks the silence only to make it seem the deeper. It does not reach the ear of the still figure standing there as if arrested in a trance. The connection between him and the common world is all but severed.

It is in the nature of monologues that they reveal springs of behaviour which remain hidden ordinarily, in the presence of others; and this one is no exception to the rule. Besides, speech eventually gives way to panto-mime; and however much we may distrust the duplicity of words, we cannot doubt the authenticity of an act performed so dreamily, with an unselfconscious absorption so complete that even the entry of Majesty goes unobserved. What is enacted here stems from the very depths of Posa's being. But it may well be that the ultimate force of this strange scene derives from its very incredibility. It is because Posa's response is so fla-grantly inappropriate to the demands of the moment and our own expecta-tions that it hits us with the full impact of its significance. At the height of the tension, on the threshold of an encounter on which the destiny of millions may well hang, we witness the incredible switch from the practical to the contemplative mode. Before our eyes, the initial impulse towards determinate action has been engulfed in the irresistible pull to-wards that totality of being which is momentarily attained in the aesthetic state. And we know: a person that responds *thus* in *this* situation cannot help himself. The impulse that governs him is his fate. Indeed, Schiller himself in his capacity as a critic supports this reading of his poetic intention. In the final pages of the *Briefe über Don Carlos*, he tells us that the ultimate cause of Posa's tragic failure lay 'in dem Bestreben, alles wegzudrängen, was das Spiel unserer Kräfte hindert'. What do these words signify if not that irresistible gravitation of the hero towards that playful equipoise which is the hallmark of the aesthetic state?

Posa wakes up from his transport, it is true, and rises to the occasion. But throughout the ensuing scene something of the self-containment of his earlier mood can be discerned. He pleads with fire and passion, to be sure. But it is a disinterested passion, curiously unrelated to the King and the great objectives that are at stake. He wants nothing, he asks for nothing. He is passionately concerned merely to fashion the occasion which chance has played into his hands into a thing of lasting and glowing significance, as the artist is passionately concerned to fashion his materials; and it is surely no accident that his speeches are permeated through and through with images drawn from the sphere of art, and that they keep coming back to the subject of creation, both in nature and in art. To endow the fleeting moment with significant form is his real purpose, a purpose avowed already in his soliloquy:

> . . . was
>
> Ist Zufall anders als der rohe Stein,
> Der Leben annimmt unter Bildners Hand?
> Den Zufall gibt die Vorsehung – Zum Zwecke
> Muß ihn der Mensch gestalten . . .

A curious metaphor this, the metaphor of the *Bildner*, if we cling to the conception of Posa as an essentially active personality. For is it not strange to describe an undertaking fraught with consequences in terms of an activity which entirely fails to point beyond itself?[36] By his own admission here and later on, his *Zweck* is that inner purposiveness which is the mark of the aesthetic activity and its creations.[37]

The King readily senses the unrelatedness of Posa's passion. He is profoundly moved, to be sure, in the way one is moved by the utterance of an artist; and significantly it is in a submerged metaphor drawn from the aesthetic sphere that he gives voice to his emotion: 'Bei Gott, er greift in meine Seele!' he murmurs, and the context of this aside leaves no doubt that he is likening his own soul to the *Saitenspiel* of which Posa has just spoken. But he does not feel moved to respond practically to Posa's revolutionary notions. They do not worry him. Intuitively he senses the strange disinterestedness of a man who, for all his fiery eloquence, has asked for neither post nor favour; and it is this quality which persuades him that it is safe to humour the 'sonderbare Schwärmer', enjoying him for what he is, a creature *sui generis*, a human being.[38]

The Marquis, in his turn, does his utmost to foster the King's belief. He seeks to explain himself, and the extraordinary effect he is having on the misanthropic monarch, in as innocuous a fashion as possible.[39] 'Kann ein Gemälde Ihre Ruhe trüben?' he asks, only to reply for the King, 'Ihr Atem löscht es aus.' And again, a little later:

> *Sie* sehn jetzt unter diesem sanftern Bilde
> Vielleicht zum erstenmal die Freiheit.

In part, no doubt, these assurances are calculated to allay the King's suspicions. But this is scarcely all. The metaphor of the picture in which the hero chooses to explain himself is an unusual one, more likely, it would seem, to perplex a man of the King's mould than to reassure him. And indeed, it stems from a different stratum of the play, far below the clash of character and the clamour of the action. These are not words primarily intended for the Monarch. In them the poet, through the mouth of his hero, addresses himself to the larger perception of his readers. Twice in rapid succession Posa likens himself to a work of art, to a picture – he whose discourse teems with aesthetic images and ideas, whose actions have all the marks of aesthetic acts, whose deepest nature the poet has finally revealed through the mediation of – a picture. Charged with such associations, the metaphor Posa invokes assumes an enhanced significance. It becomes the ultimate poetic symbol of his personality. And what better symbol than the picture for a personality so harmoniously contained within himself, so deeply set apart from the strivings of the common man? For the picture, in truth, is the most 'composed' of things.[40] Finished and complete, it rests in its own symmetries, *in* space and time, to be sure, but in its essence not *of* it.[41] So too has Posa been transported into a timeless dimension as he stands on the threshold of the fateful hour, lost in contemplation. And it is precisely that profound sense of his own timelessness which he expresses when he says to the King in what is perhaps the most hotly disputed statement of the tragedy:

> Das Jahrhundert
> Ist meinem Ideal nicht reif. Ich lebe
> Ein Bürger derer, welche kommen werden.

The gulf that separates Posa from reality cannot be spanned by a century or two. He belongs to the future no more than to the present hour, like the *Gemälde* to which a moment later he will liken himself.

As Posa sees himself, so he sees others. To him, human nature is as harmoniously self-contained, as exempt from time and change and want as a work of art. In his last conversation with the Queen he confesses that she, too, had been a work of art to him, a *Bild*, and that this is how he had looked upon the Prince. Don Carlos's love for Elisabeth was to have been his aesthetic education. The contemplation of her beauty was to have led him to perfection:

> Zur höchsten Schönheit wollt' ich ihn erheben:
> Die Sterblichkeit versagte mir ein Bild,
> Die Sprache Worte – da verwies ich ihn
> Auf *dieses* . . .   (IV. xxi)

Posa's static conception of human nature – a mistaken one as it turns out since living beings are no works of art – is of the greatest consequence, dramatically and psychologically. His whole scheme, the prime lever of the dramatic action, hinges on the assumption that those involved in it will stay in their appointed places and play the roles for which they have been cast. He makes no allowance for the incalculable, for changing situations and susceptible minds, in short, for life in time which is a continual process of metamorphosis.[42] Because his assumption is mistaken, because everyone on whom he counted – the Prince, the Queen and even he himself – responds irrationally and quite unpredictably to an unforeseen situation – his plot miscarries and catastrophe ensues. At a deeper level, Posa's misconception of human nature is the source of his inner failure and constitutes the key to the theme of the tragedy as a whole. He fails because by the very rigidity with which he clings to total freedom he ironically comes to betray freedom in himself and others. And it is precisely with the paradox that freedom and fullness of life, to be truly gained, must for ever be staked and lost, that the tragedy as a whole is concerned, as indeed is every tragedy from Schiller's pen.[43]

III

But over and above these varied significances, Posa's static conception of human nature has a profound aesthetic import; and this, its most important function, becomes readily apparent if we perceive the figure of the tragic hero within the system of stresses and tensions that make up the tragedy. As the drama unfolds, the springs of passion are coiled ever more tightly: tensions rise, converge and clash, finally to precipitate themselves into action. Twice in the two opening acts of the play Carlos runs the full gamut of emotions – from unrest through temporary composure back to renewed frustration and deepened agitation. Tension mounts in the third act as we see the King's self-control crumble under the pangs of jealousy. In the fourth act breaking-point is reached. Turmoil prevails. Gone is the Queen's tranquillity, gone Eboli's pretended poise, Don Philip is beside himself and Carlos desperate. And what of Posa? In the midst of these kaleidoscopic transmutations the central figure remains unmoved. Through all the vicissitudes he, like Fiesco before him, evinces the same harmony, the same unruffled composure.[44] It is as if, exempt from time and change, he stood transfixed in a kind of motionless grace until composure abruptly gives way to inner chaos.

This stillness of the central figure has a profound effect on characters and spectators alike. In his presence, pressures slacken, passions abate and perspectives are restored. All around him – Carlos, the King, the Queen – look to him to give them back a measure of their lost equanimity. And the spectator? Carried along on the turbulent current of the action and caught up in a vortex of conflicting interests and emotions, he all but loses his freedom as an onlooker; until suddenly all this movement comes to rest in the still presence of the central figure, in the tranquil amplitude of the central scene. The spaciousness of Posa's mood, the breadth and boldness of his vision and, above all, the demoniacal detachment of the man who, granted a moment of historic consequence, refrains from seizing it but is content, instead, to live it, shape it and to reveal its inner form: the awareness of all this filters into our consciousness and imperceptibly transmutes the very quality of it. Our tension relaxes, our sensibilities expand; and with an absorption that is yet dispassionate we experience every inflection of form and meaning of the scene that is enacted before our eyes. Thus prepared, we can see the tragedy run its course and perceive the poetry of it.

We are at the end, or very nearly. I have presented the central figure of one of Schiller's tragedies as an essentially contemplative being, fitted by precisely this character to help evoke an aesthetic response on the part of the spectator. It remains to say that what is true of Marquis Posa is true of every tragic protagonist from Schiller's pen. They are all cast in a contemplative mould. The underlying reason for this disposition varies from character to character and from play to play. As we saw in an earlier chapter, Fiesco, like Posa, is capable of a truly aesthetic response which is vitiated largely by being maintained out of season. There are genuinely aesthetic elements in Wallenstein's character, too. Nevertheless, in his case the refusal to exchange the freedom of contemplation for the determinacy of action springs, in the main, from the strength of his power-impulse; and this is true to an even greater degree of the vacillating English Queen. On the other hand, the indecision of Luise Millerin which likewise discharges itself in an excess of reflectiveness is governed by an unconscious conflict so crippling as to jeopardize all freedom of movement and decision. But however different the *psychological* motivation giving rise to a dominantly contemplative or reflective frame of mind, this disposition in each case serves the same *poetic* end. Take Fiesco, Wallenstein, the Tudor Queen, Don Manuel, Isabella or even Luise Millerin: as long as we conceive of them as being essentially active characters, they remain curiously ambiguous figures, like Posa riddled with psychological contradictions, vacillating irresolutely between incompatible courses and causes, and achieving nothing for all their seeming forcefulness. It is only when

we cease to regard their reflectiveness as an outcrop of the poet's philosophical temper and instead include it as an intrinsic part of their personality, that their characters fuse into a whole and their overall function in
the tragedies in which they figure can be adequately defined. Like Posa,
they desire *Gedankenfreiheit*, the contemplative experience of their full
potential rather than the exercise of any one power, rather than the actual –
and limiting – realization of any one purpose. For the sake of this experience they seek out those ambiguous situations in which two contrary
courses are open to them at once. Or perhaps it would be truer to say that
in order to create characters such as these, the poet time and time again
devises situations which are basically and profoundly ambiguous. To these
situations they cling tenaciously and they delight in 'feeling themselves'
in the suspense they bring. For what better way to savour the potential
range of one's power than thus to remain poised between alternative
possibilities, contemplating both yet yielding to neither? For the sake of
this experience Posa seeks out the despot without abandoning his friend.
And it is to savour this delight that Fiesco warns his enemy of the impending *coup d'état* without a thought of giving up his plot; that the Queen of
England goes to visit her rival in prison, without the slightest intention
of coming to terms with her; that Wallenstein negotiates with the Swedes
without resolving to give up the Emperor:

> Es macht mir Freude, meine Macht zu kennen;
> Ob ich sie wirklich brauchen werde, *davon*, denk' ich,
> Weißt *du* nicht mehr zu sagen als ein andrer . . .

and

> Die Freiheit reizte mich und das Vermögen.

These words of Wallenstein's formulate the deep craving of every
Schillerian hero, the craving, more or less conscious and more or less pure,
for contemplative totality of experience. It is this which irresistibly draws
him to embrace the irreconcilable, to seek the unfeasible; this which gives
a rapt intensity to his very indecision. And it is precisely this craving for
aesthetic totality that marks him out for his role as tragic hero. In a context which is seemingly far removed from the present topic Schiller
writes as follows:

> Gewisse Charaktere . . . können den Zustand der Bestimmungslosig-
> keit nicht lang' ertragen und dringen ungeduldig auf ein Resultat,
> welches sie in dem Zustand ästhetischer Unbegrenztheit nicht finden.

Dahingegen breitet sich bei andern, welche ihren Genuß mehr in das Gefühl *des ganzen Vermögens* als einer *einzelnen* Handlung desselben setzen, der ästhetische Zustand in eine weit größere Fläche aus. So sehr die ersten sich vor der Leerheit fürchten, so wenig können die letzten Beschränkung vertragen.

This distinction is then clinched as follows:

Ich brauche kaum zu erinnern, daß die ersten fürs Detail und für subalterne Geschäfte, die letzten, vorausgesetzt daß sie mit diesem Vermögen zugleich Realität vereinigen, fürs Ganze und zu großen Rollen geboren sind.

This passage comes from Schiller's chief aesthetic work, the *Ästhetische Briefe*.[45] I would venture to suggest that it represents one of the three most vital links between Schiller's philosophy of art and that art itself.[46] For this description of the predominantly aesthetic character, loath to exchange his *Gefühl des ganzen Vermögens* for any real and limited achievement – does it not correspond precisely to the picture of the tragic hero that has crystallized here and in the analysis of *Fiesco*? And has not Schiller himself forged the link between the seemingly disparate spheres of life and art when he says that the aesthetic type of personality is cut out for – *große Rollen*? But if the *Ästhetische Briefe* confirm our findings, they do nothing to explain them. Why this predilection for a special kind of character and for one, moreover, that seems so strikingly ill-suited to the temper of that most linear and energetic of art-forms, the drama? If an artist of the calibre of Schiller chooses a certain type of character, or situation, not once, but time and time again, we may be sure that he is not impelled, simply, by the obsessive force of some personal experience demanding monotonous reiteration, but that his choice is prompted by the sober awareness that this type of character or situation is peculiarly fitted to help him explore the possibilities and transcend the limitations of the genre in which he is working.

I would suggest, then, that the contemplative bent of the tragic hero is Schiller's answer to the gravest shortcoming afflicting, in his view, his chosen form of art – the genre of tragedy. For tragedy, enacting before our eyes the awful riddle of destiny, more than any other literary genre tends to imperil the aesthetic distance of the spectator. We are too moved by what we see to remain free.[47] I submit that Schiller solved this artistic problem by the consistent use he made of reflection as a technical device. In the contemplative nature of the hero, maintaining himself at an aesthetic distance from the events that assail him, he found the formal – indeed, he would have said, the epic – counter-poise to the immediacy of the tragic action. The hero's own distance acts as a filter to our response, purging it of its coarser ingredients. He enables the spectator 'auch in der heftigsten Passion seine Freiheit zu behalten'; for 'das Gemüt des Zuschauers und Zuhörers muß völlig frei und unverletzt bleiben, es muß aus dem Zauberkreise des Künstlers rein und vollkommen wie aus den Händen des Schöpfers gehn.' (*Ästhetische Briefe*, Letter XXII.) The mediation of an aesthetic response: this is the poetic function of that verbal expansiveness, of those liberal reflections on the nature of freedom which are so characteristic of the Schillerian hero;[48] reflections, moreover, which are always placed at the precise point of the drama when tensions run highest, demanding to be precipitated into action. Their true significance is not to be sought in the philosophical truths they impart – very doubtful truths at that, since the hero is labouring under an illusion about himself and the world;[49] it is to be found, rather, in the formal values they mediate to the spectator. They do not *in*form our intellect; they *trans*form our total response by lifting us out of the tragic action and the very time-stream in which it is embedded and transporting us into a timeless poetic dimension.[50] And so, too, with the other retarding elements: the hero's passionate irresolution, his endless lingering between two contemplated courses, and his deep reluctance to make an irrevocable choice. They too demand to be apprehended, not merely in their dramatic and psychological import, great though that import be: they demand, above all, to be directly experienced in their formal significance as transformers, or filters, of a response which continually threatens to fall short of the aesthetic.

Throughout Schiller's tragedies, the protagonist himself embodies this function; a function which, in his last tragedy, the poet was to assign to the chorus. And indeed, it is in the preface to *Die Braut von Messina* that Schiller finally postulates the contemplative character of the tragic hero, already implicit in *Über das Pathetische*,[51] and justifies his postulate on purely aesthetic grounds. 'Die tragischen Personen', we read there, 'stehen gewissermaßen schon auf einem natürlichen Theater, weil sie vor Zuschauern sprechen und handeln, und werden eben deswegen desto tauglicher, von dem Kunst-Theater zu einem Publikum zu reden.' The tragic hero is now openly shown to be what he has always been in fact: a contemplative being – for what else is an actor on the natural stage of life? – experiencing the tragic events that assail him at one remove as it were. But the introduction of a chorus furnished a motivation for the aesthetic distance of the tragic hero which is more palpable and, at the same time, more purely poetic than any other the poet had devised before.

Thus the formative principle of Schiller's tragedies which guarantees their character as art is built deep into their structure, into the very heart of their matter.[52] It is incorporated in the central personage, in the shape of his contemplativeness. And in his last tragedy by a further extension it becomes embodied in an independent organ, to wit, the chorus. In this fashion the poet ensured doubly and triply the purity of a response which is only mediated to us after being passed through a series of filters: the chorus, the aesthetic consciousness of the hero, and finally the formal structure of the tragedy in its totality. As he has it in *Über das Pathetische*: 'Alle Affekte sind ästhetischer aus der zweiten Hand.'[53]

Schiller is indeed the philosophical poet that history has judged him to be. But the time has come to give the old label a new significance.[54] To think of him as a genius divided, part poet, part thinker, who philosophized in his poetry when the creative power went out of him, is to condemn him and to condemn him most unfairly. To be sure, there is dualism in the man. But to explain the processes and products of the creative artist in terms of the empirical personality is to be guilty of a gross over-simplification. It is bad aesthetics and bad psychology.[55] Quite on the contrary: the reflective component so prominent in the tragedies, so far from signifying any weakness in the creative powers of the poet, testifies to their exceptional vigour and resilience. For reflection – in this relatively early play as much as in those of his maturity – is not only wholly assimilated into the aesthetic organism of his tragedies; it serves itself aesthetically to organize the materials of his art. Thus we shall do well to think of Schiller as an artist who made a seemingly intractable mass of intellectual matter available to poetry; more than that: as an artist who in theory and practice alike systematically explored the possibilities of reflection as a function of artistic form. If we can but accomplish this Copernican revolution, we shall have laid the groundwork for the appreciation of a singularly aristocratic artist and uncompromising philosopher of art.

3

Element into ornament : the alchemy of art : a reading of *Die Braut von Messina*

—————⪼⟨⟩⪻—————

If I were to be asked what association the thought of Schiller's last tragedy evoked in my mind, I should at once mention its frankly rhetorical character; by which I should mean both the majestic stance of the final choruses and, at the other extreme, those stylized and slightly ludicrous declarations that exude from the lips of the *dramatis personae* like the explanatory tapes fluttering from the figures in medieval paintings, as when Don Cesar says, 'Verachtung nicht erträgt mein edles Herz.' Above all, however, I would mention the solemn symmetries in which the opposing forces of this drama are contrapuntally composed: two choruses, two brothers, two heroines, two dreams, two oracles, two alternating backdrops – an antithetical structure which every time betokens conflict and its appeasement in the realm of figure and form.[1] In short, what would spring to my mind is the immensely formalized character of this 'tragedy in the Greek manner': the generalizing reflections of the chorus, the typifying treatment of character and motive, the power of the poetic form – all those anti-naturalistic tendencies, in fact, which have found their theoretical justification in the preface.

I doubt whether I would as promptly recall the uproariousness of the subject-matter. For unruly it is in the extreme, this fable of incestuous passion perpetuated through generations, unrecognized, until it is appeased by death; as preposterous as perhaps only one other work of art in the German tongue: Thomas Mann's *Der Erwählte*. None other is so sombre and yet so serene, none other so chaotic and so contrived, none so precariously close

to our deepest taboos and yet so self-confidently and sublimely composed.[2]
It is the combination that matters and demands to be examined. How did
Schiller handle such explosive materials?

The tragedy is set in Sicily, scene of ancient edifices and senseless
devastation, sea-girded and fire-spitting. A place of violent tensions, it
seems to be compounded of these two elements, harbingers of life and
death, each opposed to the other yet together pitted against the structures
of man's making. The characters that people this scene, too, are compounded of the same stuff. Images of the sea are used to characterize the common people of Messina – labile, accessible, bearing the short-lived imprint
of every impression and, for all the evanescence of the individual, lasting.

Imagery of water and fire is used in a more threatening fashion to build
up the principal figures of the tragedy, the ruling family of Messina, and
the relations between them. Time and time again, the hatred of the
brothers, their love of Beatrice, the intrepid and passionate way of responding that characterizes them all, is articulated in terms of this imagery.[3]
References abound to 'Lebens Glut', 'feurige Kraft', 'kochendes Blut',
'Liebesglut', 'Zwistes Flammen', 'Hasses Flammen', etc. At first these
seem to be rhetorical figures of speech, remnants from the poetic language
of the baroque which have no more than conventional significance. Undoubtedly they are rhetorical forms. But if language itself has prefigured
the connection between human passions and natural elements, it is because
that connection is basic and universally experienced; besides, the poet has
given expression to it in a sustained and personal idiom and enhanced it
by every device of repetition and antithesis. Embedded in such a context,
even petrified tropes are restored to fluid life and fresh meaning.

The metaphors and similes taken from the sphere of elements are
legion, and to recount them in full is impossible. A few selected instances
must suffice to give an indication of their force and direction. Immediately
after their father's death, Isabella tells us, the brothers' hatred came out
into the open. This is the simile she uses:

> Als er die Augen
> Im Tode schloß . . .
> . . . bricht der alte Groll,
> Gleichwie des Feuers eingepreßte Glut,
> Zur offnen Flamme sich entzündend los.
> (I. i)

This opening simile is straight away linked with the associated imagery of water. For in the preceding lines Isabella has remarked of her husband's suppression of his sons' hatred:

> . . . Der Starke achtet es
> Gering, die leise Quelle zu verstopfen,
> Weil er dem Strome mächtig wehren kann.
>
> (ibid.)

Imagery of fire and water persists and fuses in the metaphor of the sulphur stream in which Isabella describes her sons' hatred:

> − Wer möchte noch das alte Bette finden
> Des Schwefelstroms, der glühend sich ergoß?
> Des unterird'schen Feuers schreckliche
> Geburt ist alles, eine Lavarinde
> Liegt aufgeschichtet über dem Gesunden . . .
>
> (I. iv)

The chorus takes up the same image as it muses over the events it has just witnessed − the abrupt reconciliation of the brothers and the story of Don Manuel's passionate adventure:

> Auf der Lava, die der Berg geschieden,
> Möcht' ich nimmer meine Hütte bauen.
>
> (I. viii)

Isabella too associates herself with the volcanic image pattern when she speaks of her own secret and ardent hopes:

> Nichts Kleines war es, solche Heimlichkeit
> Verhüllt zu tragen diese langen Jahre . . .
> . . . und ins Herz zurückzudrängen
> Den Trieb des Bluts, der mächtig, wie des Feuers
> Verschloßner Gott, aus seinen Banden strebte?
>
> (IV. i)

Imagery of water is variously linked with imagery of fire in the composite image of a flood, or stream, of fire; not only in the instances already quoted, but, most importantly, in the twice-repeated account of the dream which culminates in the twice-repeated image of an 'ungeheurer Feuerflut' devouring the ancestral house (II. v and IV. iv). Thus, too, Isabella says of her sons:

> Vom Berge stürzt der ungeheure Strom,
> Wühlt sich sein Bette selbst und bricht sich Bahn,
> Nicht des gemeßnen Pfades achtet er,
> Den ihm die Klugheit vorbedächtig baut.
>
> (II. v)

As the peripeteia approaches and their passions begin to outrun all caution, this metaphor echoes what the chorus had earlier on anticipated:

> Jene gewaltigen Wetterbäche,
> Aus des Hagels unendlichen Schloßen,
> Aus den Wolkenbrüchen zusammen geflossen,
> Kommen finster gerauscht und geschossen,
> Reißen die Brücken und reißen die Dämme
> Donnernd mit fort im Wogengeschwemme,
> Nichts ist, das die gewaltigen hemme . . .
>
> (I. iii)

Two things emerge from these examples. Firstly, the figures of this drama are built up of the same verbal materials that are used to characterize this wild and profuse nature. The Etna is more than a scenic property. It is a symbol. Volcanic forces rage within these characters. The homogeneous verbal fabric links the natural and the human spheres, showing both to be permeated by the all-pervading element. Secondly, there is an unmistakable movement in these images. The elements are held in check and controlled at first; in the images that occur toward the end of the tragedy, they rise to the surface and irrepressibly break out. And it is part of this movement that what is true on the metaphorical plane at the beginning finally becomes true on the level of outward reality – a progressive poetic intensification of symbolic truth into reality which we commonly associate with Kleist. The eruption of pent-up elements is symbolically foreshadowed in the chorus's following Don Cesar's impetuous murder of his brother:

> In schwarzen Güssen
> Stürzet hervor, ihr Bäche des Bluts. . . .
> Stürzet ein, ihr Wände!
> Versink, o Schwelle . . .
> Schwarze Dämpfe, entsteiget, entsteiget
> Qualmend dem Abgrund! . . .
> Schützende Götter des Hauses, entweichet . . .
>
> (IV. iv)

It becomes real – with a realism which grimly eclipses the last vestiges of the symbolic – in the conflagration that destroys the sage's hut; an action which in its turn confirms the truth of the father's dream and prepares for the catastrophe about to be revealed. Thus the imagery of flood and fire may be said poetically to articulate the elemental forces within the characters, repressed at first and then uncontrollably and catastrophically released.

II

Contrapuntally pitted against these forces of the unconscious are the controlling powers of reason, symbolized in the imagery of edifices. In most of the instances which I have quoted, images of man-made structures are in fact juxtaposed to the elements, for instance bridges, dams, sluices, paths – in fact edifices of every kind which fail to check the torrential rush of the unbridled forces of nature. The walls and thresholds of the house tumble down as vapours and streams of sulphur gush forth from the earth; the men of the chorus would not build their huts on the lava of hatred. Don Manuel and Isabella, the protagonists who are most steadily associated with images of repressed elemental forces, are also most steadily associated with images suggestive of control and permanence. Isabella gives us the first intimation of her secret hopes when she says:

> Noch heute soll dies Herz befriedigt sein,
> Und dieses Haus, das lang' verödet war,
> Versammle alles, was mir teuer ist.
>
> (I. ii)

In her hour of triumph she exclaims:

> – Gegründet
> Auf festen Säulen seh' ich mein Geschlecht,
> Und in der Zeiten Unermeßlichkeit
> Kann ich hinabsehn mit zufriednem Geist.
>
> (II. v)

And in her dream, strife and peace present themselves under the double image of fire and a new edifice that will withstand the fury of the elements:

> Und wie der Eulen nachtgewohnte Brut
> Von der zerstörten Brandstatt, wo sie lang'
> Mit altverjährtem Eigentum genistet,

> Auffliegt in düsterm Schwarm, den Tag verdunkelnd,
> Wenn sich die lang' vertriebenen Bewohner
> Heimkehrend nahen mit der Freude Schall,
> Den neuen Bau lebendig zu beginnen
> So flieht der alte Haß . . .
>
> (II. v)

Don Manuel, too, is preoccupied with the 'house' into which he will introduce his bride, and images of it permeate his speeches.[4] Indeed, his very first mention of Beatrice is coupled with this association:

> – Ich sehe diese Hallen, diese Säle
> Und denke mir das freudige Erschrecken
> Der überraschten, hocherstaunten Braut,
> Wenn ich als Fürstin sie und Herrscherin
> Durch dieses Hauses Pforten führen werde.
>
> (I. vii)

And again:

> Als eine Fürstin fürstlich will ich sie
> Einführen in die Hofburg meiner Väter.
>
> (I. vii)

To perceive the full significance of such seemingly literal references, we must read them in conjunction with passages which have a clear metaphorical meaning. The enmity between elements and edifices is driven home by juxtapositions such as that of the early choruses (my italics):

> Bauen wir auf der tanzenden *Welle*
> Uns ein lustig schwimmendes *Schloß?*
>
> (I. viii)

This rhetorical question is presently answered in the negative by the recognition that the fluid element permits of no permanence:

> Auf den Wellen ist alles Welle,
> Auf dem Meer ist kein Eigentum . . .
>
> (ibid.)

and, more categorically still, by the reflection that impermanence reigns even on *terra firma*, the stablest of the elements:

> Auch auf der Erde, so fest sie ruht
> Auf den ewigen, alten Säulen,
> Wanket das Glück und will nicht weilen.
>
> (I. viii)

Wanken, schwanken – these are words perpetually used of the fluidity of wave and water, and their appearance here betokens the realization that there is no permanence to be found anywhere in the sphere of the elements. This dichotomy between element and edifice finally becomes apparent on the level of an action that has itself become pregnant with symbolic meaning, in the conflagration of the seer's hut. On the level of poetic metaphor it becomes explicit in images such as

> Des Jammers Fluten, die auf dieses Haus gestürmt
>
> (IV. ix)

or in Isabella's moving words:

> – Komm, meine Tochter! Hier ist unsers Bleibens
> Nicht mehr – den Rachegeistern überlaß ich
> Dies Haus – Ein Frevel führte mich herein,
> Ein Frevel treibt mich aus – Mit Widerwillen
> Hab' ich's betreten und mit Furcht bewohnt,
> Und in Verzweiflung räum' ich's . . .
>
> (IV. v)

This enmity and the ultimate victory of the elements over the permanence of all structures except one – the grave – was already foreshadowed in the dream of the father:

> Ihm deuchte,
> Er säh aus seinem hochzeitlichen Bette
> Zwei Lorbeerbäume wachsen . . .
> . . . zwischen beiden
> Wuchs eine Lilie empor – Sie ward
> Zur Flamme, die, der Bäume dicht Gezweig
> Und das Gebälk ergreifend, prasselnd aufschlug
> Und um sich wütend, schnell, das ganze Haus
> In ungeheurer Feuerflut verschlang.
>
> (II. v and cf. IV. iv)

The lily which turns into a flame engulfing everything around it in a flood of fire is, of course, Beatrice. Beatrice is the focus of the associated imagery of fire and water. The other figures are part element, part permanent, and that in them which strives for permanence holds in check that which is elemental. Beatrice is wholly a creature of the elements. On the level of image and metaphor, she *is* the conflagration of the father's dream. Even to the interpreting consciousness she remains the force which would reconcile the brothers' hatred 'mit *heißer Liebesglut*' * (II. v and I V. iv). Her abode is on the slopes of the volcano, and from there, from the safety of her cell, she actively breaks out twice to engulf the members of her family in destruction. The true significance of these eruptions is pointed up by the seer's symbolic action in answer to the question of where she is. His burning down of his hut, itself near the top of Etna, is the confirmation of the father's dream: there is no controlling of an elemental force. The more it is controlled, the more it will expand. Her eruptions are as irrepressible as the eruptions of the fiery element itself; and the poetic symbol is the closest the poet could devise short of letting the volcano itself erupt.[5]

Equally close is Beatrice's association with the fluidity of water. Before her birth, even, she was destined to be cast into the ocean (II. v). She belongs to the element. She lives by the shores of the sea and images evoking the sea pervade her speeches as indeed they pervade the choruses which flank her first appearance. More importantly still, her expository speeches themselves (II. i), with their irregular fluid structure, their constant shift of mood and metre, each following upon the other with a fleeting finality, by purely formal means suggest that she is of the sea and partakes of the labile fluidity of this element. As wave follows upon wave, so, in her, impression follows upon impression, and each terminates without a trace in the one that succeeds it. The very structure of her speech reflects the character of the element, by the apparent finality of each component part as well as by its evanescence. Her impressionableness is infinite. Like the crest of the wave, the contour of her every mood is sharp and, for a short moment, final; then it dissolves. But as the wave has no separate identity to separate it off from the surrounding waters –

> Auf den Wellen ist alles Welle,
> Auf dem Meer ist kein Eigentum . . .
>
> (I. viii)

– so Beatrice. There is no context of consciousness to embrace the single mood and make it hers. On the contrary, she *is* the mood. So far from her having it, it has her. She is nothing but a succession of states. This lack of encompassing consciousness is reflected in the vocabulary she uses. In-

---

* My italics.

deed, it is imprinted on the very syntax and grammar of her speeches. The sentences in which she refers to herself show the same dominant pattern. She figures not as the grammatical subject but as the object of the sentence and she uses verbs in the passive or reflexive voice. And the imagery she uses: she is the leaf torn from the tree, the prey of the waves, the victim of destructive forces. She is constantly assailed, seized, compelled, the passive recipient of violent stimuli, except when she breaks forth, actively, in order to lose herself. Only when she recounts her fatal escapades does she momentarily become the grammatical subject and choose the active voice as well as verbs connoting activity and choice.

Indeed, we might say that Beatrice is the dramatic embodiment of that philosophical abstraction which Schiller, in the *Ästhetische Briefe*, calls 'der reine Zustand'. In the twelfth letter we read:

> Indem man auf einem Instrument einen Ton greift, ist unter allen Tönen, die es möglicherweise angeben kann, nur dieser einzige wirklich; indem der Mensch das Gegenwärtige empfindet, ist die ganze unendliche Möglichkeit seiner Bestimmungen auf diese einzige Art des Daseins beschränkt. Wo also dieser Trieb ausschließend wirkt, da ist notwendig die höchste Begrenzung vorhanden; der Mensch ist in diesem Zustande nichts als eine Größen-Einheit, ein erfüllter Moment der Zeit – oder vielmehr *er* ist nicht, denn seine Persönlichkeit ist solange aufgehoben, als ihn die Empfindung beherrscht und die Zeit mit sich fortreißt.

Beatrice is this instrument and she is played upon by the world. She is the sense-drive, receptivity personified. And the passage from the *Ästhetische Briefe*, which describes this character with such extraordinary exactitude, makes us ask even at this point: how can such a being, the central figure of Schiller's drama, be made aesthetically tractable, seeing that in this poet's view the greatest problem of tragedy lies in the fact that it suffers from an excess of immediacy?[6]

The final, and perhaps most telling, token of Beatrice's lack of personhood, however, is her lack of identity, her namelessness and her ignorance about herself and her origin. This obscurity is not only her fate; it is her choice:

> Nicht kenn' ich sie und will sie nimmer kennen,
> Die sich die Stifter meiner Tage nennen . . .
> Ein ewig Rätsel bleiben will ich mir . . .

(II. i)

This anonymity is confirmed – and accepted – by both brothers. She is a mystery, 'ein Geheimnis':[7]

> Nicht forschen will ich, wer du bist – Ich will
> Nur *dich* von *dir*, nichts frag' ich nach dem andern.
>
> (II. ii)

for 'ein Verborgenes ist sich das Schöne' (ibid.). Thus Don Cesar; he is echoed by Don Manuel who confesses to the chorus that Beatrice herself does not know her origin, saying:

> Sich selber ein Geheimnis wuchs sie auf.
> Nicht kennt sie ihr Geschlecht noch Vaterland.
>
> (I. vii)

But most interesting for the light it throws on the nature of her obscurity is Don Cesar's reply to Isabella's question as to the identity of his bride-to-be:

> Fragt man,
> Woher der Sonne Himmelsfeuer flamme?
>
> (II. v)

he asks in reply, and goes on to say:

> Am reinen Glanz will ich die Perle kennen,
> Doch ihren Namen kann ich dir nicht nennen.
>
> (II. v)

Beatrice is nameless and anonymous because she is of the elements. The image of the pearl here recalls the chorus that follows her first appearance. There, too, she is likened to a pearl:

> Von den Perlen, welche der tauchende Fischer
> Auffängt, wählt er die reinsten für sich . . .
>
> (II. iv)

She is a glistening gift of the elements retrieved from the bottom of the sea, and here, in varied images of pirates and power and robbery, the lure and the danger of a beauty that is born of the elements is brought home to us.

III

They all seek out this elemental being: the mother and both her sons. They seek her out because in the effort of conquest and of controlling what they have conquered, they have denied their elemental life, and they now perceive that their existence is incomplete and bereft of grace. Beatrice represents what they lack. Indeed, she not merely represents it. The homogeneous fabric of the words tells us that her being is part of the being of Isabella, of Don Manuel and Don Cesar: she embodies their deepest elemental drives. As Don Cesar has it:

> Es war ihr tiefstes und geheimstes Leben,
> Was mich ergriff mit heiliger Gewalt . . .
> Fremd war sie mir und innig doch vertraut . . .
>
> (II. v)

By owning her, they seek to retrieve what they lack in themselves, and, therewith, wholeness of being. This is the deeper significance of that hope of reconciliation which plays such an important role in their fantasies.[8] It is, essentially, an inner regeneration these characters are seeking through Beatrice, an ultimate wholeness of what is partial and divided. This significance becomes quite evident from Don Manuel's apostrophe to the power of love:

> Allmächt'ge Liebe! Göttliche! . . .
> Dir unterwirft sich jedes Element,
> Du kannst das feindlich Streitende vermählen . . .
> Und auch des Bruders wilden Sinn hast du
> Besiegt, der unbezwungen stets geblieben.
>
> (II. v)

This faith in the regenerative power of love is voiced on all sides, and its religious quality is unmistakable. Don Cesar invokes an ancient myth when he says, as the messenger approaches with the news of Beatrice's discovery:

> Du siehst die Liebe aus des Hasses Flammen
> Wie einen neu verjüngten Phönix steigen.
>
> (I. vi)

Similarly, the dream which impels Isabella to save her unborn daughter draws its force from the soil of myth and legend:

> Ein Kind, wie Liebesgötter schön,
> Sah ich im Grase spielen, und ein Löwe
> Kam aus dem Wald, der in dem blut'gen Rachen
> Die frisch gejagte Beute trug, und ließ

Sie schmeichelnd in den Schoß des Kindes fallen,
Und aus den Lüften schwang ein Adler sich
Herab, ein zitternd Reh in seinen Fängen,
Und legt' es schmeichelnd in den Schoß des Kindes,
Und beide, Löw' und Adler, legen fromm
Gepaart sich zu des Kindes Füßen nieder.

(II. v)

Don Manuel resorts to the imagery of religious experience to express the significance of Beatrice's love:

Und wie der Pilger sich nach Osten wendet,
Wo ihm die Sonne der Verheißung glänzt,
So kehrte sich mein Hoffen und mein Sehnen
Dem einen hellen Himmelspunkte zu.

(I. vii)

Don Cesar, similarly, describes her coming as 'eines Engels Lichterscheinung' (II. ii).[9] And he assures his mother that, in falling in love with Beatrice at his father's funeral, his mind was deeply attuned to the solemnity of the occasion. For he finds love at the most solemn moment when

. . . auf den Seraphsflügeln des Gesangs
Schwang die befreite Seele sich nach oben,
Den Himmel suchend und den Schoß der Gnade.

(II. v)

The operative word here is 'Gnade'. Don Cesar, Isabella and Don Manuel all look to Beatrice for an ultimate grace that has eluded lives given over to conquest, repression and strife. Beatrice's beauty is the reflection of an inner beauty they seek: the beauty of the Phoenix, the beauty of the playing child which appeases the strife of elemental forces – the beauty of inner harmony and fulfilment which adds lustre to greatness and transcends it. Their dream is the dream of every Schillerian hero, of being reborn into a second nature, into a regenerated humanity – the dream of aesthetic totality.[10] Beatrice is the tool and the token of such totality, such beauty. To possess her means to be the *'beglückte** Besitzer der Macht'*, as the chorus has it, and the images in which that possession is described leave no doubt of its aesthetic nature. The 'beglückte Besitzer der Macht'

* My italics.

possesses 'die Perle', 'die Blume der Frauen, die das Entzücken ist aller Augen', 'die schönste Gestalt' (II. iv). And it is this aesthetic, humanizing nature of love that is expressed in the epithet *'schöne* * Liebe' which occurs so often in this tragedy.[11]

Thus each character dreams of retrieving, through Beatrice, the same long-repressed elemental stratum of his psyche, and with it, wholeness; and each dreams of incorporating this elemental force, safely and permanently, into the stable structure of his personality.

Isabella's joy at the extravagant fulfilment of her hopes finds expression in an image saturated with a sense of stability and permanence:

> – Gegründet
> Auf festen Säulen seh' ich mein Geschlecht,
> Und in der Zeiten Unermeßlichkeit
> Kann ich hinabsehn mit zufriednem Geist.
>
> (II. v)

Manuel announces his love in similar terms:

> Es zieht die Freude ein durch alle Pforten,
> Es füllt sich der verödete Palast
> Und wird der Sitz der blühnden Anmut werden.
>
> (ibid.)

And again:

> – Ich sehe diese Hallen, diese Säle
> Und denke mir das freudige Erschrecken
> Der überraschten, hocherstaunten Braut,
> Wenn ich als Fürstin sie und Herrscherin
> Durch dieses Hauses Pforten führen werde.
>
> (I. vii)

Don Cesar, a less restrained character than Isabella and Manuel and closer to Beatrice, has a finer intuition than they of the elemental power embodied in her. He reads her reticence at his courtship as an awareness of that power:[12]

> Denn ein Verborgenes ist sich das Schöne,
> Und es erschrickt vor seiner eignen Macht.
>
> (II. ii)

* My italics.

For himself, however, he lacks no confidence that he can find this mysterious force a place in his life:

> Belehret sie von ihres Standes Größe . . .

he instructs his men, continuing:

> Bald kehr' ich selbst zurück, sie heimzuführen,
> Wie's *meiner* würdig ist und ihr gebührt.
>
> (ibid.)[13]

There is *hubris* in this confidence of the rulers that they will be able to
domesticate the elemental force they are letting into their lives. It is an
uneasy confidence bred of haughtiness, suspicion and fear. How aware
both brothers are of their superior position *vis-à-vis* their nameless bride!
Notwithstanding the fact that she is beauty incarnate and that they need
her to clothe their naked power with the mantle of humanity. This ambivalence comes out very strikingly in Don Manuel's reflection:

> – Noch liebt sie nur den Liebenden! Dem Fremdling,
> Dem Namenlosen hat sie sich gegeben.
> Nicht ahnet sie, daß es Don Manuel,
> Messinas Fürst ist, der die goldne Binde
> Ihr um die schöne Stirne flechten wird.
> Wie süß ist's, das Geliebte zu beglücken
> Mit ungehoffter Größe Glanz und Schein!
> Längst spart' ich mir dies höchste der Entzücken:
> Wohl bleibt es stets sein höchster Schmuck allein,
> Doch auch die Hoheit darf das Schöne schmücken,
> Der goldne Reif erhebt den Edelstein.
>
> (I. vii)

What ambiguity in the use of the word 'hoch', repeated four times in so
many lines! What is higher: grace or greatness?[14] The glistening beauty
of the elemental, of the pearl, of the gem that is the centrepiece of a man's
crown or the firm setting in which that gem is placed and which it
adorns – his might and his dominion? Cesar and Manuel bow to the
elemental force that has seized them, and at the same time, and paradoxically, they want to raise it up to their height. Beatrice may be 'eines
Engels Lichterscheinung' to Cesar. Yet he finds it necessary to assure
this blessing from above that he is able

> . . . das Geliebte
> Mit starkem Arm zu mir emporzuheben
>
> (II. ii)

even in the worst of contingencies:

> Und wärst du selbst die Niedrigste geboren . . .
>
> (ibid.)[15]

And there is fear too, compounded with adoration and contempt. How slow is Isabella to release into life the force that she has retrieved from death; how long does she leave Beatrice buried, 'in Lebens Glut den Schatten beigesellt'![16] How vigilantly Manuel guards her safe hiding place, and how loath is he to unlock his secret! This ambivalence is reflected in the multitude of names that are showered on the nameless one. She is 'die schönste Gestalt', 'die Anmut', 'die Perle'; she is 'das Glück' and 'das Geheimnis', she is 'das Opfer' and 'der Raub'. And, indeed, as Beatrice is 'the prey', so, through the vagaries of the plot as well as through the poetic imagery, Isabella as well as her two brothers becomes associated with the image of robbers. Conquerors from the North,[17] they view the sensuous, the elemental, which they have held in subjugation and which nevertheless they covet, with dread and superstition. It is a dangerous thing from the depths, a lure towards chaos threatening the very structure of their civilizing will and intellect. Can they retrieve it from life without surrendering to its treacherousness? Can beauty and grace be snatched like a crown jewel or a pearl to adorn greatness, without surrender of dominion, and death? These are the questions this Sicilian tragedy asks, with its clash of North and South, of intellect and sense, of permanence and transience, with its precarious structures pitted against the unbridled might of the elements. It asks these questions fearfully, suspiciously and haughtily, as they have been asked by many an artist torn between a Puritan heritage and the richer life of the senses disclosed by art – by Oscar Wilde, by Thomas Mann and by Stefan George, to mention but a few.

Schiller's last tragedy answers these questions in the negative. To toy with beauty is impossible. For beauty is the gateway to the dark elemental forces of the unconscious, and thence to surrender and dissolution of forms that have become arid, 'öde'.[18] Estranged elemental force and exiled member of the house, Beatrice is doomed to destroy those who, arrogantly and too late, seek her out demanding their redemption. The attempt to incorporate the aesthetic into a rigidly structured personality

must end in catastrophe. Too long subjected and too little trusted, the
elements, once released, break out, sweeping before them all the careful
structures and fortifications of spirits bent on permanence, and leaving
devastation in their wake.[19]

IV

But if these be the thematic perspectives of the tragedy, how are we to
understand the preface 'Über den Gebrauch des Chors in der Tragödie'?
What has its message of sculptured form and aesthetic distance to do with
this tragedy of elemental uprising, of chaos and catastrophe? In this preface we read the programmatic words that it is the task of dramatic art, as
indeed of all art, to induce in the spectator 'die Freiheit des Gemüts in dem
lebendigen Spiel aller seiner Kräfte'; '. . . dadurch, daß sie eine Kraft
in ihm erweckt, übt und ausbildet, die sinnliche Welt, die sonst nur als ein
roher Stoff auf uns lastet, als eine blinde Macht auf uns drückt, in eine
objektive Ferne zu rücken, in ein freies Werk unsers Geistes zu verwandeln und das Materielle durch Ideen zu beherrschen.' Under this concept of 'roher Stoff' Schiller includes all mere matter or 'content' – the
intellectual and moral components of an aesthetic composition as well as
its emotional constituents. A little later he says quite explicitly: 'Alles,
was der Verstand sich im allgemeinen ausspricht, ist ebenso wie das, was
bloß die Sinne reizt, nur Stoff und rohes Element in einem Dichterwerk
und wird da, wo es vorherrscht, unausbleiblich das Poetische zerstören.'
   It is easy to understand how by the introduction of the chorus the poet
is enabled to deal with any excess of intellectual matter in his tragedy.
This is beautifully expressed in the analogy of the sculptor and his art
which dominates this essay, recurring time and again. The sculptor, too,
turns the materials in which his figures are clothed – his 'Stoff' – to good
artistic account.[20] He endows their texture and movement with intrinsic
charm, and he uses them to help him arrange and 'compose' the human
forms that are the centre of his work: to connect them and yet to keep
them apart, in fact, to organize them in their aesthetic space in such a
manner that they appear 'composed' (however much in movement they
may actually be) so that, perceiving them, we feel 'composed' in turn.
   This is how the lyrical language does in fact operate in the tragedy
itself. That excess of reflective matter (the 'Stoff' of the sculptor) which
cannot be assimilated into the aesthetic organization of the central
dramatic structures – the tragic characters – without impairing it, is used

to form a separate poetic structure. A fully matured aesthetic organ itself – Schiller calls it 'ein Kunstorgan'[21] – the poetic idiom provides as it were a verbal continuum in which the tragic characters and events are arranged and 'composed'. The lyrical interpolations of the chorus expatiate on the related themes of discourse, the themes of permanence, transience and beauty, and by doing so they interpret, relate and transmute the events they frame. Moreover, they hold these events apart in time, as the sculptor's mantle connects and holds apart in space the human forms it surrounds, and thus they give the characters in the tragedy, as well as its spectators, time and breathing space to recover from the impact of the action and to regain a measure of freedom.

But how does this device break the force of the affective component which is embodied in Beatrice, the central figure of the tragedy and the centre of the vortex in which all are swallowed up? She is in perpetual commotion – abducted, escaping, fainting; and this is merely the outward reflection of the incessant inner turmoil in which she lives. For she is, as we have seen, receptivity personified, pure elemental flux. We might say that she is constitutionally beside herself. How can any *surrounding* part of the structure stay the flight and still the ceaseless movement of this figure and break the force of its impact? For this and nothing less is Schiller's own ambition, an ambition he explicitly avows when he says 'daß der Künstler kein einziges Element aus der Wirklichkeit brauchen kann, wie er es findet, daß sein Werk in *allen* seinen Teilen ideell sein muß'. And how, furthermore, can any extraneous device redeem the central area of the tragic action – the brothers' incestuous entanglement with their sister, and, especially, the love-idyll between her and Don Manuel? Love-idyll indeed! The poet here handles a matter so explosive, so close to our unconscious fears and taboos and so disturbing that it is difficult to see how he could aesthetically transmute it at all. Nor does the preface answer that question, for it deals with the problem of excess intellectual matter rather than with that of excess sense-matter, 'das, was bloß die Sinne reizt': a problem which is raised but not expressly answered at all. And yet the poet succeeded. If anything, he succeeded too well, for we feel a little too emotionally distanced from his materials. What school teacher has ever stopped to wonder whether *Die Braut von Messina* makes fit reading for his sixth-form charges?[22] So we are back at the beginning. How did the poet succeed in handling his volcanic materials? How did he transform what seems 'Stoff' and 'rohes Element' *par excellence* – the elemental figure of Beatrice and the surrounding area of incestuous relationship – into mature aesthetic components, capable of functioning within the poetic organization as a whole?

V

Although the preface does not seem to hold out an answer, the commanding metaphor of the sculpture still lingers in the mind; surely, somewhere there is some connection with Beatrice!

> Aber ebenso, wie der bildende Künstler die faltige Fülle der Gewänder um seine Figuren breitet, . . . um die menschlichen Formen zugleich geistreich zu verhüllen und sichtbar zu machen, ebenso durchflicht und umgibt der tragische Dichter . . . die festen Umrisse seiner handelnden Figuren mit einem lyrischen Prachtgewebe, in welchem sich, als wie in einem weitgefalteten Purpurgewand, die handelnden Personen frei und edel mit einer gehaltenen Würde und hoher Ruhe bewegen.

The lines come to mind in which Don Manuel describes Beatrice arrayed in her bridal clothes:

> Dann zum Gewande wählt das Kunstgewebe
> Des Indiers . . .
> Und leicht umfließ' es, wie der Morgenduft,
> Den zarten Bau der jugendlichen Glieder.
>
> (I. vii)

We read the whole passage, and the scene in which it is embedded, and presently the connection we had suspected is before our eyes, important and clear. Before ever Beatrice is introduced into the tragedy as a 'handelnde Person', and before the catastrophic character of her being and her relationships is revealed, the poet, through the offices of Don Manuel, projects a verbal image of her in the stillness of a sculpted form, and 'composes' her disturbing bond with Don Manuel into an idyll of the utmost contemplative tranquillity. In other words, before the outset of the tragic action proper he introduces and uses his precarious poetic materials in such a fashion that they themselves induce a distanced aesthetic response in the spectator, an inner freedom which he is then able to sustain *vis-à-vis* a figure itself lacking in all freedom, and the action about to issue from this character. Let us see by what means the poet accomplishes this poetic transmutation.

Don Manuel introduces the description of his bride by words that clearly mark the transition from the psychological plane of empirical reality to the aesthetic plane:

> In banger Furcht ließ ich sie dort allein
> Zurück, die sich nichts weniger erwartet,
> Als in dem Glanz der Fürstin eingeholt
> Und auf erhabnem Fußgestell des Ruhms
> Vor ganz Messina ausgestellt zu werden.

$$\text{(I. viii)}$$

'Auf erhabnem Fußgestell' – 'ausgestellt' – these are strange words, fitting, not a living being, but a statue. By placing a statue on a pedestal and removing it from the ordinary space we share, we not only display it the better; we also declare that it belongs, not to life, but to the world of forms. This is exactly what Don Manuel does. He views Beatrice as he views the beauty of the Orient which is 'displayed' ('ausgestellt') in the bazaar – 'fertig und vollendet' – as a thing of beauty which is apprehended with disinterested pleasure.[23] And presently the living person – the anxious prey of impinging forces – is left behind 'in wesenlosem Scheine' and Don Manuel's words chisel, from the pedestal upwards, the being of his sister in its pure aesthetic semblance. In this composition there is no remnant of chaos, no raw material, no matter waiting to be formed. The basic constituents of living and of inorganic nature alike are inherently beautiful. Beatrice's feet are as delicate as the sandals that are to adorn them, her garments, 'Kunstgewebe' made of 'edelm Stoff', are as exquisite as the 'zarte Bau der jugendlichen Glieder' they are to clothe. The 'feine Kunstgebild' of the Orient, the wrought bracelets, the diadem, 'gefüget aus dem köstlichsten Gestein', the veil, the wreath, beautiful themselves, serve merely to enhance the native beauty they adorn – the 'schönen Arme', the 'Haarschmuck', the 'glänzende Gestalt'. There is scarcely a word that does not belong to the sphere of beauty, of art and skilled craftsmanship: 'edler Stoff', 'feines Kunstgebilde', 'zierliche Sandalen', 'zartgeformte Füße', 'Zier', 'Kunstgewebe', 'hellglänzend', 'leicht', 'zarter Bau', 'zarte Fäden', 'durchwirkt', 'reizend', 'glänzend', 'gewebt', 'schöne Arme', 'umzirken', 'gefüget', 'köstliches Gestein', 'Haarschmuck', 'glänzende Gestalt', 'helles Lichtgewölk', 'vollende', 'krönend', 'schönes Ganze'.

Where is matter here? Where nature in the raw? Where are those demonic forces that drive Beatrice to her doom? Where the elements

that she embodies? They are all there, transmuted. Nature is Beatrice's
jewel box. The pearl and the coral from the dangerous depths of the ocean
reappear fashioned into her 'Schmuck'; the 'feurig glühende Rubin'
crosses 'Farbenblitze' with the emeralds in her wrought diadem. Even
Etna itself, symbol of those pent-up elemental forces that are embodied in
Beatrice, is invoked, but invoked, significantly, as a symphony of snow and
light, of ethereal beauty suffused with spirituality. Heaviness, darkness,
matter – all those forces of the deep are transfigured. Light and lightness
reign. Nature is imbued with form, the demonic has become design, and
element is transmuted into ornament by the alchemy of art.[24] The dangerous beauty of Beatrice has been 'composed' into the tranquil perfection of the sculpted form.

   The artist is Don Manuel, and the stillness which informs his creation
is created by the verbal forms themselves. The longest of his speeches – it
takes up forty-six lines, considerably more than the account of his first
meeting with Beatrice – is almost wholly composed of nouns, adjectives
and participial forms, with a bare minimum of finite verbs. In strange
contrast to the introductory words:

> Doch nur mit ihr werd' ich beschäftigt sein
>
> (I. viii)

its syntax expresses the virtual cessation of activity; and the 'ich' of the
lover is lost in the disinterested contemplation of the object: until the end
of his speech, the personal pronoun does not appear again! It is true that
images from the dynamic sphere of nature and the elements pervade Don
Manuel's speech. But they are used ornamentally, in the measured mode
of the simile. To say, then, that Manuel evokes a verbal sculpture or a
'word picture' means more than that an actual visual image of a sculptured form is presented to our inner eye. It means, more importantly, that
language itself is here handled statically by every means in the poet's
power, and that by the consistent use of syntactical, verbal and rhetorical
forms that express such an intention the objective and distanced mode of
response is induced that is characteristic of the plastic arts.[25]

   The same aesthetic distance and contemplative tranquillity characterize Manuel's love story:

> Versunken in dich selber stehst du da,
> Gleich einem Träumenden, als wäre nur
> Dein Leib zugegen und die Seele fern . . .
>
> (I. vii)

the chorus says in what are virtually the opening words of the scene. And just as in his verbal evocation of Beatrice's beauty the initial movement terminates in stillness – we recall the 'bange Furcht' at the opening of the description – so here, too, the motionless stillness of their first encounter is enhanced by the wild chase preceding it. It is in the excited pursuit of a deer that Don Manuel chances upon his sister; and as soon as he sets eyes on her, all activity except that of perception is brought to a standstill:

> Bewegungslos starr' ich das Wunder an,
> Den Jagdspieß in der Hand, zum Wurf ausholend . . .
> . . . so stehn wir schweigend gegeneinander –
> Wie lange Frist, das kann ich nicht ermessen,
> Denn alles Maß der Zeiten war vergessen.
>
> (I. vii)

This timelessness is the mark of the true contemplative experience. Don Manuel not only presents to us his love as an essentially aesthetic phenomenon; he not only transmutes the object of his passion into a work of art, but he also communicates the aesthetic temper which informs these responses by subtler means. He transmits it to us through the timelessness and expansiveness of his speeches, by what we might call their 'heavenly lengths'. We share this timeless tranquillity with him, and permit our response to him, to Beatrice and to the relationship between them to be pervaded by a sense of pure duration and by a lit-up perceptiveness which not all the impact of characters and action can take from us again. Looked at from the outside, the aesthetic time-dimension which Don Manuel creates appears like emptiness and stagnation. And as the poet has led us into the aesthetic region by depicting the cessation of initial movement, so he gradually leads us from the aesthetic plane back on to the plane of action and involvement by letting the chorus voice the time-experience of the uncomprehending and bored outsider. Schiller must have had a twinkle in his eye when he concluded the high aesthetic venture of this scene with words which are little short of a healthy yawn:[26]

> Sage, was werden wir jetzt beginnen,
> Da die Fürsten ruhen vom Streit,
> Auszufüllen die Leere der Stunden
> Und die lange unendliche Zeit?
>
> (I. viii)

VI

Don Manuel is the author of a distilled art experience within the aesthetic experience of the tragedy as a whole. It is not the first time in these pages that we have encountered the contemplative bent of Schiller's tragic protagonists and observed the pivotal function of this disposition for the aesthetic structuring of the tragedies in which they figure. The analyses of *Fiesco* and *Don Carlos* have consistently pointed in the same direction; and so will the discussion of *Wallenstein* in later chapters. In the preface to this, his last completed tragedy, the poet at long last provides the rationale of a practice he has intuitively adopted from the very start. For here, in the preface, the ultimate function of the chorus is seen precisely in its distancing effect on the characters themselves: 'Sie stehen gewissermaßen schon auf einem natürlichen Theater, weil sie vor Zuschauern sprechen und handeln, und werden eben deswegen desto tauglicher, von dem Kunst-Theater zu einem Publikum zu reden.' The protagonist is not an agent but an actor,[27] an artist, a distanced and conscious spectator of himself as he acts out his destiny, and by that token enabled to induce just this distanced and illuminated response in the spectators once removed.[28] This near-identity of our response with that of the tragic protagonists themselves is confirmed by the striking similarity of the vocabulary which Schiller, in the preface, uses to characterize each. The spectator's '*Freiheit*',* we read there, is ensured by the 'schöne und *hohe Ruhe*,* die der Charakter eines *edeln** Kunstwerks sein muß'. And so, too, the tragic 'actor-spectators' *within* the drama move '*frei* und *edel* mit . . . *hoher Ruhe*'.* Such correspondences, in a critic who never ceases to write as a poet, deserve to be taken seriously.

Yet it is not with the distanced being of Don Manuel, the main pillar of the tragic structure, but with his own aesthetic transmutation of Beatrice, the most disruptive element in its economy, that we are here principally concerned. His ornamental handling of this elemental material does not involve a psychological sleight of hand; indeed it does not involve Beatrice as a 'handelnde Person' at all, although it modifies our perception of her. It is a purely poetic transmutation of her personality, a purely verbal staying of the fluidity and movement that is Beatrice.

In a letter to Goethe, Schiller defines the difference between the tragic and the epic action as follows: 'Die dramatische Handlung bewegt sich vor mir, um die epische bewege ich mich selbst, und sie scheint gleichsam

* My italics.

stille zu stehen'.[29] Obviously the spatial image in which the poet envisages the time patterns of the epic genre stems from the sphere of the visual arts, in fact, from the realm of sculpture. If, a moment later, the poet urges that the main danger to tragedy as an art-form lies in its excessive immediacy, and if he sees the remedy of that shortcoming in the poetic tendency of tragedy 'immer zu dem epischen Charakter *hinauf* [zu] streben', we can fully understand the aesthetic significance of the still sculpted form in Schiller's classical tragedy itself and in the introductory essay. The stylistic tendency which, here and there, finds expression in the metaphor of chiselled calm is the tendency toward epic forms as the necessary *contrepoids*, or counterpoise, to the excessive immediacy of tragedy. Thus element is turned into ornament. Beatrice attains the stillness of the statue through the transmuting force of Manuel's aesthetic perception, Don Manuel, in turn, becomes the 'actor' of his destiny *vis-à-vis* the chorus, whilst the chorus, finally, is the embodied self-awareness of the 'actors', the spectator within the play. Filters are built into filters, removes are built into removes. Such is the secret alchemy by which a work of epic stance is distilled from a tragedy of incest.

It would seem, then, as if Schiller's tragedy might be described as a polarity of forces straining in opposite directions. On the plane of theme, elemental forces dominate; on the level of structure, the energies working for form. But if we look more closely, a strange coalescence becomes apparent where we thought that we saw contrast. For is there not on the thematic level, too, a persistent preoccupation with the redeeming power of form? Did we not find the theme of the tragedy in the unremitting attempt on the part of the characters to retrieve the elemental and to incorporate it into the stable structure of the aesthetic personality? It is as if the theme of this play in its entirety were a large poetic metaphor of that formal preoccupation which drove Schiller to write his tragedy in the Greek manner: the quest for a form that would transmute the elemental immediacy of tragedy as such.

This is a strange identity. The artistic process is reflected in the final product. It is mirrored in the total conception, and it shows through in many places, making us feel that for all its force this creation is sometimes a trifle lacking in substance and opacity, perhaps, even, a little contrived.[30] The verbal evocation of Beatrice's sculpted form is one such bit of process peeping through the matter in which it is embodied, just as the metaphor of the sculptured group which dominates the preface is a bit of subject carried forward into the theoretical explication of the artistic process.

Perhaps there is a trace here of that paucity to which Schiller confessed years earlier, when he wrote to Goethe: 'Erwarten Sie bei mir keinen großen materialen Reichtum von Ideen. . . . Mein Bedürfnis und Streben ist, aus wenigem viel zu machen . . . und eine Mannigfaltigkeit, die dem Inhalte fehlt, durch die Form[zu]erzeugen.'[31] Perhaps also the severely functional character of the subject was what Humboldt had in mind when he criticized the tragedy for its lack of poetic substance.[32]

Be that as it may, the austere homogeneity of this soliloquy in the dramatic mode is also its fascination. Like Lessing in his *Emilia Galotti*, and Thomas Mann in his late work, the greatest creator-critic of all, in his last tragedy, articulates the artistic process in a creation that is transparent with consciousness. We can hold it up and grasp it, yet the mystery of it remains.

2

Irrevocability

– Schon bleibt verdorben, was verdorben ist –
was ich gestürzt habe, steht ewig niemals mehr auf –

(*Die Räuber*)

4

'A pottage of lentiles': a reading of *Die Räuber*

I

It is customary to assume that the biblical story of the Prodigal Son served Schiller as a model for his first play.[1] And, indeed, there is considerable internal evidence to support such a claim. It is because of his father that Karl turns robber in the first place, and he feels his exile to be above all a banishment from his father's love, whether it be that of the heavenly or earthly one: '. . . daß alles so glücklich ist', he reflects, 'durch den Geist des Friedens alles so verschwistert! – Die ganze Welt *eine* Familie und ein Vater dort oben! – *Mein* Vater nicht – Ich allein der Verstoßene, ich allein ausgemustert aus den Reihen der Reinen – mir nicht der süße Name Kind . . .' (III. ii). When finally he returns home, desperate, after a squandered life, it is the consciousness alone that he is avenging his father that once more fills him with a momentary sense of mission. And indeed, when first he awaits his father's letter of forgiveness, impatient to rush into his arms, Spiegelberg taunts him, saying: 'Pfui, du wirst doch nicht gar den verlorenen Sohn spielen wollen!' (I. ii). This direct allusion to the biblical motif reappears in a curious reversal at the end of the tragedy.[2] Smitten with remorse at his harshness towards his best-beloved son, Der alte Moor imagines meeting him with the same plea for forgiveness which in the Gospel of St Luke is put into the mouth of the Prodigal Son himself: 'Ich hab' gesündigt im Himmel und vor dir' – Karl's father cries: 'Ich bin nicht wert, daß du mich Vater nennst.' (V. ii.)

This seems pretty conclusive evidence in favour of an assumption that has become a commonplace of Schiller scholarship. None the less it does

not quite fit the bill. The Prodigal Son of the Bible is the younger, as well
as the preferred, son.[3] Besides — and this is vastly more important — the
reunion between himself and his father is a lasting one which inaugurates
mutual joy and happiness. In *Die Räuber* this is demonstrably not so. Der
alte Moor blesses his son not suspecting that it is Karl and, on learning his
identity, falls dead.

Indeed, the stolen blessing brings to mind another biblical story — the
story of Jacob and Esau.[4] Here is a pair of brothers whose archetypal
rivalry is better marked than in the story of the Prodigal Son, where it
remains subliminal. The younger brother, Jacob, is clearly a charismatic
figure, 'a smooth man', preferred in the sight of God to his 'hairy' brother
Esau. What he does — and some of it is morally very dubious indeed — has
the blessing of the Lord upon it and succeeds. Twice he deceives his
'faint' brother Esau: when he feeds him with a dish of lentils in return for
the elder one's birthright, and again when he steals, with his mother's
help and God's sanction, the father's blessing which is reserved for the
elder. The second of these events is clearly paralleled in Schiller's play.
Karl has no right to his father's blessing and steals it, pretending to be a
stranger. 'Und wie?' he reflects, 'Wenn ich jetzt seinen Segen weg-
haschte — haschte wie ein Dieb und mich davon schlich' mit der göttlichen Beute — Vatersegen, sagt man, geht niemals verloren.' (V. ii.) And
the first theft, the theft of the birthright? For a modern poet this would
be an impossible poetic motif to take over unchanged. But Schiller could
and did take it over and translated it into his very own poetic idiom. Karl,
like Jacob, is a charismatic figure.[5] Looks, temperament and an inde-
finable native princeliness combine to make him the first in love[6] in the
eyes of his father and all those who know him — Amalia, Daniel, and,
last but not least, his robber band, whilst Franz, 'der kalte, trockne,
hölzerne Franz', as he calls himself (I. i), goes empty-handed. A literary
descendant of Richard III, Franz is blessed with a burden of excessive
ugliness. He is nature's own stepchild. 'Ich habe große Rechte, über die
Natur ungehalten zu sein,' he reflects. 'Wer hat ihr die Vollmacht gegeben, jenem dieses zu verleihen und mir vorzuenthalten? . . . Warum
ging sie so parteilich zu Werke?' (Ibid.) In the universe of discourse of
Schiller's poetry there is no simple let alone a rational answer to this
question.[7] Some are blessed and others are not. And always this prefer-
ential treatment is expressed in terms of beauty, felicity of natural endowment and superiority of rank. The lucky ones, of whom the poet tends
to think as 'die Kinder des Hauses', are the true heirs. In terms of

Schiller's poetic imagination this means that Karl, in addition to and as a seal of his natural blessings, is his father's first-born. Unaccountably, by nature's arbitrary decree, he usurps by his very being what might be his brother's portion. He does not try for it any more than Maria Stuart tries to justify by 'works' her inborn superiority of her 'sister' Elisabeth. Legitimacy is something bestowed by nature, not something that can be earned. Here, in Karl Moor's inborn superiority over his brother Franz – a superiority of outward rank as well as of natural splendour – is Schiller's first statement of the polarity between *Charis* and *Verdienst* which will inform his every tragedy to the very last, *Demetrius*, and which has found its most memorable statement – and resolution – in the poem *Das Glück*.[8]

Karl, then, is like Jacob in that, with the help of a partial nature, he has usurped his brother's portion twice: he has stolen his birthright in that he is first in rank *and* in love; and he will steal his father's blessing at the end of the play. And this last theft, so close to the catastrophe, is embedded in a context of encompassing significance. The tragedy begins with Karl's choice to become a robber, that is to say, one who takes what does not belong to him; it ends with his revoking this initial choice. Karl voluntarily gives himself up to justice, saying: 'Was soll ich, gleich einem Diebe, ein Leben länger verheimlichen, das mir schon lang' im Rat der himmlischen Wächter genommen ist?' (V. ii.)[9] Thus I suggest that the theft of his father's blessing is crucial and points to the central theme of this tragedy. Like the story of Jacob and Esau, *Die Räuber* is – as the very title of the play implies – centrally concerned with stealing. It traces the growth of the recognition, in the relentless consciousness of one man, of the true nature of an act he had regarded as highminded. The five acts of this remarkable and remorseless tragedy are concerned with Karl's gradual discovery of what it is that he has done and what it is not; what his deed has made of him and what it has not made of him; and what it means to have made this choice and none other. The process of recognition and, ultimately, the nature of moral choice and accountability is the theme of Schiller's first tragedy – a theme which will inform the fabric of every future tragedy from this poet's pen. And with the young playwright's analysis of these basic problems of tragedy the following pages will be concerned.

II

The opening act of the drama sees the birth of two choices, Franz's and Karl's. In some way these choices are remarkably alike, in other ways they

are diametrically opposed. Both brothers are unusual characters, and both
repudiate, in terms which are strikingly similar, the laws by which
ordinary men feel themselves bound. 'Das Recht wohnet beim Über-
wältiger, und die Schranken unserer Kraft sind unsere Gesetze', muses
Franz (I. i), and: 'Es ist itzo die Mode, Schnallen an den Beinkleidern zu
tragen, womit man sie nach Belieben weiter und enger schnürt. Wir
wollen uns ein Gewissen nach der neuesten Façon anmessen lassen, um
es hübsch weiter aufzuschnallen, wie wir zulegen.' (Ibid.)[10] And in the
following scene Karl reflects: 'Ich soll meinen Leib pressen in eine
Schnürbrust und meinen Willen schnüren in Gesetze . . . Das Gesetz
hat noch keinen großen Mann gebildet . . .' (I. ii).

On the basis of this common rejection each brother makes his choice;
the one of his own free will, the other hard-pressed and impassioned.[11]
Franz chooses to clear his brother and his father out of the way. Karl,
disappointed in his hopes of reconciliation with his father, chooses to make
war on society as captain of a band of robbers. The choice of Franz is,
ultimately, a choice against nature who has in the first instance treated
him in such a miserly fashion. He rejects her heritage and abrogates the
natural instincts she has implanted in him; and instead he decrees what he
will be: 'Sie gab mir nichts mit; wozu ich mich machen will, das ist nun
meine Sache.' (I. i.) As against this, Karl quite simply loses his head. Hurt
to the quick by the unjust treatment he has supposedly received at the
hands of his father, he gives full rein to his outraged instincts and abrogates his higher censoring self. Not indeed that these instincts lack
nobility. Reverence, piety and fidelity are ingrained in their very fabric.
But these qualities of spirit have as yet remained undifferentiated. They
are developed only on a primitive emotional level, in relation to his father
who is as it were the navel-cord connecting him with the world of
spiritual values.[12] Once this cord is cut, these higher qualities run errant
and catastrophically attach themselves to a worthless cause, to wit, his
robber band to which he lends all the fire of his idealism. Of this disastrous displacement and its function in bringing about the process of
recognition we shall treat presently. First of the nature of Karl's choice.

However little the hero himself will hear of it, the poet himself tells
us that what he has chosen is the craft of thievery. Even before Moor
thinks of joining the robbers' band, Spiegelberg states his aims in words
the meaning of which is unequivocal. He wants to enter crime on a big
scale, 'das Handwerk ins Große praktizieren'. 'Du wirst gaffen! Du wirst
Augen machen!' he tells the absent-minded Karl. 'Wart', und wie man

Handschriften nachmacht, Würfel verdreht, Schlösser aufbricht und den Koffern das Eingeweid' ausschüttet – das sollst du noch von Spiegelberg lernen!' (I. ii.) This is plain enough, and the poet has stressed its significance for Karl Moor himself by a strange pantomimic interplay between those two figures at a crucial moment of the play. While Karl reads his brother's faked letter and pain and rage show in the deathly pallor of his face, Spiegelberg ecstatically enacts a drama of his own, seizing Schweizer by the throat and crying, 'La bourse ou la vie!' The two states of mind and their pantomimic expressions are, or so it would seem, as incompatible as the characters to whom they belong: one utterly detestable, the other fiery and noble. And yet the poet has silently juxtaposed them[13] and drawn our attention to their coincidence at this precise moment which is the most important moment in the tragic economy of this drama as a whole. For it is nothing less than what the later Schiller would call 'der prägnante Moment', that is to say the moment from which light is shed on past and future alike and from which the action may be seen to unfold with absolute inner necessity.[14] Karl is repudiated by his father, the sole guarantor of his spiritual values, and being in any case a creature of instinct rather than of reasoning, he feels driven to put himself out of bounds, beyond the moral law. And at that moment Spiegelberg pantomimically enacts before our eyes what outlawry means in sordid practice.

At this point of the tragedy most readers or spectators will be as unwilling as the hero himself to concede any conceivable connection between Karl's own character and actions and those of Spiegelberg, the most squalid and grotesque of his accomplices. Does Moor himself not continually and strenuously dissociate himself from his companions? And is not the dichotomy between Karl's own intentions and the outcome of those intentions at the hands of his associates the inner hub of the tragedy, a tragedy which already betrays the future disciple of Kant? This is certainly how Karl himself sees the situation. Time and again, he dissociates himself from his band, and distinguishes the integrity of his motive from the squalor of consequences he has been instrumental in inaugurating.[15] But the strange thing is that he himself fails to convince himself that he is morally exonerated by such academic distinctions. Indeed, he nullifies them by a spontaneous movement towards involvement, as we shall presently see.

When we first encounter the robber band in the Bohemian forest, Spiegelberg supplies a vivid exposition of their doings to date. We hear of his methods of recruiting new members, involving innocent men in crime

by every form of bribery, blackmail and corruption; and we hear of a raid
on a nunnery, with collective rape of the nuns thrown in afterwards for
good measure. In these activities the captain of the band, Karl himself,
occupies an ambiguous position. We are told that he openly dissociates
himself from the men who work under his command and their motives.
'Er mordet nicht um des Raubes willen wie wir,' Razmann relates; 'nach
dem Geld schien er nicht mehr zu fragen, sobald er's vollauf haben
konnte, und selbst sein Dritteil an der Beute, das ihn von Rechts wegen
trifft, verschenkt er an Waisenkinder oder läßt damit arme Jungen von
Hoffnung studieren.' (II. iii.) And the tenor of this report is confirmed by
the story of the rich count who, with the help of a cunning lawyer, won
millions in a lawsuit. Moor waylays the count, stabs the deceitful advocate
to death and turns away from the scene of the crime, proudly proclaiming: 'Ich habe das Meine getan! Das Plündern ist eure Sache.' (Ibid.)
This important bit of exposition immediately precedes the rescue of
Roller, a member of the band who, together with four others, had got
himself caught and was to be hanged that very morning. Roller is saved
at the foot of the gallows because Moor had ordered the town to be fired
in the nick of time. Returning from their exploit, the members of the
band tell gruelling stories of the death of innocent women and children
and of the looting and killing they did in the general confusion. Especially
Schufterle excels with a fine story of how he threw a helpless baby into
the fire. And again Moor dissociates himself from the activities of his men,
activities so alien to his intentions and yet sprung from them. Dismissing
the culprit, he addresses himself to the avenging powers in heaven, saying:

> Was kann ich dafür? Was kannst du dafür, wenn deine Pestilenz,
> deine Teurung, deine Wasserfluten den Gerechten mit dem
> Bösewicht auffressen? Wer kann der Flamme befehlen, daß sie nicht
> auch durch die gesegneten Saaten wüte, wenn sie das Genist der
> Hornissel zerstören soll? – O pfui über den Kindermord! den
> Weibermord – den Krankenmord! – Wie beugt mich diese Tat! Sie
> hat meine schönsten Werke vergiftet . . .

Karl dissociates himself from his deed in the most effective manner. He
degrades its executors into senseless instruments that have emancipated
themselves from the mind of their master and its intentions. And yet he
himself feels the puerility of such a distinction. A good Kantian distinction. This puerility is already apparent in his opening gambit, the typical
protestation of any child anywhere: 'Was kann ich dafür?' It is borne out

by his ensuing condemnation of himself: '. . . da steht der Knabe,
schamrot und ausgehöhnt vor dem Auge des Himmels, der sich anmaßte,
mit Jupiters Keule zu spielen, und Pygmäen niederwarf, da er Titanen
zerschmettern sollte – geh! geh! du bist der Mann nicht, das Rache-
schwert der obern Tribunale zu regieren, du erlagst bei dem ersten
Griff . . .' (Ibid.)

The recognition begins to dawn on Moor that he has arrogated to himself a task to which he is not equal. Neither he nor indeed any other
mortal, for none may control the issue of an action once it is let loose. It
is the recognition Wallenstein will formulate when he says:

> In meiner Brust war meine Tat noch mein:
> Einmal entlassen aus dem sichern Winkel
> Des Herzens, ihrem mütterlichen Boden,
> Hinausgegeben in des Lebens Fremde,
> Gehört sie jenen tück'schen Mächten an,
> Die keines Menschen Kunst vertraulich macht.
>
> (*Tod*, I. iv)

It is the recognition of the terrible finality of action in the irreversible
stream of time which is voiced by the Archbishop in *Die Jungfrau von
Orleans*:

> Fürchtet die Gottheit
> Des Schwerts, eh' ihr's der Scheid' entreißt. Loslassen
> Kann der Gewaltige den Krieg; doch nicht
> Gelehrig, wie der Falk sich aus den Lüften
> Zurückschwingt auf des Jägers Hand, gehorcht
> Der wilde Gott dem Ruf der Menschenstimme.
>
> (III. iii)

This indeed is the recognition which pervades Schiller's tragedies from
start to finish, recognition of the radical treacherousness of a world in
which good seed yields evil fruit, and the ensuing consciousness that in
such a world we must hold ourselves accountable not only for our mind's
intentions but for what becomes of them in 'des Lebens Fremde'. But this
dawning recognition in Karl's case is time and again overlaid by his outer
and inner dissociation from his doing: by his dissociation from his associates and, therewith, from the consequences of his intentions of which
his men are the chief executors.[16]

Both recognition and elusion are equally marked in Karl's encounter

with the Priest which follows upon the rescue of Roller with its accompanying atrocities. The Priest makes no nice distinction between intent
and consequences. He adjudges the band and their leader in terms of the
actions they have perpetrated, and his verdict is that they are plain thieves
and robbers: '. . . ihr Diebe – ihr Mordbrenner – ihr Schelmen . . .',
he addresses the assembled company; and, turning to Moor, he says, 'Und
du, feiner Hauptmann! Herzog der Beutelschneider! Gaunerkönig!
Großmogol aller Schelmen unter der Sonne!' (II. iii.) Karl throws the
Priest into the utmost confusion by conceding the truth of these accusa-
tions and by doing his level best to entice his companions into giving him
up to the authorities. 'Mich allein wollen sie haben, ich allein verdiene zu
büßen. Ist es nicht so, Herr Pater?' he asks. It looks as though he were
shouldering the moral responsibility for the actions committed in his
name. But this impression is misleading. He is in fact radically dissociating
himself from them. 'Ihr seid nicht *Moor*!' he exclaims: 'Ihr seid heillose
Diebe, elende Werkzeuge meiner größeren Plane, wie der Strick veräcnt-
lich in der Hand des Henkers!' (Ibid.) But of himself he says: 'Ich bin
kein Dieb, der sich mit Schlaf und Mitternacht verschwört . . . mein
Handwerk ist Wiedervergeltung – Rache ist mein Gewerbe!' (Ibid.) And
the fact that he is evading his responsibility is well expressed in the stage
direction: he turns his back on his accuser.

Even as late as Act IV, when Moor has once more returned to his home,
desperately, knowing that he is over and over sullied by his actions, he
still recoils from the devastating knowledge of the nature of his craft. He
gives his men the strictest orders not to steal: 'Wer nur eine Rube vom
Acker stiehlt, daß ich's erfahre, läßt seinen Kopf hier, so wahr ich *Moor*
heiße.' (IV. v.) For one as steeped in crime as Karl this is not being real.
It is moral posturing.

When he rescues his old father from living death in the tower in which
Franz had locked him up, he comes within a hair's breadth of perceiving
the incompatibility of the means he employs and the ends which are
motivating him: '*Itzt zum erstenmal* komm mir zu Hilfe, *Dieberei*!' he
exclaims. And the stage direction reads: '(Er nimmt Brechinstrumente
und öffnet das Gittertor . . .)' (IV. v). But again he cannot face the ugly
truth. Turning to his men, he says: '. . . das hat euch wohl niemals
geträumet, daß ihr der Arm höherer Majestäten seid? Der verworrene
Knäul unsers Schicksals ist aufgelöst. Heute, heute hat eine unsichtbare
Macht unser Handwerk geadelt! Betet an vor dem, der euch dies erhabene
Los gesprochen . . .' (Ibid.) Karl salves his conscience by shifting the

dichotomy between intent and execution from the moral to the metaphysical plane. But this is to evade the ultimate issue: that theft is his career, that by his own choice he has inaugurated a sequence of hideous actions of which he and his band are both the begetters and the executors, and for which he is accountable in their concrete psycho-dynamic entirety. It is in this state of desperate deludedness, yet torn by a sense of utmost unworthiness, that he decides to steal his father's blessing, only to learn that his true identity has become lethal.

III

But long before he returns a life which he has stolen, 'gleich einem Diebe', a counter-movement has set in. However much he tries to dissociate himself from his accomplices, and his intentions from the consequences of his doing, he is caught up in an irresistible impulse to identify himself with his choice.[17] This prompting is partly dictated by outward necessity. The consequences of his actions catch up with him and, step by remorseless step, he finds himself more deeply implicated in a situation he utterly detests. But there is an inner necessity at work as well. For, in a kind of perverse idealism, he welcomes such involvement and invests all his errant rectitude in a worthless cause.[18] Loyal to a fault, he *wants* to see through the course he has chosen and, in doing so, discover what it is that he has chosen. He *wants* to drink his bitter cup to the dregs.[19]

Even before his father's rebuff, rash actions, drink and bad company had inclined Karl along a dangerous, downward course. Such latent imbalance is retrospectively illuminated, and confirmed, at the 'prägnante Moment' of the tragedy. He receives his brother's letter; and at once he throws all constraint to the wind and gives free rein to his outraged instincts: '. . . o so fange Feuer, männliche Gelassenheit! verwilde zum Tiger, sanftmütiges Lamm! and jede Faser recke sich auf zu Grimm und Verderben!' (I. ii.) It is thus, hard-pressed from without and within, that he embarks on an irrevocable course: he gives that unconditional pledge of loyalty to his comrades which will make him walk through the mire and remorselessly bind him to the end. 'Nun, und bei dieser männlichen Rechte! schwör' ich euch hier, treu und standhaft euer Hauptmann zu bleiben bis in den Tod!' (Ibid.) The words themselves tell us how, ivy-like, this moral sense has begun to attach itself to his instinctual self. This becomes most apparent in the splendour of his concluding words: 'Fürchtet euch nicht vor Tod und Gefahr, denn über uns waltet ein unbeugsames

Fatum! Jeden ereilet endlich sein Tag, es sei auf dem weichen Kissen von
Pflaum, oder im rauhen Gewühl des Gefechts, oder auf offenem Galgen
und Rad! Eins davon ist unser Schicksal!' (Ibid.) From the lips of this poet
these are poignant words indeed. For wherever we look in his dramas,
from *Die Räuber* to *Wilhelm Tell* and beyond to *Demetrius*, the willingness to acknowledge the ultimate human destiny – death – is seen as the
ineluctable condition of living to the full. Karl has an unfailing sense of
destiny and in it he possesses the most precious guarantor of inner freedom. But instead of acknowledging mortality and being released from
care by this act of acceptance, he compulsively seeks death and the evil
fate which lies hidden, as a seed in a husk, within the choice he has blindly
made. For only by living with this unconscious choice will it reveal its
face to him.

The atrocities committed to save Roller fill Karl with disgust, and he
does his utmost to dissociate himself from his accomplices and from the
grotesque consequences of a well-intentioned action. Nevertheless we may
perceive an unmistakable counter-movement. When the news comes that
troops in overwhelming numbers have surrounded the band on all sides,
Karl reflects in a fashion entirely characteristic of him: 'Ich habe sie
vollends ganz einschließen lassen, itzt müssen sie fechten wie Verzwei-
felte.' (II. iii.) For himself as well as for others, he welcomes the therapy
of being irrevocably involved. For such coercion leaves no option but completely to identify with a choice once made and a course of action once
begun. At the end of the fight, in which Roller is killed, he pledges himself anew to his comrades, in extravagant words: 'Jeder von euch hat
Anspruch an diesen Scheitel! (Er entblößt sich das Haupt.) Hier heb' ich
meinen Dolch auf! So wahr meine Seele lebt! *Ich will euch niemals verlassen.*' (III. ii.) Schweizer's remonstrances that he may well come to
regret so irrevocable an oath elicits a pledge which is even more binding:
'*Bei den Gebeinen meines Rollers! Ich will euch niemals verlassen.*' (Ibid.)

Kosinsky's arrival, immediately after this pledge, is designed to drive
home to Karl how hasty his own choice has been. For Kosinsky is as it were
a young Karl Moor. The misfortunes they have endured are all but the
same; only the newcomer has not yet crossed the threshold to crime. Thus
in him Moor sees himself make his fatal choice all over again. As he wit-
nesses the youth's first steps toward outlawry, he realizes how far he himself has walked along the road of no return; and from the awareness that
what he has done is irreversible, there springs an altogether new sense of
responsibility, not just towards the stranger but, more importantly, to-

wards himself. '. . . Weißt du auch, daß du ein leichtsinniger Knabe bist und über den großen Schritt deines Lebens weggaukelst wie ein unbesonnenes Mädchen?' hs asks (III. ii), and: 'wie viel hast du schon getan, wobei du an Verantwortung[20] gedacht hast?' (ibid.); '. . . lern' erst die Tiefe des Abgrunds kennen, eh' du hineinspringst! . . .'; '. . . wenn dir noch ein Funken von Hoffnung irgend anderswo glimmt, so verlaß diesen schröcklichen Bund, den nur Verzweiflung eingeht . . .'; 'Man kann sich täuschen – glaube mir, man kann das für Stärke des Geistes halten, was doch am Ende Verzweiflung ist – Glaube *mir*, *mir*! und mach' dich eilig hinweg' (ibid.).

This is a new language; the adult language of a man who knows that what is done is done, who knows even that noble impulses may lend a false glamour to an intrinsically base cause, and who recognizes the nature of what he has in fact done. And yet he accepts Kosinsky as a member of the band; yet, having been reminded of what he has lost, he decides to return to his home: not indeed to regain what he has forfeited, but in order to know the better what it is. Before ever he sets foot in his father's house he says: 'Lebt wohl, ihr Vaterlandstäler! Einst saht ihr den Knaben Karl, und der Knabe Karl war ein glücklicher Knabe – itzt saht ihr den Mann, und er war in Verzweiflung.' (IV. i.) Then, thinking of Amalia, he decides to see her: 'es soll mich zermalmen' (ibid.). And once again, on the point of drawing back, he reaffirms his resolution, saying, '. . . ich muß den Gifttrank dieser Seligkeit vollends ausschlürfen, und dann . . .' (IV. iv).

Once again, after the recognition scene with Amalia, Karl is tempted to elude the consequences of his doing by committing suicide. And once again a stronger hand holds him back. He cannot even conceive of any eternity in which he would wish to evade his self such as it is: 'Sei wie du wilt, *namenloses Jenseits* – ' he exclaims, 'bleibt mir nur dieses mein *Selbst* getreu – Sei wie du wilt, wenn ich nur mich *selbst* mit hinübernehme – Aussendinge sind nur der Anstrich des Manns – *Ich* bin mein Himmel und meine Hölle.' (IV. v.)[21] Thus he resolves to drink his cup and to face this self, such as it has become, unflinchingly, here and now. 'Nein! ich will's dulden . . . Die Qual erlahme an meinem Stolz! Ich will's vollenden.' (Ibid.)

IV

This process of self-involvement and gradual recognition is gathering momentum throughout the course of the tragedy. It is a trial Karl ferociously inflicts upon himself; and his agony is at once his illness and its cure. I use the word 'illness' advisedly. For Schiller himself, in his own review of the play in the *Wirtembergischen Repertorium*, describes a moral crisis in terms of a pathological psychophysical imbalance. Apropos of Franz he writes:

> . . . ich denke . . . überzeugt zu sein, daß der Zustand des moralischen Übels im Gemüt eines Menschen ein schlechterdings gewaltsamer Zustand sey, welchen zu erreichen zuförderst das Gleichgewicht der ganzen geistigen Organisation (wenn ich so sagen darf) aufgehoben sein muß, so wie das ganze System der tierischen Haushaltung, Kochung und Scheidung, Puls und Nervenkraft durcheinandergeworfen sein müsse, eh' die Natur einem Fieber oder Konvulsionen Raum gibt.[22]

This general statement is as applicable to Karl as it is to Franz. Karl's anarchic instincts do not simply run riot any more than Franz's rational drives are able to gain unchallenged sway over the 'verworrenen Schauer des Gewissens'.[23] If this were all, both would have an easier time of it. Franz's irrational terrors as much as Karl's spiritual anguish – 'Ich will's vollenden' – leave no doubt of the fact that the equilibrium of the whole psyche is disturbed by the pathology of one of its functions.[24] Karl's higher promptings, his fidelity and his rectitude, have indeed been displaced by the upsurge of excessive instinctual drives. But so far from ceasing to function without a proper domain of their own, these moral impulses attach themselves to his anarchic instincts, surreptitiously reinforcing them until their tyranny becomes absolute and untenable and the whole diseased system breaks down. Schiller has described this process of psychological displacement with every precision, again in the *Selbstrezension der Räuber*. There we read: 'Die gräßlichsten seiner [i.e. Karl's] Verbrechen sind weniger die Wirkung bösartiger Leidenschaften als des zerrütteten Systems der guten. Indem er eine Stadt dem Verderben preisgibt, umfaßt er seinen Roller mit ungeheuerm Enthusiasmus.'[24] It is Karl's 'gute Leidenschaften', that is to say, his moral impulses, which give the obsessive and fatalistic edge to his pursuit of a worthless and lost cause until, in the end, both that cause and the instincts that bound him to it stand revealed for what they are. Delusion and the strength lent to the usurping instincts by delusion lead to their eventual collapse and that of the psychic system they have disrupted, and thus, ultimately, to recognition and cure. As in an infection the healthy blood corpuscles themselves aid the inflammation and induce the crisis, so here: Karl's moral self reinforces the operation of his instinctual drives, until, in a paroxysm, the whole diseased system collapses and balance is restored.

In precisely this fashion, throughout Schiller's tragedies, the neglected and repressed aspects of the psyche will lend their strength to reinforce the dominant ones and lead to their destruction and that of the system to which they belong. Franz's rationality is brought to a pitch where it drives him mad by the clandestine agency of the very instincts he has denied. Wallenstein's neglected feeling-side will disastrously attach itself to his rationality and drive him into an obscurantist and fallacious reliance on astrological facts; Elisabeth's denied eroticism will lead her, open-eyed, into a meeting with Maria which she knows must be fatal, whilst the repressed power-impulse of the latter will avenge itself by making her assert herself in the face of her all-powerful rival; Johanna's denied sexuality will give a compulsive tinge to her purity and drive her into asserting this purity in cruel and excessive ways. Each time, the frustrated drives themselves aid the process of recognition by thus magnifying and reinforcing a latent imbalance; and, in some cases, they inaugurate an inner catharsis. For catharsis, in the eyes of Schiller, is nothing other than the recognition of an initially unconscious choice in its full and tragic implications, and the transcendence of its compulsion through the act of acceptance.[25]

Karl has made a blind and disastrous choice in giving free rein to his impulse. In doing so, he has offended against 'die richtende Empfindung', against what Goethe calls 'das Obere Leitende' in himself: the constraints imposed by the allegiance to spiritual values. By dissociating himself from his actions and their consequences he is – so the poet tells us – committing a theft. He is trying to steal back a part of his personality he has irretrievably forfeited by giving rein to the other side of his being. This tendency, perpetually balanced by the counter-movement towards greater involvement and clearer recognition, comes to a head in his attempt to steal his father's blessing. Such spiritual sanction is something to which he has forfeited any right by his initial choice and its obdurate reaffirmation, just as he has forfeited the right to Amalia's love. It is only at the very last that he understands what he has chosen and what he has forfeited, in making this choice and none other:

O über mich Narren, der ich wähnete, die Welt durch Greuel zu verschönern und die Gesetze durch Gesetzlosigkeit aufrecht zu

halten. Ich nannte es Rache und Recht . . . aber – O eitle Kin-
derei, da steh' ich am Rand eines entsetzlichen Lebens und erfahre
nun mit Zähnklappern und Heulen, *daß zwei Menschen wie ich den
ganzen Bau der sittlichen Welt zu Grund richten würden* . . .
Freilich steht's nun in meiner Macht nicht mehr, die Vergangenheit einzuholen – schon bleibt verdorben, was verdorben ist –
was ich gestürzt habe, steht ewig niemals mehr auf – Aber noch
blieb mir etwas übrig, womit ich die beleidigte Gesetze versöhnen
und die mißhandelte Ordnung wiederum heilen kann. Sie bedarf
eines Opfers – Eines Opfers, das ihre unverletzbare Majestät vor der
ganzen Menschheit entfaltet – dieses Opfer bin ich selbst! . . .
Was soll ich, gleich einem Diebe, ein Leben länger verheimlichen,
das mir schon lang' im Rat der himmlischen Wächter genommen
ist? (V. ii)

Thus to steal, here as in every other tragedy from the pen of this poet,
means to usurp the appearance of wholeness after wholeness has been
forfeited. Karl and Franz, Fiesco, Marquis Posa, Wallenstein, Elisabeth
and Maria, Johanna, Isabella and her sons and Demetrius are usurpers in
this sense of the word, and more often than not the inner, psychological
fact has found expression in a spurious claim to outward rank or political
title.[26] And how easy it is, in the universe of discourse of Schiller's poetry,
to forfeit that most precious and fragile of gifts, wholeness of being! No
poet was more acutely aware of the terrible finality of time, that rapid and
irreversible movement into perpetual darkness. Its every moment is
fraught with irrevocable consequences leading into the unknowable;[27]
and its might is conquerable – if at all – only through the resilient strength
of the sum total of our human resources.[28] Yet how hard-pressed human
beings are, how liable to be victimized in their integrity by the unpre-
dictable pressures of the moment! From the very first, man, for Schiller,
is 'der flüchtige Sohn der Stunde', 'der leichte Raub des mächt'gen
Augenblicks'. In such a view, loss of wholeness is tragically all but inevitable, and not until his last finished drama, *Wilhelm Tell*, did Schiller
create an image of integration in which a man masters the treachery of the
moment and bows only to the ultimate human destiny – death.

Nowhere has the poet portrayed the finality of choice and action in the
stream of time with a more remorseless sense of tragedy than in this, his
first-born play. A noble character makes a heedless choice and is destroyed
by it. As long as he still claims wholeness, he is a thief. Once he recognizes

what he has irretrievably lost, he honours the forfeit. By such recognition and acceptance, he restores not only 'die mißhandelte Ordnung' in the world outside. He restores the disrupted balance within himself and, in doing so, regains wholeness in his own tormented self. This princely acceptance of loss is Moor's catharsis; and this was to be a reading of the concept of which the poet never let go again.

V

For all this tendency to dissociate himself from the consequences of his actions, Karl's final acceptance of commitment is a development which from the very first is assured. Quite early in the play one of the band says: ' . . . ich kenne den Hauptmann. Wenn er dem Teufel sein Wort drauf gegeben hätte, in die Hölle zu fahren, er würde nie beten, wenn er mit einem halben Vaterunser selig werden könnte.' (II. iii.) This characterization furnishes a vital link between the brothers. For Franz will try to save himself, precisely, 'mit einem halben Vaterunser'. Franz has opted for a wholesale repudiation of a nature who has treated him in a stepmotherly fashion and, with it, of the instincts she has implanted in men. One of the most deep-rooted of these is piety, and the rationally inexplicable bonds which spring from piety. Franz denies the reality of such ties, arguing: 'Kann ich eine Liebe erkennen, die sich nicht auf Achtung gegen mein *Selbst* gründet?' (I. i.) The logical consequence of this position would be the unhesitating infringement of the dictates of piety without any sense of being accountable. For these promptings, in his view, are based on a delusion. And this is in fact the way in which Franz lives up to his end. It is then, close to death, that his outraged instincts reassert themselves, holding up before him apocalyptic visions of the last judgement born of all the 'verworrenen Schauer des Gewissens', visions in which he is held answerable for his disbelief and the actions springing from his disbelief. And at once Franz does what Karl would never do: he dissociates himself from the course he has pursued and recants his atheism. In order to avoid being held accountable for his moral choice, he turns to God, asking to be pardoned: 'Höre mich beten, Gott im Himmel!' he prays: ' – Es ist das erste Mal – soll auch gewiß nimmer geschehen – Er höre mich, Gott im Himmel.' (V. i.)

This 'soll auch gewiß nimmer geschehen' is the strangest mental act of self-contradiction, the first of a long series of such acts we shall encounter from a galaxy of poetic characters anxious to preserve their freedom from commitment at any price. Turning to God and betraying his first choice, Franz at once dissociates himself from the second choice he is in the process of making. For if God is real and prayer is meaningful he will, after all, have to answer for the consequences of his life. And this will never do. This double betrayal expressed in Franz's recantation of his prayer is perfectly summed up by his old servant Daniel who comments: 'Mein doch! Was treibt Ihr? Das ist ja gottlos gebetet. . . . Gott sei uns gnädig. Auch seine Gebete werden zu Sünden.' (Ibid.) And, indeed, Franz's final action – his suicide – so far from signifying the acceptance of commitment, is its final repudiation. Suicide is the only way out for one who is hemmed in on all sides by consequences – consequences of evil doing, consequences of praying or of not praying – and who is driven at all costs to evade consequences in order to preserve his freedom. His brother would not pray to buy himself off from what he has done. Franz revokes his atheism in prayer because he is afraid of the consequences of his atheism, and he recants his anguished prayer because he is afraid of the finality of a religious confrontation. His last word, quite logically, is 'unentrinnbar'.[29]

VI

When Karl had first returned home, his old servant, Daniel, had identified his master by a large scar across his right hand dating back to his wild boyhood. At the height of Karl's moral crisis, after the battle in which Roller loses his life, Moor's comrade-in-arms, Schweizer, brings him some drinking water in his hat, to cool him after the heavy fighting. Schweizer is wounded and Moor, with a tender gesture, wipes his bloodstained face, explaining: 'Sonst sieht man ja die Narben nicht, die die böhmischen Reuter in deine Stirne gezeichnet haben – dein Wasser war gut, Schweizer – diese Narben stehen dir schön.' (III. ii.) It is this incident more than anything else which causes Moor to renew his pledge of loyalty to a band he knows to be rotten through and through. Later, when Moor embraces Amalia, the robbers remind him of his pledge: 'Denk' an die böhmischen Wälder! Hörst du? Zagst du? – an die böhmischen Wälder sollst du denken! Treuloser, wo sind deine Schwüre? Vergißt man Wunden so bald?' (V. ii.) And after he has murdered Amalia, to pay his associates for 'ein Leben, das schon nicht mehr euer war, ein Leben voll Abscheulichkeit und Schande . . . ' he says bitterly laughing: 'Die Narben, die böhmischen Wälder! Ja, ja! dies mußte freilich bezahlt werden.' (Ibid.)

What is the meaning of this recurrent image? Scars are consequences of actions, and reminders, most of all, of rash or regrettable actions. They are the indelible imprint actions etch on to a face, a hand, a life. This person Karl, a creature of impulse from the start, is scarred by his so being from the outset of his life. And the choice he impulsively makes, at the 'pregnant moment' of his career, irrevocably marks him and his associates, and scars both body and soul for ever. These robbers wear their past upon their faces. This impetuous man has his choice engraven on the very mirror of his soul. And thus, scarred, he accepts himself. He judges his choice and its moral worth by the ravages it has left.[30]

In this most exhaustingly scrupulous of tragedies, the worth of a moral choice and of the action ensuing from it is not assessed according to the integrity of its author's disembodied intentions. Here, as in every other tragedy from Schiller's pen, it is judged, with formidable concreteness, precision and psychological acumen, according to its total outcome, by the mark it leaves on the outer world and in the inner universe of a man's life. Maria Stuart will in the end accept the remotest reverberations of a rash action long since past as 'hers' and as a sufficient justification for her death.[31] Wallenstein chooses to go to his death for having toyed with the life of Max who is dead and done with. A man like Karl Moor, princely but heedless, will walk through a veritable hell of self-torment to ferret out what his choice was in the first place and what the mark it left has made of him and the world.

It is improbable in the extreme that a young artist who took such a fiercely committed view of moral responsibility should ever have to come to adopt the bifocal vision of transcendental idealism[32] to mediate his poetic experience of man's journey through the world, however compelling this philosophy proved to be to him as a thinker. For one thing, Kant's idiom is basically unpoetic in that it singles out a man's conscious intent at the expense of those less accessible reaches of human experience which are the artist's inalienable concern: the complex network of man's unconscious being and its secret radiation outward, into the world.[33] Besides, to those of us who have got accustomed to regarding man as a pattern-making creature, who *is* what he *does* rather than what he *thinks* he does, Kant's exclusive concern with conscious motivation may seem psychologically thin. As against this, the existentialist idiom that this incorruptibly honest young author forged for himself in his first play speaks to us authentically across the gulf of two centuries. As Sartre has it: 'L'homme . . . n'est donc rien d'autre que l'ensemble de ses actes, rien d'autre que sa vie.'[34]

5

Passions and possessions
in *Kabale und Liebe*

<hr>

I

We are no longer in the habit of regarding the major literary achievements of the *Sturm und Drang* as effusions of feelings devoid of form. The relevance of epithets such as 'sincere', as applied to art, is becoming ever more questionable as we recognize that the quality of a work of art cannot be adequately determined by reference to its author, his feelings, attitudes or intentions, but needs to be defined in terms of its own internal organization. The impression of spontaneity, immediacy, even of chaos transmitted by a poem, so far from simply reflecting the intensity or turbulence of the feelings of the poet, is a deliberate effect which comes off in the measure in which the poet has succeeded in ordering his materials. The poets themselves have been telling us so. Bürger, in the eyes of Schiller, fails to be an artist precisely because he fails to interpolate aesthetic distance – 'fernende Erinnerung' – between himself and his experience; Goethe's Werther is habitually so overcome by his emotions that his eyes brim over with tears and he can no longer see the object he would paint; whilst the fine feelings of the unforgettable young merchant Tonio Kröger meets aboard ship terminate, not in poetry, but in seasickness.

What is thus being recognized as a matter of aesthetic fact, is being increasingly confirmed by the results of critical analysis. The presence of the 'inner form' of the young Schiller's domestic tragedy has been convincingly shown.[1] What effect this drama still has on us is due, not to the dated topicality of the social problem which may indeed have excited Schiller to put pen to paper, but to the poet's creative use of the media of language and tragic form which led him, perhaps unawares, to explore deeper levels of human nature and to articulate a more lasting theme.

The theme of the tragedy is love; more precisely speaking, the limitation of the love evinced by Luise Millerin, the tragic heroine; as Ferdinand words it: 'Ich fürchte nichts – nichts, als die Grenzen deiner Liebe' (I. iv).[2] The significance of the image-pattern of music for the development of this theme is crucial. Music, in this play, is the overall symbol of love. And it is revealing how, as the tragedy unfolds, the images from the sphere of music, with all their attendant associations of harmony and fulfilment, become transferred from the figure of Luise's lover to that of her father. It is Ferdinand who, virtually in his opening words, testifies to the indestructible harmony between himself and Luise, saying: 'Wer kann den Bund zwoer Herzen lösen oder die Töne eines Akkordes auseinander reißen?' (I. iv.) But it is to Miller that the poet, near the close of the tragedy, assigns the culminating metaphor of the whole pattern: 'Ich setze die Geschichte deines Grames auf die Laute, singe dann ein Lied von der Tochter, die, ihren Vater zu ehren, ihr Herz zerriß – wir betteln mit der Ballade von Türe zu Türe, und das Almosen wird köstlich schmecken von den Händen der Weinenden . . . ' (V. i) – lines that would seem to speak of suffering, but more deeply speak of love: for in this play it is the power of love alone which kindles the universal sympathy of which Miller is here speaking.[3] Miller it is who, at the beginning of the drama, finds image upon image to express the defilation of harmony, who more than once threatens to break his instrument upon the back of his wife. Yet it is Ferdinand, enraged by the limitations of Luise's love, who finally shatters the violin he has vainly tried to play. And to him fall, in the closing scenes of the tragedy, those bitterly cynical metaphors of harmony fouled: as when he likens his last meeting with Luise to a 'verdrießlichen Duett' (V. vii), or envisages a future in which '. . . Ekel und Scham noch eine Harmonie veranstalten, die der zärtlichsten Liebe unmöglich gewesen ist' (ibid.).

By such symmetrical distribution of his image material between Ferdinand and Miller, by the gradual transference of all its positive connotations to the father and its negative associations to the lover, the poet tells us a great deal about a process of which the characters themselves are only partially aware and which embodies the underlying theme of the tragedy. The process is that of the gradual strangulation of an adult relationship caught in the coils of a filial entanglement. The theme realized in this process is that of possessive love.[4]

This theme has been formulated through yet another image-pattern, perhaps the most central of all: the imagery of monetary possessions.[5] The following pages attempt to throw some light upon this imagistic complex and its interrelation with other structures, rhetorical or dramatic, and finally to determine its specific contribution to the overall poetic meaning of the play.

II

The test of an interpretation is how much light it sheds on a work of art; how much relevance, connectedness and artistic purpose it is able to show where before there had appeared to be incoherence. For this reason, the consideration of two scenes in this play which have customarily exercised critics will be a convenient starting-point for these reflections. These scenes are not chosen at random. For in both, money is introduced in the plot; indeed, in both, and only in these scenes, money is actually introduced on the stage. The first of these (II. ii) comprises the lackey's account of the outrages committed by the ruling Prince, and ends with his indignant refusal to accept a purse filled with gold which is offered to him by Lady Milford. An important scene, this, in that it provides a historical setting which goes some way towards explaining the despotic ruthlessness so prominent in the subsequent action. The other scene (V. v) is taken up by the encounter between Luise's father and her lover, during which Ferdinand announces his impending departure and offers Miller a purse full of gold which the latter duly accepts.

The reasons for which these scenes have monopolized critical attention are not dissimilar. In both, Schiller's naturalistic tendency seems to have tempted him into an exploration of historical or psychological niceties without regard for the economy and tone of his play as a whole. We know that the incident reported by the lackey – the sale and deportation of some 7,000 young men to America – was suggested to the poet by a similar event which had occurred, not many years before, in his native Württemberg – an event which his father had actually witnessed; and this outrage was far from being the only one of its kind.[6] Neither the stage history of this scene nor indeed the critical comments it has inspired leave any doubt as to where its importance was – and still is – seen to lie: in its candid exposure and condemnation of current social and political ills. The scene was either omitted because of its topicality (as at the first, unofficial performance of the play by Grossmann's company on 13 April 1784, at which the director of the company himself had originally intended to play the part of the lackey but eventually deleted it altogether), or, for the same reason, played by leading figures such as Iffland himself, and later by K. F. Unzelmann and others.[7] And literary critics have, from the first, subscribed to this assessment of its significance.[8] We have heard a chorus in praise of its daring realism and patent sincerity; of its intrinsic merits and its function in the artistic economy of the drama as a whole we have heard nothing. But historical faithfulness and/or, for that matter, congruence with any reality outside a poem cannot of itself vindicate any element within it;[9] and as it has become increasingly apparent that this powerful tragedy of Schiller's youth cannot draw its continued poetic life from social issues which have become increasingly dated but from its treatment of the timeless problem of love,[10] we are bound to review the credentials of this celebrated scene and ask ourselves whether its appeal really derives from the faded topicality of the outer action or whether it is woven into the deeper artistic life of the drama.

Even more obviously refractory to critical endeavours is the second incident. Miller's reaction to Ferdinand's gift of money is generally held to be the most baffling and repellent feature of the tragedy.[11] Throughout the play, and especially in its expository scenes, Miller has been shown as an upright character with a strong tinge of pietistic inwardness: despising the things of this world, despising his wife for coveting them, and unhesitatingly rejecting the material benefits that have accrued to his household through Ferdinand's courtship of Luise. And here he is, accepting her lover's money with an uninhibited show of delight which strikes one as all but indecent. This is all the more puzzling in view of the fact that throughout the tragedy the most sensitive side of his character has been revealed in his relationship with his daughter. How is it possible that all of a sudden he should be so obtuse to her suffering?

Here then are two areas of the drama that have defied elucidation: one at its circumference, the other at its core. They are linked by the fact that money plays a prominent part in both. Parallelism suggests pattern, and thus poetic purpose. And indeed, looked at more closely, the parallelism between the two situations becomes more remarkable. The lackey's rejection of the Lady's offer of money serves ironically to underline the grim fact which her gesture was designed to mitigate: to the Prince, his subjects *are* material possessions. He treats living beings as saleable property. The lackey's own sons were among those whom the Prince has sold to finance his costly gifts to his mistress. 'Gestern sind siebentausend Landskinder nach Amerika fort – die zahlen alles' (II. ii), the lackey explains to Lady Milford. Now compare with this Ferdinand's words as he hands a purse full of gold to Miller: 'Mit dem Geld bezahl' ich Ihm – (*von Schauern ergriffen hält er inn*) bezahl' ich Ihm (*nach einer Pause mit Wehmut*) den dreimonatlangen glücklichen Traum von Seiner Tochter. (V. v.) There can be no doubt: Miller is offered money for the temporary grant of possession of his daughter to Ferdinand, and he accepts this money as a token of his proprietary rights,[12] just as the Prince accepts money for making over his subjects. Ferdinand's twofold hesitation to name the object of his payment – Luise – serves at once to underline the utter incongruity he perceives between the sanctity of a human relationship and monetary recompense, and to stress the fact that in the mind of the recipient no such incommensurability exists: for with these words Miller's qualms are allayed.

If any doubt as to the connection between the two scenes still remains, it is dispelled by the realization of yet another means the poet has devised to draw them together more closely. In the earlier scene, and there alone, the Prince is repeatedly called *Landesvater* and his subjects *Landeskinder*: in the circumstances a misnomer of patent irony, designed to arrest the reader's attention and to force him into the awareness that what passes on the historical circumference of the drama directly bears on its central configuration – the relationship between father and child. Is the poet's implication, then, that Miller owns his daughter and – we might add – that the President owns his son in a way comparable to that in which the tyrant owns his subjects? An examination of the image pattern centred in the events and properties of these scenes – the images of monetary possessions – will answer this question.

III

So heavily do the expository scenes of the tragedy stress the gulf between the social station of the lovers that we tend to read Luise's first speeches as expressions of a genuine resignation in the face of adverse circumstances. Her unquestioning renunciation of Ferdinand for this life, her hope of a reunion in a hereafter where 'die Herzen im Preise steigen' (1. iii) and where, thus, she will be rich – 'Ich werde dann reich sein' (ibid.) – and finally her avowal 'Ich will ja nur wenig – an ihn denken – das kostet ja nichts' (ibid.): all these we tend to accept as essentially realistic reflections on a situation, the unfeasibility of which has already been impressed on the reader.[13]

Yet the last of the above-quoted statements is so strange as to arrest our attention. Luise renounces her lover because she is poor. Poor, clearly, not in the literal sense of the word; that cannot be the meaning of 'das kostet ja nichts' in this context, for to have him in reality would presumably be more costly for him than for her! But in what sense is she poor, then? Poor of heart? The puzzle deepens when in the following scene Ferdinand likens Luise to a treasure, declaring: 'Ich . . . will über dir wachen wie der Zauberdrach über unterirdischem Golde' (I. iv).[14] Does this contradiction arise from a difference in the lovers' views, or is it indicative of some paradox inherent in Luise's situation? The puzzle is resolved in the crucial encounter between the lovers in which Luise summarily explains her intention to break off the affair between the President's son and herself with the words: 'Ich habe einen Vater, der kein Vermögen hat als diese einzige Tochter' (III. iv). Luise *is* a treasure, a fortune, and thus Ferdinand is right: she is rich. But she *has* nothing herself because she belongs to her father. And thus she is right, too: she is poor. How little she owns herself, indeed, a glance at the grammatical form of her statement reveals: it is the father who is the subject of the sentence; Luise herself is the object, passive, possessed. Small wonder that she thinks of herself as a piece of property!

The same imagery is henceforth invoked time and again, from all sides, with so varied a reference as to become the overall symbol of feeling-relationships in this play, yet with such subtle shading of connotation as to delineate the precise nature of the relation between father and daughter and to set it apart from all others. Lady Milford sums up her relation to the Prince, saying: '. . . ich habe dem Fürsten meine Ehre verkauft, aber mein Herz habe ich frei behalten' (II. i.) So too, Ferdinand counters Luise's refusal to elope with him on the ground that she is all her father possesses, saying: 'Ich gehe, mache meine Kostbarkeiten zu Geld, erhebe Summen auf meinen Vater. Es ist erlaubt, einen Räuber zu plündern, und sind seine Schätze nicht Blutgeld des Vaterlands?'[15] (III. iv.) However factual Ferdinand's references to money seem in themselves, Luise's preceding words suffice to imbue his reply with something of their own imaginative force, to make it into a significant statement of relationship. Moreover, later on Ferdinand himself returns to the subject of filial obligation, and, whilst using the same imagery, he does so, this time, in a sense that is clearly metaphorical. As he contemplates the loss he is about to inflict on Luise's father by killing his only child, his thoughts revert to his own father and the loss he too will sustain: '. . . aber auch *mein* Vater hat diesen einzigen Sohn', he muses, only to add: 'den einzigen Sohn, doch nicht den einzigen Reichtum!' (V. iv.) Thus both for Ferdinand and Lady Milford relatedness indeed entails indebtedness; but this indebtedness is strictly conditional on the inalienable right of each individual to his own life, his own soul and his own salvation. How is this imagery manipulated in connection with Luise and her father?

Miller himself spontaneously resorts to it when he confesses to Ferdinand: 'hab' meine ganze Barschaft von Liebe an der Tochter schon zugesetzt' (V. iii). Indeed, he has already used it earlier on in the same act, in his attempt to prevent Luise from seeking death together with her lover. 'Du warst mein Alles,' he begins and goes on to plead with her thus: 'Jetzt vertust du nicht mehr von deinem Eigentum. Auch ich hab' alles zu verlieren. . . . Die Zeit meldet sich allgemach bei mir, wo uns Vätern die Kapitale zu statten kommen, die wir in den Herzen unsrer Kinder anlegten – Wirst du mich darum betrügen, Luise? Wirst du dich mit dem Hab und Gut deines Vaters auf and davon machen?' (V. i.) Luise fully responds to this appeal, replying to it in the same vein: 'Nein, mein Vater,' she says, 'Ich gehe als Seine große Schuldnerin aus der Welt und werde in der Ewigkeit mit Wucher bezahlen.' (Ibid.) Ferdinand too, repeatedly takes up the same imagery: 'Rauben den letzten Notpfennig einem Bettler?' (V. iv) he muses as he discovers how much Luise means to her father; and he warns the old man of the risks of such an attachment, saying: 'Nur ein verzweifelter Spieler setzt alles auf einen einzigen Wurf' (V. v), and: 'Einen Waghals nennt man den Kaufmann, der auf *ein* Schiff sein ganzes Vermögen ladet' (ibid.). True, the fatal words spoken to him earlier on by Luise and her father's confession to him may be echoing in Ferdinand's mind and so determine his choice of image here. But this is not all. It does not explain the precise quality his own metaphors have spontaneously assumed. The fact of the matter is that in the last act of the tragedy the three principal characters have begun, in independent concert, to use the original metaphor in a significant variation. The capital investment of which Miller speaks, the debt Luise promises to pay back with high interest, the gambler's stake and the merchant's riches to which Ferdinand likens Miller's expectations of his daughter: all these add a new dimension of meaning to the image which dominated the beginning of the drama. As it becomes clear how completely Luise is possessed by her father, the symbol of this relation, inanimate and static at first, becomes invested with a kind of life of its own; it feeds on itself and grows. The successful merchant, the lucky investor or gambler, the

usurer – they all own more in the end than they had owned in the beginning. A masterly stroke, this intensification of the dominant symbol as the
tragedy gathers final momentum and catastrophe is in the air – and
sufficient proof that we are here dealing, not primarily with a stylistic
device to characterize individual speakers, but with a poetic symbol directly
controlled by the central theme and responsive to its development.[16]

IV

Luise, then, has no right to her own life. She belongs to her father in a deep
and exclusive sense. Against such ties Ferdinand is powerless. His claim
'Das Mädchen ist mein' (IV. iv)[17] comes to nought against Miller's 'Du
warst mein Alles' (V. i). This double process, in which Ferdinand is dispossessed and Miller comes into his own, is a gradual one; and it is revealing to see how, step by step, phase by phase, it is poetically implemented
by the use of images of possession. Luise's opening words almost – 'Ich
will ja nur wenig – an ihn denken – das kostet ja nichts' – contain in the
seed the essential unreality of her love[18] which will become tragically
apparent under the pressure of events. The first actual withdrawal takes
place when she refuses to live her life with her lover; a step that is explained by her statement that she is her father's only possession. The
blackmailing scene engineered by Wurm – which marks the turning-point
of the outward action – naturally enough abounds with metaphorical
references to goods to be secured and costs to be paid: 'Welchen Preis kann
er auf eine Menschlichkeit setzen?' (III. vi) Luise asks of the Prince; and
the price she eventually pays is neither her father's safety nor her own
salvation – she is not free to forfeit either – but the irrevocable betrayal
of her love: the ransom she pays is Ferdinand's peace of soul. In the end,
having abandoned the reality of a life lived with her lover, she sacrifices
the hope of an eternity shared with him so as not to remain in her father's
debt. Indeed, she goes further still. Moved by her father's entreaties to
tear up her letter to Ferdinand, she says: 'So zernicht' ich sein letztes
Gedächtnis.' (V. i.) With these words the imagery has come full circle. For,
even in the beginning, to think of Ferdinand and the love that might be
was all that Luise could afford. In the end, even this small stake has to be
withdrawn.[19]

Thus the reader's imagination is amply prepared for the tragic reversal
of fortunes which precipitates the final catastrophe, and for the causes
leading up to it. It is in the much-disputed scene between Ferdinand and

Miller that the displacement of the lover by the father becomes a palpable
dramatic reality. Once this scene is viewed in the context of the rhetorical
structure in which it is embedded, its meaning becomes apparent and the
objections raised against it vanish. It is nothing less than the transfer of
ultimate proprietary rights over Luise that is symbolically enacted in the
transfer of the money from one man to the other. At this voluntary renunciation on the part of the 'legitimate' owner, the sluice-gates of Miller's
unconscious open and his passionate possessiveness, long condemned and
now inexplicably sanctioned, wells up with elemental force.[20] The true
character of his involvement, scarcely hinted at before, now becomes manifest; witness the undisguised sensuality of his words at the sight and touch
of the promised splendour: 'Da *greif** ich ja das *bare** *gelbe** *leibhafte**
Gottesgold' (V. v), he exclaims. Nor can we wonder at the extravagance
of his actions and the violence of his speech. They reflect the storm that is
shaking this man, tossing him this way and that, now towards the object
he desires, now away from it in revulsion. For the glory that is held out
to him is sinful and sweet, diabolical and divine, and terrible in this
ambiguity. Miller's ambivalence is expressed, not only in his prolonged
wavering between acceptance and rejection of the gift, but, more intimately, through the succession of antitheses he invokes in an effort to
come to terms with the situation. *Gottesgold* is one such coinage, intensified
by the *leibhaft* that precedes the mention of God, and doubly enhanced by
the invocation of *Satanas* which follows it. Again, 'die ganze *allmächtige
Börse'** or 'der ganze *grausame Reichtum'** follow the same pattern; or,
finally, 'In *Henkers** Namen – ich sage – ich bitte Sie um *Gottes Christi**
willen – Gold!'[21] By bracketing together contraries, by piling antithesis
upon antithesis, the poet communicates the violence of the conflict
precipitated by Ferdinand's gift.

Only the realization of the symbolic nature and significance of this gift
will explain the profound revolution of values it begets in the recipient,
and the sudden and drastic change of personality he undergoes. While
Miller was dispossessed, he had despised the things of this world. Now he
has come into his own and he takes his place in it. This reversal of a behaviour pattern,[22] far from being the result of the poet's caprice, is
psychologically fully motivated and indeed required the most deliberate
and consistent handling of his poetic materials to be successfully conveyed
at all. In this connection, the symmetry between the first and last acts of
the play is remarkable. The very things Miller had despised his worldly

---

* My italics.

wife for desiring he now wholeheartedly wants himself – whether it be *Tobakschnupfen* for himself or French lessons or fineries for his daughter. He even tries his hand at French words himself, as his wife had done before him! And he does not scruple to accept what in the opening scene of the tragedy he had called 'das Geld, das mein einziges Kind mit Seel' und Seligkeit abverdient', what in its final scene he will call so again.

V

The heroine herself is dimly aware of what the imagery tells the reader: that she has no choice but to belong to her father.[23] Twice in the play, when the necessity of making a choice between him and Ferdinand is borne in upon her, she admits that she has no option. When Wurm asks her to decide between Ferdinand and her father, she bitterly rejects the very suggestion that she is free to choose between them and exclaims: 'O du weißt allzu gut, daß unser Herz an natürlichen Trieben so fest als an Ketten liegt.' (III. vi.) Again, she yields to her father's threat that a decision in favour of her lover will kill him, knowing full well that where there is such inner coercion to speak of freedom becomes meaningless. 'O mein Vater!' she cries, 'Daß die Zärtlichkeit noch barbarischer zwingt als Tyrannenwut!' (V. i.) *Ketten, barbarisch, Tyrannenwut* – these are strange words to use of one's nearest and dearest. They bring to mind, rather, the political scene that forms the background of the human drama, the sphere dominated by the Prince and his oppressed people. And, indeed, these words finally harden the connection between the two domains, already variously linked despite their seeming disparateness. There can be no doubt but that the poet tells us that Luise's life is ruled by a coercion as despotic – if not as visible – as are the lives of the *Landeskinder;* that her father's relation to her is as deeply anonymous as the ruler's relation to his subjects, in that neither is aware that he is related to adult beings with rights and needs of their own. It is no accident, indeed, that in the twofold account of the Prince's tyranny very special emphasis is laid upon his disregard of adult relationships. In this one point the two accounts overlap. The lackey's report 'wie man Braut und Bräutigam mit Säbelhieben auseinander riß' (II. ii) in the very next scene is echoed by Lady Milford's '[Er] hatte Braut und Bräutigam zertrennt – hatte selbst der Ehen göttliches Band zerrissen' (II. iii). Luise's father too, like the *Landesvater*, destroys the most sacred of bonds – the voluntary association of lovers.[24]

We may only neglect such connecting links between the inner action

and its outer setting at our peril. For they – rather than any overt statements – enable the dramatic poet to communicate his ultimate evaluation
of a human situation too fully realized, too intricate in its ramifications
and too organically inevitable in its outcome to be readily transparent to
the moral judgement. Once, however, this central situation is related to the
framework of reference within which it is placed, its contours stand out and
its moral significance becomes apparent. Through his association with the
despot, Luise's father stands condemned of what is unequivocally judged
to be a cardinal crime. Thus, those 'historical' elements which, at a superficial reading, may well be regarded as frankly propagandist excursions on
the part of the youthful poet, leading out of the play and threatening its
internal coherence, in fact lead deep into its structure, completing it and
sealing it off from the historical process in which it has its origin.

There can be little doubt that the theme of possessive love, so insistently
realized by every means at the poet's disposal – dramatic, psychological
and rhetorical – embodies the main meaning and intention of the play.
There can also be little doubt that the possessiveness of Ferdinand's passion
is a tributary to the main stream of the inner action, the relation between
father and daughter. But in the contest between the father and the lover
the father wins. As Miller himself has it: 'Um einen Liebhaber bist du
leichter, dafür hast du einen glücklichen Vater gemacht.' (V. i.)

A child of eighteenth-century rationalism, the poet himself would have
been hard put to it to define such poetic insights in discursive terms. This
does not militate against the reading put forward here. Nothing is more
indicative of the order of the imagination at work in this tragedy than the
fact that the poet forged, in the symbols of material possessions, an imaginative instrument so strong and responsive as to divine, encompass and
organize a vast area of meaning far beyond the reaches of his intellect.

6

Wallenstein's poodle : an essay in elusion and commitment

I

In scene vii of *Wallensteins Lager*, Der erste Jäger relates an intriguing episode dating back to Wallenstein's student days. Apparently the hero, in those days, was something of a hothead. One day, in circumstances the details of which are not divulged, he nearly killed his famulus and was duly sent to prison by the judges at Nürnberg:

> 's war just ein neugebautes Nest,
> Der erste Bewohner sollt' es taufen.
> Aber wie fängt er's an? Er läßt
> Weislich den Pudel voran erst laufen.
> Nach dem Hunde nennt sich's bis diesen Tag;
> Ein rechter Kerl sich daran spiegeln mag.
> Unter des Herrn großen Taten allen
> Hat mir das Stückchen besonders gefallen.

Looked at a little more closely this 'Stückchen' is really 'ein starkes Stückchen'. Especially for a budding man of war. For the soldier is professionally at risk. At every moment he must cast his bread upon the waters. 'Im Felde' – we shall hear the chorus declare in unison, at the end of the *Lager* –

> Da tritt kein anderer für ihn ein.
> Auf sich selber steht er da ganz allein.
>
> (scene xi)

And, in its concluding lines:

> Und setzet ihr nicht das Leben ein,
> Nie wird euch das Leben gewonnen sein.
>
> (ibid.)[1]

Well, the young Wallenstein clearly did nothing of the sort. He did not, in a soldierly kind of way, stand on his own two feet, stake his all and take the consequences: instead he let his poodle walk into the trap.

For a trap the prison is, first and foremost, and this is how it would certainly appear in the eyes of the wretched beast. The poodle's master was capable of knowing that he had done a bad thing, and to him the prison cell might have seemed a place of penance and, perhaps, reform. But the poodle knew none of these background complexities. To him jail meant, purely and simply, the irksome experience of extreme constriction. It meant one door slamming behind him as he entered, and no back door or side door or any other exit through which to leave. Like his more famous literary colleague, Faust's poodle, Wallenstein's dog must have discovered that he was free to walk into a place but not to walk out of it again.

And perhaps, in his simple sort of way, the poodle knows better than the police or the moral philosophers. For it is not only for our evil actions that we are asked to pay the penance of constriction. Every action, whether good or bad or neutral, every non-action equally, has its train of consequences.[2] What we do, or fail to do, excludes not only its opposite, but the unlimited possibilities that were open to us until, from amongst them, we chose this course and none other. Any determinate act – whether I sit down or stand up or walk about – entails both, an unending train of consequences which do in fact flow from it, and the exclusion of myriads of other acts, and their consequences, which might have happened in its stead. Those other uncounted acts that did not, and could not, simultaneously take place, and the uncounted trains of consequences that would have sprung from them, are so many lost worlds, like galaxies beyond the Milky Way. Of such a radical narrowing of possibility, which attends any act whatsoever, the constriction of prison is as potent a symbol as it is of the consequences ensuing from a specifically evil act. Prison, first and foremost, stands for constriction. To be confined is chastisement in itself. The poodle knows this well enough. And, at the other end of the scale, even its human master may share the beast's experience. He may legitimately feel the cruel curtailment of possibility that life perpetually exacts to be an existential ill of which moral dilemmas and the coercion they entail are but corollaries.

Actually, it is to this more generalized dialectic of freedom and necessity that the poet himself draws our attention. The young Wallenstein's misdemeanour, although almost costing a human life, is at no point morally evaluated. All that we hear is that

> . . . im Studentenkragen,
> Trieb er's, mit Permiß zu sagen,
> Ein wenig locker und purschikos . . .
> > (scene vii)

'Studentenkragen', 'locker', 'purschikos': these words suggest an excess of roaming freedom, certainly, but no moral defect; and it is to such amplitude that the sobering constriction of the prison cell is juxtaposed.

Well, Wallenstein gets away with his 'Stückchen', to say the least. For not only has he avoided tarnishing his good name. Clearly the Jäger – a real daredevil – considers the budding hero's trick to be a fair sample of the sort of action that one day was to make Wallenstein great. And we must remember here that this anecdote is told by way of initiating a brand new recruit into the mysteries of military success. Here is an example for you to emulate, the Jäger is in fact saying to the newcomer on the martial scene; this is the sort of behaviour that leads you or anyone else to the top. And look at me, the sergeant-major had similarly said to the boy, anyone who makes the grade of corporal has climbed on to the first rung of a ladder which soars to the heights – 'der steht auf der Leiter zur höchsten Macht'. What is more, look at Buttler, the sergeant-major had argued, a common soldier like himself when he began and now a major-general. Above all, look at Wallenstein, Duke of Friedland, another self-made man who is second only to the Emperor himself:

> Und wer weiß, was er noch erreicht und ermißt,
> (*pfiffig*)
> Denn noch nicht aller Tage Abend ist.
> > (scene vii)

Actually, the sun will set only twice more before the evasive Generalissimo, well and truly trapped in the fortress of Eger, will bid goodnight to Gordon, his unwilling jailkeeper, and to life itself, and will say:

> Ich denke einen langen Schlaf zu tun,
> Denn dieser letzten Tage Qual war groß.

Sorgt, daß sie nicht zu zeitig mich erwecken.

(*Tod*, V. v)

But here, in the *Lager*, at the time that his men are gossiping about him, and Octavio Piccolomini and Questenberg are having their first worried exchanges, he stands on the precarious pinnacle of his power: and indeed the image of the ladder which the Wachtmeister had used of his greatness is one of the key images by which the poet, throughout the trilogy, brings before our imagination Friedland's giddying rise and fall. Already in the Prologue, he had introduced Wallenstein as

Des Glückes abenteuerlichen Sohn,
Der, von der Zeiten Gunst emporgetragen,
Der Ehre höchste Staffeln rasch erstieg . . .

At the end of the tragedy, Gordon will take leave of him in words which still draw on the force of this opening image:

O schad' um solchen Mann! Denn keiner möchte
Da feste stehen, mein' ich, wo er fiel.

(*Tod*, IV. ii)

Then, after likening him to a tightrope walker, he will once more bid him adieu in words, almost, of a *Chorus Aestheticus*:

. . . wo große Höh', ist große Tiefe.

(*Tod*, IV. vii)[3]

Not dissimilarly, the Duchess, Friedland's hard-tried wife, had said:

O mein Gemahl! Sie bauen immer, bauen
Bis in die Wolken, bauen fort und fort
Und denken nicht dran, daß der schmale Grund
Das schwindelnd schwanke Werk nicht tragen kann.

(*Tod*, III. iv)

And already earlier and in a much more positive vein, Buttler had declared in the blunt and literal fashion that is so characteristic of him:

Nichts ist so hoch, wornach der Starke nicht
Befugnis hat die Leiter anzusetzen.

(*Pic.*, IV. iv)

But the central statement comes from Wallenstein himself. In *Piccolomini*,

II. vi, the most crucial scene of the exposition, Illo pleads with his master saying that the time for concerted action has come. Wallenstein answers in portentous words, words throbbing with inner excitement. Illo is a child of Saturn, he replies, and as such he cannot understand the grand plan of the universe, which is a living cosmic process, nor fathom 'was die Welt im Innersten zusammenhält'. He can only see 'das Irdische, Gemeine', and cleverly connect 'das Nächste mit dem Nächsten':

> Doch, was geheimnisvoll bedeutend webt
> Und bildet in den Tiefen der Natur, –
> Die Geisterleiter, die aus dieser Welt des Staubes
> Bis in die Sternenwelt, mit tausend Sprossen,
> Hinauf sich baut, an der die himmlischen
> Gewalten wirkend auf und nieder wandeln,
> – Die Kreise in den Kreisen, die sich eng
> Und enger ziehn um die zentralische Sonne –
> *Die* sieht das Aug' nur, das entsiegelte,
> Der hellgebornen, heitern Joviskinder.
>
> (*Pic.*, II. vi)

Wallenstein has hoisted the ladder of his greatness to the stars. It reaches not merely to the top of the world but to a fixed point beyond it from where he has the wisdom to understand it as well as the power to control it.[4]

Wallenstein's words here – so reminiscent of Faust's as he gazes at the sign of the Macrocosm[5] – identify the man of vision, and a vision of indubitable greatness at that. And indeed, the quality of greatness they breathe is not at all unlike that of Faust prior to his encounter with the Erdgeist and before the emissary of the latter, the black poodle, has woven circles around him to entice him into commitment and reality. It is a greatness that is inseparable from that very lack of involvement which Faust so abruptly and bitterly laments as he turns away from the sign of the Macrocosm. Both, the scholar of the *Studierstube* and the Wallenstein of the astrological tower, are outside observers of cosmic life rather than genuine participants in vital process. Only whereas the one is torn – 'Welch Schauspiel, aber ach! ein Schauspiel nur,' Faust cries – the other is serenely contented in his condition of unassailable aloofness. Like the early Faust, Wallenstein sees all and is committed to nothing in particular beyond the quest for totality of experience: neither to a cause, nor to the demand of the hour, nor to the discipline of loving. For any definitive engagement means a shutting-out of limitless potentiality and, with it, an intolerable narrowing of vision. It is tantamount to walking into a trap. And this is a price that Wallenstein is not prepared to pay.

II

We may begin to suspect that what the poet has given us in as it were the nutshell of a seemingly trifling anecdote is nothing less than the law that governs Wallenstein's existence, his overt political behaviour as much as his innermost thoughts. Wallenstein will not act decisively because he will not give up the freedom of possibility. He clings to a dream of totality of being such as any determinate choice, and the course of action springing therefrom, would irrevocably cripple. This unwillingness to forfeit latent potentiality is what has made him play a passionate and protracted double game with the Emperor and his enemies, the Saxons and the Swedes. While he keeps both courses open, he surrenders none of his sovereign freedom. More than that, he annuls the force of both possibilities. For being mutually incompatible, each rules out the other and neutralizes any overriding temptation the other might exercise over him. A pair of scales, as Schiller remarks in a different though related context, balances when each is empty. But it also balances when both are equally weighted. Thus, at the cost of total indeterminacy, Wallenstein remains totally unbound.

At a crucial place in his *Ästhetische Briefe*, Schiller writes: '. . . der Mensch spielt nur, wo er in voller Bedeutung des Worts Mensch ist, und *er ist nur da ganz Mensch, wo er spielt.*' Wallenstein – this is his greatness and his tragedy – is a political figure who wants to be 'ganz Mensch'.[6] Hence he plays and continues to play when play is out of season. To remain whole, he remains indeterminate when decisive action is demanded; and this indeterminacy is at once the reward and the price of his unwillingness to act. For to contemplate means to function as a whole. But to function as a whole also means to be restricted to a contemplative response rather than to enter into reality. Action realizes but restricts. Contemplation widens but does not mould and master the real.

This dilemma – for a dilemma is what it is in the real world of purposes whether Wallenstein chooses to know it or not – informs his every move from the political acrobatics he performs with the Catholic League and his Protestant allies, through the adroit tactics of evasion he employs with his own lieutenants, Illo and Terzky, to the smallest quirks of his personal behaviour. The very deadlock between his aloofness and the itching impetuosity of his counsellors signifies the depth of this dilemma. Terzky and Illo and the Countess spoil for action. But to their clamouring for 'entschlossne' or 'beherzte Tat' he will smoothly oppose, time and time again, the noncommittal freedom of the 'Wort',[7] to their 'Ernst' his 'Spiel' and 'Scherz'; to their unequivocal resolve his 'Masken' and 'krumme Wege'. Wallenstein is in earnest about one thing only and resolved to fight for that alone: the unlimited freedom of potentiality. He announces it plainly enough when he cuts short the remonstrances of his exasperated lieutenants, saying:

> . . . Der Kaiser, es ist wahr,
> Hat übel mich behandelt! – *Wenn* ich wollte,
> Ich könnt' ihm recht viel Böses dafür tun. . . .

and triumphantly continues:

> Es macht mir Freude, meine Macht zu kennen;
> *Ob* ich sie wirklich brauchen werde, *davon*, denk' ich,
> Weißt *du* nicht mehr zu sagen als ein andrer.
>
> (*Pic.*, II. v)

It is one thing contemplatively to savour one's full potential, stretched to one's utmost by opposing and balancing pulls. This is the mastery of neutrality. To use this potential, 'wirklich', is another thing altogether. It means the descent into reality and cruel diminution of potentiality. The 'wenn' and 'ob' and the subjunctival 'wollte' tell their own tale as to Wallenstein's view of the matter.

Even when Sesina has walked into the trap set up for him by Octavio Piccolomini, Wallenstein still powerfully protests the freedom and the essential innocence of uncommittedness:

> Wär's möglich?

he muses,

> Könnt' ich nicht mehr, wie ich wollte?
> Nicht mehr zurück, wie mir's beliebt? Ich müßte
> Die Tat *vollbringen*, weil ich sie *gedacht*,
> Nicht die Versuchung von mir wies, auf ungewisse
> Erfüllung hin die Mittel mir gespart,
> Die Wege mir bloß offen hab' gehalten? –
> Beim großen Gott des Himmels! Es war nicht
> Mein Ernst, beschloßne Sache war es nie.

> In dem Gedanken bloß gefiel ich mir;
> Die Freiheit reizte mich und das Vermögen.
>
> (*Tod*, I. iv)

Every word here counts in that it helps delineate the apparent dichotomy between the freedom of contemplation and the necessity of action:'können', 'wollen'; 'belieben', 'müssen'; 'vollbringen', 'denken'; 'Erfüllung', 'Mittel'; 'Wege' and 'offen'; 'Ernst' and 'beschlossene Sache', 'Gedanken' and 'sich gefallen'; 'Freiheit' and 'Vermögen'. And the basic weakness of Wallenstein's position is wonderfully compacted into his opening question: 'Wär's möglich?' For Wallenstein is at this moment tumbling to the paradox which is inherent in the very positing of unlimited possibility: the paradox that possibility, of its nature, is self-limiting. Wallenstein has carefully avoided a choice. He has 'saved up' the means of an 'uncertain fulfilment'. He has 'kept the ways open'. At no time has he allowed his actions, or his thoughts even, to be governed by one overriding cause or commitment. He has kept himself in neutral gear, idling unpurposively, permitting contrary impingements to step up his self-awareness and merely savouring the enhanced sense of potential resulting from such varied stimuli: and yet all this studied ineffectualness, all this non-action has been as good as any other action in that it has set in motion an unfathomable train of consequences.[8] He is trapped, and trapped in his own seeming infinity. The last words of the passage powerfully evoke the sense of his being a captive without a way out – so well known to his poodle – of being shut in by the towering wall of his own non-actions:

> Wohin denn seh' ich plötzlich mich geführt?
> Bahnlos liegt's hinter mir, und eine Mauer
> Aus meinen eignen Werken baut sich auf,
> Die mir die Umkehr türmend hemmt!
>
> (ibid.)

Wallenstein has begun to realize that there is no such a thing as potentiality that can be contemplated without this contemplation itself overflowing into reality, that his non-acts are themselves acts and that he is responsible for their consequences. Yet he is also conscious of his 'Unshuld' and his 'unverführten Willen'. And rightly so. He has refused to make a choice, let alone a decision. He has remained morally uncommitted: and to be uncommitted is to be innocent.[9] He has been morally raped, by what means we shall presently see.

Just how passionately he has sought to evade involvement is shown by a curious trait to which the poet gives repeated mention. Wallenstein refuses to give any written undertaking. 'Ich geb nichts Schriftliches von mir, du weißt's', he had rapped out to Terzky when the latter had complained, earlier on in the play, that his allies, the Saxons, were beginning to doubt the integrity of intentions he so steadfastly refused to commit to paper; for as Terzky pathetically says: 'Ich hab' nicht einmal deine Handschrift' (*Pic.*, II. v). And later, just before the great monologue, when Sesina's capture has been announced, Terzky desperately argues:

> Sie haben Dokumente gegen uns
> In Händen, die unwidersprechlich zeugen –

to which Wallenstein curtly replies:

> Von meiner Handschrift nichts. Dich straf' ich Lügen.
>> (*Tod*, I. iii)

To write is basically to leave a trace,[10] as a worm leaves a trace in the sand through which it crawls. It means perpetuating passing thoughts or momentary whims. In that sense every piece of writing is an undertaking, whether its contents happen to be promisory or not. Anyone seeing a piece of handwriting can turn round and say 'this is you'. But to be recognized is the last thing Wallenstein wants. For to identify a person by what he has written or by any other sign is, indeed, to pin him down to that intention or that thought or that momentary whim in perpetuity; and to be thus pinned down, for someone as anxious as is Wallenstein to preserve inviolate his unlimited potential, is tantamount to being trapped. And that the poodle's master cannot bear.

Not to leave a single trace in the world that might identify and trap him is this man's most haunting and obsessive need. And it is this that makes him so enigmatic, to himself as much as to others.

> Ich kann mich manchmal gar nicht in ihn finden . . .

Terzky laments to Illo:

> Er leiht dem Feind sein Ohr, läßt mich dem Thurn,
> Dem Arnheim schreiben, gegen den Sesina
> Geht er mit kühnen Worten frei heraus,
> Spricht stundenlang mit uns von seinen Planen,
> Und mein' ich nun, ich hab' ihn – weg auf einmal
> Entschlüpft er, und es scheint, als wär' es ihm
> Um nichts zu tun, als nur am Platz zu bleiben. (*Pic.*, III. i)

'. . . ich hab ihn' – Wallenstein would shudder at the very word. A beetle
or a butterfly can be caught or pinned; but not he. And indeed, neither
the Swedes nor the Saxons know what to make of him and his avowed intentions. Is he playing off one against the other? Is he using both? Is he
fooling his closest associates? None can see through him. This perplexed
guessing game is exactly what Wallenstein wants.[11] It suits him down to
the ground:

> Und woher weißt du, daß ich ihn nicht wirklich
> Zum besten habe?

he asks in reply to Terzky's remonstrances that the Saxon resents his
'krumme Wege' and his 'Masken':

> Daß ich nicht euch alle
> Zum besten habe? Kennst du mich so gut?
> Ich wüßte nicht, daß ich mein Innerstes
> Dir aufgetan . . .
>
> (*Pic.*, II. v)

These are revealing words indeed. Wallenstein does not wish to open
the doors of his innermost sanctuary. He likes nothing better than to tan-
talize others and to remain inscrutable; for this way his innermost self
remains as impregnable as an invisible fortress. Nothing he says or does is
written and signed by this, his secret self. This self remains hidden and
uncommitted, just as 'its' every manifestation remains merely public
and provisional. In this way his 'real' self eludes the others.

But it also eludes him. For uncommitted as he is, he drains his actions
of their motive force and robs them of their air of authenticity, even to
himself. He play-acts reality. 'Ernst' becomes 'Spiel', 'Sein' becomes
'Schein', 'actions' become 'acts'.[12] More and more he becomes enveloped
in a mesh of manifestations which, in his own eyes as much as in those of
others, are only half-real; and his hidden self, carefully locked away from
compromising contact with reality, becomes more and more imprisoned
and elusive. More and more, as he acts his way through life, the border
line between truth and semblance becomes blurred, even in his own perception,[13] and more and more he becomes inscrutable to himself. When,
at the height of the crisis, he plays the *paterfamilias* and makes his
daughter, anguished as she is, play to him on the zither, when he shares
his vision of 'das Ganze' with Max's Cuirassiers, or, later still, drops
apocalyptic hints to the Mayor of Eger, there is no more saying where

reality ends and play-acting begins. He is an enigma to himself. In this ambivalence lies his irresistible charm. It is the magnetism of a charismatic figure who is nourished by a powerful vision of wholeness.[14] But by clinging to that ideal out of season, and protecting his inner self from corroding contact with reality, his masks become as threadbare as the outworn garments of an old actor, and his charm gives way to clowning and to charlatanry. Worse still, there are times when the public self which he exhibits is so machine-like in its ruthlessness that one wonders whether his real self, his hidden self, has not perhaps altogether eluded him in its closely guarded captivity and become a fiction. This, however, is a question which is only finally resolved in Wallenstein's dying moments, in captivity, at Eger.

III

Friedland is by no means the only character in the trilogy to whom the coercion of actions and their consequences presents a problem and a threat. He is merely the most articulate spokesman of a problem shared by the vast majority of figures in the play.[15] Octavio Piccolomini knows and fears the curse of consequences and seeks to elude them to the best of his ability.

> Das eben ist der Fluch der bösen Tat,
> Daß sie, fortzeugend, immer Böses muß gebären. . . .
>
> (*Pic.*, V. i)

he had said to his son early on in the play. This turns out to be much too simple a statement, and Octavio is forced to review his sanctimonious wisdom when, at the end, a man who was far from bad lies murdered at the hands of one who merely did his duty, at the ultimate behest of Octavio himself who was fighting for an honourable cause. But even then he hedges and seeks to elude responsibility for events he himself had set in motion.

> Gott der Gerechtigkeit! Ich hebe meine Hand auf.
> Ich bin an dieser ungeheuren Tat
> Nicht schuldig . . .
>
> (*Tod*, V. xi)

he exclaims when Friedland's corpse is carried on to the scene. Whereupon Buttler retorts:

> Eure Hand ist rein. Ihr habt
> Die meinige dazu gebraucht.
>
> (ibid.)

His attempts to wash his hands of Wallenstein's murder *vis-à-vis* the Countess Terzky are equally unsuccessful. His spineless lament:

> O Gräfin Terzky, mußt' es dahin kommen?
> Das sind die Folgen unglücksel'ger Taten . . .
>
> (*Tod*, V. xii)

is brushed aside by the deadly reply:

> Es sind die Früchte Ihres Tuns . . .
>
> (ibid.).

It is one thing that Octavio, a man of mixed motives, should fear action and seek to evade the consequences of action as he does. But so too does Gordon, a truly kind man, to whom the poet, towards the end of the tragedy, has assigned the function almost of a tragic chorus. Gordon is sorely tempted to save Wallenstein, yet he resigns himself to passivity, arguing:

> *Ich* hab' ihn nicht ermordet, wenn er umkommt,
> Doch seine Rettung wäre *meine* Tat,
> Und jede schwere Folge müßt' ich tragen.
>
> (*Tod*, V. vi)

He has not learnt what Wallenstein has come to know: that inaction is as effective a form of action as any other.

Even the all but subhuman assassins of Wallenstein have to be carefully goaded into action by Buttler. And at the other end of the scale, even the two most wholly pure and selfless figures in the tragedy, the lovers, shudder at the mercilessness of irrevocable involvement — because all they hold sacred is at stake and because they are human.

> Soll ich dem Kaiser Eid und Pflicht abschwören?

Max desperately beseeches Thekla:

> Soll ich ins Lager des Octavio
> Die vatermörderische Kugel senden?
> Denn wenn die Kugel los ist aus dem Lauf,
> Ist sie kein totes Werkzeug mehr, sie lebt,

> Ein Geist fährt in sie, die Erinnyen
> Ergreifen sie, des Frevels Rächerinnen,
> Und führen tückisch sie den ärgsten Weg.
>
> (*Tod*, III. xxi)

And Thekla, that most lucid of all figures, knows what Goethe's Homunculus will discover: that it takes the irresistible lure of loveliness to woo an intelligent being into the 'seltne Abenteuer' of living and loving and paying the price for it:

> Aus stiller Freistatt treibt es mich heraus,
> Ein holder Zauber muß die Seele blenden.
> Es lockt mich durch die himmlische Gestalt,
> Ich seh' sie nah und seh' sie näher schweben,
> Es zieht mich fort mit göttlicher Gewalt,
> Dem Abgrund zu, ich kann nicht widerstreben.
>
> (*Pic.*, III. ix)

Only Illo and Buttler and the Countess Terzky are not afraid of action; and that is so because, being complete and hardened realists, they lack a metaphysical dimension, that awed openness to the numinous which makes the other characters both richer and more vulnerable.[16] But they are the exception. Action, for most of the figures in this tragedy, is and remains a fearful thing. They shudder to act because they are haunted by dread of the consequences of their actions; and they fear the consequences of their actions because they all share an ineradicable dread of the treacherousness of life itself and of those powers, 'die unterm Tage schlimmgeartet hausen', which attack good and bad alike and destroy them at the very core of their personhood. As Wallenstein himself has it:

> In meiner Brust war meine Tat noch mein:
> Einmal entlassen aus dem sichern Winkel
> Des Herzens, ihrem mütterlichen Boden,
> Hinausgegeben in des Lebens Fremde,
> Gehört sie jenen tück'schen Mächten an,
> Die keines Menschen Kunst vertraulich macht.
>
> (*Tod*, I. iv)[17]

Thus involvement is shunned because it leads to action. When action cannot be avoided, it may be over-hasty or it may be tardy; but always it is blind and full of anxious inner provisos. And it takes the conscious or unconscious collusion of all to pull the trigger of so dangerous an arm.

IV

This communal act of collusion is like a weird dance, intricately patterned, in which every move is designed to call forth a faster and bolder response from the partner, and so back again, in a kind of controlled *crescendo*, until all are swept off their feet and perform their appointed steps intoxicated and oblivious of their former reserve. The master of ceremonies is undoubtedly Illo.

Illo is in love with everything that is real and he is as cunning as a fox.[18] He knows that a man fights best when he is cornered, with his back to the wall. Quite early in the tragedy, he had said:

> . . . Die Menschen, in der Regel,
> Verstehen sich aufs Flicken und aufs Stückeln
> Und finden sich in ein verhaßtes Müssen
> Weit besser als in eine bittre Wahl.
>
> (*Pic.*, I. ii)

But he also knows that no one – not even a poodle – will walk open-eyed into a trap. Thus he has devised a complicated and highly ingenious machinery, designed to overcome the universal dread of action and the consequences of action: a mutual collusion by which each is left with the false belief that the other is already implicated, with the result that in the end all are implicated, as it were behind their own backs. Each in fact has his own inner provisos, the 'buts' and 'ifs' we know from Wallenstein himself. But Illo sees to it that each is under the illusion that the other's commitment is unconditional, that he can be counted upon, thus risking a less cagy response himself until all parties are caught up in the game and the original reservations are lost sight of. As with a house of cards, each is precariously propped against the other; yet together they stand. This mutual collusion operates between Wallenstein and his own officers; it is designed even to take care of the relations between the Generalissimo and the Imperial Court.

Link by remorseless link, this strategy is being hammered out in the opening scene of Act III of the *Piccolomini*. In the preceding act Wallenstein had asked for a written undertaking of unconditional loyalty from his officers:

> Parole müssen sie mir geben, eidlich, schriftlich,
> Sich meinem Dienst zu weihen, *unbedingt.*
>
> (*Pic.*, II. vi)

Terzky had pointed out that the allegiance to the house of Austria, being absolute, would always constitute a proviso, at which Wallenstein had heatedly replied:

> . . . Unbedingt
> Muß ich sie haben. Nichts von Vorbehalt!
>
> (ibid.)

As we know, Terzky turns out to have been correct. The vast majority of Wallenstein's general staff will no more bind themselves unconditionally to him than he will bind himself to this or any other allegiance. Indeed he wants from his corps of officers exactly what he himself would never dream of giving to anyone – a *written* pledge.[19] This bilateral unwillingness to enter into an unconditional commitment, Illo perceives, must at all costs be broken down. He suggests a crude opening gambit. The officers are to be made drunk and without their knowledge sign a copy of the original pledge from which the clause concerning the Emperor is left out. This move, Illo foresees, will have two results. In the first place, they will be well and truly compromised in the eyes of the Emperor:

> Gefangen haben wir sie immer – Laßt sie
> Dann über Arglist schrein, so viel sie mögen.
> Am Hofe glaubt man ihrer Unterschrift
> Doch mehr als ihrem heiligsten Beteuern.
> Verräter sind sie einmal, müssen's sein,
> So machen sie aus der Not wohl eine Tugend.
>
> (*Pic.*, III. i)

Here is the possibility of a collusion and Illo is quick to exploit his opportunity: each feels endorsed and confirmed in his own behaviour by that of the other. The generals toy with the idea of defection. The court would like nothing better than to see them guilty. This forces them deeper into commitment than they had bargained for and this, in turn, surpasses the highest expectations of the court.

But the most important consequence by far of the officers' seemingly unconditional pledge of loyalty is the free hand they thereby give to Illo to engineer a mutual and disastrous collusion between them and their own leader. Neither side in fact 'has' the other unconditionally. But let each think he 'has' the other, and he will invite the other to respond more boldly to his own emboldened step. Let Wallenstein think he has his men and act as if he had them and he will have them in the end:

Und dann – liegt auch so viel nicht dran, wie weit
Wir damit langen bei den Generalen,
Genug, wenn wir's dem Herrn nur überreden,
Sie *seien* sein – denn handelt er nur erst
Mit seinem Ernst, als ob er sie schon hätte,
So *hat* er sie und reißt sie mit sich fort.

(ibid.)

The two subjunctives – 'seien', 'hätte' – tell their own tale. Neither
believes in what he is doing, and on this double dissemblance hangs their
precarious conviction. For a double dissemblance it is: we must not over-
look the deep irony in the formulation '. . . denn handelt er nur erst mit
seinem Ernst, als ob er sie schon hätte . . .' The proviso that is being
made here is, basically, not one of time at all. It is Illo who worships time
and thinks that it will right everything, as his obsessive harping on words
such as 'erst' and 'schon' readily goes to show. But Wallenstein's being in
earnest is at all times and ineradicably hypothetical. His is the passionate
earnestness of being at play, of being whole and savouring that wholeness
in the unchallenged inwardness of contemplation; the 'als ob' earnestness
of the man who will say with unconditional conviction:

Es macht mir Freude, meine Macht zu kennen . . .

but hedges on the question '*ob* ich sie brauchen werde . . .'[20]

The masterly Illo knows how to cement this insecure alliance between
mutually deluded friends: he does so by introducing the third partner,
their common adversary. Let the conspiracy against the Emperor start,
he argues, by all means even let it start as a pretence: no matter.

Doch wißt Ihr, in der Hitze des Verfolgens
Verliert man bald den Anfang aus den Augen.
Ich denk' es schon zu karten, daß der Fürst
Sie willig finden – willig *glauben* soll
Zu jedem Wagstück. Die Gelegenheit
Soll ihn verführen. Ist der große Schritt
Nur erst getan, den sie zu Wien ihm nicht verzeihn,
So wird der Notzwang der Begebenheiten
Ihn weiter schon und weiter führen. . . .

(*Pic.*, III. i)

Thus, at the end, friend and foe are welded together in a collusion none clearly suspects, in a cause none really wants, in a network of necessity none fully foresaw. They are the intersecting parts of a clock which ticks away with remorseless precision, and the master mechanic who turns the key until the springs are taut enough to snap is Illo.

Even the common people need to be enticed into commitment by the mechanics of collusion; and here Wallenstein – himself so duped by Illo – proves to be the all too willing disciple of his diabolical master. At the height of the political gamble, while there is still hope that Prague may fall to the defectors, Wallenstein cynically announces just how he will use this probable event:

> Die Prager Truppen wissen es nicht anders,
> Als daß die Pilsner Völker uns gehuldigt,
> Und hier in Pilsen sollen sie uns schwören,
> Weil man zu Prag das Beispiel hat gegeben.
>
> (*Tod*, III. iv)

And here it is interesting to note the observation by which he introduces this strategem of mutual delusion. In such cases as this, he argues, the example is decisive:

> Der Mensch ist ein nachahmendes Geschöpf,
> Und wer der Vorderste ist, führt die Herde.
>
> (ibid.)

Wallenstein should know; for did he not once use his poodle in the same fashion? Let the guileless and the gullible that know not what they do lead the eery procession towards action and commitment. And let their example delude those that follow them into thinking that they are not accountable for what they are doing. But by a supreme irony, this is exactly the way in which, in a scene of bloodcurdling realism, Macdonald and Deveroux will follow Buttler and let themselves be eased into the awful deed – the murder of their leader:

> Wir denken *nicht* nach. Das ist deine Sache!
> Du bist der General und kommandierst,
> Wir folgen dir, und wenn's zur Hölle ginge.
>
> (*Tod*, V. ii)

Thus friend and foe, princes and people, assassins and their victims alike hoodwink one another into action in a play in which action is so dreaded that none dares face it squarely and without the deepest metaphysical misgivings.[21] In the universe of discourse of this tragedy – and this is a pattern discernible in every tragedy from Schiller's pen – to act is to walk into a trap, resolutely facing backwards. It is only when we appreciate the profound dread inspired by the thought of action and the consequences of action that we can understand the broad significance of the officers' written undertaking which is as it were the hub of the intrigue. The faked document, which is substituted for the true one and given to the officers to sign, signifies not so much the need to hoodwink decent men into a course of action which is bad; it signifies the much more primitive need to hoodwink good or bad alike into committing themselves to any all-out action at any time, in a world where action is held in dread as a trap set by the treacherousness of life. It is exactly as it is with the symbol of prison; for prison, too, signifies not merely the constriction consequent on evil doing, but the existential and much more crippling constriction that attends all doings as such.

And, indeed, the imagery of prison springs to Illo's lips when, in his drunken state, he scolds Max of all people for not signing his name and, with the prophetic insight of the drunk, voices the fears and provisos that lurk at the back of the others' minds:

> Wer nicht ist *mit* mir, der ist wider mich . . .

he apocryphally shouts, and:

> Die zärtlichen Gewissen! Wenn sie nicht
> Durch eine Hintertür, durch eine Klausel . . .
>   . . . sich salvieren können.
> Was Klausel! Hol der Teufel diese Klausel –
> <div align="right">(<i>Pic.</i>, IV. vii)</div>

In prison, as literary poodles appreciate, there is no 'Hintertür'. Once you are in, you are in. And Schiller lets this strange apostle of action speak with evangelical tongues not only because he is drunk; but because in his drunkenness he divines the apocalyptic terror attaching to choice and commitment. Only Buttler and, at the other end of the scale, Max, are masters of this dread. Buttler, because he accepts the undertaking 'mit oder ohne Klausel', saying:

> . . . Ich bin darum minder nicht entschlossen,
> Weil ich es deutlich weiß, wovon ich scheide.
> <div align="right">(<i>Pic.</i>, IV. iv)</div>

But then, in opting for decisive action, Buttler does not part from much: neither from wife and child, nor from an encompassing vision of inviolate humanity. And Max, because he has the purity of youth and every moment to him is a sacred covenant in which he signs away his all. This is why he does not need to go through the motions of Illo's written farce:

> Wie ich für ihn gesinnt bin, weiß der Fürst,
> Es wissen's alle, und der Fratzen braucht's nicht.
>
> (*Pic.*, IV. vii)

But for the others, and especially for Wallenstein himself, what anguished dithering on the threshold of action!

> Noch ist sie rein − noch! Das Verbrechen kam
> Nicht über diese Schwelle noch − So schmal ist
> Die Grenze, die zwei Lebenspfade scheidet!
>
> (*Tod*, I. iv)

Friedland muses as Wrangel is about to enter. And he can think of no better way of ingratiating himself to the foreign emissary and proving that in his heart of hearts he has always been 'gut schwedisch' than by reminding him:

> Ich hatt' euch oft in meiner Macht und ließ
> Durch eine Hintertür euch stets entwischen.
>
> (*Tod*, I. v)

Already much earlier, he had stipulated to Questenberg that he must have unlimited power and authority vested in him; for

> Wenn für den Ausgang *ich* mit meiner Ehre
> Und meinem Kopf soll haften, muß ich Herr
> Darüber sein. . . .
>
> (*Pic.*, II. vii)

But this is fooling himself. For who can master or control the issue of anything in life? Especially when, as in this play, there is no exit at the far end of the corridor.

Schiller's characters are entitled to their qualms about setting out on the road to action and commitment. For, whichever kind of way they choose, every one of them leads to disaster.[22] Octavio's and Wallenstein's 'krumme Wege' lead the one into the cul-de-sac of being the founding father of a princely lineage that is extinct; the other into assassination at

Eger. Max's 'grader Weg' does not leave a trail of damage like the straight path traversed by lightning and the cannon-ball which is Wallenstein's: it leads him to his own destruction none the less.

It is because the way is as fearful as its ineluctable goal that Wallenstein dreams up a fantasy way which is designed to be as unreal and ineffectual as are his actions. He has two ways, running side by side in opposite directions, and between them there exists a continual and clandestine intercommunication:

> Blieb in der Brust mir nicht der Wille frei,
> Und sah ich nicht den guten Weg zur Seite,
> Der mir die Rückkehr offen stets bewahrte?
>
> (*Tod*, I. iv)

he asks. His dream way is not unilateral. It is secretly circular. He never decisively sets out and he never hopes to arrive; for his way, as the Countess knows, expands as he walks and stretches into a comfortable infinity. But just as his non-actions turn out to be actions, so his non-way turns out to be a way like any other: its end lies in its beginning, it is an ever-narrowing passage that leads into a trap with no door at either end:

> Wohin denn seh' ich plötzlich mich geführt?
> Bahnlos liegt's hinter mir, und eine Mauer
> Aus meinen eignen Werken baut sich auf,
> Die mir die Umkehr türmend hemmt!
>
> (*Tod*, I. iv)

V

Thus there is no way out. Life is a trap. The poodle has learnt it, and Max will experience it in deadly earnest, before many hours have ticked away on Illo's devilish clock. For the innocent youth is trapped in the 'Notzwang der Begebenheiten' Illo has construed; first in a murderous spiritual dilemma and then in hideous reality. Resolved to die, he and his Pappenheimer storm the Swedish camp, jumping in full gallop, across the ditch behind which the enemy is encamped. But the Swedes ward them off and drive them back towards the ditch where meanwhile the infantry have taken up positions. And there they receive the intruders with a veritable wall of bayonets. What was a way in is no longer a way out:

> Nicht vorwärts konnten sie, auch nicht zurück,

> Gedrängt in drangvoll fürchterliche Enge.
>
> (*Tod*, IV. x)

It is thus cornered that Max is flung from his horse and dies, mercilessly pinned down beneath his horse's hooves. Is not the physical reality he endures exactly what Wallenstein had seen in his mind's eye[23]– that walls grow up blocking the way he had come and obliterating it?

Max's claustrophobic end is sensitively shared, and matched, in the experience of Thekla.[24] She too is trapped on all sides as she goes to her death:

> Nicht Ruhe find' ich, bis ich diesen Mauern
> Entrunnen bin – sie stürzen auf mich ein . . .
> Es füllen sich mir alle Räume dieses Hauses
> Mit bleichen, hohlen Geisterbildern an –
> Ich habe keinen Platz mehr – Immer neue!
> Es drängt mich das entsetzliche Gewimmel
> Aus diesen Wänden fort, die Lebende!
>
> (*Tod*, IV. xi)

And the hero himself?

> Er ist herein . . .

are the opening words of Act IV, set in Eger. And by these words of Buttler's, and those that follow, the Mayor's residence, in our imagination, is translated into a dreaded prison:

> Er ist herein. Ihn führte sein Verhängnis,
> Der Rechen ist gefallen hinter ihm,
> Und wie die Brücke, die ihn trug, beweglich
> Sich niederließ und schwebend wieder hob,
> Ist jeder Rettungsweg ihm abgeschnitten.
>
> (*Tod*, IV. i)

And indeed the poet, in these two final acts, has spared no means to evoke a claustrophobic atmosphere of extreme and ominous constriction. Buttler contributes to this effect and so does Gordon, an anguished man who calls himself the 'Schergen des Gesetzes' and laments a fate which has destined him of all people to turn the castle in which he received his erstwhile friend into his execution cell. But principally it is the Countess who sets the tone and who time and again conjures up a picture of intolerable oppression and anguished incarceration:

> . . . Laß uns nicht
> In dieser düstern Einsamkeit dem Ausgang
> Mit sorgendem Gemüt entgegen harren . . .
> (*Tod*, IV. ix)

she pleads when she hears that Wallenstein plans to leave Eger at cock's
crow, and to leave behind his ladies:

> Denn schwer ist mir das Herz in diesen Mauern,
> Und wie ein Totenkeller haucht mich's an,
> Ich kann nicht sagen, wie der Ort mir widert.
> (ibid.)

Hers is the dream that the room into which she came to look for him, as
she entered it, turned into the ducal family vault; the dream, too, that
she pursued him, and –

> Als ich dir eilend nachging, liefst du vor mir
> Durch einen langen Gang, durch weite Säle,
> Es wollte gar nicht enden – Türen schlugen
> Zusammen, krachend – keuchend folgt' ich, konnte
> Dich nicht erreichen – plötzlich fühlt' ich mich
> Von hinten angefaßt mit kalter Hand,
> *Du* warst's und küßtest mich, und über uns
> Schien eine rote Decke sich zu legen . . .
> (*Tod*, V. iii)

– which is, as Wallenstein explains to her, the red tapestry of his room,
the very tapestry in which, an hour hence, his dead body will be carried
across the scene. And the murder itself! Buttler's detailed instructions to
the assassins, the stage directions and verbal suggestions here and there,
combine in creating the impression that he is tracked down, trapped and
killed in the most recondite and secluded chamber of the fortress, in the
very bowels of the earth where 'falsche Mächte schlimmgeartet hausen',
from which none may escape.

VI

And yet, Wallenstein himself in these last hours is quite serene. He who
had so dreaded the prospect of being trapped has no forebodings but
tranquilly lays his head upon his pillow, certain that he is

> . . . mit den sichern Freunden eingeschlossen . . .
>
> (*Tod*, V. iv)

And lightly he recounts the story of the French king who felt the murderers' knife being twisted in his breast before it pierced him and, terror-stricken, fled from his palace, 'ins Freie'. The horror tale does not tell him what it tells the Countess; it does not touch him.[25] In the extremest captivity he is serene and free.

To say – and it has been said – that Friedland is serene because he is obtuse is nonsense.[26] To say that he is serene because he has undergone a moral catharsis in the ordinary understanding of that term is equally far off the mark.[27] To argue that he is serene because he is free, and that he is free because he accepts constriction, comes nearer to the truth.[28] But such serenity as Wallenstein exudes in these dying scenes has no tinge of resignation about it. On the contrary, his words breathe a buoyant confidence and a sense of enlargement and liberation so positive and so radiant that we must find a different explanation.[29]

In mourning the passing of his young friend, Wallenstein has come to accept his actions and their consequences as his own.

> . . . mir fiel
> Der liebste Freund, und fiel durch meine Schuld . . .
>
> (*Tod*, V. iv)

he says; and there is no trace of equivocation in this verdict. He knows that he has sacrificed Max for the sake of the course he has steered, and in resolving to remain loyal to that course, he also remains loyal to Max, and therewith to himself. He has learnt what his daughter knew all along:

> Wie du dir selbst getreu bleibst, bist du's mir.
>
> (*Tod*, III. xxi)

But the self to which Wallenstein remains faithful is a very complex self indeed; and nowhere has the poet triumphed more than in the Janus-faced ambiguity of his hero in these final scenes. Twice more, for all his steadfast resolve to accept the consequences of his doing, the old uncommitted self rears its head. First, when he declares himself accountable for Max's death and at once reverts to the barbaric superstition that by sacrificing another he has purchased immunity for himself:

. . . Der Neid
Des Schicksals ist gesättigt, es nimmt Leben
Für Leben an, und abgeleitet ist
Auf das geliebte reine Haupt der Blitz,
Der mich zerschmetternd sollte niederschlagen.

(*Tod*, V. iv)

Is this not still the Wallenstein who sent his poodle ahead of him so that
he might elude punishment? And once again we glimpse him at the very
end, at the precise moment when he learns the meaning of loyalty. When
Gordon begs him to give himself up and thus to regain the Emperor's
favour, Wallenstein, in great emotion, answers:

– Blut ist geflossen, Gordon. Nimmer kann
Der Kaiser mir vergeben. Könnt er's, ich,
Ich könnte nimmer mir vergeben lassen.
Hätt' ich vorher gewußt, was nun geschehn,
Daß es den liebsten Freund mir würde kosten,
Und hätte mir das Herz wie jetzt gesprochen –
Kann sein, ich hätte mich bedacht – kann sein
Auch nicht . . .

This is the old inscrutable Wallenstein, the lover of subjunctives who
lives in a hypothetical world, refusing to be pinned down to any definitive
reality. But the ruthless ambivalence of this 'kann sein auch nicht' is not
his last word. It is embedded in the unshakeable resolve at long last to
pay his debt to life. For he continues thus:

. . . Doch was nun schonen noch? Zu ernsthaft
Hat's angefangen, um in nichts zu enden.
Hab' es denn seinen Lauf.

(*Tod*, V. iv)

At long last, Wallenstein has accepted the poodle's fate – the fate of any
living creature. He willingly walks into his trap. Wallenstein has learnt
to die.

Has Wallenstein changed, or has he merely come to accept the iron law
of his being? What, for Schiller, is acceptance? The answer is not a simple
one. The man who here speaks has metamorphosed. He has found new
words for new ranges of experience. Yet all the time the lineaments of
his old character are showing through. Only they have become more

lightly drawn and are all but transparent now. The compulsion has gone out of what he has come to accept, he is himself and not himself. He has become, almost, a symbol.

As Friedland comes to accept his doing and its consequences as his own, 'ernsthaft', he experiences a sudden and overwhelming influx, an enrichment and a liberation which transform his whole being. For he has retrieved that vast area of action and interaction with the world outside from which his inner self had cut itself off. And this was in fact most of himself, since most of himself – a very extrovert self indeed – was in fact involved in the world.[30] While he was uncommitted, that whole world, in which he in fact moved and which he had in fact helped to build, had remained suspect and alien. He had denied his identity with it. His relation to all without him had remained aloof and as it were provisional. He had looked upon it as the public forecourt to an inner sanctuary in which his real self was secretly enshrined. And all the while that incapsulated self had been starved and shrunk. Now, in outward captivity and about to die, this inner lock has sprung open and this inner attrition has come to an end. His whole being expands as never before. Freedom and plenty are his, perhaps for the first time since he sent his poodle into the trap, eluding commitment, reality and, almost, his own self. Almost, during these dying moments, he might give praise in the words of Faust when *his* poodle had led him into the greater freedom of commitment:

> In dieser Armut welche Fülle!
> In diesem Kerker welche Seligkeit!

3

Integration

Wäre die sinnliche Natur im Sittlichen immer
nur die unterdrückte und nie die mitwirkende
Partei, wie könnte sie das ganze Feuer ihrer
Gefühle zu einem Triumph hergeben, der
über sie selbst gefeiert wird?

(Über Anmut und Würde)

7

Bread and wine : a reading
of *Maria Stuart*

———————————⋯⋯⋯———————————

I

Powerfully and swiftly, Schiller's *Maria Stuart* rises to its appointed climax
in the encounter between the hostile Queens. Their clash marks what the
poet would call the *punctum saliens* of the tragedy. Before it, the issue of
Maria's execution lay in the balance. By her shortlived triumph over the
English Queen, in the presence of Leicester, she has sealed her fate.
Elisabeth has no option but to clear her rival out of the way.

It is indeed a clash of opposites. We may say that in his mosaic of the
two Queens Schiller has used no colour and no shape for the one which does
not have its exact counterpart in the other, contradictory or complementary as the case may be. The one, incarcerated, impotent, young, lovely,
labile and susceptible in the highest degree; the other, 'frei . . . wie die
Luft auf den Gebirgen' (IV. x), a sovereign wielding barely disguised
dictatorial rights, plain to the eye, and possessed of an astonishing power
of self-control. The first two acts preceding the fatal collision have patiently
built up that interlocking picture, colour by colour and stone by stone.
Maria's unenviable condition is palpably brought before our eyes, first by
the prizing open of her secret casket, and then in speech upon speech by
Kennedy and Paulet, the one lamenting the ungracious bareness of the
prison walls in which she is fated to live, 'lebendig eingemauert', the
other suspecting the capacity of even these stout walls to hold one as
volatile and as dangerous as their inhabitant:

Kein Eisengitter schützt vor ihrer List

Maria's hard-tried prison warder says:

> Weiß ich, ob diese Stäbe nicht durchfeilt,
> Nicht dieses Zimmers Boden, diese Wände,
> Von außen fest, nicht hohl von innen sind
> Und den Verrat einlassen, wenn ich schlafe?
>
> (I. i)

To this outward condition of captivity there corresponds Maria's enslave-
ment by her own sensual beauty.[1] Still lovely and irresistibly seductive –
as Mortimer's arrival soon testifies – we hear of her earlier thraldom to
Rizzio and Bothwell, the murderer of her husband Darnley. Desire en-
slaved and totally blinded her. We hear of the 'Wahnsinn blinder Liebesglut' subjugating will and reason to the shameless seducer 'der dies Band
um Eure hellen Sinne wob' (I. iv). And all this, not because she was bad,
but because she was feminine, unguarded and yielding:

> Weich
> Ist Euer Herz gebildet, offen ist's
> Der Scham – der Leichtsinn nur ist Euer Laster.
>
> (ibid.)

And indeed, 'weich', 'zart', 'offen' – these are the key-words which with
the force of a leitmotif recur throughout these opening scenes, used both
of Maria and of those who may become dangerous to the State because
they are not proof against her charms.

As against that, Elisabeth. The second act opens with the description of
the coy tournament given in her honour, on the occasion of the French
royal marriage suit: the chaste fortress of English beauty beleaguered by
French desire – attacked by a battery of bouquets and fine fragrances
shot from dainty cannon – yet victoriously withstanding the siege:

> Umsonst! die Stürme wurden abgeschlagen,
> Und das Verlangen mußte sich zurückziehn.
>
> (II. i)

And although Kent confidently predicts that the fortress will have to surrender in the end, Elisabeth's own response to the ambassador's urgent
pleading scarcely supports such optimistic expectations. If Maria is in thrall
to men who ruthlessly subjugate and master her, the English Queen is, if
anything, in thrall to her own virginal freedom. There is passion in her
desire to be known by future generations as 'die jungfräuliche Königin';
passion in her sallies against that 'Naturzweck',

> Der *eine* Hälfte des Geschlechts der Menschen
> Der andern unterwürfig macht –
> (II. ii)

and there is genuine anxiety in her apprehension lest the ring she is about to send to her royal suitor should bind her:

> – Bringt seiner Hoheit dies Geschenk. Es ist
> *Noch* keine Kette, bindet mich noch nicht . . .
> (II. ii)

And such anxiety is powerfully reflected in the following scene when Elisabeth cuts short Shrewsbury's musings on the frailty of woman with a royal apophthegm which, to present-day readers, smacks of her successor's 'We are not amused':

> Das Weib ist nicht schwach. Es gibt starke Seelen
> In dem Geschlecht – Ich will in meinem Beisein
> Nichts von der Schwäche des Geschlechtes hören.
> (II. iii)

Altogether, this scene with her State councillors forcibly supports the impression left by her handling of the French ambassador. If Maria is impressionable to such a degree that her 'unverwahrte Brust' becomes a habitation for impulses stronger than herself, Elisabeth's emotional control seems impeccable. Coolly she steers her course through opposing opinions of others as well as through her own contradictory responses – curiosity and fear, resentment and desire – until, at the end, she comes up with an unruffled face and a smooth phrase purporting to reconcile what is irreconcilable:

> . . . Wir werden Mittel finden,
> Was Gnade fordert, was Notwendigkeit
> Uns auferlegt, geziemend zu vereinen.
> Jetzt – tretet ab!
> (II. iv)

II

And yet the very nicety of the opposition between these two rival Queens suggests some underlying connection. They are not merely different. They are like the positive and the negative of one and the same picture. And indeed, there is a secret meeting-point: for their hearts are inhabited by one man whom both love, who woos them both – Leicester. Not only does such shared attraction argue some as yet inexplicable closeness of personality structure; the figure of Leicester himself seems to be a careful compound of the dominant qualities of the two Queens. Impressionable like Maria, he has the sang-froid and the addiction to contrary courses of the English Queen. A picture of Maria will throw him into raptures. Yet, to save his skin, he turns on Mortimer callously – later on in the drama, Elisabeth will turn on Davison with equal callousness – and with positive glee plays a nimble, intrepid and protracted double game. And, indeed, further scrutiny strengthens the suspicion that the two Queens may in fact be more intimately connected than appears at first sight. Maria herself is anxious to stress not only their equality but their kinship. 'Meine Blutsverwandte' and 'meine Schwester', she calls her repeatedly, and she intimates the existence of a fateful bond between herself and her rival[2] when she counters Mortimer's assurance that Elisabeth will not shrink from having her executed, saying:

> Sie könnte *so* die *eigne**** Majestät
> Und aller Könige im Staube wälzen?
>   (I. vi)

At the end, Maria's intuition is confirmed by Shrewsbury, the most far-sighted and objective figure in the play, to whom the poet has assigned the function of the chorus in Greek tragedy. Commenting, in the final lines of the drama, upon *Maria*'s execution, he says to Elisabeth:

> Ich habe *deinen**** edlern Teil
> Nicht retten können . . .
>   (V. xv)

This is a startling statement. It goes far beyond anything so far explicitly stated. Yet coming at the very end of the play and from one so just, we are bound to consider it in all the gravity of its implications.[3]

Shrewsbury, so it seems, is suggesting nothing less than a relation of partial identity between the enemies. He is confirming that overlap of ostensibly separate and hostile personalities which the poet had indicated on the level of the plot through the two women's shared attachment to one and the same man: Leicester. And indeed, the play as a whole lends support to the suggestion made by its outer action and its final comment alike: the

* My italics.

Queens are not two separate persons. More precisely speaking, Maria is the palpable dramatic embodiment of her 'sister's' clandestine erotic drives. This connection is forged on a number of levels, and by a great variety of verbal links of which, for our present purpose, we need consider only one or two.

Throughout the course of the drama, Maria is associated with the imagery of fire. Words such as 'Fackel', 'Feuer', 'brennend', 'glühend' or 'heiß' abound in descriptions of her by all hands. Their enumeration would be as lengthy as it is tedious. But the many single impressions combine to create a powerful image of a conflagration which only the severe bounds of her captivity prevent from spreading abroad and setting everything ablaze.[4] Even such cool and level-headed characters as Paulet and Burleigh concur in this somewhat mythical view of her. When her nurse Kennedy complains that Maria is altogether too closely confined to have been able to do harm to the land where she is detained as a captive, Paulet replies:

> Doch wußte sie aus diesen engen Banden
> Den Arm zu strecken in die Welt, die Fackel
> Des Bürgerkrieges in das Reich zu schleudern . . .
>   (I. i)

Picking the very same image to describe the menace represented by the Scottish Queen, Burleigh startlingly stresses its erotic aspect!

> – Und in dem Schloß zu Fotheringhay sitzt
> Die Ate dieses ew'gen Kriegs, die mit
> Der Liebesfackel dieses Reich entzündet.
>   (II. iii)

And Elisabeth? For all her cool composure she not only entertains the idea of crowning the Duke of Anjou's courtship by lighting 'die freud'ge Hochzeitfackel'; for ten long and degrading years she has played a cat and mouse game with Leicester, ruthlessly toying with the affections of the man

> Der mir der Nächste stets am Herzen war,
> Dem ich verstattete, an diesem Hof
> Sich wie der Herr, der König zu betragen . . .
>   (IV. v)

yet – as the 'wie' betrays – in reality keeping him captive to every 'Wechsel ihrer Sultanslaunen', so that he looks upon himself

> Wie ein Gefangener vom Argusblick
> Der Eifersucht gehütet . . .

As she despotically subjugates her desire, so too with the object of her desire:

> . . . Unterworfen
> Ist alles, unterm Schlüssel eines Weibes,
> Und jedes Mutes Federn abgespannt.
>   (ibid.)

And, with it all, she is the slave of her slave, 'der Sklave seines Sklaven', as Schiller has it in the *Ästhetische Briefe*. For what power has this weak and vacillating man over her! It is because she must shine in his eyes that, in an unconscious collusion, she seduces him into seducing her to do what she knows she must not do: to meet Maria face to face. And even before the incredulous eyes of Mortimer she dangles the prospect of nocturnal trysts and silent pleasures; playful promises, no doubt, yet not entirely baseless, for the young man who sizes her up shrewdly enough does not hesitate to interpret them in a literal fashion:

> Erhöhen willst du mich – zeigst mir von ferne
> Bedeutend einen kostbarn Preis – Und wärst
> Du selbst der Preis und deine Frauengunst!
> Wer bist du, Ärmste, und was kannst du geben? . . .
> Das *eine* Höchste, was das Leben schmückt,
> Wenn sich ein Herz, entzückend und entzückt,
> Dem Herzen schenkt in süßem Selbstvergessen,
> Die Frauenkrone hast du nie besessen,
> Nie hast du liebend einen Mann beglückt!
>   (II. vi)

Attracting and repelling, lascivious and brittle by turns, Elisabeth indecisively toys with her instincts and those of others, neither fully mastering nor yet trusting them. And as a result she is as gullible as she is liable to be hurt.

If thus Maria is the candid personification of the 'Wahnsinn blinder Liebesglut' which governs her, her flirtatious rival conceals that same 'Glut' in the depths of her uncommitted self. It is Maria herself who, at the end of her fatal encounter with the Virgin Queen, uncovers this unwelcome fact. 'Von Zorn glühend, doch mit einer edeln Würde', she replies to her rival's merciless taunts:

Ich habe menschlich, jugendlich gefehlt,
Die Macht verführte mich, ich hab' es nicht
Verheimlicht and verborgen, falschen Schein
Hab' ich verschmäht mit königlichem Freimut.
Das Ärgste weiß die Welt von mir, und ich
Kann sagen, ich bin besser als mein Ruf.
Weh Euch, wenn sie von Euren Taten einst
Den Ehrenmantel zieht, womit Ihr gleißend
Die wilde Glut verstohlner Lüste deckt.

                                      (III. iv)

Thus, the same desire which brightly and visibly burns in Maria smoulders
in Elisabeth, concealed and captive to her conscious will. The Scottish
Queen in her prison is as it were a part-image of her rival's clandestine
eroticism,[5] blown up to full-size dimensions and candidly projected onto a
vast screen. Incarcerated herself and guarded by a vigilant censor, Maria
is the magnified embodiment of her 'sister's' incarcerated desires. And so,
too, conversely: in the figure of Elisabeth the poet has embodied, and
enlarged, those constraining forces of conscience which in Maria herself
have remained rudimentary, condemned to linger beneath the threshold
of her consciousness. Each, we may say, is the palpable embodiment of
those drives which in the other have remained undifferentiated and un-
internalized.

It is with this secret connection in mind that we must approach the
fatal encounter between the Queens. Their meeting does not merely, or
even principally, signify the head-on collision between two separate and
hostile figures who are irreconcilably opposed on political, intellectual and
temperamental grounds. More importantly, it signifies a confrontation of
each with herself; more precisely, with the repressed and undeveloped aspect of her psyche which uncomfortably faces her in the shape of her
kindred, yet hostile, *alter ego*. The issue confronting the two Queens is
basically whether, by coming to terms with and accepting the other, each
can come to face and to accept that part of herself which she has denied.
For only by reconciling to herself what she has inwardly rejected, can
either become a psychologically viable whole. Thus the encounter that
is the inner axis of the play serves as a decisive test of the willingness and
the capacity on the part of each Queen to internalize what has remained
extraneous, to integrate it with those qualities which are dominant in her
make-up, and thus to achieve fullness and maturity of being.

III

If the actual encounter of the two Queens is the *punctum saliens* of the tragedy, the 'pregnant moment' from which this fateful development has sprung is Maria's request to be granted a personal interview with her enemy. This request is made as early as I. ii, when Maria hands a letter to her prison-keeper, Paulet, explaining:

> . . . Ich bitte
> In diesem Brief um eine große Gunst –
> Um eine Unterredung mit ihr selbst,
> Die ich mit Augen nie gesehen . . .

And here it is important to note that it is in the same terms – the terms of a face-to-face and eye-to-eye meeting – that this request is henceforth referred to on all sides. Paulet, laying the letter into the hands of the English Queen, faithfully reports Maria's demand in the same terms of a face-to-face encounter in which she herself had phrased it:

> Sie bittet
> Um die Vergünstigung, *das Angesicht*
> *Der Königin zu sehen.**
>
> (II. iv)

Already before her request had been formally made known, Shrewsbury had supported the idea, urging:

> Verbündet hat sich alles wider sie,
> *Du selber hast ihr Antlitz nie gesehn,**
> Nichts spricht in deinem Herzen für die Fremde.
>
> (II. iii)

Burleigh heatedly responds to Maria's request – and once again in the same terms:

> Die Gunst *des königlichen Angesichts**
> Hat sie verwirkt . . .
> . . . Unwürdig ist's der Majestät,
> *Das Haupt zu sehen,** das dem Tod geweiht ist . . .
>
> (II. iv)

and, later on in the same scene:

* My italics.

> Du *kannst* sie nicht begnadigen, *nicht* retten,
> So lade nicht auf dich verhaßten Tadel,
> Daß du mit grausam höhnenden Triumph
> *Am Anblick deines Opfers dich geweidet.* *
> (ibid.)

Leicester immediately recognizes the force of Burleigh's argument; and this is precisely why, swept off his feet by Maria's picture, he hatches the plan of having the two meet, face to face and eye to eye:

> Vielleicht, daß ich durch List sie überrede,
> *Das Angesicht der Gegnerin zu sehn,* *
> Und dieser Schritt muß ihr die Hände binden.
> Burleigh hat recht. Das Urteil kann nicht mehr
> Vollzogen werden, *wenn sie sie gesehn.* *
> (II. viii)

Caught by the Queen in the middle of his deliberations with Mortimer, he turns his embarrassment to good account and answers her question:

> Was ist Euch, Lord?
> So ganz betreten?

by purporting to be dazzled by her charms:

> . . . Über deinen *Anblick!* *
> *Ich habe dich so reizend nie gesehn,* *
> Geblendet steh' ich da von deiner Schönheit.
> (II. ix)

This, together with the rankling recollection of Shrewsbury's praises of her rival, gives the Queen the opening they both want; she muses:

> Und ist's denn wirklich wahr, daß sie so schön ist?
> So oft mußt' ich die Larve rühmen hören,
> Wohl möcht ich wissen, was zu glauben ist.
> Gemälde schmeicheln, Schilderungen lügen,
> *Nur meinen eignen Augen würd' ich traun.* *
> (ibid.)

This veiled counter-demand gives Leicester the chance to translate his plan into action. Mercilessly he goads Elisabeth to go to *see* her rival and to score a devastating triumph over her:

* My italics.

> – Die Freude wünscht' ich mir, ich berg' es nicht,
> Wenn es ganz in geheim geschehen könnte,
> *Die Stuart gegenüber dich zu sehn!* *
> Dann solltest du erst deines ganzen Siegs
> Genießen! Die Beschämung gönnt' ich ihr,
> *Daß sie mit eignen Augen* * – denn der Neid
> Hat scharfe Augen – *überzeugt sich sähe,* *
> Wie sehr sie auch an Adel der Gestalt
> Von dir besiegt wird, der sie so unendlich
> In jeder andern würd'gen Tugend weicht.
>
> (ibid.)

And, a little later, when Elisabeth concedes with studied carelessness:

> *Man peinigt mich ja, sie zu sehn* * –

Leicester continues in the same malicious vein:

> Sie fordert's
> Als eine Gunst, gewähr' es ihr als Strafe!
> Du kannst sie auf das Blutgerüste führen,
> Es wird sie minder peinigen, als sich
> *Von deinen Reizen ausgelöscht zu sehn.* *
> Dadurch ermordest du sie, wie sie dich
> Ermorden wollte – *Wenn sie deine Schönheit*
> *Erblickt,* * durch Ehrbarkeit bewacht, in Glorie
> Gestellt durch einen unbefleckten Tugendruf . . .
>   . . . dann hat
> Die Stunde der Vernichtung ihr geschlagen.
> Ja – *wenn ich jetzt die Augen auf dich werfe* * –
> Nie warst du, nie zu einem Sieg der Schönheit
> Gerüsteter als eben jetzt . . .
>
> (ibid.)

Thus we may say that the meeting between the two Queens, which is here being engineered with everybody's connivance except that of Burleigh, is a contest of beauty carried out under six watchful eyes: Elisabeth's, Maria's and Leicester's. The remarkable and unanimous emphasis, from every side, upon the physical act of seeing and of being seen permits of no other interpretation. And, indeed, the stage directions

* My italics.

and words of this climactic scene leave no doubt that this is the reading the
poet himself intended. Elisabeth, on first sighting her quarry, 'fixiert mit
den Augen die Maria' whilst continuing to speak to Paulet. Maria, in
turn, who had been close to fainting, 'erhebt sich jetzt, und ihr Auge
begegnet dem gespannten Blick der Elisabeth'. Shrewsbury introduces
Maria, saying:

> Laß dich erbitten, königliche Frau,
> *Dein Aug auf die Unglückliche zu richten,* *
> Die hier vergeht *vor deinem Anblick.* *

Maria, shuddering, pleads:

> Löst *mir* das Herz, daß ich das Eure rühre!
> *Wenn Ihr mich anschaut mit dem Eisesblick,* *
> Schließt sich das Herz mir schaudernd zu, der Strom
> Der Tränen stockt, und kaltes Grausen fesselt
> Die Flehensworte mir im Busen an.
>
> (ibid.)

Elisabeth hypocritically rejoins:

> . . . Ich vergesse
> Die Königin, die schwer beleidigte,
> Die fromme Pflicht der Schwester zu erfüllen,
> *Und meines Anblicks Trost gewähr ich Euch.* *
>
> (ibid.)

Turning to Leicester to humiliate Maria with her biting taunts in front
of his eyes, Elisabeth 'sieht sie lange mit einem Blick stolzer Verachtung
an', whilst of Maria's spirited reply Elisabeth later recalls:

> Mit welchem Hohn sie auf mich *niedersah,*
> *Als sollte mich der Blick zu Boden blitzen!* *
>
> (IV. x)

And when the impassioned Maria has emptied her arsenal of insults, we
read: 'Elisabeth, für Zorn sprachlos, schießt wütende Blicke auf Marien.'
(III. iv.) Finally, Maria sums up the situation in the following scene when
she triumphantly exclaims:

> Vor *Leicesters Augen* hab ich sie erniedrigt!
> *Er sah es,* * er bezeugte meinen Sieg!
>
> * My italics.

Wie ich sie niederschlug von ihrer Höhe . . .

(III. v)

And indeed Leicester did see it all. He witnessed Maria emerge victorious in a contest of physical and moral beauty. He himself had foretold no less than that, and this was precisely the dilemma he had prepared for the English Queen who had so blithely assumed that she could juggle the opposing claims of 'Gnade' and 'Notwendigkeit'. Already at the State council Burleigh had put his finger on this dilemma. He had urged:

Unwürdig ist's der Majestät,
Das Haupt zu sehen, * das dem Tod geweiht ist.
Das Urteil kann nicht mehr vollzogen werden,
Wenn sich die Königin ihr genahet hat,
Denn Gnade bringt die königliche Nähe –

(II. iv)

And, later in the same scene:

. . . Raube dir nicht selbst
Die Freiheit, das Notwendige zu tun.
Du *kannst* sie nicht begnadigen, *nicht* retten,
So lade nicht auf dich verhaßten Tadel,
Daß du mit grausam höhnendem Triumph
Am Anblick deines Opfers dich geweidet. *

(ibid.)

The dilemma Burleigh perceives – of which Leicester is well aware – is this: either Elisabeth, after meeting her defeated enemy face to face, shows mercy and Maria has won in that her life is saved; or she refuses to do so and Maria, dying, shows off her rival's moral shoddiness. Whichever course Elisabeth takes, Maria is bound to win: either physically or else morally. This is why, earlier on in the play, Burleigh had, in his view quite justifiably, tried to help Elisabeth evade an intolerable choice by seeking to persuade her jailer Paulet to have Maria done away with secretly:

Die Welt
Glaubt nicht an die Gerechtigkeit des Weibes,
Sobald ein Weib das Opfer wird. Umsonst,
Daß wir, die Richter, nach Gewissen sprachen!

* My italics.

> Sie hat der Gnade königliches Recht.
> Sie muß es brauchen; unerträglich ist's,
> Wenn sie den strengen Lauf läßt dem Gesetze!
>
> (I. viii)

It seems that Elisabeth's womanhood which she had been so contemptuously rejecting in the end is her undoing. For a woman – as Burleigh and Leicester and Shrewsbury and, above all, Maria know – is accountable to an altogether different code from that which is binding on a man. She has no option but to show mercy. For a woman is made to be soft and responsive.

> Nicht Strenge legte Gott ins weiche Herz
> Des Weibes . . .
>
> (II. iii)

as Shrewsbury has it. She is in a special sense the guardian of a humanity which so readily becomes brutalized at the hands of men in the fight for self-preservation and even justice.[6] In her, head and heart, feeling and intellect, are united by a stronger and more lasting bond, never to be broken; and the badge of such mellowed humanity is grace, physical and moral. For a woman to see is to be moved and melt, as Maria melted when she saw Rizzio and Bothwell and as, at the end of the play, she will be moved by the plight of those who loyally served her. Similarly, for a woman that is worthy of the name to be seen means to be moving, as Shrewsbury and Mortimer and Leicester find out to their peril. To be thus readily moved, and moving, is to accept a troubled heritage. It means frailty and moral confusion, it means 'der Wahnsinn blinder Liebesglut' to which Maria, Mortimer and Leicester all succumb; it means certain suffering and, in the world of Schiller's tragedies at least, it means loss of property or life. But it also signifies that the channels between head and heart, sense and sensibility are not blocked, and such a gracious union is the shining token of humanity.

This, then, is the nature of the contest between the two women.[7] Maria wants to be seen, to move and to be moved. Elisabeth wants to watch the spectacle and to remain icily unmoved. Yet, paradoxically, she wants to move the man who is watching her. Maria had formulated her expectations early on in the play when she had first told Paulet of her desire for a personal confrontation with her

> Die ich mit Augen nie gesehn –

urging:

> Man hat mich
> Vor ein Gericht von Männern vorgefordert,
> Die ich als meinesgleichen nicht erkennen,
> Zu denen ich kein Herz mir fassen kann.
> Elisabeth ist meines Stammes, meines
> Geschlechts und Ranges – Ihr allein, der Schwester,
> Der Königin, der Frau kann ich mich öffnen.
>
> (I. ii)

She pleads with her 'sister' to allow this intercourse of mercy, to move her so that she in turn may move her heart to forgiveness:

> O Gott im Himmel!

she had exclaimed:

> Steht nicht da, schroff und unzugänglich, wie
> Die Felsenklippe, die der Strandende
> Vergeblich ringend zu erfassen strebt.
> Mein Alles hängt, mein Leben, mein Geschick
> An meiner Worte, meiner Tränen Kraft;
> Löst *mir* das Herz, daß ich das Eure rühre!
> Wenn Ihr mich anschaut mit dem Eisesblick,
> Schließt sich das Herz mir schaudernd zu, der Strom
> Der Tränen stockt, und kaltes Grausen fesselt
> Die Flehensworte mir im Busen an.
>
> (III. iv)

But Elisabeth watches Maria in her humiliation and her eyes remain dry. Her earlier tears at her rival's downfall – 'Was ist das Glück der Erde!' – turn out to have been no more than the crocodile tears she is willing to shed on her behalf at the end.[8] Asked by her 'sister' to stretch out her hand in mercy and to raise her from her degradation she replies:

> Ihr seid an Eurem Platz, Lady Maria!
> Und dankend preis' ich meines Gottes Gnade,
> Der nicht gewollt, daß ich zu Euren Füßen
> So liegen sollte, wie Ihr jetzt zu meinen.
>
> (ibid.)

She gloats over her rival, seeing all with the eye of envy and forgiving nothing:

Das also sind die Reizungen, Lord Leicester,
Die ungestraft kein Mann erblickt, daneben
Kein andres Weib sich wagen darf zu stellen!
Fürwahr! *Der* Ruhm war wohlfeil zu erlangen:
Es kostet nichts, die *allgemeine* Schönheit
Zu sein, als die *gemeine* sein für *alle*!

(III. iv)

She has come to do exactly what Burleigh knew she should not do and
Maria thought she could not do –

Um Euer Opfer grausam zu verhöhnen.

(ibid.)

But she has been seen and judged.

IV

Like the earlier tournament with which the action proper opens, this
second, and crucial, contest of beauty is symbolic. It is a moral contest in
which visible beauty and the allied capacity to see and be moved are the
tokens of the humanity which is at stake. For here, as in every drama from
Schiller's pen, visible, physical beauty and that swift responsiveness we
call grace are the guarantors of spiritual beauty. Their mingling is suggestive of that sacred communion between sense and spirit which is the ultimate seal of our humanity.[9]

In this contest, Maria bows to her opponent and is willing to abrogate
all those rights which she herself has forfeited by throwing away the
freedom of self-discipline. She pleads with her 'sister' to raise her from
the depth of her degradation:

Laßt mich nicht schmachvoll liegen, Eure Hand
Streckt aus, reicht mir die königliche Rechte,
Mich zu erheben von dem tiefen Fall.

(III. iv)

By doing so, she is showing her willingness not only to be reconciled to her
opponent, but also to face the enemy within herself. She is ready to restore
the inner integrity she herself has violated by violating her own conscience.

In an image surprisingly similar to the one Maria uses here, Shrewsbury had begged the English Queen to hold out a helping hand to her defeated rival:

> O Königin! Dein Herz hat Gott gerührt,
> Gehorche dieser himmlischen Bewegung!

he had urged; and, later on:

> Reich' ihr die Hand, der Tiefgefallenen;
> Wie eines Engels Lichterscheinung steige
> In ihres Kerkers Gräbernacht hinab . . .
>
> (II. iv)

This gesture which he, too, asks of Elisabeth is more than one from one enemy to another. It is the compassionate gesture of self-acceptance, the acceptance, in Elisabeth's case, of a joyless youth spent, ostracized, 'in des Towers Nacht', 'nur das Grab zu deinen Füssen'. It is the acceptance, ultimately, of the 'wilde Glut verstohlner Lüste' which has tainted her very birth and continues to smoulder in her, clandestine and unsanctioned by her puritanical self. But the inner rift between one half of her divided self – the self which lies before her, prostrate, in the shape of her kindred asking to be pardoned – and the self she has chosen to be is too great to be bridged. She is incapable of yielding to 'dieser himmlischen Bewegung'; she is capable – as Leicester is not – of gazing at the image of her fallen self 'mit unbewegten Blicken' and of remaining stony-eyed (V. x). And for all her feigned willingness to descend to Maria's depths –

> Dem Trieb der Großmut folg' ich, setze mich
> Gerechtem Tadel aus, daß ich so weit
> Heruntersteige . . .
>
> (III. iv)

– she is no more capable of descending to her downcast 'sister' than of descending to her own unhallowed depths and of redeeming them by an act of inner acceptance.

> Ihr seid an Eurem Platz, Lady Maria!
>
> (ibid.)

she says. And the concealed moral flaw Maria uncovers at the end is none other than the deep and incurable inner rift between 'Schein' and 'Sein', between native endowment and moral pose[10] which the Virgin Queen herself has betrayed by the unbending rigidity of her virtuous stance:

> Ich habe menschlich, jugendlich gefehlt,
> Die Macht verführte mich, ich hab' es nicht
> Verheimlicht und verborgen, falschen Schein
> Hab' ich verschmäht mit königlichem Freimut.
> Das Ärgste weiß die Welt von mir, und ich
> Kann sagen, ich bin besser als mein Ruf.
> Weh Euch, wenn sie von Euren Taten einst
> Den Ehrenmantel zieht, womit Ihr gleißend
> Die wilde Glut verstohlner Lüste deckt.
> Nicht Ehrbarkeit habt Ihr von Eurer Mutter
> Geerbt: man weiß, um welcher Tugend willen
> Anna von Boleyn das Schafott bestiegen.
>
> (III. iv)

Just before Maria speaks those fateful words, Elisabeth exclaims, 'höhnisch lachend':

> Jetzt zeigt Ihr Euer wahres
> Gesicht, bis jetzt war's nur die Larve.
>
> (ibid.)

By a supreme irony, it is her own, Elisabeth's, moral mask that Maria's words proceed to tear off her face. She needs to wear a mask; for the Virgin Queen is plain – 'schimmerlos', as she herself has it – and in the universe of discourse of Schiller's dramas physical ugliness always signifies being bereft of inner, moral grace as well.

V

For in the world of this poet, the outward and plainly visible is at all times the objective correlative of the hidden truth of the spirit. This correspondence is cruelly driven home by the contest of beauty between the two Queens, from which the younger and the lovelier of the two emerges as the rightful winner. It is established beyond a shadow of a doubt by the religious framework in which the action is embedded.

In the opening scenes of the tragedy – those which are dominated by Paulet – this parity between the visible and the spiritual is strenuously denied. The puritanical dichotomy between remorse and vanity, between Bible and mirror, between the 'Christus in der Hand' and the 'Hoffart' and the 'Weltlust in dem Herzen' (I. i), seems complete and is gainsaid only by the involuntary grace and the matchless dignity of the holy sinner's bearing.

It is Mortimer, the youthful convert to Catholicism, who first lends words to an opposing creed. Bred in 'der Puritaner dumpfe Predigt-stuben', reared 'in strengen Pflichten' and 'in finsterm Haß des Papsttums', the young man has been driven away from home by an irresistible instinct, 'das gepriesene Italien mit heißem Wunsche suchend'. We might almost add the echoing words 'Das Land der Griechen mit der Seele suchend'; for to do so is to protect us from the start against the erroneous belief that Schiller, in this play, is eulogizing the bigotry of fanaticism.[11] And there, in Rome, he sees the truth with his own dazzled eyes:

> Es haßt die Kirche, die mich auferzog,
> Der Sinne Reiz, kein Abbild duldet sie,
> Allein das körperlose Wort verehrend.
>
> (I. vi)

In eternal Rome – the Rome which Schiller knew through his great pagan friend in Weimar – he feels the power of art and through it comes to perceive a communion between inspiration and medium, between sense and spirit, more gracious than that he had imbibed at home with his mother's milk. He comes to realize the innate kinship between what is physical and visible and the spiritual realm, and with it the possibility that mind itself may descend to the depth of matter to redeem and to transfigure it:

> Wie wurde mir, als ich ins Innre nun
> Der Kirchen trat und die Musik der Himmel
> *Herunterstieg* * und der Gestalten Fülle
> Verschwenderisch aus Wand und Decke quoll,
> Das Herrlichste und Höchste, gegenwärtig,
> Vor den entzückten Sinnen sich bewegte,
> Als ich sie selbst nun sah, die Göttlichen,
> Den Gruß des Engels, die Geburt des Herrn,
> Die heil'ge Mutter, die *herabgestiegne* *
> Dreifaltigkeit, die leuchtende Verklärung . . .
>
> (I. vi)

And the miracle of music and indeed of the divine itself descending to embrace the earthly – the very miracle of compassion and redemption which Elisabeth rejects – is matched by the more tender miracle of a great spirit

* My italics.

descending to his lowliness in order to initiate him into the mysteries of
the true faith and its Church. The Cardinal of Guise

> . . . *ließ selber sich herab,* *
> Die hohen Glaubenslehren mir zu deuten
> Und meines Herzens Zweifel zu zerstreun.
>
> (ibid.)

And what is the heart of that doctrine? It is the faith, surely, in the
sacramental kinship, inaugurated by the event of the Incarnation, between
the visible and the invisible, between the truth of the spirit and what the
physical eye may see:

> Er zeigte mir, daß grübelnde Vernunft
> Den Menschen ewig in die Irre leitet,
> Daß seine Augen sehen müssen, was
> Das Herz soll glauben, daß ein sichtbars Haupt
> Der Kirche not tut . . .
>
> (ibid.)

It is true, Mortimer's fervour will presently confuse the earthly Maria
with her heavenly counterpart – just as Maria herself, in her very last
moments, will by a supreme and touching irony mistake her former lover's
arms for the arms of Christ spread out to receive her[12] – and he will confuse the blessings awaiting him in eternity with the sweetness of the
fleeting moment. He will presently prostitute the woman whom hot
desire and the proximity of death have made anonymous; and this degrading translation of the '*allgemeine* Schönheit' to the '*gemeine*' which is
free for all will retrospectively lend substance to the taunt Elisabeth has
levelled at her rival. But also he will find it possible to choose death, in a
swift and manful transition from the 'irdischen Maria' back to the
heavenly Queen, and from the anonymity of bodily desire to the encompassing anonymity of a sensuous and soaring faith. For, as Maria herself
has it:

> – Die Kirche ists, die heilige, die hohe,
> Die zu dem Himmel uns die Leiter baut;
> Die allgemeine, die katholische heißt sie:
> Denn nur der Glauben aller stärkt den Glauben;
> Da wird die Glut zur Flamme, und beflügelt
> Schwingt sich der Geist in alle Himmel auf.
>
> (V. vii)

* My italics.

VI

That Mortimer's aberration is the price of truth the concluding scenes of
the tragedy establish beyond a shadow of a doubt. The Maria of the fifth
act is reconciled to her fate. She is all festive and prepared to die. Yet she
bitterly longs for a priest empowered to give her the last sacraments and
to grant her absolution from her sins. Before she knows that Melvil has
taken holy orders so that he may be able to do her this very last service,
she laments:

> Ach Melvil! Nicht allein genug ist sich
> Das Herz, ein irdisch Pfand bedarf der Glaube,
> Das hohe Himmlische sich zuzueignen.
>
> (V. vii)

And she continues thus:

> Drum ward der Gott zum Menschen und verschloß
> Die unsichtbaren himmlischen Geschenke
> Geheimnisvoll in einem sichtbarn Leib.
>
> (ibid.)

Nostalgically she recalls Holy Mass and the bell announcing the heart of
its mystery,

> Das hohe Wunder der Verwandlung . . .
>
> (ibid.)

In easy stages Melvil prepares Maria for the knowledge which is the innermost law governing her life – that the invisible, spiritual reality lies incarnate in the visible, physical one which is at hand:

> . . . der dürre Stab
> Kann Zweige treiben in des Glaubens Hand!
> Und der die Quelle aus dem Felsen schlug,
> Kann dir im Kerker den Altar bereiten,
> Kann *diesen* Kelch, die irdische Erquickung,
> Dir schnell in eine himmlische verwandeln.
>
> (ibid.)

and, a little later on:

> Hier sei kein Priester, sagst du, keine Kirche,
> Kein Leib des Herrn? – Du irrest dich. Hier *ist*

Ein Priester, und ein Gott ist hier zugegen.

(ibid.)

After her confession, he celebrates Holy Communion. He gives Maria
the host, saying:

Nimm hin den Leib, er ist für dich geopfert!

(ibid.)

He offers her the wine, saying:

Nimm hin das Blut, es ist für dich vergossen!

(ibid.)

And in doing so, he visibly enacts the mystery of the communion between
sense and spirit and the ultimate mystery of their kinship which is the
central import of this tragedy and, indeed, at the heart of every other
drama Schiller ever wrote.[13]

Melvil's concluding words are:

> Und wie du jetzt dich in dem ird'schen Leib
> Geheimnisvoll mit deinem Gott verbunden,
> So wirst du dort in seinem Freudenreich,
> Wo keine Schuld mehr sein wird und kein Weinen,
> Ein schön verklärter Engel, dich
> Auf ewig mit dem Göttlichen vereinen.

(ibid.)

Much earlier in the play Shrewsbury had begged Elisabeth to descend
into her enemy's nocturnal prison 'wie eines Engels Lichterscheinung'
(II. iv). But the Queen had refused to be the messenger of mercy. Even
now, on realizing that Melvil is a priest and thus empowered to grant her
absolution, Maria exclaims, in an upsurge of extravagant gratitude:

> O so muß an der Schwelle selbst des Todes
> Mir noch ein himmlisch Glück bereitet sein!
> Wie ein Unsterblicher auf goldnen Wolken
> Herniederfährt, wie den Apostel einst
> Der Engel führte aus des Kerkers Banden,
> Ihn hält kein Riegel, keines Hüters Schwert,
> Er schreitet mächtig durch verschloßene Pforten,
> Und im Gefängnis steht er glänzend da –
> So überrascht mich hier der Himmelsbote . . .

(V. vii)

This heavenly messenger, as Melvil well knows, is neither he, nor could it have been Mortimer, nor indeed Elisabeth. They are only tools of redemption, the one recalcitrant, the others willing instruments. The angel – Schiller seems to imply – is none other than Maria herself, transformed in the irresistible glory of a humanity grown consummate and whole. Her spirit, sure of its kinship with its mortal part, lovingly descends to it; and in that majestically humble gesture which is the poet's very own, they embrace and together are carried aloft, through the gates of death to final transfiguration.

This gesture transcending a divided self was needed by one who could create two hostile Queens, 'sisters', yet poles apart, and let the one refuse to forgive herself in the other. It is a gesture of innermost compassion; we meet and recognize it time and again in Schiller's work, from Karl Moor's fiercely tender farewell embrace of his Amalia to the parting words of Don Cesar in Schiller's last completed tragedy:[14]

> Ein mächtiger Vermittler ist der Tod.
> Da löschen alle Zornesflammen aus,
> Der Haß versöhnt sich, und das schöne Mitleid
> Neigt sich, ein weinend Schwesternbild, mit sanft
> Anschmiegender Umarmung auf die Urne.
> Drum, Mutter, wehre du mir nicht, daß ich
> Hinuntersteige und den Fluch versöhne.
>
>   (*Die Braut von Messina*, IV. ix)

8

Die Jungfrau von Orleans : a saint out of season

I

To approach Schiller's 'romantic tragedy' takes a more conscious suspension of disbelief than we are normally required to make with this poet. In an age when countries are struck off the map one day and others appear on it the next, where anti-heroes are less suspect than heroes, where saints are demoted and celibacy is challenged by large sections of the priesthood, the story of the heroic maiden who saved her country clad in sanctity seems altogether too simple readily to engage our sympathies. And coming from Schiller, too, from the universe of discourse of the *Wallenstein* trilogy and *Maria Stuart*, we seem to be regressing rather than progressing. For there, in *Wallenstein*, the poet had led us deep into the labyrinthine complexities of action in a life which is inscrutable and treacherous, where good seed yields bad fruit and the consequences of our doing or non-doing are equally disastrous. In *Maria Stuart*, too, both the rashness of the heroine and the uncommittedness of her rival had borne bitter fruit. Moreover, we had found ourselves transported into an uncomfortably topsy-turvy world of values. For all her earnest striving to do her duty and to uphold her reputation, the English Queen had emerged as a moral imposter, whilst her seductive rival, laden with guilt and striving for nothing in particular, had snatched the laurels of victory.

How different in this *Romantische Tragödie*! All the complexities of our own life which the poet had so faithfully reflected in his earlier work seem to be shed and forgotten. We seem to be entering the harmless realm of fairytale.[1] Like a sleep-walker or an angel, Johanna takes up her patriotic mission and marches onward to her goal, armed with simple sanctity. Only momentarily does she err, a lapse too small to be detected by the naked eye which appears mercilessly magnified only to her imagination and is made good before it can erode her moral integrity.[2] And after this short and sharply felt aberration – too quickly registered, some say, to carry conviction[3] – she commits a deed of heroism and dies wreathed in clouds of glory.

And yet the poet has set the apparently simple career of the Maid of Orléans in a scene of the utmost complexity. It is a scene of disintegration; and disintegration, like the decaying body of a natural organism, is a highly complex condition. France is a country in the throes of chaos. War and inner division have corroded all long-term bonds and, with them, all those basic human values that depend on peace and stability to flourish. A royal mother has turned against her son and fights him from the enemy's camp, upholding her right to unlimited licence, a veritable she-devil strutting about in man's clothing, a scourge to friend and foe alike. Karl's cousin, the Duke of Burgundy, has turned his back on his own kith and kin, forswearing a sacred allegiance for personal vengeance's sake and leading the enemy into the midst of his native France. But in his self-inflicted exile the springs of wholehearted action have dried up, he is torn hither and thither, too sapped spiritually to be either wholly good or wholly bad. Even the English camp in the midst of France is rent with inner strife – the pretender they have placed upon the throne of the diseased old king is a mere stripling of a boy. The deposed and rightful heir, Karl, is reduced to a state of impotence. Desperate, he has retreated into a never-never land of courtly make-believe, as exquisite as it is degenerate. While his cities are ransacked by the 'ländergewaltige Burgund', while his armies are bled white and his subjects let themselves be killed for him, the 'länderlose König' lives, a 'Fürst der Liebe',

> . . . umringt von Gaukelspielern
> Und Troubadours, spitzfind'ge Rätsel lösend
> Und der Sorel galante Feste gebend,
> Als waltete im Reich der tiefste Friede!
>
> (I. i)

The King's resistance is at an end, his power is draining away. The woman who sustains his waning strength is not his wife but his mistress, whilst his staunchest peer, impatient of his weakness and about to leave him to his fate, is a bastard. Without a vital centre, weakness and strength run errant side by side and make the strangest pair of bedfellows.

As with the peers and their King, so with the people and their country. France is split from east to west. Down to the Loire it has fallen into the hands of the enemy. Its face is changing day by day. Cities and villages are pillaged, the fields are being burnt. Hamlets, towns and whole regions, together with their inhabitants, change hands from the French to the English and back again, with the changing luck of battle. What is there today may have vanished by tomorrow. The very opening words of the Prologue are spoken by one who stands on the slender crest of time where each moment is swallowed by the next and today's wave is tomorrow's trough:

> Ja, liebe Nachbarn! Heute sind wir noch
> Franzosen, freie Bürger noch und Herren
> Des alten Bodens, den die Väter pflügten;
> Wer weiß, wer morgen über uns befiehlt!
>
>   *(Pr.* I)

This is why Thibaut wants to see his daughters speedily married, without asking after the young couples' worldly goods:

> Wer *hat* jetzt Schätze? Haus und Scheune sind
> Des nächsten Feindes oder Feuers Raub —
> Die treue Brust des braven Manns allein
> Ist ein sturmfestes Dach in diesen Zeiten.
>
>   (ibid.)

A man's heart is a safe roof in storm-tossed times; or, as in Johanna's case, a helmet such as Bertrand is presently going to produce — 'ein stählern Dach fürs Haupt' (III). Or Mother Earth herself. For even that most conservative of mortals, the French peasant, abandons all material goods and gives up all thought of permanence in the face of such total chaos as is sweeping France. This is why Thibaut, towards the end of the Prologue, resigns himself to enduring whatever comes, to accepting whichever king the luck of war will toss upon the throne, and admonishes his young family to care only for the nearest and the farthest:

> — Kommt an die Arbeit! Kommt! Und denke jeder
> Nur an das Nächste! Lassen wir die Großen,
> Der Erde Fürsten um die Erde losen;

> Wir können ruhig die Zerstörung schauen,
> Denn sturmfest steht der Boden, den wir bauen.
> Die Flamme brenne unsre Dörfer nieder,
> Die Saat zerstampfe ihrer Rosse Tritt –
> Der neue Lenz bringt neue Saaten mit,
> Und schnell erstehn die leichten Hütten wieder!
> (*Pr.* III)

But it is not only the peasant, he who has not much to lose, that speaks thus. War and change have imprinted the spectre of impermanence on every mind. In war, time is a swifter and more merciless killer even than usual. What has gone, has gone. The moment is as precious as it is costly. As Burgund returns to his King and receives a tumultuous welcome from the crowd, Karl marvels:

> . . . Wie schnell
> Vergessen ist's, daß eben dieser Herzog
> Die Väter ihnen und die Söhne schlug!

And he adds:

> Der Augenblick verschlingt ein ganzes Leben.
> (III. ii)

And a little later, when his vassal embraces him, speechless at his own faithlessness, he replies:

> Vergeßt es! Alles ist verziehen. Alles
> Tilgt dieser einz'ge Augenblick.
> (III. iii)

Later still, the Archbishop pays moving homage to the terrible power of the moment, so swiftly come and gone and so fraught with irrevocable consequence. Peace has returned, he says, the villages and cities which now lie waste will be built up again, the fields too will yield a new crop:

> Doch, die das Opfer eures Zwists gefallen,
> Die Toten stehen nicht mehr auf; die Tränen,
> Die eurem Streit geflossen, *sind* und *bleiben*
> Geweint! Das kommende Geschlecht wird blühen,
> Doch das vergangne war des Elends Raub,
> Der Enkel Glück erweckt nicht mehr die Väter.
> Das sind die Früchte eures Bruderzwists!

> Laßt's euch zur Lehre dienen! Fürchtet die Gottheit
> Des Schwerts, eh ihr's der Scheid' entreißt. Loslassen
> Kann der Gewaltige den Krieg; doch nicht
> Gelehrig, wie der Falk sich aus den Lüften
> Zurückschwingt auf des Jägers Hand, gehorcht
> Der wilde Gott dem Ruf der Menschenstimme.
> Nicht zweimal kommt im rechten Augenblick
> Wie heut' die Hand des Retters aus den Wolken.
>
> (III. iii)

Here, as in *Wallenstein*, every moment is a pregnant moment, powerfully asking to be seized and used, yet pregnant with future; and this is a dilemma which nothing less than the highest consciousness and the nimblest self-mastery of the whole person can mitigate. This is perhaps the special lesson of war. But basically the power of time and the need for resilience in the face of its terrible evanescence and finality is an experience which is woven deep into the very fabric of life, whatever its special conditions; and it is to this ultimate human experience that Burgund, newly returned to Karl and finding himself embracing the man who has murdered his father, lends unforgettable words:

> – Umarmt mich, Du Chatel! Ich vergeb' Euch.
> Geist meines Vaters, zürne nicht, wenn ich
> Die Hand, die dich getötet, freundlich fasse.
> Ihr Todesgötter, rechnet mir's nicht zu,
> Daß ich mein schrecklich Rachgelübde breche!
> Bei euch dort unten in der ew'gen Nacht,
> Da schlägt kein Herz mehr, da ist alles ewig,
> Steht alles unbeweglich fest – doch anders
> Ist es hier oben in der Sonne Licht.
> Der Mensch ist, der lebendig fühlende,
> Der leichte Raub des mächt'gen Augenblicks.
>
> (III. iv)

II

Above all this impermanence and flux the figure of the heroine towers immobile, like a monument of bygone times. Raymond's very first words – the first description we have of Johanna – convey an impression of an over-life-sized and statuesque tranquillity:

> Jetzt liebt sie noch zu wohnen auf den Bergen,
> Und von der freien Heide fürchtet sie
> Herabzusteigen in das niedre Dach
> Der Menschen, wo die engen Sorgen wohnen.
> Oft seh' ich ihr aus tiefem Tal mit stillem
> Erstaunen zu, wenn sie auf hoher Trift
> In Mitte ihrer Herde ragend steht,
> Mit edelm Leibe, und den ernsten Blick
> Herabsenkt auf der Erde kleine Länder.
> Da scheint sie mir was Höh'res zu bedeuten,
> Und dünkt mir's oft, sie stamm' aus andern Zeiten.
>
> (*Pr.* II)

Standing there at her height and viewing the world from above, Johanna is totally unaware of the confused nature of reality. *Sub specie aeternitatis* is how she sees the role of a kingship in which mercy flows from a might the real King so patently does not possess; *sub specie aeternitatis* is how she views her rent and pillaged and burning land: 'Ihr Toren!' she says to the trembling Montgomery:

> Frankreichs königliches Wappen hängt
> Am Throne Gottes; eher rißt ihr einen Stern
> Vom Himmelwagen als ein Dorf aus diesem Reich,
> Dem unzertrennlich ewig einigen! . . .
>
> (II. vii)

And *sub specie aeternitatis* she views her own life, flawlessly spread out beneath her, all in one, without the hazards and delays of organic growth. It is her father who reminds her that a human life, and the life of a woman at that, has its seasons like every other thing on earth:

> – Ich sehe dich in Jugendfülle prangen,
> Dein Lenz ist da, es ist die Zeit der Hoffnung,
> Entfaltet ist die Blume deines Leibes;
> Doch stets vergeben harr' ich, daß die Blume
> Der zarten Lieb' aus ihrer Knospe breche
> Und freudig reife zu der goldnen Frucht!
> O das gefällt mir nimmermehr und deutet
> Auf eine schwere Irrung der Natur!
> Das Herz gefällt mir nicht, das streng und kalt
> Sich zuschließt in den Jahren des Gefühls.
>
> (*Pr.* II)

But Johanna knows of no season except the season of sanctity. Three times she has been called by the Holy Virgin to take up her flag and her sword and to lead the King to Rheims; and at the third call she has responded and left her flock. Purity, the Virgin had told her, is the condition of her vocation; she had said:

> . . . Eine reine Jungfrau
> Vollbringt jedwedes Herrliche auf Erden,
> Wenn sie der ird'schen Liebe widersteht.
> Sieh *mich* an! Eine keusche Magd wie du
> Hab' ich den Herrn, den göttlichen, geboren,
> Und göttlich bin ich selbst! . . .
>
> (I. x)

And obediently Johanna had pledged herself to fulfil her mission in purity and, by that delicate confusion of her own subjective reality with an objective one – a type of confusion which, years before, Goethe had so sensitively traced in his *Bekenntnisse einer schönen Seele*,[4] she had gradually identified herself with the divine cause she serves. 'Sieh *mich* an,' she says to Montgomery as she explains to him the inevitability of his – and her – death, echoing the words of the Holy Virgin; the sword she asks of the King is embossed with the lilies which had surrounded the heavenly apparition – the lilies of the Virgin and of Valois, symbol of purity and power; and embroidered on her flag is an image of the Heavenly Queen, the Holy Virgin who in Johanna's vision had been clad in the dress of a shepherdess, just like herself.

When Johanna exhorts the French troops to attack, crying:

> 'Gott und die heil'ge Jungfrau führt euch an!'
>
> (I. ix)

when she tells the English herald:

> Die Jungfrau kommt vom Könige des Himmels,
> Euch Frieden zu bieten oder blut'gen Krieg . . .
>
> (I. xi)

and when she bursts into the adversaries' camp, crying

> Gott und die Jungfrau!
>
> (II. iv)

it is impossible to tell whether she is referring to the Virgin Mary or herself. By the time she pleads with Burgund to join the sacred cause of the

French, all distinctions between vision and reality, between herself and
the heavenly hosts, have become blurred:

> Ich selbst, die Gottgesandte, reiche dir
> Die schwesterliche Hand. Ich will dich rettend
> Herüberziehn auf unsre reine Seite! –
> Der Himmel ist für Frankreich. Seine Engel –
> Du siehst sie nicht – sie fechten für den König,
> Sie alle sind mit Lilien geschmückt;
> Lichtweiß wie diese Fahn' ist unsre Sache,
> Die reine Jungfrau ist ihr keusches Sinnbild.
>
> (II. x)

It is impossible to make out whether the 'reine Jungfrau' is the heavenly
one depicted on the flag or she herself, and which of them is the chaste
symbol of the sacred cause to which she is rallying the traitor: all is
'lichtweiß', chaste and pure, each refers to all, and all flows into all.

In the entirety of her conscious being, Johanna is identified with the
divine cause, and she knows of no portion of her self which is not so identified.[5] She does not *represent* that divine cause: she *is* it.[6] Tirelessly and
changelessly, she is pledged to it. There is a strange quality of archaic
tranquillity about her as she moves through a troubled and kaleido-
scopically changing world, referring to herself, simply, as 'die Jungfrau'
or even '*der*** Retter'. But with it, also, an alarming restlessness and
impersonality. One asks oneself whether the woman who sees herself
thus, from the outside, really knows the forces that propel her.[7] Suspicion
is aroused long before she meets Lionel and falls in love with him. The
robot-like obsession with which she pursues and kills the hapless Montgomery is startling. The historical Johanna did not engage in battle; in
the play, even the most ardent admirers of the Maid of Orléans, Dunois
and La Hire, are uneasily aware that in her remorseless pursuit of her
victims she is transgressing against a law as natural as it is sacred.[8] The
warning of the Black Knight goes unheeded.[9] Time and again, an uneasy
comparison between her own unnaturalness and the unnatural cruelty of
the monstrous Isabeau, another woman in man's clothing, flits across the
horizon of our consciousness.[10]

Most startling of all is the strange quality of the compassion she evinces
for her young victim – and indeed for herself – which makes it appear as
if there were two separate persons: the one obsessed and forced to kill, the

* My italics.

other looking on, helplessly and even tenderly, like her own ghost, across an unbridgeable gulf. Impersonally she kills him and impersonally she calls him 'friend':

> Stirb, Freund! Warum so zaghaft zittern vor dem Tod,
> Dem unentfliehbaren Geschick? Sieh *mich* an! Sieh!
> Ich bin nur eine Jungfrau, eine Schäferin
> Geboren; nicht des Schwerts gewohnt ist diese Hand,
> Die den unschuldig frommen Hirtenstab geführt.
> Doch weggerissen von der heimatlichen Flur,
> Vom Vaters Busen, von der Schwestern lieber Brust,
> Muß ich *hier*, ich *muß* – mich treibt die Götterstimme, nicht
> Eignes Gelüsten – *euch* zu bitterm Harm, *mir* nicht
> Zur Freude, ein Gespenst des Schreckens, würgend gehn,
> Den Tod verbreiten und sein Opfer sein zuletzt.
>
> (II. vii)

The heavy emphases tell their own story. This is not the voice of a united person who knows what she is doing and why. It is the strident voice of one who is divided, now compelled by forces in herself the very existence of which she does not recognize and now, momentarily, identified with those unknown forces and looking upon her habitual self as though it were a stranger. What these forces are, Montgomery's words tell us:

> Dort die Fürchterliche, die verderblich um sich her
> Wie die Brunst des Feuers raset . . .
> . . . Dort erscheint die Schreckliche!
> Aus Brandes Flammen, düster leuchtend, hebt sie sich,
> Wie aus der Hölle Rachen ein Gespenst der Nacht,
> Hervor. – Wohin entrinn' ich! Schon ergreift sie mich
> Mit ihren Feueraugen, wirft von fern
> Der Blicke Schlingen nimmer fehlend nach mir aus.
> Um meine Füße, fest und fester, wirret sich
> Das Zauberknäul, daß sie gefesselt mir die Flucht
> Versagen! . . .
>
> (II. vi)

Burgund will use that very same imagery when he meets Johanna to do battle with her and exclaims, over-confidently as it turns out:

> . . . Verwahrt
> Ist mir das Ohr vor deiner Rede Schlingen,

Und deines Auges Feuerpfeile gleiten
Am guten Harnisch meines Busens ab.

(II. x)

It is the imagery of fire which Schiller has used in *Fiesco* and *Don Carlos*
and *Maria Stuart*, and which he will use once again with overwhelming
effect in *Die Braut von Messina* to signify the open or concealed force of
sexual desire.[11] By a seductiveness, the existence of which is totally unknown to herself, Johanna here ensnares and masters men stronger than
herself. She will meet these desires face to face when, finally, she will

Für meines Landes Feind entbrennen . . .

(IV. i)

and herself be ensnared by the seductive melodies which accompany her
lament, from behind the scene.

Meanwhile, she is far from consciously encountering that other self.
But the monologue following Montgomery's slaying tells us with extraordinary precision of the channels into which its repressed energies are
being forced: utterly dissociated from her conscious self, they become a
tool of destruction; they have entered her unerring sword:

Erhabne Jungfrau, du wirkst Mächtiges in mir!

she exclaims:

Du rüstest den unkriegerischen Arm mit Kraft,
Dies Herz mit Unerbittlichkeit bewaffnest du.
In Mitleid schmilzt die Seele, und die Hand erbebt,
Als bräche sie in eines Tempels heil'gen Bau,
Den blühenden Leib des Gegners zu verletzen;
Schon vor des Eisens blanker Schneide schaudert mir,
Doch wenn es not tut, alsbald ist die Kraft mir da,
Und nimmer irrend in der zitternden Hand regiert
Das Schwert sich selbst, als wär' es ein lebend'ger Geist.

(II. viii)

III

Still, by her extraordinary and strenuous identification with what Goethe
would call 'das Obere Leitende' in herself, Johanna has achieved outward
victory. The English are decisively beaten; Talbot, their leader, is killed;

Burgund has returned to his liege lord, and peace, at long last, is at hand. But now too the season of sanctity is over. Reconciliation between enemies and relaxation amongst friends are the order of the day. Burgund has embraced his father's murderer and has given voice to the universal knowledge that only in death are finality and permanence to be found:

> Da schlägt kein Herz mehr, da ist alles ewig,
> Steht alles unbeweglich fest – doch anders
> Ist es hier oben in der Sonne Licht.

For:

> Der Mensch ist, der lebendig fühlende,
> Der leichte Raub des mächt'gen Augenblicks.
>
> (III. iv)

The moment has come for Johanna, too, when she is called upon to respond to the exigencies of a changed situation. She is, or so it seems, a creature of flesh and blood like everyone else. Two honourable men are in love with her and offer her their hand in marriage. The hour has arrived for her to share in the general rejoicing. Instead, at the end of the great reconciliation scene, a visibly irritated Karl terminates the tense gathering, saying:

> Brecht ab. Es ist umsonst, sie zu bewegen.
>
> (ibid.)

And indeed, throughout this scene which had begun under such happy auspices, Johanna is as remote and restless as an imprisoned ghost. It is Burgund who can say:

> Mein Herz ist weiches Wachs in ihrer Hand.
>
> (ibid.)

She, the woman, is unmoved as if her heart were dead or absent. Or as if the incredible and startling words she had addressed to Montgomery were true after all:

> Gleichwie die körperlosen Geister, die nicht frei'n
> Auf ird'sche Weise, schließ' ich mich an kein Geschlecht
> Der Menschen an, und dieser Panzer deckt kein Herz.
>
> (II. vii)

Impervious to the mellow radiance of all around and to the demand of this

rare and happy hour, she remains the same impersonal self; monoton-
ously prophesying and preaching, without showing the slightest regard
for the ineptness of her response in a group so finely tempered as this
group at this moment.[12] She is incapable of understanding the King's
meaning when, taking her by the hand, he reminds her that everything
has its season, war and peace, self-denying service and love, the public and
the personal:

> Dich treibt des Geistes Stimme jetzt, es schweigt
> Die Liebe in dem gotterfüllten Busen.
> Sie wird nicht immer schweigen, glaube mir! . . .
>   . . . dies Herz,
> Das jetzt der Himmel ganz erfüllt, wird sich
> Zu einem ird'schen Freunde liebend wenden –
> Jetzt hast du rettend Tausende beglückt,
> Und, *einen* zu beglücken, wirst du enden!
>   (III. iv)

This reminder of the power and the frailty of the moment is lost on
Johanna. She cannot yield to change. She is, as she has been, wedded to
the universal cause. She *is* that cause, in all its abstract austerity, and
quite incapable of striking a personal, let alone a feminine and gracious
note. All she desires is to flee from a gathering that, to her, is threatening
in its relaxedness. Full of anguish, she will exclaim:

> Befiehl, daß man die Kriegstrommete blase!
> Mich preßt und ängstigt diese Waffenstille,
> Es jagt mich auf aus dieser müß'gen Ruh
> Und treibt mich fort, daß ich mein Werk erfülle,
> Gebietrisch mahnend meinem Schicksal zu.
>   (III. iv)[13]

Evidently, Johanna needs a heart plated with armour.
   In her plea for Du Chatel she had said:

> Was irgend gut ist und von oben kommt,
> Ist allgemein und ohne Vorbehalt,
> Doch in den Falten wohnt die Finsternis!
>   (ibid.)

A little later, she had concluded her unsolicited prophecy of the King's
future with the words:

> . . . von den niedern Hütten, wo dir jetzt
> Der Retter ausging, droht geheimnisvoll
> Den schuldbefleckten Enkeln das Verderben!
>   (ibid.)

In both instances, Johanna, however unconsciously, is also speaking of herself. It is *her* identification with the universal goods which come from above and *her* secret terror of the dark and dangerous forces stirring within herself to which she gives unwitting expression. And indeed, when the King urges her to choose a husband from amongst her suitors, she bursts out with a hysterical stridency which betrays her lack of inner freedom:

> Dauphin! Bist du der göttlichen Erscheinung
> Schon müde, daß du ihr Gefäß zerstören,
> Die reine Jungfrau, die dir Gott gesendet,
> Herab willst ziehn in den gemeinen Staub? . . .
> Und ihr erblickt in mir nichts als ein Weib. . . .
> Kein solches Wort mehr, sag' ich euch, wenn ihr
> Den Geist in mir nicht zürnend wollt entrüsten!
> Der Männer Auge schon, das mich begehrt,
> Ist mir ein Grauen und Entheiligung.
>   (ibid.)

Even here, long before she meets Lionel and before she transgresses against the warning of the Black Knight, Johanna's guilt is established. It is the hubris of being identified with the highest, and rejecting the natural side of herself, in a tragically unavailing effort to reach out for absolute integrity.[14] Integrity springs from integration. It is the ability to respond appropriately to any given situation, with any and all of the manifold resources which are available to a many-faceted being of flesh and blood. By the most tragic of ironies, Johanna, an idealized Elisabeth, fails in this initial test of moral integrity. She will only use the top string of her fiddle and its tone is brash. She cannot draw from it the more tempered chords of a mature humanity. To be able to do so, she will have to practise the bass.

IV

This chance comes to her when she encounters Lionel and instantly falls in love with him. The man for whom she finally falls is bound to be the enemy of the universal cause; for her desires and, for that matter, her very femininity are inimical to the forces with which she identifies herself, so inimical indeed that she altogether denies their existence.[15]

It is customary to regard Johanna's response to Lionel as her crucial lapse, as the outbreak of her moral disease. I would argue, on the contrary, that their meeting marks the outbreak of her moral health. As she finds herself face to face with him, she at last encounters her hidden self, those drives which had been so repressed as to be altogether dissociated from her conscious mind, manifesting themselves merely in the unerring agency of her emancipated sword. Now at last she looks these desires in the face and immediately – and this is moving – she finds their features to be noble. And as soon as those hidden drives enter her consciousness, they lose their compulsion. Her sword refuses to serve her and is duly taken from her hands.

In meeting Lionel, Johanna, for the first time in her saintly career, comes face to face with her conflict and thus within reach of its resolution. It is a conflict which had been so deeply denied as to fall altogether outside the ken of her conscious personality. It had manifested itself only indirectly, in her strenuous and inflexible identification with the divine, in her visionary gift and in the supernatural power of her sword. In all this she had felt herself ruled by an outside agency. This divine automatism had betrayed the operation of concealed inner driving forces, the very existence of which was unknown to her. And in a twofold fashion this lack of recognition had marred her sanctity. She had pursued her sacred mission unaware of the fact that there was any portion of herself she must indeed offer as a sacrifice; and she had pursued it unaware of the fact that this very part provided the impure motive-springs which mercilessly propelled her along her course. Thus, unconscious and obsessed, she had always overshot the mark. Now this force has entered the arena of her consciousness and the two aspects of a deeply divided and warring self meet. Prior to her 'fall', her conflict had possessed her. Now that she has 'fallen', it is she that possesses her conflict; and thus she is able to come to grips with the moral challenge it represents.[16]

This signal progress is reflected in the development of an image pattern which is familiar to us.[17] Before her loving encounter, Johanna had been a seer. She had seen the world lying far away, deep below her feet, she had seen the remote destinies of the great. But her visions had been public and impersonal and what she saw had left her unmoved and, for all her dedication, strangely uninvolved. She had remained a bystander to her own prophetic zeal. Her visionary powers had in fact covered up a deeper blindness, the sort of blindness which had manifested itself in the extraordinary lack of tact and insight she had displayed in the reconciliation scene. Now, face to face with Lionel, she perceives concretely for the first time. The stage directions read: 'In diesem Augenblicke sieht sie ihm ins Gesicht, sein Anblick ergreift sie, sie bleibt unbeweglich stehen und läßt dann langsam den Arm sinken'; and, later on: 'erhebt das Schwert mit einer raschen Bewegung gegen ihn, läßt es aber, wie sie ihn ins Gesicht faßt, schnell wieder sinken.' She sees and she is moved by what she sees. Not that she wants to be; as she tells Lionel to run for his life, she speaks 'mit abgewandtem Gesicht', and her words bear out the meaning of her gesture: 'Rette dich!' she pleads:

> Ich will nichts davon wissen, daß dein Leben
> In meine Macht gegeben war.
>
> (ibid.)

But of course she sees, and of course she responds to what she has seen; what is more, her seeing ushers in the realization that when she had thought she saw before, she was in fact blinded. It means the unwelcome consciousness of her twofold self and, with it, the power and necessity of choice.[18] In her monologue, Johanna tells us so herself:

> Warum mußt ich ihm in die Augen sehn!
> Die Züge schaun des edeln Angesichts!
> Mit deinem Blick fing dein Verbrechen an,
> Unglückliche! Ein blindes Werkzeug fordert Gott,
> Mit blinden Augen mußtest du's vollbringen!
> Sobald du *sahst*, verließ dich Gottes Schild,
> Ergriffen dich der Hölle Schlingen!
>
> (IV. i)

Only in her interpretation of the event does Johanna as yet go wrong. A blind tool is not the agent of the divine, and a sanctity which needs to rely on the protection of such blindness is specious. It is the prerogative of human beings to see; and it is the special prerogative of the gentler sex to be moved by what it sees. Schiller has said so in *Don Carlos* and again, more insistently and specifically, in *Maria Stuart*.[19] In *Würde der Frauen* he celebrates 'die fühlende Seele der Frau' and her capacity to be moved to tears. Women

> Löschen die Zwietracht, die tobend entglüht,
> Lehren die Kräfte, die feindlich sich hassen,
> Sich in der lieblichen Form zu umfassen,
> Und vereinen, was ewig sich flieht.

Such pacification of sense and spirit is the seal of mature humanity. And this, indeed, is the sole spring of sanctity.

Johanna, who had shot fiery glances at men, ensnaring them by their power, sees and melts and is herself ensnared. In this unwelcome recognition of her 'lower' self lies her chance. For only by experiencing this self in the first place is she enabled to choose what kind of a self she wants to be. For the moment, she repudiates her 'higher' self, the self which had presumed unaided to reach for the divine:

> Nimm, ich kann sie nicht verdienen,
> Deine Krone, nimm sie hin!

(IV. i)

she cries to the heavenly Queen. Now she rejects her sacred mission as, before, she had rejected everything that was indifferent to this mission, saying:

> Ach! Es war nicht meine Wahl!

This is a temporary choice, as immature and as far from signifying integration as her earlier conviction of being a divinely chosen instrument had been. But at least it is *her* choice, and the action springing from that choice – the silence she maintains in the face of her father's and Heaven's own indictment of her presumption – is *her* action.[20] Before, she had been a puppet in the hands of unknown powers, and her actions had been as blind and hasty and destructive as those which make up the chequered weave of war. In the monologue following her encounter with the night side of herself, Johanna, for the first time in her saintly career, uses the personal pronoun 'I' in its proper signification: as an expression of that sense of conscious identity which is the basis of adult personhood.

Johanna does not spare herself in recognizing the implications of her choice. The self for which she has momentarily opted is undifferentiated in the extreme. It is the self she had denied and, projecting outward, had known only in the shape of her country's enemies. This self is indifferent and even inimical to the common cause with which she had so exclusively identified herself, and from which now, abruptly, she feels ostracized and severed. Already in her monologue she had lamented that she alone was excluded from the 'allgemeine Lust':

> Mich rührt es nicht, das allgemeine Glück
> (IV. i)

she had confessed. In her ensuing encounter with Sorel she tastes the
bitter fruits of her choice.

The King's mistress accepts the limitations of her femininity. She too
is not moved by the public cause; she is filled with the private rapture of
her love:

> . . . Nicht der Ruhm des Vaterlandes,
> Nicht der erneute Glanz des Thrones, nicht
> Der Völker Hochgefühl und Siegesfreude
> Beschäftigt dieses schwache Herz . . .

she confesses:

> Es ist
> Nur *einer*, der es ganz erfüllt, es hat
> Nur Raum für dieses einzige Gefühl:
> *Er* ist der Angebetete, *ihm* jauchzt das Volk,
> *Ihn* segnet es, *ihm* streut es diese Blumen,
> Er ist der Meine, der Geliebte ist's.
> (IV. ii)

But Johanna, with a moral sensitivity that has become sharpened by her
shattering experience, puts her finger on the difference between the love of
the King's mistress and her own. In Sorel, the particular and the universal
meet and marry in a true act of participation which is private *and* public,
personal *and* objective at once. In herself, they are at war:

> O du bist glücklich! Selig preise dich!
> Du liebst, wo alles liebt! . . .
> Dies Fest des Reichs ist deiner Liebe Fest . . .
> Eins bist du mit der allgemeinen Wonne,
> Du liebst das Allerfreuende, die Sonne . . .
> (ibid.)

Johanna is here lending voice to that supreme tragic irony which lies at
the heart of moral endeavour; an irony which Schiller had articulated on
a lower level in the figure of the English Queen and to which he will give
surpassing utterance in *Demetrius*. Unconditional upward striving – this
is the poet's unshakeable conviction – of necessity defeats itself.[21] Johanna
who had thought that

Was irgend gut ist und von oben kommt,
Ist allgemein und ohne Vorbehalt . . .
(III. iv)

who had likened these universal goods to the sun's rays, tragically finds herself excluded from partaking of this universal radiance; she has omitted to rise to the abstraction of the universal by the fearless acceptance of the concrete and particular: *her* own feeling and *her* own femininity. She is mercilessly correct in her elevation of Sorel and in the repudiation of her own state of dividedness which is implicit in it:

Du bist die Heilige! *Du* bist die Reine!
(IV. ii)

V

In the sequel Johanna no longer mentions her shattering experience with Lionel. But she symbolically enacts her descent to the buried strata of her psyche, which this encounter has revealed to her, and her acceptance of what she has discovered in her depths. In a tumultuous tempest which reflects the chaos in her own nature no less than the disintegration into which her country has once again been plunged, she finally descends to the 'niedern Hütten' from which she had issued and which, for so long, she had shunned, those very 'Hütten' which she had prophetically seen as the cradle of far-away future insurgence. Humbly, led by Raymond, the despised companion of her youth – she had not once addressed him in the Prologue – she wanders through nature's own hell and seeks refuge in a humble charcoal-burner's hut. This nocturnal Odyssey marks a vital phase of Johanna's moral education. More precisely, and to begin with, it resumes the education of her senses and natural instincts which had been so cruelly cut short by her call to sanctity. When Raymond urges that she needs him by her side to help and tend her in the wilderness, she replies:

Ich kenne alle Kräuter, alle Wurzeln;
Von meinen Schafen lernt' ich das Gesunde
Vom Gift'gen unterscheiden – ich verstehe
Den Lauf der Sterne und der Wolken Zug,
Und die verborgnen Quellen hör' ich rauschen.
Der Mensch braucht wenig, und an Leben reich
Ist die Natur.
(V. iv)

Coming from the most presumptuous of mortals who had relinquished the pastures and repudiated the jurisdiction of nature, these words are some of the most moving in the entire play. Johanna learning from her sheep indeed! There is a new wisdom, a new humility and fluidity in these words. The stars are no longer pinned to the sky, the clouds are drifting and the springs – hidden springs – are murmuring. Johanna has come to terms with the eternal flux of things. She has come to understand that there is a season for everything.

Not indeed that this is a season for sanctity. As the charcoal-burners flee from her presence, and the English, led by the devilish Isabeau, capture her, she sadly observes:

> Kein Gott erscheint, kein Engel zeigt sich mehr,
> Die Wunder ruhn, der Himmel ist verschlossen.
>
> (V. vi)

And, indeed, she needs a rest from miracles as they need a rest from her. But even as her prophetic vision fails her, her natural vision reaches a new pitch of perfection. Incarcerated and impatiently listening to the English soldier who reports on the progress of the battle from the ramparts, she exclaims:

> Hätt' er *mein* Auge oder stünd' ich oben,
> Das Kleinste nicht entginge meinem Blick!
> Das wilde Huhn kann ich im Fluge zählen,
> Den Falk erkenn' ich in den höchsten Lüften.
>
> (V. xi)

This is the voice of the simple shepherdess, of the girl who single-handedly snatched her lamb from the jaws of the tiger-wolf. It is a creature of flesh and blood who is speaking here, one who is proud of her natural skills. 'Jetzt bin ich geheilt', she had modestly said;

> . . . und dieser Sturm in der Natur,
> Der ihr das Ende drohte, war mein Freund,
> Er hat die Welt gereinigt und auch mich.
> In mir ist Friede . . .
>
> (V. iv)

This is the voice, not indeed of holiness, but of one beginning to be whole. Sanctity has gone out of her, and simple sober sanity has taken its place.

When Johanna's enthusiasm is kindled again, it springs from those 'verborgnen Quellen' she had discovered in nature. It wells up from the depth of frailty and constriction and from her acceptance of this, the human condition.

> Und ihr erblickt in mir nichts als ein Weib . . .
>> (III. iv)

she had indignantly exclaimed when the King had reminded her of her femininity. Now she accepts this troubled heritage:

> Erschreckt dich ein gefessel Weib?
>> (V. x)

she asks before ever she is put in chains; and again, later:

> Und ich bin nichts als ein gefessel Weib!
>> (V. xi)

As she accepts the fetters of womanhood and, ultimately, of mortality, a new strength comes to her. She transcends what she has accepted. From the bottom of an anguished and loyal heart she desires liberation; and, falling to her knees, she prays:

> Höre mich, Gott, in meiner höchsten Not!
> Hinauf zu dir, in heißem Flehenswunsch,
> In deine Himmel send' ich meine Seele.
> Du kannst die Fäden eines Spinngewebs
> Stark machen wie die Taue eines Schiffs,
> Leicht ist es deiner Allmacht, ehrne Bande
> In dünnes Spinngewebe zu verwandeln –
> Du willst, und diese Ketten fallen ab,
> Und diese Turmwand spaltet sich – du halfst
> Dem Simson, da er blind war und gefesselt
> Und seiner stolzen Feinde bittern Spott
> Erduldete. – Auf dich vertrauend faßt' er
> Die Pfosten seines Kerkers mächtig an
> Und neigte sich und stürzte das Gebäude . . .
>> (ibid.)

And it is after this prayer that she finds the strength to break her iron chains.

VI

We should be wary of describing Johanna's heroic liberation – of herself, her King and her country – as an act of sublimity. This word, so glibly used, has taken on an ugly divisive ring, suggesting the inhuman triumph of one portion of the self over the other.[22] No single concept that is current in Schiller scholarship has done more to obscure a true perception of this poet's meaning. Johanna's sublimity – if we insist on so calling the final phase of her development - wears the graceful features of a child peacefully asleep:

> Seht einen Engel scheiden!

Burgund says of the dying heroine:

> Seht, wie sie da liegt,
> Schmerzlos und ruhig wie ein schlafend Kind!
> (V. xiv)

Sublimity thus lightly worn is the ultimate triumph of a person in whom sense and spirit are united. This is Johanna's consummate humanity; this – in the view of a profoundly humanistic poet deeply committed to our modern values – is the only viable basis of sanctity. Her nature has been redeemed and is able to share the triumph of the spirit over its earthly bounds. Her self-immolation becomes a truly liberating act because it is a voluntary act, desired and endorsed by her whole being. As Schiller has it in *Über Anmut und Würde*: 'Wäre die sinnliche Natur im Sittlichen immer nur die unterdrückte und nie die mitwirkende Partei, wie könnte sie das ganze Feuer ihrer Gefühle zu einem Triumph hergeben, der über sie selbst gefeiert wird?'

4

Health

Sorget für eure Gesundheit, man kann ohne
das nicht gut sein.
(Written in mortal illness, recorded by
Karoline von Wolzogen)

9

'Heiliger Dankgesang
eines Genesenen an die Gottheit' :
a reading of *Wilhelm Tell*

I

The sun, as it sinks below the horizon, may for one last fleeting moment touch a whole landscape with a transient splendour. Just so the last gesture of a dying man may sometimes illuminate the darkening landscape of a mind. Schiller on his deathbed, taking his last leave of his youngest child, made a gesture of this kind.

When he was already close to death he expressed a wish to see Emilie, his youngest. 'Er wandte sich mit dem Kopfe um' – we are told – 'nach dem Kinde zu, faßte es an der Hand und sah ihm mit unaussprechlicher Wehmut ins Gesicht. Die Schillern sagte mir, es wäre gewesen, als ob er das Kind habe segnen wollen. Dann fing er an bitterlich zu weinen und steckte den Kopf ins Kissen und winkte, daß man das Kind wegbringen möchte.'[1] No one who knows and loves Schiller can fail to be moved by this scene. This wordless taking of leave is at least as eloquent as Marfa's more famous monologue. This gesture carries the plain signature of this man's spirit.

What was going on in him as he gazed at his daughter, knowing it must be for the last time? He felt a father's love, no doubt; no doubt sadness too that he should be parting from a creature so young, whose life was only just beginning. But there was much more in this gazing at her 'with inexpressible sadness': all his knowledge of the world, his love for it, his renunciation of it. We may picture this most conscious of men gazing on this totally unconscious life for the last time and in that gesture taking leave of nature – nature which had been no more than a stepmother to him, nature which had long been spurned by his lofty and demanding intellect, and which only at the end he had painfully learned to cherish and to honour. Was he taking leave of the vision he had continued to nurse in his mind even as his body was failing him, of a humanity of the future fully restored to its pristine nature? There had been years of intellectual tension and pitiless philosophical self-punishment; now this more natural and relaxed fruit of his genius signified a healing of the spirit. And, barely restored to health, he had to die. The eyes of his child returning his gaze for the last time were those of such a restored humanity, in all its innocence and unboundedness. Was it for this vision that he gave his blessing and felt this profound sadness?

He had not long since written the last lines of his *Wilhelm Tell*, and this play is his song of thanksgiving for the healing powers of nature. Let us listen to it.

The closeness of man and nature in every aspect of this play must be apparent to every reader.[2] It is manifest throughout in two modes; equally in the way men are seen to belong to a natural environment, and in the human character of external nature itself.

We are concerned again, as in *Don Carlos* and *Die Jungfrau von Orleans* and in *Demetrius*, with a people's destiny – the actualization of a spiritual value glimpsed as a new form of freedom.[3] But in this play how simple, how close to physical nature, are the events which make history! An oath sworn by a tiny group of men meeting under the stars in a meadow; an experienced marksman piercing an apple that had been taken by the tyrant from the nearest branch and placed on his son's head; a bold leap to the shore from a boat, by a man for whom it was only possible because every inch of the ground was as familiar to him as his own hand; the final placing of his arrow in the heart of the tyrant, and a peasant jubilation. Whatever the moral character of such events, they are all plainly close to nature and rooted in a natural form of existence.[4] The history of this people exhibits this same character: the history of a race of settlers, the saga of an obstinate battle waged by men against the elements, the gradual humanization of nature by them. Melchthal's journeys on behalf of the cause of freedom take him into the heart of the mountains, and we feel him drawing power and wisdom from them along with the glacier-milk that quenches his thirst. Johanna, in the *Jungfrau*, too, had been restored and strengthened in this way. 'Ein harmlos Volk von Hirten' is how these Swiss again and again refer to themselves[5] – a term that not only describes their chief occupation but points also to the protectiveness that informs their relationship with the natural and animal world, and gives its colour to their perception of human relationships. The parson is *their* shepherd, and Tell, when he is suspected of intending to keep himself to himself, counters with the rhetorical question:

> Der Tell holt ein verlornes Lamm vom Abgrund,
> Und sollte seinen Freunden sich entziehen?
>
> (I. iii)

No one is ashamed to use symbols drawn from nature in speaking of human acts and failures. Tell compares the tyrant's power to the shortlived rage of the Föhn or a mountain storm, or to the sting of a serpent that someone has provoked. All the innocence of this man comes out in the (in fact misleading) harmlessness of these metaphors, in which what is specifically evil in the world of men is not fully grasped. Tell is already wiser when he says, a little later, to his son,

> Ja, wohl ist's besser, Kind, die Gletscherberge
> Im Rücken haben als die bösen Menschen.
>
> (III. iii)

But even the sacred cause of freedom is unaffectedly referred to in metaphors drawn from the natural and animal world:[6]

> Jedem Wesen ward
> Ein Notgewehr in der Verzweiflungsangst:
> Es stellt sich der erschöpfte Hirsch und zeigt
> Der Meute sein gefürchtetes Geweih,
> Die Gemse reißt den Jäger in den Abgrund –
> Der Pflugstier selbst, der sanfte Hausgenoß
> Des Menschen, der die ungeheure Kraft
> Des Halses duldsam unters Joch gebogen,
> Springt auf, gereizt, wetzt sein gewaltig Horn
> Und schleudert seinen Feind den Wolken zu.
>
> (I. iv)

How close and intimate the relationship with nature must be for images such as these to be chosen to lend expression to their most elevated spiritual concerns! The ox is 'der sanfte Hausgenoß' of his human masters; then what could be more telling than the ambiguity of the relative pronoun in the following clause?

> . . . der sanfte Hausgenoß
> Des Menschen, *der* die ungeheure Kraft
> Des Halses duldsam unters Joch gebogen . . .

What does the 'der' that I have italicized refer to? To the ox, to a people
oppressed by the yoke of tyranny, or to Tell himself, 'der . . . das
Härteste erduldet' – a liberator whose final deed springs from his super-
human endurance much as his adversary is tossed by the horns of the ox
and as the bolt flies from the tautened spring? Man and beast are not
distinguished here. What is asserted of the beast is asserted of the 'companion to men' and even of man himself because of the ambiguous grammatical reference. Beast and man are participants in one destiny and one
nobility: the humble nobility of the people, 'das so bescheiden ist und doch
voll Kraft'; finally the nobility of Wilhelm Tell, 'who endured the worst'
(V. i).

And just as man is turned sympathetically towards nature, nature itself
has a human face. The very first scene tells us this – indeed, does it tell us
anything else? Could one ever imagine that Schiller's aim was merely to
provide local colour? It tells us that humanity is latent in every animal
and requires to be recognized and honoured. 'Das Tier hat auch Vernunft',
the huntsman agrees with the shepherd; and its intelligence, its dignity,
its pride are known to them both. The cow that Ruodi admires has her
own name, and ceases to eat if she is deprived of her 'Halsschmuck'. Wounded honour is more powerful than a mere instinct. Melchthal sizes up the
situation similarly when the bailiff's men unhitch his oxen, 'die schönen
Tiere', from the plough:

> Dumpf brüllten sie, als hätten sie Gefühl
> Der Ungebühr, und stießen mit den Hörnern
> (I. iv)

he reports, and carries on with a *non sequitur* entirely characteristic of that
closeness to nature which pervades the play:

> Da übernahm mich der gerechte Zorn,
> Und meiner selbst nicht Herr, schlug ich den Boten.
> (ibid.)

Granted, Melchthal is himself here still in the thrall of a blind instinctive
drive. He is 'not master of himself'. But equally, later on when he is able
to say

> Urteilt, ob ich mein Herz bezwingen kann:
> Ich sah den Feind und ich erschlug ihn nicht.
>
> (II. ii)

he is again comparing the self-defence of a man in dire moral straits with the animal's own reaction to danger.

Even so remote a part of the natural world as the plants have their share in humanity and feel with the human. A mysterious bond between man and forest is brought out into the open in Tell's conversation with his son.

> Vater, ist's wahr, daß auf dem Berge dort
> Die Bäume bluten, wenn man einen Streich
> Drauf führte mit der Axt?

Walther asks his father, who confirms this and adds a further striking claim:

> So ist's, und die Lawinen hätten längst
> Den Flecken Altdorf unter ihrer Last
> Verschüttet, wenn der Wald dort oben nicht
> Als eine Landwehr sich dagegen stellte.
>
> (III. iii)

Just as the beasts themselves have the power of reason and a sense of what is unfitting, so the trees too are part and parcel of the animal and even the human realm: they bleed, they are like a 'Landwehr' in protecting one among the primeval settlements mentioned in the scene on the Rütli meadow. These settlements had been wrested by man from the elements, and constitute a sacred domain where man and nature enter by covenant into an indissoluble unity. A crime committed by a man against nature is also a crime against himself – for the man who raises his axe against a tree of the 'Bannwald' and makes it bleed will find his hand will grow from out of his grave. Everywhere we find this same *rapprochement* between man and nature, this gentle raising up of the natural realm on to the higher level of the specifically human.

The elements themselves are drawn into this secret bond. The storm unleashed by Geßler's crime is nature's answer to the outrage that has occurred:[7] the victory of what in man is against nature.

> Zu zielen auf des eignen Kindes Haupt,
> Solches ward keinem Vater noch geboten!

> Und die Natur soll nicht in wildem Grimm
> Sich drob empören . . .
>
> (IV. i)

And when the fisherman, terror-stricken, cries out into the gale,

> Ihr wilden Elemente werdet Herr,
> Ihr Bären kommt, ihr alten Wölfe wieder
> Der großen Wüste, euch gehört das Land . . .
>
> (IV. i)

his words conjure up an image of disintegration, in which the process of civilizing, the subject of Stauffacher's allocution on the Rütli, is progressively reversed, step by step, gain by gain. Stauffacher has recalled that process:

> — Wir haben diesen Boden uns erschaffen
> Durch unsrer Hände Fleiß, den alten Wald,
> Der sonst der Bären wilde Wohnung war,
> Zu einem Sitz für Menschen umgewandelt . . .
>
> (II. ii)

Now the 'wild elements' again hold sway, the bears and the primordial wolves return to their 'savage dwelling' in the ancient forests, and the soil again reverts to an untamed waste: 'der alte Urstand der Natur kehrt wieder'. An ancient covenant is dissolved, precisely that 'uralte Bündnis' to which the Swiss when they forgathered on the Rütli had appealed as the ground of their eternal right to freedom: the alliance, centuries old and wrought by unceasing toil, between nature and man, between the cultivator and the soil he had 'wrested from the ancient waste'. Such an alliance can only subsist for as long as the inner relation between man and nature is kept intact. The outrage perpetrated by the tyrant sets loose something within the human realm which is against nature; and thereby the blind forces of primordial nature are unleashed; elemental chaos returns again.

The existence of this precarious bond between nature and man is reflected back to us again in the figure of Tell, the pivotal figure in this dramatic poem. Tell's own nature has been brutally violated by Geßler's inhuman demand; this fact is brought home to us by a symbol deriving again from the Rütli scene. As in that scene we had been told:

> Die Brut des Drachen haben wir getötet,

> Der aus den Sümpfen giftgeschwollen stieg,
> (II. ii)

so now Tell bitterly mediates:

> Du hast aus meinem Frieden mich heraus
> Geschreckt, in gärend Drachengift hast du
> Die Milch der frommen Denkart mir verwandelt . . .
> (IV. iii)

Within Tell too there rises again the ancient chaos, the chaos which only unremitting civilizing labour over centuries had tamed and kept in bondage. The inner situation reflects the external: from nature in revolt there emerges a man grown savage and alienated from himself.[8] It is as if a chasm had opened up within Tell and was threatening to destroy his own inner cohesion.

II

Plainly what Schiller's last completed play is about is the bond between man and nature, nature both within him and around him. This bond is expressed above all in a coherent set of symbols from which the characteristic stamp in the linguistic structure of the work derives. Time and again, in the most varied dramatic contexts and formal configurations, there recur in the verbal texture words such as 'Herz', 'Haupt', 'Auge' or 'Arm' – honest to goodness, apparently homely words, lacking in resonance, giving the statements in which they are used an appearance of robust simplicity of meaning. This appearance, looked at more closely, can be seen to be deceptive. Schiller – to adapt a saying of Hofmannsthal's – has concealed his profundity on the surface;[9] he was able to conceal it on the surface of the natural, physical sphere of existence, precisely because that sphere, for Schiller, stands in the closest *rapport* with the realm of the spirit. These words, seemingly so easy to grasp, resolve themselves at a closer look into metaphors for spiritual processes, concealing within themselves an import as perpetually fleeting as it is profound. For what naïve significance could be read into utterances such as this of Geßler's –

> . . . der ist mir der Meister . . .
> Dem's Herz nicht in die Hand tritt noch ins Auge . . .
> (III. iii)

or this of Fürst's, speaking of Rudenz –

> Sein wiederkehrend Herz
> Verdient Vertraun . . .
>
> (IV. ii)

or into the visionary words of Attinghausen's —

> Aus diesem Haupte, wo der Apfel lag,
> Wird euch die neue beßre Freiheit grünen;
>
> (ibid.)

let alone into Melchthal's tortured variations on the theme of the eye —

> Welch Äußerstes
> Ist noch zu fürchten, wenn der Stern des Auges
> In seiner Höhle nicht mehr sicher ist?
>
> (I. iv)

and

> O, weil ihr selbst an eurem Leib und Gut
> Noch nichts erlitten, eure Augen sich
> Noch frisch und hell in ihren Kreisen regen
> So sei euch darum unsre Not nicht fremd . . .
>
> (I. iv)

None of this is really current homely speech. In such words the spirit of these men finds direct expression; and it is a spirit that in defiance of all potential estrangement and danger knows its oneness with the body, and has the power to be heard through the symbolism of the body.

The poet achieves three things through such symbolism. In the first place, he has found, in the language of the body, an extremely concise and yet the most universally valid idiom in which to express psychic events. In the second place, this symbolism is the key to a coherent structuring of the dramatic content of the poem. It becomes clear, for instance, as one reads and rereads the drama, that not only individual personages but whole groups of characters, whole social orders, are pre-eminently associated with one or the other symbol, the links being created both by repetition and by the use of *synecdoche*. Melchthal is always associated in this way with the word 'Herz', and along with him the whole peasant order that he represents. Rudenz — and along with him the order of the nobility — are linked just as regularly with the symbol of the head. Now, just as the single members or functions of a body point to the organism to which they are subordinate and from which they derive their existence, so with the personages and groups that are identified in this way: they point beyond themselves to others that complement and complete them, and in combination with whom they comprise an organic whole.[10] Melchthal and Rudenz, heart and head, are linked with each other in this way by an inescapable necessity, but so are the classes that they represent. And such external relationships as these also serve continually to point to parallel harmonies or divisions within the individual himself. Moreover, as we have already seen in considering the Rütli scene, the bond – the confederation – that is at issue is not only something linking this man and that, this class and that, but in the last resort is a bond that aims to be consummated at a deeper level: the effective union of different strata within the individual psyche, linking and uniting the human spirit with its sensuous nature. Passage after passage could be quoted to illuminate this dimension of *depth*. Look at Attinghausen's words of warning to Rudenz:

> – O lerne fühlen, welches Stamms du bist! . . .
> Das Haupt zu heißen eines freien Volks,
> Das dir aus Liebe nur sich herzlich weiht,
> Das treulich zu dir steht in Kampf und Tod –
> *Das* sei dein Stolz, *des* Adels rühme dich –
> Die angebornen Bande knüpfe fest,
> Ans Vaterland, ans teure, schließ dich an,
> Das halte fest mit deinem ganzen Herzen.
> Hier sind die starken Wurzeln deiner Kraft;
> Dort in der fremden Welt stehst du allein,
> Ein schwankes Rohr, das jeder Sturm zerknickt.
>
> (II. i)

The power of these lines is drawn from the changing significance given the word 'Stamm'. Almost imperceptibly Attinghausen moves from the idea of the 'stem' – the racial stock – in which the concrete meaning of the word is all but lost, on to the simile of a tree with its stem – its trunk – its roots, its branches and its 'head'. Within the logical structure firmly established by this simile, 'head' and 'heart' are no longer referred to as distinct entities; they are parts subservient to one and the same organic whole. They designate merely the highest and deepest strata within one and the same vital system, and such words as 'Bande', 'festknüpfen', 'anschließen' characterize the cohesive force by which the organic constituents are drawn, and held, together.

A third implication is carried for the poet by the symbolism of the physical organism. It ensures that the inner development and diverse fortunes affecting the peripheral figures in the drama are constantly related to the main spiritual event, the enacting of which constitutes the central area of the drama: namely the exfoliating (to use the same symbol) of an organically structured psyche in the figure of Wilhelm Tell himself. Heart and head, Melchthal and Rudenz, are embodiments in dramatic form of the strata existing within Tell, so that the developing relation between Melchthal and Rudenz implies and reflects the process of integration taking place in the hero of the play.

III

As so often in Schiller's writing, so here too words like 'Haupt' and 'Herz' in passages such as those we have just considered are a shorthand for the spiritual and the sensuous, the 'spontaneous' and the receptive part of man. As against that, the eye designates the point of intersection where the two realms within the human psyche meet and interact. This singular position, between mind and sense, assigned to the eye is in accord with Schiller's philosophical views, and in fact corresponds to the idea that other poets have traditionally held on this subject. Throughout the whole history of dramatic poetry the eye has possessed a quite unique symbolic force. It emerges as the ultimate poetic symbol for human awareness or unawareness, knowledge or delusion, and for a spiritual vision which is bound to be tragic in that it is ineluctably rooted in physical existence. One need only consider Sophocles' *Oedipus*, Shakespeare's *King Lear*, Milton's *Samson Agonistes*, Goethe's *Egmont*, Schiller's own *Wallenstein*, or Kleist's *Amphitryon* – indeed, the entire dramatic and epic work of that poet.

The eye is one of the human organs of perception and as such belongs to the domain of the senses; the most fragile in its structure and the most vulnerable of them all. Yet by this very token it is also the most differentiated, the most selective, the most intellectual of our sense-organs. Since its functioning actually requires spatial distance, it achieves a remoteness from the object of perception, enhanced by the ability to relegate that object to the periphery of its field or to shut it out altogether – an ability not shared for instance by the ear – and thus, effectively, liberates us from the direct physical force of what we perceive and helps engender psychical distance and, eventually, the free play of activity within the mind.[11] Thus the eye, in Schiller's drama, becomes the ultimate symbol of our double nature, which is a compound of spirit and sense. We can in effect read off what stage Melchthal's inner development has reached by considering the significance to him of this act of perception. When for instance he is still at the mercy of blind instinctuality driving him on, vision is for him a predominantly sensuous and vegetative experience:

> . . . Alle Wesen leben
> Vom Lichte, jedes glückliche Geschöpf –
> Die Pflanze selbst kehrt freudig sich zum Lichte.
> Und er muß sitzen, fühlend, in der Nacht,
> Im ewig Finstern – ihn erquickt nicht mehr
> Der Matten warmes Grün, der Blumen Schmelz,
> Die roten Firnen kann er nicht mehr schauen . . .
>
> (I. iv)

Perception shades off precariously into tumultuous passion in the words with which Melchthal opens his report in the Rütli meeting:

> Die Hand hab' ich gelegt auf seine Augen,
> Und glühend Rachgefühl hab' ich gesogen
> Aus der erloschnen Sonne seines Blicks.
>
> (II. ii)

It is only a little later that he can say, when suffering has brought him to a new maturity,

> Urteilt, ob ich mein Herz bezwingen kann:
> Ich sah den Feind, und ich erschlug ihn nicht . . .
>
> (ibid.)

and thus show his new power of distinguishing the act of seeing from the feeling it arouses, and both from the decision to act out his emotional response. But in between such increasingly sober statements Melchthal's language gathers force, and time and again issues in towering metaphors, carried aloft by powerful surges of feeling; illumination bordering on insanity in which, taut with suffering, he attempts to say the ultimate about the human eye and the significance of its possession and its loss:[12]

> Welch Äußerstes
> Ist noch zu fürchten, wenn der Stern des Auges
> In seiner Höhle nicht mehr sicher ist?
>
> (I. iv)

And:

> Ihr selbst seid Väter, Häupter eines Hauses
> Und wünscht euch einen tugendhaften Sohn,
> Der . . . euch den Stern des Auges fromm bewache.
>
>   (ibid.)

And again:

> O, weil ihr selbst an eurem Leib und Gut
> Noch nichts erlitten, eure Augen sich
> Noch frisch und hell in ihren Kreisen regen,
> So sei euch darum unsre Not nicht fremd.
>
>   (ibid.)

The apple of the eye – a 'star', in its orb of jelly and bone! In this image, an image of an explosiveness and obsessive force to match Kleist's, the highest and the deepest, the brightest and darkest, the most spiritual and the most earthy, the most lasting and the most fragile, are united. The human eye participates in two realms; it is by its nature, as the word 'Stern' tells us, related to the luminous sphere of the

> . . . ew'gen Rechte,
> Die droben hangen unveräußerlich
> Und unzerbrechlich, wie die Sterne selbst . . .
>
>   (II. ii)

and at the same time it is as vulnerable and unprotected as anything can be in the whole of nature. For precisely this reason, that it stands on the frontier of two realms, it is a fitting symbol for that inner, psychophysical unity in which the dignity of our human existence is comprised. That is why the blinding of Melchthal's aged father is experienced as a desecration of humanity itself, and as an ultimate violation such as to waken every sacred power of resistance in men.

It is this precarious unity of spirit and nature in men which is the mark of their human dignity and which the play is really about. Geßler's obdurate malice is directed against it; his purpose is to destroy this dignity. Indeed he makes this explicit when he plants his ridiculous hat for passersby to salute:

> Ich hab' ihn aufgesteckt, daß sie den Nacken
> Mir lernen beugen, den sie aufrecht tragen –
> Das *Unbequeme* hab' ich hingepflanzt
> Auf ihrem Weg, wo sie vorbeigehn müssen,

Daß sie drauf stoßen mit dem Aug' und sich
Erinnern ihres Herrn, den sie vergessen.

(IV. iii)

By every word and deed this tyrant strives to degrade the nobility with
which any man is endowed when he is at one with his nature; for he both
fears and despises nature, and knows nothing of its inborn dignity. He will
bow men's necks so that they are on a level with the animals – never
realizing that animals too are noble in themselves. His entirely material-
istic image of the eye – 'daß sie drauf stoßen mit dem Aug' ' – precisely
denies the innate spirituality of human vision which resides in its need for
distance, and reduces it to the blind and groping level of the lower senses.

Thus too the testing shot he invented for Tell is designed to humiliate
this man and to prove to him and the rest of the world, once and for all, that
nature is never to be relied on. The soft-hearted Tell he is sure will fail;
and he desires to reveal nature in all her baseness, and to tear up any
claim to sovereign dignity that the human spirit at peace and unity with
nature might make; he will make a mock of the concept of the man at
unity with himself.

The target he sets for Tell is ostensibly his child's heart. But in a deeper
sense it is Tell's own heart, 'denn auf den Schützen springt der Pfeil
zurück'. By forcing Tell to exact from his own nature what is sheer against
nature,[13] he aims to provoke the instincts to rebel against the mind that
could impose such a command; and this very treachery of nature is the
wedge he would use to burst the inner unity of Tell's personality asunder,
and expose the impotence of a mind that is allied with nature.

Once again the question really at issue here – the question of real
freedom, who is really lord and master of himself – is posed and resolved
through the image of the human eye.

Du rühmst dich deines sichern Blicks! Wohlan!
Hier gilt es, Schütze, deine Kunst zu zeigen . . .
Das Schwarze treffen in der Scheibe, das
Kann auch ein andrer – der ist mir der Meister
Der seiner Kunst gewiß ist überall,
Dem's Herz nicht in die Hand tritt noch ins Auge.

(III. iii)

Is the eye a true ally of the mind? Or will it not, as soon as heart and
instincts are up in arms asserting themselves against it, fall victim to the

tyranny of the senses from which it after all stems, and desert the mind which places its confidence in it?

For one moment only Geßler has all the appearance of being proved right; it seems that nature will turn out after all to be the master. Tell is already standing with his bow tensed, ready to let loose the bolt, when Stauffacher's anxiety communicates itself to him and he feels giddy. Literally, 'his heart invades his hand and his eye'. Tell 'läßt die Armbrust sinken' and mutters 'Mir schwimmt es vor den Augen'; he bares his breast and offers *his* heart to the Governor. Only the challenging words uttered by his son restore him to himself. And while Rudenz struggles with his 'überschwellend und empörtes Herz',[14] Tell succeeds in dominating his own, and aims his bolt at the child.

The inner event which culminates in this act takes place in complete silence, not a word being spoken.[15] But it is visibly enacted before us in the demeanour of Tell's boy. Of course Walther is a little person in his own right. But within the verbal structure of the play he is also something besides: he is an embodiment of Tell's vital force, of his instinctual nature. In the ability of this child to control himself, the nature of Tell's own inner self-conquest is first made manifest to us. For what is it that the child masters in himself if not the most direct and instinctive expression of his physical being, those aspects of behaviour that are least amenable to voluntary control? He wills himself not to breathe, not to allow an eyelid to flicker. Unmanacled and with eyes wide open is how he wills himself to face his father's arrow.

From this free, deliberate and conscious participation of his son, and from nothing else, we can measure the true significance of Tell's act. Tell does not dominate his inner drives. His drives control themselves. So full has been the permeation of his nature by his spirit that there is no depth in him so remote, so inaccessible, but that it too has been penetrated; no stratum that is not free and participating, or that resists the categorical 'it has to be' dictated by his conscious mind. His whole being endorses his action, as the text makes clear: 'Tell stand mit vorgebognem Leib, als wollt' er dem Pfeil folgen.' After that he falls to the ground, 'kraftlos'.

The natural self in Tell remains true and loyal in its alliance with his mind. So too in reverse. What is therefore perilous for Tell is Stauffacher's ratiocination, his 'foresight'; this threatens his integrity no less than the rebellion of his own inner drives. Stauffacher is reflective – he looks ahead, he calculates, he is articulate; these are characteristics he shares with Rudenz, and Tell's own wife Hedwig. Mind and imagination, in these personages, push their terrain beyond what is real, and reach out into remote regions of the future.[16] Stauffacher 'foresees' with great clarity the potential horrors of a war. Hedwig is perpetually 'seeing' her husband in danger of every kind:

> Ich sehe dich im wilden Eisgebirg,
> Verirrt . . .
> > . . . seh', wie die Gemse dich
> Rückspringend mit sich in den Abgrund reißt . . .
> > (III. i)

and

> Und lebt' ich achtzig Jahr – Ich seh' den Knaben ewig
> Gebunden stehn, den Vater auf ihn zielen,
> Und ewig fliegt der Pfeil mir in das Herz.
> > (IV. ii)

Rudenz 'sees' beyond the encompassing mountains, and lauds his own impulse to penetrate into the infinite beyond as 'weise Vorsicht'. This contemplative character – Schiller calls it 'Besonnenheit' – is a decisive feature in the make-up of Schiller's *tragic* heroes – in a Fiesco, a Posa, a Wallenstein, an Isabella or Demetrius – but is utterly alien to Tell,[17] and for a profound reason. He never, like those others, aspires to the pinnacle of vision from which he can survey the whole realm of existence. Neither are circumspection and caution his style. On the contrary: what is characteristic of him is a quite deliberate constriction and narrowing of the field of vision; and this is something he himself continually refers to. 'Wär' ich besonnen, hieß' ich nicht der Tell . . .', he tells Geßler at the very start of the apple scene; and the act of taking deliberate aim at his son is feasible later for him only because his mind imposes on itself a discipline no less stern than that his instinctive responses impose upon themselves. Here as always Geßler's words, though meant ironically, hit the nail on the head:

> Ei, Tell, du bist ja plötzlich so besonnen! . . .
> Ein andrer wohl bedächte sich – du drückst
> Die Augen zu und greifst es herzhaft an.

Just this is in fact what Tell does.[18] 'Fore-sight' is something he deprives himself of: it is precisely by restricting his vision and narrowing the focus down to the utmost limits that he succeeds, 'herzhaft', in achieving his task. His eye and his heart, his sensual nature and his mind work here in flawless unity, each oriented to the other, each lending support and strength to the other, and each renouncing that self-assertiveness and claim to autonomy which would have done a hurt to the others and to the whole.

Time and again we are shown this conscious limiting by Tell of his mental perspective, and nothing could be further from the truth than to interpret this as a sign of good-natured obtuseness on his part. Time and again some imperious instinct bids him harness his mental resources strictly to the demands of what is real and present, the here and now. He tells Stauffacher, quite early in the play,

> Doch was ihr tut, laßt mich aus eurem Rat,
> Ich kann nicht lange prüfen oder wählen;
> Bedürft ihr meiner zu bestimmter Tat,
> Dann ruft den Tell, es soll an mir nicht fehlen.
>
> (I. iii)

When his wife expresses her forebodings, he counters by saying:

> Wer gar zu viel bedenkt, wird wenig leisten
>
> (III. i)

and when the fisherman is idly inquisitive he rebuffs him, saying:

> Ist es getan, wird's auch zur Rede kommen.
>
> (IV. i)

But nothing is more illuminating than the laconic dismissal he gives to Stauffacher's plea for discussion with him.

> Mir ist das Herz so voll, mit euch zu reden

Stauffacher pleads; to which Tell replies,

> Das schwere Herz wird nicht durch Worte leicht.

But Stauffacher will not leave off:

> Doch könnten Worte uns zu Taten führen

he insists; to which Tell replies with the astounding claim that

> Die einz'ge Tat ist jetzt Geduld und Schweigen.[19]
>
> (I. iii)

Astounding; because it is one thing to present the discipline of silence, say, as a preliminary and necessary preparation for action; but Tell goes well beyond this in asserting that for him such voluntary restriction of the mind is itself a form of action. For him the energizing of reflection by action, of mind by sense and will, is complete; as complete as the interaction between the ordering activity of the mind and the instinctual drives in his sensuous nature.

How can we doubt that what confronts us here is a psychic organism whose individual powers are intimately attuned to each other and supportive of each other? The symbolisms of head and heart, of eye and arm, are enough in themselves to tell us that for Schiller here the human psyche is an ideal unity in the same way as a physical organism is – an ideal unity which in the man Tell has become tangible and real. Any detailed consideration of this figure, moreover, brings out at every point a reciprocal action of the individual functions, and an economy in the whole psychical system, such as is only to be found in a whole which is organically structured. Whatever Tell's mind and spirit lack in breadth is the very source in him of the tension and motivation to action, and all returns again to his spirit as intellectual energy, fed back by the circulation pervading the whole man. Whatever, on the other hand, his sense-drive lacks in intensity is nourishment for his mental powers, and in turn enriches his senses by bringing discrimination and differentiation to them.[20] Can one doubt that what we see embodied before our eyes in Tell's mental structure is that reciprocal action, *Wechselwirkung*, which is the crowning concept in the *Ästhetische Briefe*,[21] that mutual action upon one another of our sense-drive and our form-drive, *Stofftrieb* and *Formtrieb*, of mind and nature, of the sensuous and rational parts of man – a situation in which 'die Wirksamkeit des einen die Wirksamkeit des andern zugleich begründet und begrenzt, und wo jeder einzelne für sich gerade dadurch zu seiner höchsten Verkündigung gelangt, daß der andere tätig ist'? Again, can one doubt that what is before us here is that 'wirkliche Vereinigung und Auswechslung der Materie mit der Form und des Leidens mit der Tätigkeit . . .',[22] which constitutes the essence of the aesthetic state, and which brings home to us the compatibility of our two natures and hence the very possibility of humanity at its most sublime, 'die Möglichkeit der erhabensten Menschheit'?

Passage after passage could be quoted from the *Ästhetische Briefe* to read like a running commentary on the aesthetic structure of Tell's personality. Not that this is to be understood either as idle persistence in an attitude of indifference to matters of real moment, or indeed as a pendulum swing from a dreamlike state of contemplation to determinate action.[23] On the contrary. What is meant by 'aesthetic' is precisely a steady interpenetration of the two dominant drives of the psyche. Through this interpenetration both are at the same time preserved and superseded, and there flowers from their integration a 'Drittes, Neues, Höheres, Unerwartetes',[24] a sensitive aesthetic distance and inner freedom in the form of play, which – Schiller assures us – will carry 'das ganze Gebäude der ästhetischen Kunst und der noch schwierigern Lebenskunst', and which struck him as being even capable of subtly transforming 'den doppelten Ernst der Pflicht und des Schicksals'.[25]

In this decisive sense of the word, Tell is an aesthetic personality; that is, he is the master of his destiny. He is free, and completely so, because in him thought, feeling and action, so far from being at odds with each other, are at one, each being at once the support and the corrective of the others; because in every manifestation of his being his total personality, in a flexible hierarchy of forces, is 'at stake'. Such is the supple wholeness of this person that not even the internal struggle which Geßler set out to provoke in him is capable of causing his disintegration.

This self-sufficiency and equilibrium of his psyche are sufficient to explain Tell's personal decision to stand aside and remain uninvolved in the affairs of the community.[26] Tell is all of a piece; whereas the nation is so only potentially, and in the future. The last words spoken on the Rütli are a true generalization for the nation as a social group.

> Denn Raub begeht am allgemeinen Gut,
> Wer sich selbst hilft in seiner eignen Sache.
>
> (II. ii)

But Tell can set as a counterpoint to this his belief in the self-sufficiency of the individual:

> Ein rechter Schütze hilft sich selbst.
>
> (III. i)

Tell can serve the common cause by serving his own. The very independence of action, which in the case of anyone else would signify a betrayal of the common cause, for him and for him alone is a higher duty. His inner organization is already more complex and specific than that of the nation with its multitude of members. For him to have identified himself wholly with that more primitive and diffuse organism would have meant sacrificing the inner dynamic balance, the completeness of which is the source of his enhanced power and ultimately the guarantor for the act of deliverance itself. He is himself well aware of his anomalous position. Expressly he says:

> Verbunden werden auch die Schwachen mächtig.
> Der Starke ist am mächtigsten allein.

> (I. iii)

This self-regulative economy has itself found a palpable embodiment in the symbol of the crossbow.[27] There is a hint of this as early as the scene with the apple. Rudenz warns Geßler that he ought to withdraw his unnatural demand:

> Herr Landvogt, weiter werdet Ihr's nicht treiben,
> Ihr werdet nicht . . .

> . . . Zu weit getrieben
> Verfehlt die Strenge ihres weisen Zwecks,
> Und allzu straff gespannt zerspringt der Bogen.

> (III. iii)

It is plain to see how the crossbow – the instrument of which Tell possesses the mastery – has become at this point a symbol of his psychic span and power. And, looked at closely, the metaphor confirms all that we have said about his own psychic structure. The feature that makes a bow what it is resides in the fact that the string and the frame – its two component parts – though clearly opposed to each other, derive their elasticity and strength only from this opposition. Individually and separately the string and the frame are nothing. Only through their being firmly held together can that 'Wechselwirkung' be achieved by virtue of which each develops its potential to the highest pitch – through, and only through, the effect of the opposing tension of the other. Schiller's definition of the reciprocal action of the two dominant drives of the human psyche may be lifted straight from its context and be used without modification, to describe the interaction of string and frame: '. . . wo die Wirksamkeit des einen die Wirksamkeit des andern zugleich begründet und begrenzt, und wo jeder einzelne für sich gerade dadurch zu seiner höchsten Verkündigung gelangt, daß der andere tätig ist'.

The symbolic meaning of the crossbow is brought out even more clearly in Tell's monologue beside the sunken lane, when he is premeditating the murder of Geßler. Tell addresses his bowstring in the following words:

> . . . Und du,
> Vertraute Bogensehne, die so oft

Mir treu gedient hat in der Freude Spielen,
Verlaß mich nicht im fürchterlichen Ernst.
Nur jetzt noch halte fest, du treuer Strang,
Der mir so oft den herben Pfeil beflügelt –
Entränn' er jetzo kraftlos meinen Händen,
Ich habe keinen zweiten zu versenden.

(IV. iii)

'Treu', 'halte fest': what else is this if not an earnest invocation addressed
to his own sensible nature to 'hold on' loyally, and stand by the spirit
which now for the second time is about to do it violence? 'Not to desert
him': if his senses and instincts abandoned him in this emergency and
broke away from their alliance, the self-regulative system of forces that
makes him both self-sufficient and invincible would be destroyed, and his
life would flow away from him. Let these impulses, on the contrary, hold
on to their alliance with the mind, because they are 'loyal' to him in the
same way that he is unshakeably loyal to them, ever protecting and
strengthening them. Throughout the entire play, certain words of powerful emotional displacement – words like 'treu', 'vertraut', 'festhalten' –
are used not only to point to external relationships but through and beyond them to the inner reciprocity of relationship which obtains between
the various psychic drives. At this moment of climax for the action, and for
Tell's inner development, this image of the bowstring tensed to its utmost
limit and Tell's moving plea that it hold fast tells of the peril involved for
the hero's whole mental equilibrium in the excess of tension threatening
to destroy it.

Even when Tell's thoughts turn to the outer world, to the past, to his
children, to the act of murder which he will be obliged to justify in their
eyes, his words retain none the less the same quality of inwardness implicit
in the very form of the monologue.[28] His remembering his children is an
act of 'er-innern'; seated anxiously above the sunken lane he is holding a
dialogue with his innermost nature. In demanding from himself what is
absolutely against nature – the act of committing a murder – he is assur-
ing himself of his profound unity with his own nature.[29] He is violating
nature only to protect her. He is committing murder only to save life.[30]
Close to the very act of violence, Tell's mind, inwardly composed and pro-
tective, embraces tortured nature with the same passion with which he
pressed his own son to his bosom after taking deliberate aim at him, the
same fervour with which later on amid the turmoil of the elements he

knelt down to embrace Mother Earth. Only, this time, at the very climax of his struggle, the violence of his suffering is strangely transmuted to pity; his passion has become *com*passion, that mode of feeling which for all its vigour retains a perceptible distance from the suffering self, and thereby makes manifest that it belongs in the aesthetic domain.[31] It was not so much in the promised section of the *Ästhetische Briefe* but here, in the extreme situation in which he placed his tragic figure, Wilhelm Tell, that Schiller demonstrated the possibility of making an aesthetic response to the 'twofold demands of duty and destiny'.

This intimate alliance of the psychic powers is given palpable reality in the final bringing together of mutually hostile estates to form one nation. The bond of friendship forged between Melchthal and Rudenz is the signal for the greater alliance between the nobility and those who cultivate the land, and for the initiation of a new aristocracy: the 'Herr-lichkeit' of a peasant nobility. More than this: Attinghausen's dying words conjure up before the inward eye a vision of a dance in which the castles of the nobility fall, cities arise and flourish, what is ancient and aristocratic declines, what is new and vital powerfully arises. The implicit action of the play draws to a harmonious close with just this rhythmic alternation of forces sinking and rising, with the act of finding, seizing and holding fast of all by all, and with, at the very end, the sacramental words of Attinghausen's, 'Seid einig – einig – einig –'.[32]

It was years since Schiller had given so much of himself to any work. Of this his favourite play he himself said that the best thing in it was Tell's monologue preceding his killing of the tyrant; the emotional appeal of the play, he wrote to Iffland, lay in the situation for which Tell found words in that soliloquy: 'und es wäre garnicht gemacht worden, wenn nicht diese Situation und dieser Empfindungszustand, worin sich Tell in diesem Monolog befindet, dazu bewogen hätten.'[33]

We can see it clearly. The spiritual gesture which becomes speech in that monologue is the gesture of Schiller's last dramatic poem as a whole, and indeed more generally of his last and greatest maturity. It is the gesture of someone restored to health: the tender and noble gesture of acknowledgement and respect paid by the spirit to its first source – to the holiness of nature, to childhood, to innocence: there are many names we can choose to express what Schiller himself, in his gratitude, found many names to express.

It is that selfsame gesture with which, a little later, he bade farewell to life itself.

10

'Die Kinder des Hauses': a model of Schiller's poetic imagination

It is well known what an insuperable aversion Schiller's essay *Über Anmut und Würde* had implanted in Goethe. Even when, full of gratitude, he celebrates the new spring which Schiller's friendship inaugurated in his own life, he prefaces his eulogy by observing that this essay was not one to reconcile him with its author:

> Sein Aufsatz über *Anmut und Würde* war ebensowenig ein Mittel, mich zu versöhnen. Die Kantische Philosophie, welche das Subjekt so hoch erhebt, indem sie es einzuengen scheint, hatte er mit Freuden in sich aufgenommen; sie entwickelte das Außerordentliche, was die Natur in sein Wesen gelegt, und er, im höchsten Gefühl der Freiheit und Selbstbestimmung, war undankbar gegen die große Mutter, die ihn gewiß nicht stiefmütterlich behandelte.[1]

In the essay *Einwirkung der neueren Philosophie*, written three years later, after an intensive study of Kant, he again criticizes his friend and once again his irritation is focused on *Über Anmut und Würde*:

> . . . er predigte das Evangelium der Freiheit, ich wollte die Rechte der Natur nicht verkürzt wissen. Aus freundschaftlicher Neigung gegen mich, vielleicht mehr als aus eigner Überzeugung, behandelte er in den ästhetischen Briefen die gute Mutter nicht mit jenen harten Ausdrücken, die mir den Aufsatz über *Anmut und Würde* so verhaßt gemacht hatten.[2]

And no wonder he harboured resentment. For had not Schiller seemed to attack Goethe's private life with a malice explicable only in terms of a deep-seated unconscious ambivalence? Had he not made fun of the in-accessible man's love relation with Christiane Vulpius and of the birth of an illegitimate son to that union?[3]

But surely Goethe's irritation was caused by something more funda-mental than Schiller's insinuation that, when nature gets the upper hand over mind, creativity may at times regress into the singular business of physical procreation![4] Goethe writes in *Glückliches Ereignis*:

> Anstatt sie selbständig, lebendig vom Tiefsten bis zum Höchsten, gesetzlich hervorbringend zu betrachten, nahm er sie von der Seite einiger empirischen menschlichen Natürlichkeiten. Gewisse harte Stellen sogar konnte ich direkt auf mich deuten, sie zeigten mein Glaubensbekenntnis in einem falschen Lichte; dabei fühlte ich, es sei noch schlimmer, wenn es ohne Beziehung auf mich gesagt worden; denn die ungeheure Kluft zwischen unsern Denkweisen klaffte nur desto entschiedener.[5]

The poet of the 'Künstlergedichte' who had early on sung the indivisible oneness of creation in all its manifestations, the author of the Roman Elegies who had learned, as well as loved, in Italy, the poet-scientist who held fast to the credo 'daß die höchste und einzige Operation der Natur und Kunst die Gestaltung sei'[6] – how could such a one but feel repelled by the prudish sterility of Schiller's opposition between creativity in its physical and in its mental aspects?

However, what would most inescapably bring home to Goethe 'die ungeheure Kluft' gaping between Schiller and himself were those scarcely conscious sallies against the great Mother herself which seem to creep into Schiller's argument to undermine the position he is overtly adopting. How often does 'die gute Mutter' appear condescendingly coupled with tell-tale words such as 'bloß' and 'nur': 'Architektonische Schönheit' is defined as 'diese von der *bloßen** Natur . . . gebildete Schönheit';[7] '. . . wo die *bloße** Natur herrscht,' we read, 'da muß die Menschheit verschwinden';[8] 'Die Temperamentstugend sinkt also im Affekt zum *bloßen** Natur-produkt herab'.[9] How could such formulations but gall one who saw works of art and works of nature as one great continuum and proclaimed of both alike: 'Da ist Gott'?[10] How could a man of Goethe's differentiated sen-suousness do other than shrink from Schiller's melodramatic description of affect and its coarsening influence?[11] What was the creator of Felix and

* My italics.

Friedrich, and of Mignon performing her egg-dance in a trance-like perfection, to make of the twice-repeated absurdity that 'mere' nature unaided by freedom cannot flower into grace? 'Bewegungen, welche keine
andere Quelle als die Sinnlichkeit haben,' Schiller declares, 'gehören bei
aller Willkürlichkeit doch *nur** der Natur an, die für sich allein sich nie
bis zur Anmut erhebet. Könnte sich die Begierde mit Anmut, der Instinkt
mit Grazie äußern, so würden Anmut und Grazie nicht mehr fähig und
würdig sein, der Menschheit zu einem Ausdruck zu dienen.'[12] But, if so,
what about the 'schwarzäugige, schwarzlockige Knabe' of Goethe's *Novelle*
who, 'mit anmutigen Tönen', 'fortsingend und anmutig', accomplishes
effortlessly what all the moral fastidiousness of a Honorio could not
achieve – the pacification of the elemental? The untutored children of
nature, in this story, do not merely represent humanity: they point forward
to possibilities of humanization which gently put to shame the heroic ideal
of the society into which they have strayed.

Or again Goethe might read: 'Grazie ist immer nur die Schönheit der
durch Freiheit bewegten Gestalt, und Bewegungen, die *bloß** der Natur
angehören, können nie diesen Namen *verdienen.'**[13] What was the
author of Philine's incomparably graceful and modest 'Wenn ich dich
liebe, was geht's dich an?' to make of the obstinate wrong-headedness of
this 'verdienen', or indeed of the greater travesty of defining grace as 'ein
persönliches Verdienst'?[14] How could one who sincerely believed in 'inborn merits' but shrug his shoulders at the younger man's elevation of
conscious effort and merit at the cost of nature's unsolicited gifts? In the
course of a comparison between the two great favours bestowed by nature –
beauty and genius – Goethe could read:

> Wie diese, so ist auch jenes ein *bloßes** Naturerzeugnis, und nach
> der verkehrten Denkart der Menschen, die, was nach keiner Vor-
> schrift nachzuahmen und durch kein Verdienst zu erringen ist,
> gerade am höchsten schätzen, wird die Schönheit mehr als der Reiz,
> das Genie mehr als erworbene Kraft des Geistes bewundert. Beide
> Günstlinge der Natur werden bei allen ihren Unarten (wodurch sie
> nicht selten ein Gegenstand verdienter Verachtung sind) als ein
> gewisser Geburtsadel, als eine höhere Kaste betrachtet, weil ihre
> Vorzüge von Naturbedingungen abhängig sind und daher über alle
> Wahl hinaus liegen.[15]

And yet this is only one side of the coin, and Goethe knew it. Resentful

* My italics.

denigration of nature does *not* set the tone of *Über Anmut und Würde* as a whole and even less so in the *Ästhetische Briefe*. The latter are pervaded by the belief, so characteristic of the Age of Enlightenment, in the amenableness of our total human nature – our emotional and instinctual drives no less than our reason – to education; indeed the whole ameliorative venture they propose, the education of man to political freedom through the offices of art,[16] rests on this presupposition. The mature Goethe who had fled to Italy to be reborn into a second nature subscribed from the depths of his heart to Schiller's *dictum*: '. . . die Philosophie selbst, welche uns zuerst von ihr abtrünnig machte, ruft uns laut und dringend in den Schoß der Natur zurück . . .'[17] For was not the course Schiller was here theoretically advocating the very course Goethe himself had intuitively taken?[18] In the earlier essay, too, he no doubt heartily welcomed Schiller's stand against Kant's moral rigorism and the clear signs that the younger man was feeling his way towards a less dualistic and potentially more unitary position. 'Nicht um sie wie eine Last wegzuwerfen,' he could read,

> oder wie eine grobe Hülle von sich abzustreifen, nein, um sie aufs innigste mit seinem höhern Selbst zu vereinbaren, ist seiner reinen Geisternatur eine sinnliche beigesellt. Dadurch schon, daß sie ihn zum vernünftig sinnlichen Wesen, d.i. zum Menschen machte, kündigte ihm die Natur die Verpflichtung an, nicht zu trennen, was sie verbunden hat, auch in den reinsten Äußerungen seines göttlichen Teiles den sinnlichen nicht hinter sich zu lassen und den Triumph des einen nicht auf Unterdrückung des andern zu gründen.[19]

Moreover, did he not owe his conception of a 'schöne Seele', which was to be embodied in the central character of Book VI of *Wilhelm Meisters Lehrjahre*, to the very essay that had so irked him?

If, then, by and large, Schiller pays homage to the great Mother in essays the tone of which, none the less, left Goethe unconvinced, his dramas certainly seem to bear out a more generous interpretation. For throughout them we find the free gifts of nature – youth, beauty and charisma – bestowed on those characters who in the course of the action come to claim our sympathy. Moreover, these qualities – *Talente* and not *Verdienste* as the author of *Über Anmut und Würde* would have insisted – turn out to be part and parcel of the characters' basic human and moral potential. Karl Moor, Don Carlos, Max Piccolomini, Maria Stuart – they all have physical splendour and the fiery feelings of youth on their side and they know how to love and to be loved, qualities some or all of which are offset against those of their more problematic counterparts: for Franz Moor is a latter-day Richard III, Elisabeth's 'schimmerlos Verdienst' is mercilessly outshone by her younger rival's radiance, and they and their likes are strangers to love which is the very element of their opponents' being. What is more, the protagonists' warm impulsiveness is associated with a capacity, altogether lacking in the others, for single-minded devotion. True, their enthusiasm leads them into hasty action, irrevocable entanglement and guilt. But it also leads them unhesitatingly to atone for their errors, and selflessly to identify themselves with a cause they have recognized to be binding; and we cannot separate our recognition of their inborn generosity from the human and moral homage we are forced to pay them in the end. Most important of all, the poet has given his sanction to their specific qualities – gifts freely showered upon her darlings by a maternal nature and totally removed from human effort or choice – by associating them with nobility of rank and indeed with kingship. Carlos is both,

> . . . eines großen Königs Sohn und *mehr*,
> Weit mehr als das, schon in der Fürstenwiege
> Mit *Gaben** ausgestattet, die sogar
> Auch Ihres *Ranges** Sonnenglanz verdunkeln.

(II. viii)

Maria Stuart

> . . . überstrahlte blühend alle Weiber,
> Und durch *Gestalt** nicht minder als *Geburt**. . .

(II. iii)

It is they and not Posa or Elisabeth who are the born and true heirs to the throne. Wallenstein is an upstart whilst of Max Thekla may truly say:

> Was wir geworden sind, ist *er* geboren.

(*Pic.*, III. viii)

It is the gentle and loving Karl who, for all his obvious failings, is the 'geborne' or 'angestammte König' of his native France.

Peripheral figures in the dramatic fragments strengthen such association of physical and moral grace with outward rank. Eduard Plantagenet in *Warbeck* and Romanow in *Demetrius* are obviously envisaged as pure

* My italics.

and lovable characters who are at the same time rightful pretenders to the crown, and by all appearances Britannicus, in *Agrippina*, was to be modelled on the same pattern. In fact we know scarcely more of these characters than these two sets of facts, and their steady concurrence argues some underlying connection. 'Romanow ist eine reine, loyale, edle Gestalt, eine schöne Seele':[20] this marginal note on the rival of Demetrius could, one feels, have served as a model for the hapless pretenders in the other fragments, and indeed it goes a long way towards describing the rightful heirs that figure in the completed dramas, in the final phase of their human development.

This legitimacy of the protagonists' claims is underscored by yet another fact. Their counterparts are without exception usurpers. Franz Moor – '*Herr* muß ich sein, daß ich das mit Gewalt ertrotze, wozu mir die Liebenswürdigkeit gebricht' (I. i) – King Philip, Elisabeth of England and for a short time, if only in thought, Marquis Posa, Wallenstein, Warbeck and Demetrius: they all lay claim to a place which by rights belongs to another; and if we add to this list Fiesco, Präsident von Walther and the ducal family of Messina, we arrive at a pattern of remarkable constancy which, by contrast, serves to strengthen the association between natural princeliness and legitimacy.

Schiller, then, has linked a legitimate and indeed royal status with nature's seal of majesty, a richness and generosity of the characters' emotional, instinctual and even physical being which are independent of choice, effort or indeed merit. And the sacramental dignity of the protagonists' kingship effectively cuts short all arguments as to

> . . . was des Verdienstes Stolz dem Stolze
> Des Glücks entgegensetzen kann . . .
> (*Don Carlos*, II. v)

Thus, paradoxically, Schiller himself in his dramas seems to have joined the ranks of those he so severely scolds in *Über Anmut und Würde*, who '. . . nach der verkehrten Denkart der Menschen, . . . was nach keiner Vorschrift nachzuahmen und durch kein Verdienst zu erringen ist, gerade am höchsten schätzen . . .'[21] He himself sides with those 'Günstlinge der Natur' who, for all their frailty and for all their obvious failings, are looked up to as though they were 'ein gewisser Geburtsadel, . . . eine höhere Kaste . . . , weil ihre Vorzüge von *Naturbedingungen abhängig* und daher *über alle Wahl hinausliegen*' *.[22]

* My italics.

It is in fact precisely this, the recognition of their 'Geburtsadel' – those gifts which a magnanimous nature has showered upon her favourites – which is the stake in the protagonists' fight for their royal title and heritage. And it is in virtue of this inborn aristocracy that we may designate them 'die Kinder des Hauses'.[23]

'Die Kinder des Hauses': at first sight, these words may perhaps not call forth a great wealth of associations. They stem from the dramatic fragment of that name on which Schiller began work immediately after the completion of *Wallenstein*, and which was sporadically to claim his attention until well after he had settled for *Demetrius*. From there, the mind may travel back to Wallenstein's plea to Max not to leave him, a plea which culminates in the words:

> Sie alle waren Fremdlinge, *du* warst
> Das Kind des Hauses – Max! Du kannst mich nicht verlassen!
>
> (*Tod*, III. xviii)

Perhaps, too, we may recall the words Don Carlos addresses to the Duke of Alba when he seeks a private audience with the King, his father:

> Den Vortritt hat das Königreich. Sehr gerne
> Steht Carlos dem Minister nach. Er spricht
> Für Spanien – ich bin der Sohn des Hauses.
>
> (II. i)

What do these words mean? The question obtrudes itself because neither Wallenstein's assurance nor Carlos's assertion can be taken at its face value. Only a few scenes earlier, Wallenstein had scornfully rejected Max's suit of Thekla and in no uncertain terms called it a *mésalliance*. 'Nun ja!' he had conceded,

> Ich lieb' ihn, halt' ihn wert; was aber
> Hat das mit meiner Tochter Hand zu schaffen?
>
> (*Tod*, III. iv)

And, a little later:

> Ließ ich mir's so viel kosten, in die Höh
> Zu kommen, über die gemeinen Häupter
> Der Menschen weg zu ragen, um zuletzt
> Die große Lebensrolle mit gemeiner
> Verwandtschaft zu beschließen? . . .
>
> (ibid.)

And Don Carlos, in his turn, at the end of the preceding act had reminded his newly arrived friend of the heir apparent's humiliating position at the foot of the throne:

> Berede dich, ich wär' ein Waisenkind,
> Das du am Thron mitleidig aufgelesen.
> Ich weiß ja nicht, was Vater heißt – ich bin
> Ein Königssohn . . .

(I. ii)

Thus neither Wallenstein's words nor those of Don Carlos have reference to any palpable external reality. But what the first act preceding Don Carlos's haughty remark *has* made clear, through a variety of situations, is the depth of a passion and the articulacy of emotions he prizes as the most sacred part of his humanity. Is it perhaps this inner legacy he is claiming when he rebuffs the clueless Alba? And Wallenstein? It will not be long before Max lies dead, trampled underfoot by horses, and thus suffers in reality what had been Wallenstein's most dreaded dream.[24] It will not be long before Wallenstein's yearning for Jupiter, the star that shone upon his life, will merge with the recollection of his dead young friend and he will recognize that in Max he has lost a part of himself, perhaps the most precious part. For Max is the child in him – 'denn er stand neben mir wie meine Jugend'; he is the vulnerable feeling-portion which in Wallenstein himself has remained rudimentary and untended, grown to full and noble maturity.

Thus in the case of both dramas we may say that to be 'the child of the house' does not necessarily designate any outward status or relationship. It may be a kind of shorthand acknowledging a basic quality in a person's make-up, such as some innate emotional articulacy; and with this possibility in mind we once again turn to the essay *Über Anmut und Würde*.

Schiller's notorious tendency to philosophize when he would write poetry and to let the imagination speak when he would write philosophy[25] has its compensations. For even in a discursive context he will continue to speak in terms of the images and symbols familiar from his dramatic work, thus giving them a firm intellectual basis. This is especially marked in *Über Anmut und Würde*, and nowhere more so than in that section of the essay with which we are concerned. All those political and social estates, for instance, that in Schiller's dramas furnish the basis of the outer action – the monarchy of Elisabeth's England, the anarchy of Maria Stuart's Scotland or Johanna's France, the rule of terror in the Germany of Karl Moor

– make their appearance in Schiller's moral philosophy, but now with a
microcosmic signification: for here political and social configurations are
candidly used as analogies for the possible relation in which the individual
human psyche can stand to itself. 'Es lassen sich in allem dreierlei Verhältnisse denken, in welchen der Mensch zu sich selbst, d.i. sein sinnlicher
Teil zu seinem vernünftigen, stehen kann,' Schiller postulates and thence
continues:

> Der Mensch unterdrückt entweder die Forderungen seiner sinnlichen
> Natur, um sich den höhern Forderungen seiner vernünftigen
> gemäß zu verhalten; oder er kehrt es um und ordnet den vernünf-
> tigen Teil seines Wesens dem sinnlichen unter . . .; oder die
> Triebe des letztern setzen sich mit den Gesetzen des erstern in
> Harmonie, und der Mensch ist einig mit sich selbst.[26]

A few paragraphs further on, Schiller proceeds to illustrate these inner-
psychological configurations by comparing them with models of relationships drawn from the political and social sphere:

> Das erste dieser Verhältnisse zwischen beiden Naturen im Men-
> schen erinnert an eine Monarchie, wo die strenge Aufsicht des
> Herrschers jede freie Regung im Zaum hält; das zweite an eine
> wilde Ochlokratie, wo der Bürger durch Aufkündigung des Gehor-
> sams gegen den rechtmäßigen Oberherrn so wenig frei, als die
> menschliche Bildung durch Unterdrückung der moralischen
> Selbsttätigkeit schön wird, vielmehr nur dem brutaleren Despo-
> tismus der untersten Klassen, wie hier die Form der Masse, an-
> heimfällt. So wie die Freiheit zwischen dem gesetzlichen Druck und
> der Anarchie mitten inne liegt, so werden wir jetzt auch die
> Schönheit zwischen der *Würde*, als dem Ausdruck des herrschenden
> Geistes, und der *Wollust*, als dem Ausdruck des herrschenden
> Triebes, in der Mitte finden.[27]

It is into this microcosmic context that Schiller places his tribute to the
moral rigorism of Kant and his apology for the sensible side of our nature:

> Er ward der Drako seiner Zeit, weil sie ihm eines Solons noch nicht
> wert und empfänglich schien. Aus dem Sanktuarium der reinen
> Vernunft brachte er das fremde und doch wieder so bekannte
> Moralgesetz, stellte es in seiner ganzen Heiligkeit aus vor dem
> entwürdigten Jahrhundert und fragte wenig darnach, ob es Augen
> gibt, die seinen Glanz nicht vertragen.[28]

But after the tribute, the burning question: 'Womit aber hatten es die Kinder des Hauses verschuldet, daß er nur für die Knechte sorgte?'[29] As earlier the inner-psychological concept had been explicated in terms of political structures, so here in reverse: the social imagery of children and heirs versus servants is used as an analogue of psychic functions: 'Weil oft sehr unreine Neigungen den Namen der Tugend usurpieren, mußte darum auch der uneigennützige Affekt in der edelsten Brust verdächtig gemacht werden?'[30] Impure inclinations, we see, are associated with serfdom and usurpation; on the other hand, the pure and unselfish affect is associated with the status of the child and heir, and with aristocracy of nature.[31]

This association, familiar to us from the dramas, remains constant. Psychic patterns are once again elucidated in terms of social status:

> Weil der moralische Weichling dem Gesetz der Vernunft gern eine Laxität geben möchte, die es zum Spielwerk seiner Konvenienz macht, mußte ihm darum eine Rigidität beigelegt werden, die die kraftvollste Äußerung moralischer Freiheit nur in *eine rühmlichere Art von Knechtschaft** verwandelt? Denn hat wohl der wahrhaft sittliche Mensch eine freiere Wahl zwischen Selbstachtung und Selbstverwerfung als der Sinnen*sklave** zwischen Vergnügen und Schmerz? Ist dort etwa weniger Zwang für den reinen Willen als hier für den verdorbenen?[32]

And now, stroke upon stroke, he penetrates into the abstract heart of the problem.

> Mußte schon durch die imperative Form des Moralgesetzes die Menschheit angeklagt und erniedrigt werden und das erhabenste Dokument ihrer Größe zugleich die Urkunde ihrer Gebrechlichkeit sein? War es wohl bei dieser imperativen Form zu vermeiden, daß eine Vorschrift, die sich der Mensch als Vernunftwesen selbst gibt, die deswegen allein für ihn bindend und dadurch allein mit seinem Freiheitsgefühle verträglich ist, nicht den Schein eines fremden und positiven Gesetzes annahm – einen Schein, der durch seinen radikalen Hang, demselben entgegen zu handeln (wie man ihm schuld gibt), schwerlich vermindert werden dürfte![33]

The immense pathos of this passage is in part explained by the footnote

* My italics.

appended to it. For here Schiller alludes to the fact that Kant, in his latest essay, proclaims man's radical disposition towards evil. And indeed, the religious resonances of Schiller's own position become audible as soon as we remember the derivation of the terms with which he operates. The juxtaposition of *Kinder* and *Knechte* occurs in the central portion of St Paul's *Epistle to the Romans*: 'Denn welche der Geist Gottes treibt, die sind Gottes Kinder,' St Paul writes in Chapter 8:

> Denn ihr habt nicht einen knechtischen Geist empfangen, daß ihr euch abermals fürchten müßtet; sondern ihr habt einen kindlichen Geist empfangen, durch welchen wir rufen: Abba, lieber Vater! Derselbe Geist gibt Zeugnis unserm Geist, daß wir Gottes Kinder sind. Sind wir denn Kinder, so sind wir auch Erben, nämlich Gottes Erben und Miterben Christi, so wir anders mit leiden, auf daß wir auch mit zur Herrlichkeit erhoben werden.[34]

What an intrepid transposition into a new key! Schiller, it will be seen, has retained the nomenclature of St Paul's argument, but has invested it with a new, inner-psychological meaning which is incompatible with the meaning the same terms carry for St Paul. For St Paul, as many are the children of God as are led by the spirit of God, that is to say, as are not in the flesh. 'Because the carnal mind *is* enmity against God: for it is not subject to the law of God, neither indeed can be. So then they that are in the flesh cannot please God.'[35] For Schiller, on the other hand, the 'flesh' is redeemable: it is precisely those animated by the 'uneigennützige Affekt in der edelsten Brust' who are freed from the spirit of bondage, and are the children and true heirs of the house. For St Paul, grace is the redemption of the spirit *from* nature. For Schiller, grace – natural and moral – is the redemption *of* nature, and the regeneration of the whole person *through* nature. St Paul unconditionally opposes to each other grace (in his sense of the term) and works – in Luther's rendering *Verdienste*. Schiller retains this opposition but shifts the discussion on to an altogether new plane. For St Paul, it is the inscrutable will of God which decrees 'I will have mercy on whom I will have mercy, and I will have compassion on whom I will have compassion. So then *it is* not of him that willeth, nor of him that runneth, but of God that sheweth mercy.'[36] For Schiller, it is the inscrutable will of nature which predestines no less inexplicably who shall be in bondage and who shall be the true child of the house, that is to say, who shall be blessed with a nature capable of flowering into grace, independently of works or merit. The flesh is heir to the

spirit; and it is with all the religious fervour of St Paul that Schiller postulates his own radically opposed tenet – the oneness of human nature and
the innate sanctity of our sensible self. 'Wäre die sinnliche Natur im
Sittlichen immer nur die unterdrückte und nie die mitwirkende Partei,'
he urges, 'wie könnte sie das ganze Feuer ihrer Gefühle zu einem Triumph
hergeben, der über sie selbst gefeiert wird?'[37] It is those who, because of
the generosity of their very instincts, willingly rally to the cause of the
spirit that are the chosen ones; and the outward sign of their redemption
through nature is their physical grace on the one hand and, on the other,
the divine grace which visibly rests upon their anointed heads.[38]

Thus, the essay which for Goethe had smacked of ingratitude towards
the great Mother, does also, by the boldest reversal of a crucial Pauline
argument, hail the redemptive power of nature and pay homage to 'the
children of the house', those in whom her heritage runs strong. They are
justified, not by their works, but by the effortless grace of their being.
They alone can become *schöne Seelen*.

What a stupendous ambivalence! Elevating man's natural side after
bitterly chastising it, speaking of the good Mother with suspicion and contempt, as though she were some sort of monster whose gifts could never
be trusted, and then again extravagantly praising her and ascribing to her
the power of regenerating our humanity! This ambivalence which Goethe
had so unerringly spotted pervades Schiller's work from *Die Räuber* onward to *Demetrius*;[39] and we may gain a better understanding both of his
dramas and of the basic problem from which they are fed, by pursuing the
motif of 'the children of the house' a little further.

I have shown elsewhere to what extent Schiller, throughout his
dramatic work, employs the poetic device of externalization.[40] That is to
say, he embodies the undeveloped side of one character in the separate
being of another, in such a fashion that the outward relationship between
the two characters reflects the relation in which each of them stands to the
repressed drives within his own psyche. For example, Wallenstein's initial
rejection and retrospective acceptance of Max, on which we touched
earlier, reflects the initial repression and ultimate recognition of his own
feeling-side of which Max has been the embodiment. Similarly, Maria
Stuart's dominant character, as we saw in an earlier chapter, is furnished
by those instinctual drives which lie hidden in the unconscious recesses of
her rival's being. I shall assume then that Schiller does make extensive
and systematic use of this technique of externalizing internal configurations through interpersonal relationships, and shall merely add, by way

of corroborating evidence, that we have seen Schiller employ precisely this technique in *Über Anmut und Würde*.[41]

It is then an inner-psychological signification we must bear in mind when we speak of 'die Kinder des Hauses'. They are the outward embodiments of the 'uneigennützige Affekt in der edelsten Brust', and by extension those who, trusting nature's heritage, feel at one with themselves and 'at home' in their own skin. True, the image does not expressly occur in every one of Schiller's dramas; but nevertheless, what a potent motif it is! Do not the words sum up all the anguish of fiery natures at having incurred exile through their own excess, and their longing to be re-established and recognized as worthy, by others and in their own conscience? Whether one thinks of Karl Moor, Maria Stuart, Johanna, Don Cesar or Melchthal, the basic structure of the experience with which they are confronted remains unchanged. 'Die ganze Welt *eine* Familie und ein Vater dort oben! *Mein* Vater nicht! – Ich allein der Verstoßene . . . mir nicht der süße Name Kind':[42] these words of Karl Moor could equally well be spoken by any of the others; for they give expression to the poignant need to be sanctioned – not merely or even mainly by others, but by themselves and in their own judgement – which is their common share.

But however passionate the need for self-recognition and self-acceptance, the act of recognizing the true self and of accepting it is not an easy one. For, strange to say, in Schiller's tragedies 'the children of the house' are always, and as it were by definition, exiled. Thus the motif becomes basically tragic. In greater or smaller measure, all doubt their own intrinsic worth. Some, such as Johanna and Warbeck, doubt their station. Others, such as Beatrice or the principal characters of *Die Kinder des Hauses*, are totally unaware of their origins and unknown to themselves. By thus uprooting and alienating 'the children of the house', both mentally and physically, the poet complicates their relation to themselves and that of others to them. They no longer appear what they are, and thus they stand at one remove from themselves. Their true self is disguised by the role, forced upon them by circumstances, of outcast or beggar or exile or orphan; and for themselves as much as for others it is difficult to be sure of what lies behind their mask. In short, by the fiction of outer or inner exile, the poet has created a series of progressively more complicated situations designed to disrupt his characters' naïve and unquestioning acceptance of themselves.

It is significant that Schiller first gave the motif of 'the children of the house' its decisive twist in the fragment entitled *Die Kinder des Hauses* which claimed his attention immediately after completion of *Wallenstein* and only lost its hold on him in the final stages of his work on *Demetrius*. In this fragment the basic problem, which has been implicit in the motif from Schiller's first use of it in *Die Räuber*, makes its appearance: the problem of hidden identity. Saintfoix and Adelaide are the children and heirs of Pierre Narbonne, but nobody, including themselves, knows of this fact. For after poisoning his brother Pierre, Louis Narbonne had instigated the murder of his brother's children, too, but unknown to him they were saved. Adelaide lives with a gipsy woman whom she fears and whom she suspects of being her mother, whilst Saintfoix returns to his uncle's house where he is kept as a poor relation. 'Er hält sich für den Sohn schlechter Eltern.'[43] On the one hand he has the natural *grandezza* we have come to associate with 'die Kinder des Hauses'. Schiller notes:

> Er zeigte ein trefflich Naturell des Kopfs und Herzens, zugleich aber auch einen gewissen Adel und Stolz, der ihm wie angeboren ließ und dem armen aufgegriffenen Waisen, der von Wohltaten lebte, nicht recht zuzukommen schien. Er war voll dankbarer Ehrfurcht gegen seinen Wohltäter, aber sonst zeigte er nichts Gedrücktes noch Erniedrigtes, er schien, indem er Narbonnes Wohltaten empfing, sich nur seines Rechtes zu bedienen.[44]

On the other hand, he is not sure of himself and his worth: 'Dabei hat er etwas Geheimnisvolles, Unsicheres, Scheues, Gewaltsames, was aussieht wie Gewissensangst. Besonders scheint er sich eines großen Undanks gegen Narbonne anzuklagen.'[45]

This initial ignorance of their identity on the part of the 'children of the house' is a motif which, in his later years, Schiller took up time and time again. 'Das Götterkind der heiligen Natur' (III. i), the Johanna of the Prologue, is shown to us in a state of primordial innocence, 'wie eine niedre Magd', ignorant as yet of her calling and herself. 'Sich selber ein Geheimnis wuchs sie auf', Don Manuel says of Beatrice (I. vii); and this lack of conscious identity is stressed twice again, by the central character herself who praises an exile which led Don Manuel to find her and vows 'Ein ewig Rätsel bleiben will ich mir' (II. i), and by Don Cesar who, mistaking Beatrice's terror at his appearance for modesty, comments: 'Denn ein Verborgenes ist sich das Schöne' (II. ii). In a prose draft of Margareta's account of Warbeck's past, the poet writes: 'Er verrichtete niedere Dienste am Hofe des englischen Königs, wo er hätte herrschen sollen, er war unter den Jagdbedienten des Königs, fern von dem Gedanken, daß er im Hause

seiner Väter sei.'[46] And if her testimony is not trustworthy, we have
Adelaide's account of the pretender's past state of idyllic ignorance; and
this, being born of love, is presumably closer to the truth:

> Dir selbst verborgen, gingst du durch die Welt,
> Mit harmlos glücklicher Unwissenheit
> Dich in dem . . . Menschenstrom verlierend.
>
> (I. vi)

Finally, Richard himself who – so the poet tells us – momentarily believes
in everything he says and does,[47] 'erinnert sich mit Rührung an seine
vorige Unbekanntheit mit sich selbst und vergleicht jenen sorglosen
Zustand mit seiner jetzigen Lage.'[48] Even more emphatically, Demetrius
stresses his initial ignorance of his identity:

> Kein Jahr ist's noch, daß ich mich selbst gefunden,
> Denn bis dahin lebt' ich mir selbst verborgen,
> Nicht ahnend meine fürstliche Geburt.
>
> (I)

And, a little further on in the same account:

> Ich kannt' mich nicht. Im Haus des Palatins
> Und unter seiner Dienerschar verloren
> Lebt' ich der Jugend fröhlich dunkle Zeit.
> Mir selbst noch fremd . . .
>
> (I)

Indeed, the original first act, in its entirety, is designed to enact before the
reader the dawning of self-recognition on the part of the young Russian
who has come to the Woiwod's court, 'namenlos'.

But this awakening of consciousness does not in any deeper sense dispel
the sense of obscurity that beset the character before: on the contrary, it
inaugurates a state of even greater confusion and complexity. Johanna's
sense of mission, kindled by her country's agony, soon gives way to a profound sense of unreality (especially in IV. ix)[49] and to doubts as to whether
she is worthy to serve the cause with which she has identified herself.
Beatrice's own lack of a sense of identity is plain enough.[50] It is underscored by the different identities ascribed to her by the other characters
throughout a drama which – this is surely significant – takes its title from
a strictly nonexistent person. Adelaide well sums up the state of deepened
perplexity which ensues from Warbeck's self-recognition when she says:

> Du hattest keinen Namen, doch dein Herz war dein . . .
> Du fandest dich und hast dich selbst verloren!
>
> (I. vi)

It is indeed in this fragment and in *Demetrius* that the poet has most deeply delved into the crisis of identity which follows upon the awakening of consciousness; and to them we must now turn.

Both Warbeck and Demetrius are pretenders to the throne, but the claims of neither are beyond dispute. Warbeck is recognized neither by the Lancasters in England nor by Stanley, England's ambassador at the court of Margareta, Duchess of Burgundy. More importantly, he himself is painfully conscious of being a fraud; and, indeed, the poet, in his prose drafts, freely refers to him as such. Against this, Demetrius believes in his royal birth; and by the strength of this belief he sweeps along all except Sapieha and, significantly, Marina, the woman who rules him emotionally. But in both cases, that of the apparent fraud as well as that of the seemingly sincere pretender, the poet pursues the problem of the characters' real identity to a point where it is recognized as independent of their own conscious conviction. Time and again he asks: is he a born prince and heir to the throne? And time and again he formulates this question in terms of another one: is his inborn nature princely? What are the credentials which nature herself has given to these two pretenders in their quest for legitimacy and crown? For, as Hereford has it in *Warbeck*:

> Der Majestät geheiligtes Gepräge
> Erlügt sich nicht . . .
>
> (I. i)

The answer seems to be in the pretenders' favour. Both Warbeck and Demetrius are noble, good-looking youths, the evident darlings of nature. Both, moreover, bear a striking physical resemblance to the royal families to which they claim to belong. Warbeck has the face and voice of King Edward IV, and Demetrius's right arm is shortened, like that of the Tsarovich. 'Es müßte ganz so aussehen, daß der Betrug ihm nur den Platz angewiesen, zu dem die Natur ihn bestimmt hatte,' Schiller writes to Goethe about Warbeck;[51] and of Demetrius Marina says, in the original first act:

> Doch wahrlich, ist er edel nicht geboren,
> So war's ein großer Mißgriff der Natur,
> Die ihm das große Herz . . . [52]

Evidently Schiller envisaged portraying the two pretenders as seemingly graceful figures capable of rising to greatness in marginal human situations. 'Er [Warbeck] muß wirklich das Entzücken aller Zuschauer sein, wenn er kommt', Schiller jots down: '. . . seine Popularität macht ihn liebenswürdig, sein Schicksal spricht zu allen Herzen, indem sein Anstand, seine hohe Graziosität Ehrfurcht gebietet. Ein gewisser Zauber ist in seinem Betragen, der ihn unwiderstehlich macht.'[53] Similarly, the poet intended to introduce Demetrius 'in einem unschuldigen, schönen Zustand, als den liebenswürdigsten und herrlichsten Jüngling, der die Gnade Gottes hat und der Menschen.'[54]

But is this natural state of grace genuine or faked? Or, to ask the same question in the terms used in *Über Anmut und Würde*: are Warbeck and Demetrius 'children of the house'? And indeed, in both these dramas, the poet has answered this question in exactly these terms; but the answer he gives is ambiguous. Warbeck and Demetrius, he tells us, are *like* the children of the house: 'Er ist *wie** der wiedergefundene Sohn des Hauses, der verloren war', Schiller writes of Warbeck;[55] whilst of Demetrius he says 'Der Woiwod behandelt ihn *wie** ein Kind des Hauses',[56] and, at a later point, 'Er ist ein Gott der Gnade für alle, kommt *wie** das Kind des Hauses'.[57]

'Wie das Kind des Hauses': the poet's answer allows equally for the possibility that the pretenders' excellence of nature is true or that it is faked. How is this question resolved in the two dramas? As we have already seen, Warbeck himself is conscious of being a fraud. Yet he must appear 'als zu seiner Rolle geboren', as Schiller stipulates in a letter to Goethe.[58] Similarly, amongst the poet's drafts, we find the following note: 'Solang er den Richard vorstellt, *ist* er Richard; er ist es auch gewissermaßen für sich selbst . . . Es ist notwendig, daß alles, was er in dem Stück als Richard tut, augenblicklich wahr sei, daß er sich des Betruges nicht mehr bewußt sei . . .'[59] His consciousness of playing a part becomes blurred and shades off into 'eine gewisse poetische Dunkelheit, die er über sich selbst und seine Rolle hat . . .'[60] Disguise and art unaccountably merge in a second nature. But this is only possible because he is in fact all along playing as a role what he is in reality. And indeed, at the end Warbeck's royal origin is revealed: he is a natural son of Edward IV, and the instinctive knowledge of this has in fact determined his character and bearing from the start: 'Ein Hauptmotif im Stück ist Warbecks wirkliche Abstammung von den Yorks, welche *dunkel mächtig** in ihm wirkt . . .'[61] 'Sein

* My italics.

deutliches Bewußtsein verdammt ihn, ein dunkles Gefühl rechtfertigt ihn. Er antizipiert nur seine wahre Person . . . Das Yorkische Blut hat in ihm gehandelt.'[62] 'Immer muß der geborene Fürst, der Yorkische Abkömmling unter dem Betrüger und Adventurier versteckt liegen und durchschauen.'[63] Thus, Warbeck's protestations are the strangest web of conscious falsehood and unconscious truth. On meeting Hereford, he exclaims, in an older version:

> Ja ich bin euer – ich erkenne mich
> Als einen York, und *mächtig** in der Brust
> Fühl' ich . . .[64]

In a prose-draft, he says: 'Nichts kann die *mächtige* Stimme des Bluts in mir unterdrücken – Es ist ein *mächtig** heilig Band, das mich an euch gewaltig bindend zieht – Ihr seid mein.'[65] And thus, too, Margareta's deliberate fiction of the pretender's past turns out to be substantially true, down to the instinctive knowledge she ascribes to him of his high origin and down to the words she chooses to describe the force of such unconscious promptings:

> – – – Doch das York'sche Heldenblut,
> Das in den Adern dunkel *mächtig** floß,
> Durchbrach die engen Schranken seines Glücks . . .
> (I. iii)

It will be seen that the problem which the poet has articulated in terms of Warbeck's wavering political pretension is a problem of consciousness and, ultimately, one of identity. For from the moment he assumes his role to the moment he finds that he play-acted reality, he is in a state of total perplexity. What is his true self? The person he dimly senses himself to be, the role he has assumed or the second nature which this role has become to him? What is the relation of this second nature to his inborn nature and of both to his role? What is he in truth, apart from what his aspirations have made of him? Is he a true 'Kind des Hauses'? And how can he tell since always, behind the mask he has assumed, his true self must 'versteckt liegen' as well as 'durchschauen'? These are the real problems that lurk behind the question of his political legitimacy. Warbeck is much too radically alienated from his original self to put his trust in it. An exile from himself, he relies, not on the grace of his *Geburtsadel*, but on works. Expressly he says: 'Ich habe . . . ein Geburtsrecht an England, aber ich

* My italics.

will es als ein Soldat geltend machen, ich will es meinem Arm und eurer
Treue zu danken haben.'[66] This, together with the relief he experiences
at the discovery of his royal birth, is the measure of the crisis through which
he has passed.

> Nichts gleichet der Empfindung Warbecks, wenn er sich als einen
> gebornen York erkennt und die unerträgliche Last der lang' getra-
> genen Lüge nun auf einmal von sich werfen kann. An dem heftigen
> Grade seiner Freude erkennt man erst, wie unerträglich ihm der
> Betrug bisher gewesen sein mußte. . . . Er eilt zu den Engländern,
> die er herbeiruft und in freudiger Verwirrung entdeckt, daß er nicht
> Richard sei und dennoch ein York sei.[67]

But then, what is this deception and this lie? Is it anything outside the
condition of consciousness itself? A consciousness which has disrupted
Warbeck's original innocence and not yet flowered into a second innocence?
Consciousness, in this play, is conceived as an unaccountable and tormenting alienation from our instinctual self, as an exile from preconscious
grace which may miraculously be transcended by a grace which lies at the
other end of knowingness.[68] In the end Warbeck achieves what is a truly
formidable goal. He accomplishes a second spontaneity, a final transcendence of 'art' by a new nature.[69] This is the goal that Schiller himself had
long ago envisaged as his own ultimate salvation. At the beginning of his
work on *Wallenstein*, after a long and rigorous philosophical discipline, he
had written:

> Die Kritik muß mir jetzt selbst den Schaden ersetzen, den sie mir
> zugefügt hat. Und geschadet hat sie mir in der Tat, denn die Kühn-
> heit, die lebendige Glut, die ich hatte, eh mir noch eine Regel bekannt
> war, vermisse ich schon seit mehreren Jahren. Ich sehe mich jetzt
> erschaffen und bilden: ich beobachte das Spiel der Begeisterung, und
> meine Einbildungskraft betrgt siäch mit minder Freiheit, seitdem sie
> sich nicht mehr ohne Zeugen weiß. Bin ich aber erst so weit, daß
> mir Kunstmäßigkeit zur Natur wird, . . . so erhält auch die Phan-
> tasie ihre vorige Freiheit zurück . . .[70]

In returning to his origin, Warbeck achieves that conscious unconscious-
ness which the Schiller of the *Ästhetische Briefe* deems the ultimate goal
of a philosophy grown mature; that breathtaking feat of a willed naïvety
which the poet hails in the distich *Das Höchste*:

Suchst du das Höchste, das Größte? Die Pflanze kann es dich lehren.
Was sie willenlos ist, sei du es wollend – das ist's![71]

Warbeck is redeemed from the torment of consciousness in that he
wills what he already is. In his end lies his beginning. After all, the great
Mother has endowed him with what is good, a princely nature which is
unmistakably attested by 'der Majestät geheiligtes Gepräge'.[72]

In *Demetrius* for the sake of which he finally shelved *Die Kinder des
Hauses* and *Warbeck*, the poet has taken this crisis of consciousness yet
one step further. Contrary to the English pretender, Demetrius believes
his claim to royal rank to be legitimate. In fact he is under an illusion. He
is an unwitting impostor. He learns that he was the companion of the
true Tsarovich who was murdered at the behest of Boris Godunow. And
again we ask: does the illegitimacy of Demetrius's political claim reflect a
flaw in his nature? Is he a true 'Kind des Hauses' or does the twice-repeated
'*wie* das Kind des Hauses' suggest that, from the outset, he is a moral
fraud?

It is customary to argue that Demetrius's character undergoes a radical
change the moment he discovers the secret of his birth and murders the
man who has told him the truth.[73] This theory seems plausible enough,
and it is supported by the fact that the murderous act sets in motion a
train of reactions which are at variance with his previous behaviour. None
the less, there are a number of signs that the perepeteia serves to reveal
the character Demetrius has, rather than to inaugurate a new one. In the
first place, we have seen the steady association, in the characters from
Schiller's pen, between a rich natural heritage and the potential for love.
In Demetrius, this pattern is disturbed; Demetrius pledges himself to
Marina who is expressly stated to be an embodiment of ambition and who,
moreover, does not love him. Nor indeed does Demetrius love her. Schiller's
marginal notes tell us so: 'Nicht sowohl Liebe, als Ehrgeiz'[74] he writes,
and 'Seine Neigung ist eine Kühnheit'.[75] But even without such explicit
statements we would know it from the way in which Schiller formulates
the hero's response to her: 'er erhebt die Augen zur Tochter seines Herrn',
the poet writes; and these words recur time and again.[76] Now Schiller
took a very literal view of 'Neigung'. Ever since his beginnings his imagination was geared to the model of love he was finally to formulate in *Über
Anmut und Würde*, where he distinguishes between love and respect,
saying: 'Liebe ist ein Herabsteigen, da die Achtung ein Hinaufklimmen
ist.'[77] Demetrius lifts up his eyes to his master's daughter; and in this

detail we at once recognize the gesture of aspiration, not of love. Furthermore he declines the pure love of the humble Polish girl, Lodoiska; and when he does love it is Axinia, bride-to-be of the true heir. Thus his love, like that of Franz Moor, of King Philip, of the old Duke of Messina and Narbonne, is defined as an unnatural act of usurpation.

In the second place, Demetrius is devoid of those filial feelings which are by definition associated with the true child, and heir, of the house. He lacks them towards Russia, towards his mother and towards nature. In Schiller's notes for the original first act we read: 'Alles, was nach Knechtschaft schmeckt, ist ihm ganz unerträglich . . .'[78] A sketch for the scene at Tula, immediately preceding his entry into Moscow, makes the same point: 'Demetrius verschmäht das knechtische Bezeugen der Russen und spricht davon, daß er es abschaffen werde. In diesem schönen Zug', the poet adds significantly, 'liegt der Keim eines unglücklichen Betragens.'[79] It is this moral pride which prompts his impatient desire to make a sweeping reform of Russian customs.[80] Already in the first act King Sigismundus has pleaded that Russia is not yet ready for freedom:

> Dort herrscht des *Vaters* heilige Gewalt,
> Der Sklave dient mit leidendem Gehorsam,
> Der Herr gebietet ohne Rechenschaft.

He has solemnly reminded Demetrius of his first filial duty:

> Drum zeiget Euch als Moskaus wahrer Sohn,
> Indem Ihr Achtung tragt vor seinen Sitten.

But Demetrius declares:

> Die schöne Freiheit, die ich – – –
> Will ich verpflanzen – – –
> Ich will aus Sklaven – – Menschen machen,
> Ich will nicht herrschen über Sklavenseelen.

He spurns the king's reminder:

> Tut's nicht zu rasch und lernt der Zeit gehorchen.

By this 'Voreilende in seiner Natur' – these are the words in which, many years later, Goethe was to describe Schiller himself[81] – by this ineradicable moral impatience Demetrius jumps the primitive stage of the development of the people whose son he is. Indeed, he jumps the more primitive strata of his own nature. For do we not know from *Über Anmut und Würde* that the social images of *Knechte* and *Sklaven* signify an internal reality, namely the presence of 'unreine Neigungen' in his breast? In dissociating himself from the political and social organization of his native land, Demetrius is dissociating himself from what he deems uncivilized in his own nature.

But he not only rejects his own primitive instincts. He declares war on nature herself; and this is poignantly brought home in his encounter with his mother, Marfa. Marfa has accepted the fact of Demetrius's reappearance; at first in the belief that he is in truth her son –

> Der wahre Zar, der rechte Erbe kommt . . .
>
> (II. i)

– then in the readiness to accept him in her son's stead:

> Doch wär' er auch nicht meines Herzens Sohn,
> Er soll der Sohn doch meiner Rache sein . . .
>
> (II. i)

She wills him to be her son:

> Es ist mein Sohn, ich will daran nicht zweifeln. . . .
> Er ist mein Sohn, ich glaub an ihn, ich will's.
>
> (II. i)

But when eventually she encounters him in the flesh, a strange man surrounded by warlike pomp, all her conscious intentions come to nought: 'Der kleine Rest der Hoffnung in Marfas Herzen schwindet ganz beim Anblick des Demetrius. Ein Unbekanntes tritt zwischen beide, die Natur spricht nicht, sie sind ewig geschieden.'[82]

Marfa's deference to the verdict of instinct and nature is the foil against which, with great deliberation, Schiller has set the response of Demetrius. When he realizes that the voice of nature is silent and that his mother does not recognize her son in him, he appears to bow to this judgement. 'Die Stimme der Natur ist heilig und frei,' he says as Marfa continues to be silent; 'ich will sie weder zwingen noch erlügen.'[83] And: 'Ich hasse die Gaukelei, ich mag nicht mit den heiligen Gefühlen der Natur spielen und Gaukelwerk treiben.'[84] But presently he begins to plead with her in a very different vein: 'Laß deines Willens freie Handlung sein, was die Natur, das Blut dir versagt. Ich fordre keine Heuchelei, keine Lüge von dir, ich fordre wahre Gefühle. *Scheine du nicht meine Mutter, sei es* . . .'[85] What else is this if not the most stupendous violation by his will of what no human will can influence or force? We may note that Demetrius's

response here is the exact obverse of the one Warbeck evinces in a similar
situation. 'Sie lasse mir das Herz groß werden,' Warbeck muses in an
imaginary conversation with Margareta, 'so werde ich *scheinen*, weil
ich *bin*.'[86] Warbeck does not pervert the promptings of feeling and instinct
as does Demetrius. They are true enough; but he dare not trust them
because the Duchess does not sanction them. 'Sie . . . behandelt ihn
immer nur als einen Imposteur, sie nimmt ihm alle Kräfte zu seiner Rolle,
weil sie ihn erniedrigt.'[87] As against this, Demetrius treats feeling and
instinct as of no consequence and in their stead imposes the dictates of the
conscious will.

> Die schöne Freiheit, die ich – – –
> *Will* ich verpflanzen – – –
> Ich *will* aus Sklaven – – Menschen machen,
> Ich *will* nicht herrschen über Sklavenseelen . . .

Demetrius had cried before the Polish Diet. The meaning of this aspiration
has now become apparent. Demetrius has not only declared war on what
is barbaric in his people's nature or in his own: he has declared nature
herself null and void and has implanted in her soil the foreign and arbitrary
yoke of the will. The engaging utterance of the young pretender who
claimed moral grace before he had a title to do so leads straight to the
desperate words of the disillusioned fraud: 'In einer Lüge bin ich befangen,
zerfallen bin ich mit mir selbst! Ich bin ein Feind der Menschen, ich und
die Wahrheit sind geschieden auf ewig!'[88]

In the figure of Demetrius, the idealist crisis of consciousness and
identity, which Schiller articulated in ever more radical forms, has become
absolute. If Demetrius believes in himself, it is because his conscious will
has altogether usurped the unconscious life of feeling and instinct. He
mistakes his aspiration for the promptings of a nature he has effectively
silenced. Nature cannot speak within him any more than the voice of
nature can tell his mother that he is her son. For nature in him is
extinct and his 'belief' in himself is, and from the beginning has been,
the most gigantic and tragic fraud.[89] Warbeck's second nature is real in
that it is rooted in his instinctual self. Demetrius's second nature is a
fiction in an existential void. With him, the advent of consciousness does
not signify the transition from grace to grace. It is the final fall from innocence, the final falsification of any inner reality he might once have had.
Where is his true self, the bedrock of his being which is incontrovertibly
real, and good if only because it is his? Where is the authentic voice of

feeling and impulse? There is no answer from his ravaged depths. All that remains are hollow will and twisted aspiration and what they have made of him. As Schiller himself has it, in the poem *Der Genius*:

> . . . Vermessene Willkür
> Hat der getreuen Natur göttlichen Frieden gestört.
> Das entweihte Gefühl ist nicht mehr Stimme der Götter,
> Und das Orakel verstummt in der entadelten Brust.

As Demetrius has denied nature so nature has denied herself to him. He is not Russia's rightful king any more than he is 'das Kind des Hauses'.

And his creator, Schiller himself? Surely Goethe was right in spotting his friend's deep ambivalence toward the great Mother. On the one hand, there was the need to sanction what nature had given him and to find it worthy, if only (one sometimes suspects) so as not to fall foul of an ideal of totality which claimed his intellectual and moral allegiance. On the other hand, there was profound dread of what he might find in his depths. This distrust, we have seen, mounted towards the end of his life when sickness overshadowed him and he might well doubt the motherliness of a nature who had given him such a spirit in such a body. Nevertheless it is pertinent at least to ask which of these factors – ill health or distrust – may have been the primary one. Did he suspect nature because she had equipped him in a miserly fashion, or did his health fail him because, for some reason, he had dissociated himself from his instinctual being in the first place? Goethe at any rate had no doubt but that Schiller's sickness was an act of his mind.[90]

To help us answer this question for ourselves, it may be useful to take another look at *Demetrius*, the precipitate of the poet's final insights. Demetrius's conscious memory sets in with two impressions: the first of these is his flight, amidst flames, from Uglitsch; the other is the awareness of the royal cross hanging from his neck. Twice he expressly declares:

> Doch weiß ich keiner Zeit mich zu besinnen,
> Wo ich das Kleinod nicht an mir getragen . . .[91]

and in the prose draft of the original act he adds, with even greater finality: 'Es ist so alt als mein Bewußtsein.'[92] The dawning of self-awareness thus seems to be bound up with two contents of consciousness: one, a traumatic event; the other, a symbol of power. One could easily adduce parallels from Schiller's other dramas showing the same basic configuration. We need only think of *Die Jungfrau von Orleans*, where the threat to the town of Orléans and the appearance of the helmet together act as catalysts of Johanna's self-awareness. It is idle to speculate which one of these mental events is prior to the other. More important is the realization of how closely they interlock: that the experience of being vulnerable for Schiller is at once associated with shying away from the hazards of sentience and striving upward, toward power and control. I would suggest that some early and traumatic awareness of the discrepancy between what he was and what he could trust himself to be opened up that inner hiatus between nature and aspiration which left its mark on the unconquerable loftiness of his mind and the incurable frailty of his body; a rift which has grown to deadly dimensions in his last drama and which indeed informs the last words of it, the very last he ever wrote:

> O warum bin ich hier geengt, gebunden,
> Beschränkt mit dem unendlichen Gefühl!
> (*Demetrius*, II. i)

In the prose draft of the scene showing Demetrius in prison at the Woiwod's court, we read:

> Es ist ein Mensch darzustellen, der zu der *außerordentlichsten** Rolle aufbehalten wird, wenn er schon glaubt zu enden. Das Tiefste im Menschen wird in solchen Augenblicken sichtbar; bei ihm ist der Ehrgeiz, *das ungeheure Streben ins Mögliche** durch eine gewisse Götterstimme gerechtfertigt.[93]

Perhaps this diagnosis of an inborn and overpowering upward drive, which contains the germ of greatness, stress and tragedy, is not altogether different from Goethe's retrospective account of his friend's mental history which I quoted at the outset of this chapter.

> Die Kantische Philosophie, welche das Subjekt so hoch erhebt, indem sie es einzuengen scheint, hatte er mit Freuden in sich aufgenommen; sie entwickelte *das Außerordentliche, was die Natur in sein Wesen gelegt,** und er, *im höchsten Gefühl der Freiheit und Selbstbestimmung,** war undankbar gegen die große Mutter, die ihn gewiß nicht stiefmütterlich behandelte.[94]

But did not the great Mother who had implanted in him the dangerous seed of greatness treat him in a stepmotherly fashion after all? Was it not ironical that he did not have the time to complete *Die Kinder des Hauses*

* My italics.

and *Warbeck*, with their promise of a non-tragic vindication of maternal nature? And was it not the supreme irony that death itself cut short *Demetrius*, Schiller's last, grandest and starkest justification of nature's fearful might?

Despite her severity, he had paid her the most moving homage, in *Wilhelm Tell* and in such poems as *Der philosophische Egoist, Der spielende Knabe, Der Genius, Der Spaziergang* und *Das Glück*. Such ardent love as these poems shower upon the favoured ones, the children of nature, is moving just because it came from one who was himself fated to remain an exile. Perhaps it was this capacity to transcend himself which Goethe had in mind when he remarked: 'Ihr seid viel zu armselig und irdisch für ihn.'[95]

5

Productivity

. . . der Geist kann nichts, als was Form ist,
sein eigen nennen.

(*Über Anmut und Würde*)

11

The pregnant moment :
Wallenstein's debt to Laocoon

I

On 1 July 1797, in the midst of the *Balladenjahr* and intensive discussions with Schiller on matters aesthetic and poetic, Goethe was visited in Weimar by one Aloys Hirt. Hirt, Professor of Archaeology in Berlin, had recently returned from Rome where he had been living since his early twenties. Goethe had got to know him well at the time of his second Roman stay during which Hirt, equally at home with the architecture and sculpture of the classical and more modern periods, had acted as his indefatigable and devoted guide. Hirt, so Goethe reported to Schiller a few days later,[1] had brought along with him an essay from his own hand on the Laocoon group, directed against Winckelmann's and Lessing's formalistic conception of beauty and designed to equate the beautiful in art with the characteristic. Hirt's essay reminded Goethe of one he himself had written as a twenty-year-old in 1769, when he had first seen the statue in the *Antikensaal* of the museum in Mannheim. However, he could not find the manuscript – which indeed is lost to us – and so, stimulated by the challenge of Hirt's thesis, he set about reformulating what he remembered of the earlier draft in a new treatise which embodied Schiller's and his own mature aesthetic convictions.

From Weimar, Hirt proceeded to Jena and duly reported to Schiller. The two men had concentrated talks stretching over some three days, no doubt on a topic which was uppermost in the illustrious friends' minds and preoccupying them, especially Goethe, almost to the point of distraction: the subject-matter that is appropriate to a given form of art. Schiller wrote to Goethe, on 4 July, that in the main Hirt appeared to see eye to eye with them and Heinrich Meyer – with whom Goethe was equally busy investigating this same burning topic from the angle of the visual arts – and adds, somewhat nostalgically, that he would have dearly liked to have listened in on Hirt's conversations with Goethe, 'weil ich ein Gespräch über bildende Kunst aus eigenem Mittel nicht lange unterhalten, wohl aber mit Nutzen zuhören kann.'

On 5 July Goethe dispatched Hirt's essay to Jena, followed by his own findings on the Laocoon group three days later. Schiller's reaction was enthusiastic. 'Sie haben', he wrote on 10 July, 'mit wenig Worten und in einer kunstlosen Einkleidung herrliche Dinge in diesem Aufsatz ausgesprochen und eine wirklich bewundernswürdige Klarheit über die schwere Materie verbreitet. In der Tat, der Aufsatz ist ein Muster, wie man Kunstwerke ansehen und beurteilen soll, er ist aber auch ein Muster, wie man Grundsätze anwenden soll.' To which he added: 'In Rücksicht auf beides habe ich sehr viel daraus gelernt.' The following day, Schiller took Goethe's manuscript back with him to Weimar where he stayed at his friend's house for a week's exchange of ideas. On his return to Jena, he wrote one of those movingly grateful 'thank-you's' in which his letters to Goethe abound. 'Ich kann nie von Ihnen gehen,' we read, 'ohne daß etwas in mir gepflanzt worden wäre, und es freut mich, wenn ich für das viele, was Sie mir geben, Sie und Ihren innern Reichtum in Bewegung setzen kann.' And then, clearly echoing his first reaction to Goethe's essay:

. . . Die schönste und fruchtbarste Art, wie ich unsre wechselseitige Mitteilungen benutze und mir zu eigen mache, ist immer diese, daß ich sie unmittelbar auf die gegenwärtige Beschäftigung anwende und gleich produktiv gebrauche. Und wie Sie in der Einleitung zum Laokoon sagen, daß in einem einzelnen Kunstwerk die Kunst ganz liege, so, glaube ich, muß man alles Allgemeine in der Kunst wieder in den besondersten Fall verwandeln, wenn die Realität der Idee sich bewähren soll. Und so, hoffe ich, soll mein Wallenstein und was ich künftig von Bedeutung hervorbringen mag, das ganze System desjenigen, was bei unserm *Commerzio* in meine Natur hat übergehen können, *in Concerto* zeigen und enthalten.[2]

Wallenstein as a practical implementation of the aesthetic principles underlying Goethe's *Laokoon* study: to us this suggestion may seem somewhat startling; but evidently it did not surprise Goethe.[3] For already on 8 July, on sending his own essay to Schiller, he had prophesied that the findings of his own little treatise could easily be extended to cover the field of the classical formative arts and more, and that, by doing so, 'man dem, der im Felde der Tragödie arbeitet, sehr erwünscht entgegenkommen würde.' And six days later he wrote to Meyer that in composing his essay he had, from the beginning, had in mind Schiller and his preoccupation with tragedy. And indeed, Schiller confirmed his indebtedness to the *Laokoon* essay for the composition of his *Wallenstein* as late as October 1797. In a letter dated 2 October he inquired how Goethe was getting on with the study on Greek sculpture of which the *Laokoon* essay was to be the spearhead. 'Ich habe diesen', he wrote, 'neuerdings wieder mit der höchsten Befriedigung gelesen und kann gar nicht genug sagen, auf wie viele bedeutende fruchtbare Ideen, die Organisation ästhetischer Werke betreffend, er leitet. Hermann und Dorothea rumorieren schon im stillen . . .' This handsome tribute figures in a highly specific and significant context. For earlier in the same letter Schiller had announced that he had just returned to his trilogy after an enforced interruption caused by the necessity of completing the 1798 issue of the *Musenalmanach*, and on returning to his work afresh, had taken stock of his achievements to date. He was well pleased with it. A colossal amount of work was still looming ahead, he wrote; 'aber soviel weiß ich, daß es keine *faux frais* sein werden, denn das Ganze ist poetisch organisiert, und ich darf wohl sagen, der Stoff ist in eine reine tragische Fabel verwandelt.' Clearly he had done what he said he was doing in the earlier letter: he had applied Goethe's general insights into the *aesthetic* organization of works of art to the job in hand, namely the *poetic* organization of his own dramatic materials. And indeed, in that same letter the most important operative term linking the two spheres, the sphere of visual art and that of poetry, made its appearance: 'Der Moment der Handlung ist so prägnant,' Schiller continues his assessment of *Wallenstein*, 'daß alles, was zur Vollständigkeit derselben gehört, natürlich, ja in gewissem Sinn notwendig darin liegt, daraus hervor geht.'

'Der prägnante Moment': clearly, this term had already 'im stillen rumoriert' for a while. Schiller had first introduced it in a fundamental context a couple of weeks earlier. In a letter dated 15 September he had exhorted Goethe to clarify, together with H. Meyer, his ideas 'über die Wahl der Stoffe für poetische und bildende Darstellung', urging that here was indeed a cardinal concern of art and that any general principles they might hammer out between them could readily be applied to actual works of art. The leading concept in this connection is, he suggests, the 'Begriff der *absoluten Bestimmtheit des Gegenstandes*'. For, as he points out, all artistic failures caused by a faulty choice of subject-matter can in fact be traced to a basic lack of artistic definition and the fortuitousness of treatment arising therefrom. But whether or not a given subject-matter qualifies for such flawless definition in turn depends on whether the artist has put his finger on the 'prägnanten Augenblick'. As the outstanding example of success Schiller cites *Hermann und Dorothea*. It could be shown, he argues, that the choice of any other moment, or angle, of the action would have left something or other artistically undefined and blurred. But even before that first and basic formulation of Schiller's, Goethe had used the term. In a letter to H. Meyer dated 6 June, he had apodictically declared: 'Alles Glück eines Kunstwerks beruht auf dem prägnanten Stoffe, den es darzustellen unternimmt.'

It is difficult to describe the anguished tone of Goethe's utterances, especially in his letters to Meyer, about the imperative need to discover the suitability of given subject-matters for given art forms. Schiller shared this passion and insisted on being kept fully informed of Goethe's and Meyer's findings. And no wonder. To discover principles that would reliably guide them in their productions was a matter of burning concern for two poets determined to achieve the mastery of their craft and to replace the blind gropings and false starts of youth by the utmost economy of directed effort. We may assume then that in their ruminations the term 'prägnanter Moment', which is indeed the crux of the problem, had become an important shorthand which was equally understood by both.

II

The term derives from Lessing's treatise on *Laokoon*. Having defined, in Chapter XV which launches the argument from first principles, simultaneous objects in space as being the proper objects of the arts and successive actions in time as being the proper objects of poetry, Lessing concedes that in so far as objects in space also endure in time and stand in a causal nexus, they also can be the objects of poetry, 'andeutungsweise'. 'Die Malerei kann in ihren koexistierenden Kompositionen nur einen einzigen Augenblick der Handlung nutzen, und muß daher den prägnantesten wählen, aus welchem das Vorhergehende und Folgende am begreiflichsten wird.' Clearly Lessing is concerned to enlarge the territory of the visual artist which his main thesis has forced him radically to curtail. By the choice of the 'prägnante Augenblick' which contains, as in a nutshell, past and future, the visual artist is enabled to mediate an experience which is virtually sequential. Here, as well as in his earlier observations on the fruitful moment and its counterpart, the transitory moment, which must at all costs be avoided, Lessing exploits the continuous existence in time of objects in space. Although all 'there' and given to us simultaneously, the object is experienced as unfolding in time; and accordingly the fruitful moment is the one in the rising scale of possible moments which allows for this extension of vision forward as well as backward, whilst the transitory moment, coming at the end of the range, confronts us with an experience which is both extreme and discontinuous.

From the definitions which eminent critics have advanced of the 'prägnante Moment' as used by Goethe and Schiller, it would seem that their concern is likewise with the quality of continuity captured in and by the single moment. Emil Staiger, with admirable precision, writes: ' "Praegnans" heisst "schwanger": Der Augenblick ist schwanger von Vergangenheit und insbesondere schwanger von Zukunft.'[4] And elsewhere: 'Er meint einen Moment, der es "in sich hat", der ergiebig ist, vor allem den Moment, der die Handlung eröffnet, sie gleichsam aus sich entläßt.'[5] Not dissimilarly, Wilhelm Emrich, in his study of *Faust II*, writes: 'Bedeutsame, "prägnante Momente" entstehen immer dort, wo lange labil ruhende Schichten und unterirdisch stille Entwicklungen plötzlich spontan hervorbrechend einen ganzen, weiten Umkreis sichtbar werden lassen und dadurch symbolkräftig werden.'[6]

It is generally accepted that Goethe, in his *Laokoon* essay, is centrally concerned with isolating the 'prägnante Moment' at which the sculptors have arrested the agitated group. Again I quote Staiger for a concise and authoritative statement on the matter: 'Goethe hat einen prägnanten Moment ausführlich in der Untersuchung *Über Laokoon* beschrieben, und er mag von dem antiken Bildwerk sagen, was er will, sein Ruhm läuft stets darauf hinaus, daß es den Künstlern gelungen ist, Vergangenes und Künftiges in das Gegenwärtige in ungewöhnlichem Masse einzubeziehen.'[7] What is more, Goethe himself, in summarizing his own intentions, leaves no doubt that here lay the centre of his concern. In the *Anzeige der Propyläen* of 15 December 1797 we read, under the heading *Laokoon*: 'Der in diesem Kunstwerk dargestellte Moment wird anders als bisher gesehen bezeichnet.'[8] In the same announcement, he justifies the pains he has taken to demonstrate the sculptors' outstanding achievement by pointing out that it is the business of any visual artist to isolate one single moment and to make that moment 'so prägnant als möglich . . .'[9] And immediately after completion of the essay, Goethe writes to H. Meyer,

asking 'ob . . . ich das Kunstwerk richtig gefaßt und den eigentlichen
Lebenspunkt des Dargestellten wahrhaftig angegeben habe'.[20] 'Lebenspunkt', in the *Goethewortschatz*, is defined as 'Keimpunkt, d.h. der Punkt
aus dem sich Lebendiges entwickelt'. Thus its meaning is synonymous
with that of the 'pregnant moment'; and indeed, in later life, Goethe used
the two interchangeably. It is a word we shall meet again.

Although the word 'prägnant' does not actually occur in the essay
itself, Goethe's argument incessantly and insistently circles around the
artistic problem it designates. Having stated generically that visual art
'immer für den Moment arbeitet' and that it is the artist's task to discover 'den höchsten darzustellenden Moment', Goethe launches his detailed analysis with the words: 'Äußerst wichtig ist dieses Kunstwerk
durch die Darstellung des Moments.' After a searching discussion of the
kind of moment which is fruitful, to which we shall presently turn, Goethe
states his contention that the group in fact excels in having arrived at the
'Gipfel des vorgestellten Augenblicks'. He proceeds to isolate this 'Einen
Moment des höchsten Interesse' by experimentally modifying, in diverse
ways, the configuration in fact chosen by the sculptors. Thus, by a process
of elimination, he demonstrates 'daß sie gegenwärtig auf dem höchsten
Punkt steht, . . . und daß kein Augenblick gefunden werden kann, der
diesem an Kunstwert gleich sei.'

The operative word here which immediately and sharply distinguishes
Goethe's position from that of Lessing, is 'Kunstwert'. Lessing's aesthetic
argument is largely informed by a representational theory of art, and this
furnishes the criterion of value with which he operates in his discussion of
the Laocoon group. The 'prägnante Moment' is prized, basically, because
it is informative. It tells the full story behind the single picture. It is as it
were the most telling snap in a film strip, the one which most vividly
suggests the action captured by the strip as a whole.[11] Goethe, on the other
hand, is exclusively concerned with the artistically consummate moment,
that is to say, the moment of optimal expressiveness. How is such expressiveness achieved?

Here a seeming paradox of Goethe's position becomes apparent. It
stamps his approach, not only in the *Laokoon* essay, but quite as much
in the contemporaneous *Der Sammler und die Seinigen*. Goethe urges that
for all its tragic pathos, or rather because of it, the Laocoon group, along
with any work of art that is worthy of the name,[12] must be possessed of
'Anmut'. By 'Anmut' he designates everything pertaining to the formal
arrangement of the group, such as the interrelations of its parts, their

symmetries, correspondences, variations and contrasts, all of which are carefully composed in a continuous gradation. 'Anmut', we may say, is the effect of such total and overall 'composedness'.[13] On such composedness the expressive potential of a work depends. And both – maximal expressiveness and maximal composedness – are only capable of being achieved when the artist has isolated, from the diverse possibilities offered by his subject-matter, the precise 'prägnante Moment' in which his composition culminates and from whence it flows in its entirety. The 'prägnante Moment' – and here Goethe seems to echo Lessing – is the point of intersection between past and future;[14] it is also the unique point of concurrence between the maximal life of the parts and the maximal life of the whole. By seizing on this singular moment, the artist is enabled flawlessly to define the inner movement of his subject and to unfold the wealth of its internal relations. As Schiller has it in connection with his own discovery of the 'prägnante Moment' in *Wallenstein*: 'Es bleibt nichts Blindes darin, nach allen Seiten ist es geöffnet.'[15]

Thus, the apparent incongruity, so vehemently strictured by the guest in *Der Sammler und die Seinigen*, of ascribing 'Anmut' to a subject as starkly tragic as the Laocoon group or indeed any Sophoclean tragedy, is resolved by a volte-face which betokens the pure and thorough-bred artist. Both in the *Laokoon* essay and in this contemporaneous work, Goethe gives voice to the unshakeable conviction that where there is art there is 'Anmut', i.e. an ultimate harmony springing from composedness.[16] '. . . wenn Laokoon wirklich so vor unsern Augen stünde wie Sie ihn beschreiben,' the speaker replies to the horrific description of the guest, 'so wäre er wert, daß er den Augenblick in Stücken geschlagen würde.'[17] This uncompromising judgement is nourished by a quite definite theory of artistic creation and perception; and this is brought to light when the speaker replies to the representations of the guest – in whom it is easy to recognize Aloys Hirt – that the Greek tragedies are of their essence horrible. 'Freilich,' he rejoins, 'wenn man in der Poesie nur den Stoff erblickt, der dem Gedichteten zum Grund liegt, wenn man vom Kunstwerk spricht als hätte man, an seiner Statt, die Begebenheiten in der Natur erfahren,' dann lassen sich sogar Sophokleische Tragödien als ekelhaft und abscheulich darstellen.'[18] From the first, Goethe is in fact telling us, the percipient of art and, to an infinitely greater degree, its creator, experience the subject before them *qua* art. From its first impact as art, they experience it not as an ordinary event in reality, but as an aesthetic event taking shape within a given artistic medium and within a given art form and tradition. It is in fact an experience that is different in kind, set within a different framework of reference, and nourished by an awareness which is subtly different both in its quality and in its source.

It is this aesthetic position, implicit throughout the *Laokoon* essay and pinpointed by the word 'Kunstwert', that distinguishes Goethe's conception of the culminating moment as sharply as is possible from Lessing's, hampered as the latter is by a largely representational theory of art.[19] But Goethe's most fascinating statement on the relation between reality and art – and, within it, between the horrible and the graceful – is to be found in *Der Sammler und die Seinigen*, again in the closest connection with the Laocoon group. Having failed to convince the speaker of its supposed horrors, the guest, in a last attempt to retrieve his position, produces the incontrovertible example of Niobe: '. . . denn', he triumphantly asks, 'wo wütet Schrecken und Tod entsetzlicher als bei den Darstellungen der Niobe?' To which the speaker replies: 'Sind die toten Töchter und Söhne der Niobe nicht hier als Zieraten geordnet? Es ist die höchste Schwelgerei der Kunst! Sie verziert nicht mehr mit Blumen und Früchten, sie verziert mit menschlichen Leichnamen, mit dem größten Elend, das einem Vater, das einer Mutter begegnen kann . . .'[20]

The highest orgy of art: art is a revel in that it forms the experience that is knocking at the doors of consciousness, be that experience even transience and death. It speaks of death, it speaks through death, and out of dread and death it fashions an adornment and an object of delight. It composes the very elements of transience into an image of transience which is consummate and enduring. But, as in the case of the Greek sarcophagus, art is a revel also in that the more intricately it structures its materials, the wider it opens the sluice-gates of awareness, allowing the artist to explore reaches of experience which, but for his shaping power, would have remained unguessed at and unsung. The pathos of the Laocoon group and the agony of the 'menschliche Leichname' surrounding the figure of Niobe would have remained muted but for the grace of form which transcends what it releases and releases what it transcends. This doubled creativity surely is the ultimate triumph of art; and Goethe well sums it up when he says, towards the end of Letter VI: 'Es gibt keine Erfahrung, die nicht produziert, hervorgebracht, erschaffen wird.'[21]

The artistically fruitful moment, then, is the moment when feeling and form fuse and, in unending mutual enhancement, bring forth an object which is felt and formed and expressive through and through. This is the 'prägnante Moment', and the artist who knows how to tread upon this tightrope is empowered to say the ultimate about the human condition, to wrest grace even from gruesomeness and to invest with delight even the spectre of decay.

III

For, let there be no mistake about it: when Goethe speaks of the 'prägnante Moment' he is concerned, basically, with the consummation and conquest of transience. The very essence of the pregnant moment, as he isolates it in the *Laokoon* essay, lies in the fact that it is transient.[22] In order to produce in a work constricted to a single point of time the illusion of movement, '. . . muß ein vorübergehender Moment gewählt sein; kurz vorher darf kein Teil des Ganzen sich in dieser Lage befunden haben, kurz nachher muß jeder Teil genötigt sein, diese Lage zu verlassen; dadurch wird das Werk Millionen Anschauern immer wieder neu lebendig sein.' But is not Goethe here concerned, precisely as Lessing had been before him, with conquering the isolation of the single point of time by making it pregnant with past and future? Is he not, exactly as Lessing had done, annulling the discreteness of the moment by the discovery within it of continuity and duration? What, for him, is the significance of the transient moment?

Towards the end of the section dealing with the precise moment chosen by the sculptors Goethe writes, in a more general vein:

> Hier sei mir eine Bemerkung erlaubt, die für die bildende Kunst von Wichtigkeit ist; der höchste pathetische Ausdruck, den sie darstellen kann, schwebt auf dem Übergange eines Zustandes in den andern. Man sehe ein lebhaftes Kind, das mit aller Energie und Lust des Lebens rennt, springt und sich ergötzt, dann aber etwa unverhofft von einem Gespielen hart getroffen oder sonst physisch oder moralisch heftig verletzt wird; diese neue Empfindung teilt sich wie ein elektrischer Schlag allen Gliedern mit, und ein solcher Übersprung ist im höchsten Sinne pathetisch, es ist ein Gegensatz, von dem man ohne Erfahrung keinen Begriff hat . . . Bleibt alsdann bei einem solchen Übergange noch die deutliche Spur vom vorhergehenden Zustande, so entsteht der herrlichste Gegenstand für die bildende Kunst, wie beim Laokoon der Fall ist, wo Streben und Leiden in einem Augenblick vereinigt sind.

Already before, Goethe had emphasized that in the present posture of

Laocoon there remains an 'Überrest der vorhergehenden Situation oder Handlung' ensuing in a 'Zusammenwirkung von Streben und Fliehen, von Wirken und Leiden, von Anstrengen und Nachgeben, die vielleicht unter keiner andern Bedingung möglich wäre.' And illustrating his point by yet another example – he imagines Eurydice stung by a serpent as she is gathering flowers in a meadow – he surmises that this subject, too, would have the makings of a 'sehr pathetische Statue . . . , wenn . . . durch die Richtung aller Glieder und das Schwanken der Falten der doppelte Zustand des fröhlichen Vorschreitens und des schmerzlichen Anhaltens ausgedrückt werden könnte.'

There is an unmistakable progression in the terms Goethe employs to develop his idea. Starting from the innocuous-sounding concept of 'ein vorübergehender Moment', he presently refines it as meaning the 'Übergang eines Zustandes in den andern'. From there, he presses on to the notions of 'Übersprung' and 'Gegensatz', and these are finally explicated as the 'Zusammenwirkung' of opposing impingements, as a 'doppelte Zustand' springing from a sharp dialectic of contrary pulls.

Clearly the concern with the basic continuity of the pregnant moment – so central to Lessing – for Goethe has become peripheral. Of course the pregnant moment, for Goethe as much as for Lessing, is the precarious ridge between past and future. But the specific function of it that he is pinpointing is not that it acts as a fluid transition within a continuum. Quite on the contrary: it is its *disruptive* nature that he singles out because of its fruitfulness to the tragic artist.[23] On his viewing, the pregnant moment appears as a point of reversal and clash, and its essence lies in its discreteness, in the fact that it exhibits not a simple continuity, but a radical discontinuity contained within a seemingly unbroken sequence.

At first sight, this may seem profoundly un-classical and profoundly un-Goethean. Was not *vis formae superba* one of the poet's most cherished watchwords?[24] Was not his active life, his art-making as well as his scientific thinking, pledged to the task of wresting the permanence of *Gestalt* from the flux of the ephemeral? Did he not live, and work, in the conviction 'daß die höchste und einzige Operation der Natur und Kunst die Gestaltung sei'?[25] Clearly Staiger cannot be gainsaid when he relates the pregnant moment, in which past and future are contained, to the 'klassischen Moment, worin Vergangenheit beständig, Künftiges voraus lebendig ist'.[26] That indeed is the poet's 'Vermächtnis'. But we must press on and ask: what, for Goethe, is 'beständig', and what, for him, is the nature

of that most articulated of forms, the organic *Gestalt?* 'Der Deutsche',
Goethe writes,

> hat für den Komplex des Daseins eines wirklichen Wesens das Wort
> Gestalt. Er abstrahiert bei diesem Ausdruck von dem Beweglichen,
> er nimmt an, daß ein Zusammengehöriges festgestellt, abgeschlossen
> und in seinem Charakter fixiert sei.
>
> Betrachten wir aber alle Gestalten, besonders die organischen, so
> finden wir, daß nirgends ein Bestehendes, nirgends ein Ruhendes,
> Abgeschlossenes vorkommt, sondern daß vielmehr alles in einer
> steten Bewegung schwanke. . . . Das Gebildete wird sogleich
> wieder umgebildet. . . .[27]

The knowledge of the scientist found unforgettable utterance in the
poem *Dauer im Wechsel*. The message of the title is plain enough. Form is
not foisted on flux. It is found, if at all, deep within it. Who could forget
the haunting lines:

> Ach, und in demselben Flusse
> Schwimmst du nicht zum zweitenmal . . .

or the lament that rises to the poet's lips as he sees his wasting hands?

> Jene Hand, die gern und milde
> Sich bewegte wohlzutun,
> Das gegliederte Gebilde,
> Alles ist ein andres nun.
> Und was sich an jener Stelle
> Nun mit deinem Namen nennt,
> Kam herbei wie eine Welle
> Und so eilts zum Element.

Horrifyingly, the 'gegliederte Gebilde', the human hand and the encompassing organism of which it forms part, are likened to the evanescence of
the wave. And indeed, throughout the poem, any comfort and sense of
stability the poet might hope to derive from the procession of durable
objects that pass before his mind, is undermined by their insidious association with the most fugitive of elements – water. 'Blütenregen', 'Regen-
guß', 'Fluß', 'Welle', 'Element': where, in such flux, is durability? Even
the most highly articulated of objects, the human form, deceives us by a
false show of permanence and identity. True, it occupies one and the same
place, just as the statue of Laocoon seems stationary, and the name by
which we call it remains unchanged. But within such precarious framework, what inconstancy! 'Die Gestalt ist ein Bewegliches, ein Werdendes,

ein Vergehendes.'[28] Every cell within that 'gegliederte Gebilde', the human hand, is perpetually broken down as another forms to replace it. The only thing that is enduring is the pattern governing this constant coming and going of the elements of which it is compounded.

We are now better able to appreciate that when Goethe stipulates that a work of plastic art must single out a transient moment in order to create the illusion of movement, he is motivated by reasons vastly different from those which induced Lessing to call for the 'prägnante' or 'fruchtbare Augenblick'. Goethe is bound to emphasize the transitoriness of the moment which Lessing seeks to minimize. He must do so because he considers it the business of the artist, not indeed to imitate reality, but 'wetteifernd mit der Natur, etwas geistig Organisches hervorzubringen'.[29] Standing there in space, a stationary object carved in imperishable marble, the sculpture must yet *seem* to move because every *Gestalt*, even the ostensibly most enduring, is in deep and terrifying flux.[30]

Transience within permanence, discontinuity within continuity, death within life: this is the all-pervasive organic rhythm which the 'prägnante Moment' exhibits and articulates; and in the *Laokoon* essay Goethe has given voice to this, its function, in two images of devastating precision. Momentarily suspended between 'Streben und Fliehen', 'Wirken und Leiden', 'Anstrengen und Nachgeben', the group stands, 'ein fixierter Blitz, eine Welle, versteinert im Augenblicke da sie gegen das Ufer anströmt.' Transfixed like lightning, an elemental phenomenon as etched as it is evanescent, and as continuous as it is discrete; like a wave frozen at the moment when it breaks upon the shore. As I have shown elsewhere, Goethe's use of the imagery of water is so all-pervasive and so accurate that it is worth pursuing the implications of the latter image a little further.[31]

A wave is a travelling configuration of more or less constant volume, modelled by the force of the wind. As it speeds across the waters' surface heading towards the shore, we are impressed by the continuity of its shape and motion. We are hardly aware of the fact that its actual substance is constantly changing, in that every drop of the water of which it is composed is momentarily swept up into its travelling shape and presently left behind to form its trough. Every moment in the life of a wave sees such a re-formation, a breaking-up and a regrouping. Only the relation of the changing parts, its overall shape, remains constant.[32] There is one moment, however, when this discontinuity within continuity becomes visible: this is the moment when the surf breaks against rock and shore. As the wave towers, topples and breaks, its form disintegrates and its force disperses. Some of its water assaults the beach. Some of it is sucked back by the undertow to rush seaward from whence it came. And in the commotion engendered by these comings and goings we may discern the beginnings of another wave.

As with the petrified wave, so with the sculpted group. The artists have frozen it at the moment of clash and impending reversal, when shapeliness and disintegration, continuity and discontinuity are poised in a fleeting balance as consummate as it is untenable. As the glassy wall of the wave must break, so too with the sculpted group: in the seeming finality of the 'moment' we feel its solid structure trembling on the knife-edge of dissolution, and we perceive that transience is of its very essence.[33]

In the organizing energy of the 'prägnante Moment' as Goethe conceived of it, the artist reaches the high-watermark of his shaping power. Like the forms of nature, the forms of art that spring from this secret 'Lebenspunkt' are fraught, not only with life, but with death and decay at the very heart of vital process. In the pregnant moment, the artist distils the essence of transient life and from it fashions an imperishable image. Thus, and only thus, by exhibiting transience, does he stay and conquer it. The artist who dares create such passing forms knows transience and mourns it as none other; but also he knows 'die höchste Schwelgerei der Kunst': adorning such life as he creates, no longer with flowers or with fruits, but with the bodies of the human dead.

IV

That Schiller's dramatic colossus is centrally concerned with transience – its grievousness and the exhilaration of its conquest – the Prologue establishes beyond a doubt. Four times in all, and in four widely differing contexts, the poet articulates the dialectic between form and flux which is the groundbass of Goethe's *Laokoon* essay: first, in relation to the contemporary historical scene, characterized as it is by the dissolution of the 'alte feste Form' which had been wrested from the chaos of the Thirty Years War; then in relation to that time itself, a period of tumultuous upheaval which forms the backcloth of Wallenstein's meteoric career; then again in relation to the hero himself, whose indomitable will built an evanescent empire out of chaos and confusion; and, finally, in relation to art 'die jedes Äußerste . . . begrenzt und bindet' and, especially, to the art of the actor which makes such a strange contrast to the constancy of its setting. For the actor's performance is 'des Augenblicks geschwinde Schöpfung', as consummate as it is fugitive, creating an intangible shape which vanishes as soon as it is perceived.

Is it accidental that the poet has embedded his reflections on the inconstancy of the historical scene in reflections on the perdurability of art? Is there any connection between the flight of phenomena on 'des Lebens Bühne' which is momentarily stayed by Wallenstein's will, and the flight of phenomena which the poet and the actor hold up to the imagination on the 'Schattenbühne' of art? Could the poet be telling us that Wallenstein himself is an actor on the stage of life,[34] bent upon permanence and grieving at its passing as do the actor and the poet? And, if so, is he perhaps in secret league with his creator who in this Prologue so persistently invokes the spectre of transience and the possibilities of its conquest, both as an artist and as a participant in historical process? We must see whether the trilogy will furnish answers to questions so eloquently raised in its opening lines.

This much is clear: from the start, the poet was urgently concerned with the 'prägnante Moment'. We have seen that Schiller claimed to have isolated this moment and therewith to have accomplished the total poetic organization of his recalcitrant material. And there are other documents that testify to the importance he attached to this matter: '. . . Nebenher entwerfe ich ein detailliertes Szenarium des ganzen Wallensteins', he writes to Goethe on 4 April 1797, 'um mir die Übersicht der *Momente* und des Zusammenhangs auch durch die Augen mechanisch zu erleichtern.' A year and a half later, he is still at it. On 21 September 1798, he writes to Goethe in connection with the *Lager* (which at that time was still referred to as 'der Prolog'): 'Ich denke, in der Gestalt, die er jetzt bekommt, soll er als ein lebhaftes Gemälde eines historischen Moments und einer gewissen soldatischen Existenz ganz gut auf sich selber stehen können.' Soon after, in a letter to Goethe dated 6 October 1798, we again read: 'Das Motif mit der Zeitung wäre passend zu einer vollkommenern Exposition des Moments . . .' Moreover, Goethe himself, in a preliminary review of *Die Piccolomini* which was written with Schiller's connivance and in full awareness of his artistic intentions, not surprisingly concentrates on the moment singled out by Schiller's composition:

> Wollte man das Objekt des ganzen Gedichts mit wenig Worten aussprechen, so würde es sein: die Darstellung einer phantastischen Existenz, welche durch ein außerordentliches Individuum und *unter*

*Vergünstigung eines außerordentlichen Zeitmoments** unnatürlich
und *augenblicklich** gegründet wird, aber durch ihren notwendigen
Widerspruch mit der gemeinen Wirklichkeit des Lebens und mit der
Rechtlichkeit der menschlichen Natur scheitert und samt allem,
was an ihr befestigt ist, zugrunde geht.[35]

The 'prägnante Moment' that is the organizing centre of the trilogy has
been rightly identified as the moment of Questenberg's arrival at Pilsen.[36]
The emissary of the Emperor, he has brought with him the imperial order
that eight of the regiments under Wallenstein's command be forthwith
despatched to accompany the Cardinal Infant on his journey from Milan
to the Netherlands. This is a stratagem designed to weaken the Generalissimo's power by forcing him into a decision. For years Wallenstein has been
in clandestine negotiations with the Emperor's enemies, who are willing
to reward his offices with the Bohemian crown. At the same time, he has
avoided an open break with his liege lord and instead has wielded absolute
authority over the Emperor's armies. Thus he has enjoyed, both literally
and metaphorically, the power and the total freedom from responsibility
of an uncrowned king.[37] Of this extraordinary concatenation of power
Questenberg's arrival marks the end. It forces Wallenstein to declare
colour. He has three choices open to him: he must obey, he must rebel, or
he must altogether abdicate.
    We see that the poet, very much like the sculptors of the Laocoon
group, has concentrated on a climactic configuration, that is to say one
which is about to disintegrate. By playing a double game, Wallenstein has
from the beginning arrogated to himself mutually incompatible powers
and liberties. He has led 'eine phantastische Existenz', built upon founda-
tions which are 'unnatürlich und augenblicklich'. Questenberg's arrival
marks the peak point of this situation in that it sheds light both on the
limitless sovereignty Wallenstein has hitherto enjoyed and on the unten-
ableness of a configuration which is compounded of incompatible elements.
His coming pinpoints the 'prägnante Moment' in the precise sense in
which Goethe had used this concept in his *Laokoon* essay: the moment of
clash, reversal and disintegration at which the future may be seen to have
been latent in the past. It is the moment when the towering wave over-
hangs and breaks and we perceive that transience was of its essence all
along. In the tragic sequence, this moment of reversal is extended long
enough retrospectively to reveal the full measure of the totality for which

* My italics.

the hero had reached, and to enable us to witness to the end the collapse
of an undertaking which had been doomed from the very start. It shows
Wallenstein in a protracted agony of reverse: still sensible of his might as
never before it was critically threatened and still carried forward by its
momentum, yet already stunned by the force which has impinged upon
him and recoiling, like a wounded animal, or a wave as it splinters upon
the rocks. Like Laocoon, freshly stung by the serpent, Wallenstein is
temporarily arrested in a double condition 'von Streben und Fliehen, von
Wirken und Leiden, von Anstrengen und Nachgeben', which no other
moment could have captured with comparable poignancy. Like the child
that is abruptly foiled in its forward surge by a blow, he stands transfixed, as if paralysed by an electric shock.

Goethe, in his *Laokoon* essay, had been quick to seize upon the aesthetic
merit of the serpents palsying the human group. 'Durch dieses Mittel der
Lähmung', he writes, 'wird, bei der großen Bewegung, über das Ganze schon
eine gewisse Ruhe und Einheit verbreitet.' If even the subliminal tremor
reverberating through the sculpted form needs to be pacified, how much
more so the violent movement of tragedy which, unfolding in a sequential order, whips time before it on its breakneck rush towards catastrophe!

Schiller was quick to take Goethe's point. The moment of reversal at
which Wallenstein is shown is a long-drawn-out moment during which all
purposive activity, and with it time itself, seems gradually to grind to a
halt. Procrastinating and planning, advancing and regressing in turn,
Wallenstein is mesmerized more and more into an agitated yet aimless
state of contemplation. He is both free and frozen to the spot.[38]

And, indeed, such an arrest was precisely what Schiller needed. Early on
in his work on the trilogy he had complained that the hero's misfortune
was as yet too much of his own making.[39] A year later, and significantly in
the same letter in which he announced that he had discovered the 'prägnante Moment' of the action, he reported to Goethe that his principal
character was now essentially 'retardierend'.[40] What might at first sight
appear to be two separate developments are, in fact, two facets of the
identical breakthrough. For the pregnant moment is precisely that dia-
lectical moment of clash and reversal in which all movement is halted. By
thus suspending his hero at a timeless moment between his rise and fall,
the poet made him into the principal if unconscious tool of his own artistic
requirements. For only by halting the rush of the action and holding it up
to our contemplation, immobile, could he hope to fashion an enduring
image of it.

The connection between the retarding character of the principal figure and the retarding stance of the drama as a whole has been rightly noted.[41] It is telling that the development in both these directions should have taken place at the same time. Telling because both the immobilization of the hero and the new 'epische Geist' which began to pervade the characters as well as the poetic idiom of the trilogy spring from one and the same source. Both grew out of the poet's conviction that tragedy must seek to approximate to the epic genre and use as many epic correctives as it can muster to preserve a modicum of aesthetic freedom amidst the pressures generated by its action.[42]

Already during an early phase of his work on *Wallenstein*, Schiller repeatedly and proudly remarks on the fact that, contrary to his usual enthusiastic approach, he treats his poetic materials 'mit der reinen Liebe des Künstlers'.[43] The word 'Künstler', it has been pointed out, in those days was still firmly reserved for the visual artist.[44] I would suggest that the key to this way of viewing himself lies in the fructifying force of Goethe's preoccupation with the visual arts, and of the *Laokoon* essay in particular. The uncanny stillness emanating from the central personage at the climactic moment is a projection, into the dimension of drama, of the very visual device to which Goethe's analysis had drawn attention: the sculpted group paralysed in the coils of the snakes. Such indeed was the strength of the impression this made on Schiller that it left two lingering after-images in the play. Twice in rapid succession, during the most agonized moment of the tragedy, the poet resorts to images of snakes:

> Ich zog
> Den Basilisken auf an meinem Busen,
> Mit meinem Herzblut nährt' ich ihn, er sog
> Sich schwellend voll an meiner Liebe Brüsten . . .
> (*Tod*, III. xviii)

Wallenstein cries when Octavio's treachery has come to light; and Max despairingly asks:

> Warum muß
> Der Väter Doppelschuld und Freveltat
> Uns gräßlich wie ein Schlangenpaar umwinden?
> (ibid.)

Coming at the crest of unendurable anguish, this doubled echo surely hints at the poetic law Schiller was observing time and again in the writing of his tragedy: to counteract, as the sculptors of the Laocoon group had done before him, the dangers of excessive agitation by a corresponding tendency towards stasis and thus to freeze the action at its passing peak.

V

Even *Wallensteins Lager* is tightly organized from the commanding centre of the pregnant moment. On the one hand, we are made to perceive the full extent of the Generalissimo's power – the extraordinary cohesion of the chequered masses assembled under his banner from all the corners of Europe who are as one in their devotion to him. We are made to sense – even the Kapuziner must tacitly concede this – that they are the giant body of which he is the animating spirit. On the other hand, we are also made aware of the fissures running through this motley conglomerate and we foresee that elements of such disparity cannot for long be held together.[45] The whole panorama is dominated by the news of Questenberg's arrival. And already at this early stage, the event shows how narrow is this ridge of a present, leading precariously from the past into the future. The rumours concerning Questenberg's mission cement the solidarity of Wallenstein's troops with their leader. At the same time, the soldiers' speculations give rise to a wide variety of reactions, and we see the secret cracks opening up. Thus Questenberg's coming highlights both the climactic character and the precariousness of the configuration of which Wallenstein is the centre. We are impressed in equal measure by its immense cohesive force and its impending dissipation.

To these conflicting tendencies within one and the same situation the poet has given voice through a number of interlocking means of which we may mention a few. The solidarity *within* Wallenstein's army is paradoxically based on the chaos *outside* it and the resultant absence of any other loyalties. The army is the only framework of security for the large variety of characters we encounter; and the impression of unity is brought home by the soldiers' canon at the end of the play in which all join alike, and by the homogeneity of the stylistic devices the poet employs throughout: the rough and racy mode of characterization, the broad humour and, last but not least, the *Knittelvers* binding all and sundry together.

The impression of disparity which the poet is equally busy creating springs from the patent variety of characters and the accompanying incongruity of background, motives and values. Disparity is significantly implicit in the very feature which also makes for homogeneity – the all-pervading sense of transience and uprootedness which suggests that loyalties may well be as shortlived as they are exclusive.

But the principal means by which the poet brings home the precariousness of the massive configuration clustered around Wallenstein is the ambivalence of the imagery he uses to describe it. There is no doubt that the army is more than the 'Schattenbild' of its leader. The same lines in the Prologue also speak of 'die kühnen Scharen, die sein Geist beseelt'; and throughout the *Lager*, and indeed until deep in the third part of the trilogy, Schiller builds up a picture of Wallenstein's army as a composite and living whole or body of which he himself is the organizing heart or intelligence. 'Das Ganze': this vague and somewhat mystifying word recurs with the force of a leitmotif which is persistently sounded throughout the *Lager*. The counsel of the Wachtmeister 'Man muß immer das Ganze überschlagen' leads on to the first Jäger's 'Ja, ja, im Ganzen, da sitzt die Macht!', and this in turn gives rise to the comparison of the parts of the army with the fingers of a hand: cut off one and – 'Pros't Mahlzeit! da fällt das Ganze gleich'. And from here there is a fluid transition to Wallenstein's repeated expression of concern for 'Europas großem Besten' (*Pic.*, I. iv), 'des *Ganzen* Heil' (*Pic.*, II. vii) and to his solemn if cryptic declaration 'Mir ist's allein ums Ganze' (III. xv).[46]

Much of the time, this whole is envisaged as an encompassing organic unity. This is already adumbrated in the Wachtmeister's 'Exempel' of the fingers and the hand and in his reference to 'der Geist, der im ganzen Korps tut leben', with its *double entendre* of 'Korps' and 'Körper'. Such chords – and there are many – are finally gathered up in Wallenstein's resounding declaration of faith at the moment of his lowest ebb:

> Es ist der Geist, der sich den Körper baut,
> Und Friedland wird sein Lager um sich füllen. . . .
> . . . Wenn Haupt und Glieder sich trennen,
> Da wird sich zeigen, wo die Seele wohnte.
>
> (*Tod*, III. xiii)

At times, the exact nature of this biological bond is differently defined: Wallenstein is not so much the organizing intelligence of the multiple body he inhabits; rather he is seen as the father and fosterer of the forces under his command. 'Ein Soldatenvater', the first Kürassier calls him; and this description adumbrates Max's filial relation to Friedland and is supported by the vision which Buttler, of all unlikely people, expounds to the incredulous Questenberg:

All dieses Volk gehorcht Friedländischen
Hauptleuten. Die's befehligen, sind alle
In *eine* Schul' gegangen, *eine* Milch
Hat sie ernährt, *ein* Herz belebt sie alle.

(Pic., I. ii)

But then such a definition in organic terms of the bond obtaining between the troops and their leader gives way, sometimes in an abrupt
manner, to images suggesting an altogether different kind of cohesion. In
the very same speech in which Buttler speaks of a virtually maternal bond
between Wallenstein and his men, he compares their rapport to the swift
and unfailing contact between lightning and lightning conductor! And
already in the *Lager* the poet uses images suggestive of a mechanical
aggregate rather than of the cohesion of a living organism. Asked about
her unexpected appearance before Pilsen, the Marketenderin explains
that she is

Heute da, Herr Vetter, und morgen dort –
Wie einen der rauhe Kriegesbesen
Fegt und schüttelt von Ort zu Ort . . .

(scene v)

And the Wachtmeister, who of all the figures in the *Lager* evinces the
shrewdest grasp of Wallenstein's character and outlook, defines 'the
whole' of which Friedland is the centre in terms which consistently fall
short of the organic. Who has the intelligence and the might, he asks,

Diese gestückelten Heeresmassen
Zusammen zu fügen und zu passen?

(scene xi)

And again, later in the same scene:

Nun! und wer merkt uns das nun an,
Daß wir aus Süden und aus Norden
Zusammen geschneit und geblasen worden?
Sehn wir nicht aus wie aus *einem* Span?
Stehn wir nicht gegen den Feind geschlossen,
Recht wie zusammen geleimt und gegossen?
Greifen wir nicht wie ein Mühlwerk flink
In einander, auf Wort und Wink?

Wer hat uns so zusammengeschmiedet,
Daß ihr uns nimmer unterschiedet?
Kein andrer sonst als der Wallenstein!

(scene xi)

Flakes of snow or specks of dust blown or swept together; chips of wood glued to one another or dovetailed by the carpenter; wheels engaging with wheels; scraps of metal welded together: there is a clear progression from the absolutely fortuitous aggregate to a solid structure. But the breath of life which unites these particles by a bond only death can sever is missing.[47]

Thus the poet dismisses us from the *Lager* in a questioning frame of mind. What is the nature of the concatenation he has put before us? Has it the resilience and the strength of an organic whole or is it fortuitous? And, most of all: will it stand up to the strains which Questenberg's arrival so patently precipitates?

VI

Presently the configuration of forces which are clustered around Wallenstein begins to change. In part the impression that this is so is due to the fact that the poet, in *Die Piccolomini*, adopts a different focus. The common soldiers that have crowded the panorama are dismissed, not to reappear until the crucial scene in *Wallensteins Tod* in which the Cuirassiers part company with their general, soon to be followed by their own commander, Max. Instead, Schiller concentrates on Friedland's bond with his fellow officers. As with a powerful telescopic lens, the poet moves in on his central subject, with the result that we see more about less. Inevitably, the field of vision seems to contract.

But even within this narrowed frame changes subtly occur. The total configuration seems at the same time to be strengthened and to crumble. Max's love for Thekla is revealed and furnishes a new bond between Wallenstein and his most popular officer. Questenberg's representations fail to dent the generals' loyalty and Friedland's mock abdication releases a surge of renewed devotion. This is cleverly conducted into written channels and the officers' pledge to their commander, although recognized by some as a fake, makes the bond tying them to him all but unconditional. Octavio's preliminary overtures to Buttler fall on deaf ears.

These are the positive assets of the situation, and they are carefully balanced against its debit side. Gallas's defection is brought to our knowledge in the opening scene and Buttler's words

Ich fürchte,
Wir gehn nicht von hier, wie wir kamen . . .
(Pic., I. i)

awaken a sense of foreboding. Octavio, the kingpin of Wallenstein's universe, presently reveals where his true loyalties lie, and soon after produces the imperial patent outlawing Friedland and appointing Piccolomini as commander-in-chief of the armed forces in his stead. The lovers are shown to inhabit an inner world of their own, remote from the world of *Zwecke* over which Wallenstein rules and, as Thekla soon realizes, threatened by it. Sesina's capture is announced and finally Max, who has quixotically refused to sign the written pledge, is forced to question his hitherto unquestioned allegiance to his leader.

Of all these adverse changes Wallenstein himself knows nothing. To him, the configuration of his fortune seems permanent and eminently predictable. He seems to be riding aloft on the same wave, only the crest is higher. And indeed, the configuration as a whole may still be the same in that the balance of forces has remained, roughly, constant. But within that frame, what insidious shifting! Some elements that had carried him have irrevocably dropped out and are beginning to form a secret undertow. Others have been swept into his course and momentarily swell his fortune.

If Wallenstein will have none of this, Illo, in one of the pivotal scenes of the drama, puts his finger on it. Illo realizes that the climactic moment is at hand and that Wallenstein's power is at its peak; and he begs him to stop procrastinating and to act now, 'mit entschlossener Tat'.

O! nimm der Stunde wahr, eh' sie entschlüpft . . .

he implores him:

> So selten kommt der Augenblick im Leben,
> Der wahrhaft wichtig ist und groß. Wo eine
> Entscheidung soll geschehen, da muß vieles
> Sich glücklich treffen und zusammenfinden –
> Und einzeln nur, zerstreuet zeigen sich
> Des Glückes Fäden, die Gelegenheiten,
> Die, nur in *einen* Lebenspunkt zusammen
> Gedrängt, den schweren Früchteknoten bilden.
> Sieh! wie entscheidend, wie verhängnisvoll
> Sich's jetzt um dich zusammenzieht! – Die Häupter

Des Heers, die besten, trefflichsten, um dich,
Den königlichen Führer, her versammelt,
Nur deinen Wink erwarten sie – O! laß
Sie so nicht wieder aus einander gehen!
So einig führst du sie im ganzen Lauf
Des Krieges nicht zum zweitenmal zusammen.
(*Pic.*, II. vi)

We have met the word 'Lebenspunkt' before. Goethe had used it when, after the completion of his *Laokoon* essay, he had inquired of Meyer whether he had 'den eigentlichen Lebenspunkt des Dargestellten wahrhaftig angegeben'.[48] And here this aesthetic term appears on Illo's lips! Of all unlikely people, the poet has chosen this ruthless creature of the moment to act as his spokesman.[49] He knows what Wallenstein refuses to accept: that the pregnant moment has come and that, in life at least, it cannot be stayed in that, being the climactic moment, it is fraught with its own disintegration.

Illo's knowledge of transience is fully driven home by the extended metaphor which dominates the closing portion of his speech:

Die hohe Flut ist's, die das schwere Schiff
Vom Strande hebt – Und jedem einzelnen
Wächst das Gemüt im großen Strom der Menge.
Jetzt hast du sie, jetzt noch! Bald sprengt der Krieg
Sie wieder aus einander, dahin, dorthin –
In eignen kleinen Sorgen und Intressen
Zerstreut sich der gemeine Geist. Wer heute,
Vom Strome fortgerissen, sich vergißt,
Wird nüchtern werden, sieht er sich allein . . .
(ibid.)

This is the imagery of water through which Goethe, in the *Laokoon* essay, had voiced the essential lability of every *Gestalt*, even the most articulated of configurations, the human form, carved though it be in eternal marble. And we may well ask with Illo and his creator: if that most structured of forms cannot survive disintegration, what hope has the fortuitous and vulnerable configuration of Wallenstein's fortune of doing so?

In the opening scene of *Wallensteins Tod*, just before the news of Sesina's capture comes to his ears, Wallenstein decides that the constellation

of the stars is at long last favourable and that the time for action has
arrived:

> Nicht Zeit ist's mehr, zu brüten und zu sinnen,
> Denn Jupiter, der glänzende, regiert
> Und zieht das dunkel zubereitete Werk
> Gewaltig in das Reich des Lichts – Jetzt muß
> Gehandelt werden, schleunig, eh' die Glücks-
> Gestalt mir wieder wegflieht überm Haupt,
> Denn stets in Wandlung ist der Himmelsbogen.
>
> (*Tod*, I. iv)

He has begun to understand the evanescence of any optimal moment,
begun to see that, like the wave, a human life is a moving configuration
for ever speeding past its zenith. Too late to save the situation, it is true,
for by a supreme tragic irony the very next scene brings the peripeteia of
the action, the *punctum saliens* as Schiller liked to call it. But even before
those fateful knocks are heard pounding on the door and the final reversal
sets in, what nostalgia is expressed in the word 'Glücks-Gestalt', stretching across two lines so that in the very saying of it, it breaks! Is this not
almost the knowledge of Helena, about to return to the elements from
whence for the short duration of the classical moment her *Hochgestalt* had
crystallized, the knowledge that

> . . . Glück und Schönheit dauerhaft sich nicht vereint?

VII

And, indeed, the high configuration of Wallenstein's fortune disintegrates before our eyes. Reverses follow one another like so many blows.
The emissary of the Swedes, Wrangel, is well aware of Sesina's capture
and thus able to enforce his terms on Friedland. Eger and half of 'his'
capital, Prague, are going to be occupied by the Swedes whom he hates,
who were to help him realize his dream and instead have robbed it of its
bloom, who tainted his 'Glücks-Gestalt' and instead have offered him a
sordid 'Konjunktion'. Wallenstein sees himself forced to tread the loath-
some path of high treason, and his own defection is presently followed by
his own generals deserting him. Isolani abandons the sinking ship; Buttler
is won over by Octavio to wreak dreadful vengeance on the unsuspecting
Friedland; Deodat, Maradas, Esterhazy, Götz, Coalto and Kaunitz have
vanished.

But for all those losses nibbling away at the periphery of his fortune, Wallenstein still feels that he is whole and that the 'Glücks-Gestalt' of his life is substantially intact. For while he thinks that he still 'has' the Piccolomini, he has himself. And he is right: they are part of him. The configuration on the firmament is the visible token of the basic configuration which does in fact govern his life – his relation to Octavio and Max. There, if anywhere, lies his inviolateness and integrity.[50]

This vital link between Wallenstein and his most intimate associates the poet has forged in a variety of ways. For us the principal one of these is the astrological motif which caused Schiller himself so much difficulty for so long. And to this we must now turn.[51]

As Max first enters the scene to greet Octavio, Questenberg joins hands with father and son and hails them thus:

> Octavio – Max Piccolomini!
> Heilbringend, vorbedeutungsvolle Namen!
> Nie wird das Glück von Österreich sich wenden,
> So lang' zwei solche Sterne, segenreich
> Und schützend, leuchten über seinen Heeren.
>
> (*Pic.*, I. iv)

This metaphor is reiterated and strengthened in the first greeting Wallenstein himself extends to the young warrior:

> Sei mir willkommen, Max. Stets warst du mir
> Der Bringer irgend einer schönen Freude,
> Und, wie das glückliche Gestirn des Morgens,
> Führst du die Lebenssonne mir herauf.
>
> (*Pic.*, II. iv)

Nor indeed does Wallenstein restrict the association with the stars to Max alone. Two scenes later he reveals to Terzky that his own planetary constellation is identical with that of Octavio:

> Wir sind geboren unter gleichen Sternen . . .
>
> (*Pic.*, II. vi)

On this mysterious interlacing of their fortunes he bases his unquestioning faith in father and son. Of them he is as sure

> Wie meiner selbst. *Die* lassen nie von mir.
>
> (ibid.)

There is intimacy in this '*Die*', but it is an intimacy mingled with contempt. Wallenstein feels that he 'has' the Piccolomini in the way in which he insists that he must 'have' his officers: unconditionally. 'Unbedingt muß ich sie haben', he stipulates no sooner than he has expressed his faith in the Piccolomini; and indeed, this request gives Terzky the idea of extracting from Wallenstein's staff a written pledge of absolute loyalty, by fair means or foul. Octavio Piccolomini is well aware of the nature of Wallenstein's attachment to himself and his son. When Max argues that Wallenstein puts his trust not only in political adventurers like Illo and Isolani, but in him and his father as well, the latter replies 'Weil man uns glaubt zu haben . . .' (*Pic.*, V. i). Octavio knows that Wallenstein's unquestioning reliance on him and his son does not spring so much from respect and love as from inner sloth and is motivated by the need to have something predictable in a welter of uncertainties. He 'has' them, once and for all, and that means that he can safely ignore them as a serious factor in his calculations.[52] And also as a serious factor in his inner life. For he does not hesitate to use father and son as pawns in his own dishonourable game and to sacrifice the better of the two. He only trusts in that he trusts the faithfulness of others.[53] And in this lack of emotional differentiation lies the ultimate cause of his downfall. He is not heartless, like Buttler; but he neglects his 'schlimmverwahrte Herz' (*Pic.*, I. iii). He is as vulnerable as he is ruthless. 'You mean to murder him', Gordon asks of Buttler, 'Der Euer Treu vertraut!' To which Buttler replies: 'Sein böses Schicksal!' (*Tod*, IV, vi). And this indeed it is.

Thus Wallenstein is not in truth aquainted with the inner constellation which governs his life; and that is, precisely, why he projects it on to the firmament, out into empty space. But to us the poet reveals, step by remorseless step, the identity of the outer and the inner; and here again, the astute Illo – the most underrated figure in this drama by far – points the way:

> O! du wirst auf die Sternenstunde warten,
> Bis dir die irdische entflieht!

he urges; and continues:

> . . . Glaub' mir,
> In deiner Brust sind deines Schicksals Sterne.
> (*Pic.*, II. vi)

The precise meaning of this statement is revealed in Octavio's crucial encounter with his son. As he prepares to let Max into his secret and to show him the imperial patent which will seal Wallenstein's fate, he says, 'nach einer Pause':

> Herzog Friedland
> Hat seine Zurüstung gemacht. Er traut
> Auf seine Sterne. Unvorbereitet denkt er uns
> Zu überfallen – mit der sichern Hand
> Meint er den goldnen Zirkel schon zu fassen.
> Er irret sich – Wir haben auch gehandelt.
> Er faßt sein bös geheimnisvolles Schicksal.
>
> (*Pic.*, V. i)

And what is this 'bös geheimnisvolle Schicksal' he is about to touch as he reaches for the stars? Octavio continues:

> Mit leisen Schritten schlich er seinen bösen Weg,
> So leis' und schlau ist ihm die Rache nachgeschlichen.
> Schon steht sie ungesehen, finster hinter ihm,
> Ein Schritt nur noch, und schaudernd rühret er sie an.
>
> (ibid.)[54]

Already earlier Octavio had said to Questenberg:

> . . . Überraschen
> Kann er uns nicht, Sie wissen, daß ich ihn
> Mit meinen Horchern rings umgeben habe;
> Vom kleinsten Schritt erhalt' ich Wissenschaft
> Sogleich – ja mir entdeckt's sein eigner Mund.
>
> (*Pic.*, I. iii)

To which Questenberg had replied:

> Ganz unbegreiflich ist's, daß er den Feind nicht merkt
> An seiner Seite.
>
> (ibid.)

Illo's prophecy has come true. The 'Schicksals Sterne', which Wallenstein had looked for far away, are indeed 'in seiner Brust'. They are the enemy by his side, stalking him as relentlessly as Wallenstein had pursued Octavio, gradually closing in on him, finally to reveal himself as the 'Rache-Engel' in his innermost heart.

Wallenstein himself makes precisely this discovery when Octavio's treachery has come to his knowledge. What had at first appeared to be an emissary from another world, then the friend by his side, in the end steps forth from himself, from his very heart of hearts:

> Mir sandte
> Der Abgrund den verstecktesten der Geister,
> Den Lügekundigsten herauf und stellt ihn
> Als Freund an meine Seite. Wer vermag
> Der Hölle Macht zu widerstehn! Ich zog
> Den Basilisken auf an meinem Busen,
> Mit meinem Herzblut nährt' ich ihn, er sog
> Sich schwelgend voll an meiner Liebe Brüsten . . .
> Am Sternenhimmel suchten meine Augen,
> Im weiten Weltenraum den Feind, den ich
> Im Herzen meines Herzens eingeschlossen.
>
> (*Tod*, III. xviii)

And Max? Does Wallenstein not discover his secret identity with him[55] when the constellation that had shone upon his life is finally blanketed by gloom, and his grief at its passing, in one of the most consummately fluid and lyrical transitions in the German tongue, turns into sorrow at the passing of his dead young friend? Does he not know that they were one when Max suffers the very fate which had been Friedland's nightmare? At the end he knows that through the loss of Max he has irrevocably lost part of himself, perhaps his best part. Over and over again he voices the same sense of bereavement – *his* bereavement:

> Die Blume ist hinweg aus *meinem**** Leben . . .
> Denn er stand neben mir wie *meine**** Jugend . . .
> Was ich *mir**** ferner auch erstreben mag,
> Das Schöne ist doch weg, und kommt nicht wieder,
> Denn über alles Glück geht doch der Freund,
> Der's fühlend erst erschafft, der's teilend mehrt.
>
> (*Tod*, V. iii)

When Octavio had left Wallenstein, he had compared himself to a tree shorn of its foliage but still intact and full of living pith. The passing of Max goes to his very marrow. He has lost his wholeness, and he can only regain integrity by shouldering the burden of that loss. And that he does. He does so by remaining faithful to his course and thereby to Max who

* My italics.

suffered because of it. But also he does so, and perhaps more deeply yet, by accepting at long last that nothing in life is permanent and bidding adieu to his dream. 'Wohl weiß ich, daß die ird'schen Dinge wechseln,' he says to Gordon; and his forebodings and, a little later, Seni's, cause him to smile – and these are the only times throughout the tragedy that he does so. Well may he smile. For the acceptance of total powerlessness in the face of transience has brought him that sense of release and overflowing bounty which so often transfigures the dying moments of Schiller's heroes.[56] It is not hubris or defiance of death, but the deep acceptance of it that makes Wallenstein speak to Gordon as he does:

> Es treibt der ungeschwächte Mut
> Noch frisch und herrlich auf der Lebenswoge . . .
> Zwar jetzo schein' ich tief herabgestürzt,
> Doch werd ich wieder steigen, hohe Flut
> Wird bald auf diese Ebbe schwellend folgen . . .
> (Tod, V. iv)[57]

We know the image which, all unbidden, springs to Friedland's lips. It is the imagery of water which Illo had used to remind Wallenstein that the pregnant moment is at hand and will pass as quickly as it had come; the imagery, too, which the author of the *Laokoon* essay had so tellingly employed. By letting his hero resort to it here, the poet intimates that Wallenstein now accepts that no configuration can be arrested, least of all the optimal one; for every climax is fraught with its own dissolution.

At the end, Wallenstein is supremely aware, not only of the power of time, but also of its nature.

> Für ihn ist keine Zukunft mehr, ihm spinnt
> Das Schicksal keine Tücke mehr . . .
> Und unglückbringend pocht ihm keine Stunde . . .
> Wer aber weiß, was uns
> Die nächste Stunde schwarzverschleiert bringt . . .
> Denn ihn besiegen die gewalt'gen Stunden . . .
> Und in dem Heute wandelt schon das Morgen . . .
> (Tod, V. iii)

Every one of these formulations crystallizes the sheer dread of time so familiar to Schiller and Goethe even at the high noon of their classicism: a dread born of the realization that the present moment, or hour, or day, inevitably dies in and for the one succeeding it.[58]

VIII

As with time, so with life. There is, in the *Wallenstein* trilogy, a vast body of imagery drawn from the sphere of organic existence, imagery of seed and fruit or indeed of pregnancy and birth. The more intimately we become acquainted with the verbal texture of the play, the more ominous the implications carried by these images seem to grow.[59]

Characteristically, and for the longest time, Wallenstein believes in the predictableness of life, and of human behaviour in particular. He knows his Piccolomini to the core, he argues, and from such trees the fruit must be good:

> – Des Menschen Taten und Gedanken, wißt!
> Sind nicht wie Meeres blindbewegte Wellen.
> Die innre Welt, sein Mikrokosmos, ist
> Der tiefe Schacht, aus dem sie ewig quellen.
> Sie sind notwendig, wie des Baumes Frucht,
> Sie kann der Zufall gaukelnd nicht verwandeln.
> Hab' ich des Menschen Kern erst untersucht,
> So weiß ich auch sein Wollen und sein Handeln.[60]
>
> (*Tod*, II. iii)

As we know, Wallenstein's optimism is presently disproved. Octavio chooses to sacrifice him whilst his son chooses to sacrifice himself: perhaps the general did not trouble to know his Piccolomini and their complex motivation sufficiently well to forecast the future correctly.

But in a sterner sort of way, the tragedy seems to bear out Friedland's underlying assumption that 'a good tree bringeth forth good fruit, but a corrupt tree bringeth forth evil fruit'. True, wherever we look in this play, the fruits seem to be evil. But so too seem to have been the intentions from which they have sprung, and there is a grim logic in the final reckoning.

> Ihr sätet Blut
> Und steht bestürzt, daß Blut ist aufgegangen . . .

the remorseless Buttler replies to Octavio's protestations of innocence over Wallenstein's corpse (*Tod*, V. xi); and presently the Countess Terzky joins the chorus: in reply to Piccolomini's

> Das sind die Folgen unglücksel'ger Taten

she raps out

> Es sind die Früchte Ihres Tuns . . .
> (*Tod*, V. xii)

And indeed, she is only telling Piccolomini what he already knows. For it is he who, much earlier in the play, had told his son:

> Das eben ist der Fluch der bösen Tat,
> Daß sie, fortzeugend, immer Böses muß gebären.
> (*Pic.*, V. i)

More importantly, Wallenstein himself knows and accepts the law of causality and the justice of the retribution it entails. As after agonized and protracted indecision he finally resolves to commit high treason, portentous words break from his lips:

> Nicht hoffe, wer des Drachen Zähne sät,
> Erfreuliches zu ernten. Jede Untat
> Trägt ihren eignen Rache-Engel schon,
> Die böse Hoffnung, unter ihrem Herzen.
> (*Tod*, I. vii)

More startling still are the concluding words of that same speech. They probe into obscurer territories of experience and give voice to a dread which is more insidious yet. 'Frohlocke nicht', he warns the Countess as he orders Wrangel to be fetched:

> Frohlocke nicht!
> Denn eifersüchtig sind des Schicksals Mächte.
> Voreilig Jauchzen greift in ihre Rechte.
> Den Samen legen wir in ihre Hände,
> Ob Glück, ob Unglück aufgeht, lehrt das Ende.
> (*Tod*, I. vii)

The simple and morally unimpeachable correlation between intention and consequence here has given way to a profound metaphysical doubt as to whether there is any such logic at all. And, indeed, this doubt forms the steady groundswell of Wallenstein's thinking and draws from him utterances which are tinged with horror and awe. Early on, when Illo had urged that the pregnant moment was at hand, he had replied:

> . . . des Menschen Tun
> Ist eine Aussaat von Verhängnissen,

Gestreuet in der Zukunft dunkles Land,
Den Schicksalsmächten hoffend übergeben.

And, with a shudder of superstition, he had added:

Da tut es not, die Saatzeit zu erkunden,
Die rechte Sternenstunde auszulesen,
Des Himmels *Häuser* forschend zu durchspüren,
Ob nicht der Feind des Wachsens und Gedeihens
In seinen *Ecken* schadend sich verberge.
Drum laßt mir Zeit.

(*Pic.*, II. vi)

But the seriousness of even these words is dwarfed by the gravity of the words he will speak in the great monologue which Goethe called the axis of the play:

Nicht ohne Schauder greift des Menschen Hand
In des Geschicks geheimnisvolle Urne.
In meiner Brust war meine Tat noch mein:
Einmal entlassen aus dem sichern Winkel
Des Herzens, ihrem mütterlichen Boden,
Hinausgegeben in des Lebens Fremde,
Gehört sie jenen tück'schen Mächten an,
Die keines Menschen Kunst vertraulich macht.

(*Tod*, I. iv)

Such dread as this stems from reaches of consciousness that lie beyond good and evil. It is the existential dread we know from the *Laokoon* essay, dread of vital process as such which is at every moment pregnant with disintegration and death.[61] It is the dread which gripped the poet of *Dauer im Wechsel* when he gazed upon his wasting hand and perceived, behind the homely change from youth to age, the much more terrifying change from moment to moment, as cells break down to re-form and structures are continually depleted of their elements to be replenished by new and strange ones. The experience of continuity, of the inexorable progress from seed to fruit, is uncanny and frightening enough. But at the core of Schiller's tragedy lies the greater terror at the discontinuity within such continuity, terror at the evanescence of every atom in every configuration and, worse still, terror at the indifference to its immediate neighbour of each link in the chain of life. The fruit is autonomous, as independent of the seed from which it sprang as the child is of its begetter; and the only thing which we may safely predict about the relation between the generations is this, 'except the seed die', the fruit cannot live; the fruit must rot so that the seed in it may come to fruition. For '. . . in dem Heute wandelt schon das Morgen': and when the morrow comes, what was present and real and living only now is past and done with. Today's wave is tomorrow's trough.

This vision of vital process as procreation pregnant with death has found poetic expression in two dramatic metaphors that seem worlds apart: the one macrocosmic, so deeply anchored in reality that we scarcely register its symbolic overtones, the other microcosmic, so tender and so charged with feeling that we resist grasping it as part of an overriding intellectual pattern. At the circumference of the action, there is the broad panorama of the army; at its inner heart, the tragedy of Max.

We have seen that, from the start, the poet has projected an image of the army as an organic whole animated and sustained by its leader. Thus it is not surprising that he should speak of this giant configuration in the same terms in which he speaks of every other: through images drawn from organic life – seed and harvest, propagation and destruction.

For all the protestations of Wallenstein that peace is his business, his army, like all armies, is an instrument of destruction. As the first Jäger has it:

> Ein Reich von Soldaten wollt' er gründen,
> Die Welt anstecken und entzünden . . .
> (Lager, vi)

This is one of many statements driving home an obvious and brutal truth. Yet, paradoxically, this instrument of extinction is persistently spoken of in images suggesting that it is a productive and even a creative force. True, it stems from chaos; it engenders chaos; but it is an ordered and self-maintaining cosmos none the less. Questenberg puts his finger on this paradox when he exclaims:

> In kein Friedländisch Heereslager komme,
> Wer von dem Kriege Böses denken will.
> Beinah' vergessen hätt ich seine Plagen,
> Da mir der Ordnung hoher Geist erschienen,
> Durch die er, weltzerstörend, selbst besteht,
> Das Große mir erschienen, das er bildet.
> (Pic., I. i)

This paradoxical association of the army with both, destructiveness and creativity, recurs persistently. But what is the nature of this double association, and, in such context, what is the meaning of creativity?

> Die Armee sich immer muß neu gebären . . .

the Jäger comments as his eyes fall upon the 'Soldatenjungen', the illegitimate offspring of the Marketenderin, a product of war and cannon-fodder for the future.

> Der Krieg ernährt den Krieg. Gehn Bauern drauf,
> Ei, so gewinnt der Kaiser mehr Soldaten . . .
> > (*Pic.*, I. ii)

Isolani replies in answer to Questenberg's representations that the army is the scourge of the land off which it lives. And Octavio Piccolomini draws an unforgettable picture of the soldiers' parasitic existence, a picture in which life and death, accretion and depletion, creation and destruction are ominously and inextricably mingled:

> In Hast und Eile bauet der Soldat
> Von Leinwand seine leichte Stadt, da wird
> Ein augenblicklich Brausen und Bewegen,
> Der Markt belebt sich, Straßen, Flüsse sind
> Bedeckt mit Fracht, es rührt sich das Gewerbe . . .

– and then, without a full stop even to mark the watershed between life and death:

> Doch eines Morgens plötzlich siehet man
> Die Zelte fallen, weiter rückt die Horde,
> Und ausgestorben, wie ein Kirchhof, bleibt
> Der Acker, das zerstampfte Saatfeld liegen,
> Und um des Jahres Ernte ist's getan.
> > (*Pic.*, I. iv)

All these statements – and there are many – point in the same direction: Wallenstein's army is a giant image of life as we know it from every page, and on every level, of Schiller's tragedy: like the pregnant moment, this miscreation is informed with death, endlessly propagating itself and proliferating, feeding on the life that sustains it, in turn destroying the life on which it feeds until, finally, it is itself destroyed.

> Das eben ist der Fluch der bösen Tat,
> Daß sie, fortzeugend, Böses muß gebären . . .
> (Pic., V. i)

Octavio, sanctimoniously if correctly, says to his son. But it is not only the curse of the evil deed that from its womb it brings forth deadly fruit. In the universe of discourse of this tragedy, it is the law of life itself, and the law of the monstrous force which is the overall dramatic symbol of such life.

From its periphery to its heart, the *Wallenstein* trilogy is shot through with dread of vital process. It informs the facts, the figures and the very fabric of its words.[62] This dread has found surpassing expression in the tragedy of Max's coming of age.

Since his earliest childhood, Max has been Friedland's ward. In the poignant plea that Max stay with him which culminates in the words

> Sie alle waren Fremdlinge, *du* warst
> Das Kind des Hauses – Max! du kannst mich nicht verlassen!
> (*Tod*, III. xviii)

Wallenstein eloquently describes the nature of the bond between his young friend and himself; and strangely enough it turns out that he has not only been a father to him but, in essential truth, a mother:

> Ich selbst war deine *Wärterin*,*

he reminds Max:

> nicht schämt' ich
> Der kleinen Dienste mich, ich pflegte deiner
> Mit *weiblich** sorgender Geschäftigkeit,
> Bis du, von mir erwärmt, an meinem Herzen
> Das junge Leben wieder freudig fühltest.
> (ibid.)

These are strong words and we cannot doubt their sincerity; for they come from the depth of Wallenstein's preoccupation with organic process and with birth.[63] And it is with all the natural right of the world on his side that he pleads with his creation not to relinquish its creator.

But Max has come of age. 'Mein Sohn ist mündig', Octavio had rapped out when Terzky had pressed him to make his unwilling offspring sign

* My italics.

the pledge of unconditional loyalty to Wallenstein which everyone else had signed. And when, later in the play, Max returns to Friedland to seek final clarity about his leader's intentions, he prefaces the moral battle in which he is about to engage with the grave and solemn words:

> Mein General! – Du machst mich heute mündig.
> (*Tod*, II. ii)

To be 'mündig' here means to be autonomous and obliged as well as able to pick one's path through the wilderness of the moral scene.[64] As Max comes of age and emancipates himself from the configuration of Wallenstein's fortune of which he had formed part, he acts out the biological tragedy of new life deserting old, the universal tragedy of birth, of the fruit leaving the tree or indeed of the cell separating from the structure to which it once belonged. And the deepest tragedy is that this new life too is so shortlived, gained only, it seems, to be engulfed in a devouring and impenetrable future.

When the life process is experienced thus, as a death within birth, its every manifestation is shot through with horror. In the end, every 'Stunde' is 'schwarzverschleiert', every 'Frucht' is an 'Unglücksfrucht', every 'Tat' is an 'Untat' and every 'gute Hoffnung' turns into a 'böse Hoffnung'.

Such profound and ineradicable distrust of life is stamped upon every page of Schiller's greatest tragedy. It has found shattering utterance in words, the ultimate significance of which reaches far beyond the occasion on which they are spoken and far exceeds the speaker's conscious grasp:

> Wer das Vertraun vergiftet, o der mordet
> Das werdende Geschlecht im Leib der Mutter.
> (*Tod*, III. i)

IX

We have seen, in two examples, the tremendous organizing energy of the pregnant moment, that slender ridge between rise and decline, past and future, power and dissipation, from which the artist may unfold a mighty human landscape. Small wonder that Goethe and Schiller considered it to be the Archimedean point, the hinge of the whole vexed problem of how to define artistically any given subject-matter and how to determine its appropriateness to a given form of art. Both these great artists, in all their major works – written, in some cases, before their theory was developed – unerringly fastened on the climactic moment when permanence becomes pellucid with transience and stable structures are seen inexorably to dissolve. Take Goethe's *Faust*, *Wilhelm Meister*, *Hermann und Dorothea*, *Iphigenie*, *Tasso* or indeed *Die natürliche Tochter*: they are all organized around the critical moment when the hero sheds the cocoon of study or home or childhood or temple or creative engrossment or aesthetic semblance to step forth into a world demanding constant metamorphosis and fraught with the incessant threat of disintegration.[65] And who would doubt that the poet of *Maria Stuart*, *Die Jungfrau von Orleans*, *Die Braut von Messina*, *Wilhelm Tell* and *Demetrius* is centrally concerned with the breaking-up of 'die alte feste Form', the dialectic of movement and stasis?

> Die Zeit ist eine blühende Flur,
> Ein großes Lebendiges ist die Natur,
> Und alles ist Frucht, und alles ist Samen.

These words come from *Die Braut von Messina*. They might have come from any drama after *Wallenstein*. Schiller's sense of transience, basically a legacy of the age of baroque, is more absolute than that of Goethe who had the forward-looking theory of natural types powerfully to sustain him. But even for him the bulwark of nature was not impregnable. There is the agonized struggle with *Die natürliche Tochter*, the tragedy of loveliness and life stepping forth, not into the fullness of being, but into a veritable chasm of decay; and the closing lines of the *Elegie* of Marienbad tell their own story. But even there the rejection of nature's balm gives way to renewed harmony and reconciliation; and Goethe was unable to complete the most unmitigated tragedy he ever contemplated whilst Schiller wrote one after the other.

However crucial these differences, both men knew that transience is the very stuff of life. They faced it to the end and shaped and conquered it through the surpassing power of form; and in their unflinching acceptance of the human condition and the courageous and creative response with which they countered existential dread lies the secret of their living classicism. *Memento vivere* was their answer to our *Angst*, and this is as good an answer as any. It is as impressive as it is touching that Schiller should have used the very imagery of seed and flower and fruit which *within* his tragedy is fraught with death, as an aesthetic category defining the 'Lebenspunkt' from which a work of art may germinate steadily, organically and imperishably. 'Mit dem Ende des 2ten Acts', he writes of his *Wallenstein*, 'ist die ganze Exposition gegeben, und alle Charaktere, die bedeutenderen ohnehin, eingeführt; so daß nach Beendigung dieser zwei ersten Acte die 3 übrigen nur als Entwickelung aus diesem *stamen* anzusehen sind.'[66] Similarly, we read of *Warbeck* and again almost verbatim of *Die Prinzessin von Celle*: the pregnant moment of the action 'ist eine aufbrechende Knospe; alles, was sich ereignet, lag schon darin'.[67] And in his letters to Weimar, how often does he give thanks for the *fruitfulness* of the aesthetic ideas Goethe has implanted in him – the very ideas which enabled him to give poignant utterance to the *fearfulness* of life!

For a similarly Janus-faced view of the productive force, in and out of art, Goethe's *Winckelmann* essay comes to mind. In the section headed *Schönheit*, we read:

> . . . das letzte *Produkt** der sich immer steigernden Natur ist der schöne Mensch. Zwar kann sie ihn nur selten *hervorbringen,** weil ihren Ideen gar viele Bedingungen widerstreben, und selbst ihrer Allmacht ist es unmöglich, lange in Vollkommnen zu verweilen und dem *hervorgebrachten** Schönen eine Dauer zu geben. Denn genau genommen kann man sagen, es sei nur ein Augenblick, in welchem der schöne Mensch schön sei.
>
> Dagegen tritt nun die Kunst ein, denn indem der Mensch auf den Gipfel der Natur gestellt ist, so sieht er sich wieder als eine ganze Natur an, die in sich abermals einen Gipfel *hervorzubringen** hat. Dazu steigert er sich, indem er sich mit allen Vollkommenheiten und Tugenden durchdringt, Wahl, Ordnung, Harmonie und Bedeutung aufruft, und sich endlich bis zur *Produktion** des Kunstwerkes erhebt . . . Ist es einmal *hervorgebracht,** steht es in seiner idealen Wirklichkeit vor der Welt, so *bringt** es eine dauernde Wirkung, es *bringt** die höchste *hervor:** denn indem es aus den gesamten Kräften sich geistig entwickelt, so nimmt es alles Herrliche, Verehrungs- und Liebenswürdige in sich auf, und erhebt, indem es die menschliche Gestalt beseelt, den Menschen über sich selbst, schließt seinen Lebens- und Tatenkreis ab, und vergöttert ihn für die Gegenwart, in der das Vergangene und Künftige begriffen ist.[68]

Eight times in this short passage does Goethe use the words 'hervorbringen', 'Produkt' and 'Produktion'; and every time they signify transience in life, and permanence in art. For its sense of inconstancy at the heart of vital process this classical pronouncement is overwhelming. It is paralleled only by the early statement of the self-devouringness of life which

* My italics.

occurs in Goethe's review of Sulzer's work,[69] and by Werther's famous
lament of 18 August. Such evanescence is only stayed and conquered in
the 'ideale Wirklichkeit' of the work of art, which rests on the still pivot
of the pregnant moment. But it is stayed only in the artistic product, which
is autonomous of its begetter. For even the climactic configurations of
creativity in the life of the artist wane, as does all living form. This the
creator of *Faust* and *Tasso* knew in abundant measure;[70] and to Schiller
it was poignantly brought home when he had come to the end of his
Herculean labour on *Wallenstein*: 'Ich habe mich schon lange vor dem
Augenblick gefürchtet, den ich so sehr wünschte, meines Werks los zu
sein,' he writes to Goethe; 'und in der Tat befinde ich mich bei meiner
jetzigen Freiheit schlimmer als der bisherigen Sklaverei. Die Masse, die
mich bisher anzog und fest hielt, ist nun auf einmal weg, und mir dünkt,
als wenn ich bestimmungslos im luftleeren Raume hinge. Zugleich ist
mir, als wenn es absolut unmöglich wäre, daß ich wieder etwas hervorbringen könnte . . .'[71]

Thus, only the work of art itself remains. In the inviolateness of its life
Goethe discovered permanence in flux, 'Dauer im Wechsel'. The concluding lines of this poem invoke the grace of form which alone stays the
gruesome flight of the moment and transcends even death and decay:

> Laß den Anfang mit dem Ende
> Sich in Eins zusammenziehn!
> Schneller als die Gegenstände
> Selber dich vorüberfliehn.
> Danke, daß die Gunst der Musen
> Unvergängliches verheißt,
> Den Gehalt in deinem Busen
> Und die Form in deinem Geist.

Schiller too knew himself to be 'der flüchtige Sohn der Stunde'. Like his
Wallenstein at the end, he faced mortality; like him, he could say:

> Wohl weiß ich, daß die ird'schen Dinge wechseln

and proudly surrender what he could not call his own. He once wrote:
'Der Geist kann nichts, als was Form ist, sein eigen nennen'. It is enough
to live by.

6
Ripeness

. . . denn still allmählich reift das Köstliche!

(*Die Jungfrau von Orleans*)

12

The art of dying : on the sublime and
the noble in Schiller's tragedies

━━━━━━━━━━━━━━━━ ⊰⊱ ━━━━━━━━━━━━━━━━

I

In what must surely be some of the most moving lines written by Schiller,
Hanna Kennedy, Maria Stuart's nurse, says to Melvil, former master of
the royal household who has now returned to administer the last sacraments to his Monarch:

> – O Sir! Wir litten Mangel, da wir lebten,
> Erst mit dem Tode kommt der Überfluß zurück.
> (V. iii)

These words are spoken in reply to Melvil's unasked question as to the
meaning of the splendour by which he sees himself surrounded:

> . . . was soll
> Das Prachtgerät an diesem Ort des Todes?
> (ibid.)

And indeed, Maria's prison, so stark and bare in the opening scenes of the
tragedy, is being filled, almost to overflowing, with lovely and precious
things, vessels wrought in silver and in gold, various looking-glasses,
paintings, Maria's jewel box and other treasures being carried in before
our eyes. When a few moments later Maria herself enters, she is clad in
festive white, her Agnus Dei framing her neck as though it were an
adornment, a crucifix in her hand and a diadem in that silken hair of hers
of which young Mortimer had dreamed and raved not many hours before.
The tableau with which the poet presents us here, close to the end of the

tragedy, seems both a confirmation and a refutation of the harsh words
Sir Paulet had levelled at the Queen in its opening scene:

> . . . Den Christus in der Hand,
> Die Hoffart und die Weltlust in dem Herzen.

A confirmation in that these worldly luxuries are clearly meaningful to
Maria, even at the door of death; a refutation in that it is patent that
such outward riches are no longer treasured for their own sakes.

The deep solemnity of the occasion – and the fact that she so readily
gives away what has just been returned to her – make it clear that they
are the visible tokens of some other, invisible bounty granted to Maria
even as death lays its shadow over her. Kennedy tells Melvil of its approach,
of those poignant seconds when the signals of life and death first got
momentarily crossed. At dawn a violent knocking was heard in the castle:

> Wir glauben, die Befreier zu vernehmen,
> Die Hoffnung winkt, der süße Trieb des Lebens
> Wacht unwillkürlich allgewaltig auf –
> Da öffnet sich die Tür . . .

(V. i)

and in comes Sir Paulet to say that the scaffolding for Maria's execution
has been erected in the hall below. Needless to say, this is a situation
fraught with tragic irony, a 'fürchterliche Wechsel' such as Kennedy and
Melvil perceive it to be. But not only that. The influx of life at the moment
of death is not just a macabre misunderstanding. The splendour of the
décor, Maria's outward apparel and, most of all, the festive solemnity of
her bearing throughout these final moments of her earthly career tell
their own tale. They suggest that life and death are not the mutually
exclusive opposites they appeared to be at first sight; that at times they
entwine so closely as to become inseparable; that the very approach of
death may release an enhanced, indeed an extravagant, sense of being
alive. After long and cruel privation, Maria at long last experiences

> Der Erde Glanz auf meinem Weg zum Himmel.

Hanna Kennedy's words about the flowering of life in the face of death
are not only moving in that they give voice to an age-old paradox – the
paradox of 'whosoever shall seek to save his life shall lose it; and whosoever
shall lose his life shall preserve it' (Luke 17: 33). If they communicate
afresh an old and universal truth it is because Schiller, himself so familiar

with death, has made it his own in a special degree. One thinks of Posa's parting words to the Queen in which he seems to discover for the first time the full glory of being alive; of the rising tide of Wallenstein's life as he is about to die; or indeed of the concluding words of *Wallensteins Lager* about having to stake one's life in order to gain it which, from afar, foreshadow the dying hero's mysterious sense of enrichment.

Towards the end of *Maria Stuart*, then, the threads of life and death intermingle. Nor is this tangled skein cut abruptly, like the Gordian knot. True, Hanna Kennedy, expatiating on Maria's reaction to the 'fürchterliche Wechsel' which had surprised her that morning, pronounces the famous words:

> Man löst sich nicht allmählich von dem Leben!
> Mit *einem* Mal, schnell, augenblicklich muß
> Der Tausch geschehen zwischen Zeitlichem
> Und Ewigem, und Gott gewährte meiner Lady
> In diesem Augenblick, der Erde Hoffnung
> Zurückzustoßen mit entschloßner Seele
> Und glaubenvoll den Himmel zu ergreifen.
>
> (V. i)

These words are traditionally regarded as giving a true account of the final phase of Maria's development, if only because of their close correspondence to an equally familiar passage in *Über das Erhabene*:

Das Erhabene verschafft uns also einen Ausgang aus der sinnlichen Welt, worin uns das Schöne gern immer *gefangen* halten möchte. *Nicht allmählich* (denn es gibt von der Abhängigkeit keinen *Übergang* zur Freiheit,) sondern *plötzlich* und durch eine Erschütterung reißt es den selbständigen Geist aus dem *Netze* los, womit die verfeinerte Sinnlichkeit ihn *umstrickte*, und das um so fester *bindet*, je durchsichtiger es *gesponnen* ist.[1]

It is perhaps worth quoting some more extracts from this passage and to note not only the repeated stress on the suddenness of the liberating experience afforded by the sublime act but also the prevalence and tenor of the images denoting captivity, both of which I shall italicize as I have done before:

. . . oft [ist] *eine einzige* erhabene Rührung genug, dieses *Gewebe des Betrugs* zu zerreißen, dem *gefesselten* Geist seine ganze Schnellkraft *auf einmal* zurückzugeben. . . . Die Schönheit unter der

Gestalt der Göttin Kalypso hat den tapfern Sohn des Ulysses *bezaubert*, und durch die *Macht ihrer Reizungen* hält sie ihn *lange Zeit* auf ihrer Insel *gefangen*. *Lange* glaubt er einer unsterblichen Gottheit zu huldigen, da er doch nur in den Armen der Wollust liegt – aber ein erhabener Eindruck ergreift ihn plötzlich unter Mentors Gestalt: er erinnert sich seiner besseren Bestimmung, wirft sich in die Wellen und ist *frei*.[1]

To be free here means to cast off the captivity of the senses. The twice-repeated word *gefangen* – and its many synonyms – has entirely negative associations. To love, conversely, is to lie in the arms of sensual slavery. We shall meet the image of the arms again. But ought we really to allow the words of the thinker to dictate our understanding of the kind of liberation one of his poetic characters is about to achieve? Maria's prison, at the end, becomes a more and more consecrated place; and it is *in* prison thus transfigured that we witness her final redemption, even as the angel sought out the apostle Peter *in* captivity –

> Und *im** Gefängnis steht er glänzend da . . .
> (V. vii)

Besides – and this is the chief point at issue – does Maria really exchange the temporal for the eternal 'mit *einem* Mal, augenblicklich' as Kennedy would have us believe and after the fashion that the poet himself, in his essay, insists that the sublime is achieved? Far from it. These words are spoken at the outset of the last act and they do indeed foreshadow the manner in which, an hour or so hence, Maria will finally bid farewell to life, gracefully and swiftly. But we must also remember that they point back to a wider context. They echo the words Hanna Kennedy had spoken to, and of, this Queen at the beginning of the tragedy; namely that there are

> . . . böse Geister,
> Die in des Menschen unverwahrter Brust
> Sich augenblicklich ihren Wohnplatz nehmen,
> Die schnell in uns das Schreckliche begehn
> Und zu der Höll' entfliehend, das Entsetzen
> In dem befleckten Busen hinterlassen.
> (I. v)

* My italics.

Maria's crime exactly matches her expiation (which begins on the anniversary of that crime). Both are the impulsive acts of one that is deeply and helplessly involved in temporality. This enmeshment ends only with time and life itself. And nothing tells us more eloquently of the tenacious hold, on the heroine, of temporal life than those final scenes which follow upon Hanna Kennedy's words to Melvil. They portray the slow maturing – step by step – of a resolution bravely born the instant the executioners were heard knocking at the door.

The Maria we encounter after the final reversal of her hopes shows every sign of composure and acceptance. 'Mit ruhiger Hoheit im ganzen Kreise umhersehend', as the stage direction has it, she marvels at her friends' grief, asking them to rejoice with her rather than to pity her. She hails death, the 'ernste Freund' who is about to 'cover her shame with his black pinions'. She seems reconciled to her fate. And yet her stance here is not entirely convincing. The image of death covering up her misdeeds sets us wondering; for in this play *decken* and *bedecken* are throughout associated with the concealment of realities not fully faced. One need only think of the culminating taunt Maria flings at Elisabeth – the taunt for which she will have to pay with her life:

> Weh Euch, wenn sie von Euren Taten einst
> Den Ehrenmantel zieht, womit Ihr gleißend
> Die wilde Glut verstohlner Lüste deckt.
>
> (III. iv)[2]

And, indeed, after her majestic entry, how full of bitterness and hurt pride are her words! How sensual is her leave-taking from her maids of honour, and how unabashedly geared to physical objects and physical experience is this scene, looked at closely in its entirety!

> Dein Mund brennt heiß, *Gertrude* – Ich bin viel
> Gehasset worden, doch auch viel geliebt!
> Ein edler Mann beglücke meine Gertrud,
> Denn Liebe fordert dieses glühnde Herz . . .
>
> (V. vi)

Just as in Maria's own mind the boundary lines between her who is about to die and those around her who will go out into life are blurred, so too we, the readers, are sensible of Maria herself even as she speaks of another; for throughout the drama we have come to associate words like *heiß* and *glühend* with none other than Maria herself.[3] By such glimpses into her mind the poet prepares us for the communion, itself a sensuous event of the most poignant significance and the culmination of the reliving, in confession, of Maria's turbulent career.

What an incredible conception this communion scene and the scenes that form the coda of Maria's life are! Not only, or even mainly, because of the audacity with which the poet has presented the central cultic act of the Christian faith upon the stage – with this venture and the organic necessity for it in the context of the thematic structure of the play I have dealt in another chapter.[4] But incredible because in these closing scenes the poet has stepped up the rhythmic alternation between spiritual equanimity and an ever-renewed assault, upon the tragic heroine, by the forces of time and life so sharply that, but for the absolute assurance with which we see him steer his heroine through a series of the most devastating false starts, we might well feel that he is allowing her to lapse from the sublime to the ridiculous. Time and again in these concluding scenes Maria reiterates the same claim – the claim that she has come to terms with her death – and time and again this claim is exploded, at least in the finality with which she has stated it, by vivid glimpses the poet affords us of the undiminished and tenacious hold life in fact still has on this woman. The words with which Maria opens her confession –

> Ich habe alles Zeitliche berichtigt . . .
>
> (V. vii)

– are presently belied by the burning bitterness of her sense of exile here and now. During and after this confession she repeatedly protests that she has surrendered her love and hate, in particular her passion for Leicester:

> Es war der schwerste Kampf, den ich bestand,
> Zerrissen ist das letzte ird'sche Band . . .
>
> (V. vii)

she says, and again when warned that the time for her execution – and meeting her executioners, one of whom is Leicester – is at hand:

> Ich fürchte keinen Rückfall. Meinen Haß
> Und meine Liebe hab' ich Gott geopfert . . .
>
> (V. vii)

and yet a fourth time, as she is about to make her exit:

> Nun hab ich nichts mehr
> Auf dieser Welt . . .
>
> (V. ix)

After these emphatic declarations – four in all – that she is now immune to the lures of life, the poet has treated us to the most ironic of spectacles which has, to my knowledge, never been discussed in the seriousness of its implications for anyone eager to identify Schiller's conception of sublimity as it emerges from his tragedies themselves. She has resolved to take the step into death at the hand of her nurse who, in her arms, carried her into life:

> Sie trug auf ihren Armen mich ins Leben,
> Sie leite mich mit sanfter Hand zum Tod.
>
> (ibid.)

She has besought her redeemer to receive her in *his* outstretched arms:

> Mein Heiland! Mein Erlöser!
> Wie du am Kreuz die Arme ausgespannt,
> So breite sie jetzt aus, mich zu empfangen.
>
> (ibid.)

At this moment her eyes alight on Lord Leicester and it is into *his* arms that, in a temporary swoon, she falls. She herself pinpoints this event and its incongruousness at this moment when she says:

> . . . Ihr verspracht
> Mir Euren Arm, aus diesem Kerker mich
> Zu führen und Ihr leihet ihn mir jetzt!
>
> (ibid.)

It is still from her erstwhile lover's arms that she announces, and renounces, that which she had wanted most from life – *his* love; from this compromising position of the utmost weakness that she declares her weakness at long last conquered; and from his encircling embrace that she finally walks straight to her death, saying, and now for the fifth time

> Lebt wohl! – Jetzt hab' ich nichts mehr auf der Erden!
> (ibid.)

Looking back to the passage from *Über das Erhabene* we may say then that, Hanna Kennedy's account of Maria's bearing notwithstanding, the differences between theory and poetic practice, in this one instance at least, are considerable. In the philosophical essay the achievement of sublimity is presented as an instantaneous event in which the spirit impatiently casts off the bondage of the senses to obey its supernatural calling.

Here, in Schiller's tragedy, the achievement of sublimity is envisaged as a process in time, and a process, moreover, moving in the opposite direction; for the resolve of the spirit is carried out, not in disregard of the senses, but with their consent, by a person who has permitted her emotions, senses and even instincts to become aroused to the utmost degree. Nothing could show this more clearly than Maria's request to go to her death at the hand of her erstwhile nurse. The humble association of her heroic bearing now with the helplessness of infancy is proof of the fact that Maria does not harden herself to feeling in the hour of moral triumph. Quite on the contrary, she exposes herself to it, fearlessly and recklessly, and at the risk of that regression – *Rückfall* – which so palpably takes place when she falls into Leicester's arms. Such total sensitization of the person, such regression even, the poet seems to be telling us through this last episode of Maria's life, need not weaken or endanger a person's moral fibre. For it is from this lapse, from this encircling pair of arms, that she effortlessly rises to meet her destiny. And, indeed, if we look closely, do not all the characters from Schiller's pen that attain to sublimity step forth to their death from the embrace of what they hold dearest? Karl Moor from Amalia's embrace, Marquis Posa from Don Carlos's, Don Carlos from the Queen's, Max from Thekla's, and, finally, Don Cesar from Beatrice's. In the passage from *Über das Erhabene* the son of Ulysses finds that what he thought to be the clasp of eternal beauty was no more than the encircling arms of *voluptas* holding his spirit in degrading captivity. Schiller's use of the same image in the dramas themselves, however, suggests that the repudiation of the life of the senses may not be necessary for man to rise to ultimate freedom of the spirit. On the contrary, their ultimate victory seems to flower from such final affirmation.

II

Is then this slow and sensually saturated farewell to life not entirely limited to this one character, Maria? Have we by chance hit upon a rhythm which is rooted, not so much in the individual psychology of this or that figure but in the tragic process itself? A look at Schiller's other tragedies confirms that we may indeed have identified a general pattern and the question suggests itself at once what function such a steady alternation of spiritual composure and self-inflicted exposure to the onslaught of life could possibly have. But before we try to find an answer to that problem, let us quickly demonstrate the recurrence of the basic rhythm itself. To begin with *Die Räuber*, that rich quarry of all the themes and techniques which Schiller was to employ through his poetic career: we have traced in an earlier chapter the alternation, in the hero, of attempts to evade the truth about himself with an ever-deepened consciousness of his real condition. This is closely entwined with the rhythmic alternation of spiritual composure and of exposure to emotional realities. Deep down Karl Moor knows that he is forfeiting his right to life and sealing his doom the moment he forms his robber band; and even at this early point he readily accepts death for his destiny: 'Nun dann, so laßt uns gehn! Fürchet euch nicht vor Tod und Gefahr, denn über uns waltet ein unbeugsames Fatum! Jeden ereilet endlich sein Tag, es sei auf dem weichen Kissen von Pflaum, oder im rauhen Gewühl des Gefechts, oder auf offenem Galgen und Rad! Eins davon ist unser Schicksal!' (I. ii). There are a number of such stoical statements, each seemingly final: at the banks of the Danube, before and after Kosinsky's arrival (III. ii and IV. i), after the recognition scene with Amalia when he rejects the idea of suicide (IV. v), and at the end when he resolves to give himself up to the law. But such high points of resolution are undermined, time and again, by an irrepressible tendency to make things more difficult for himself and seek out situations sure to stir up the very emotions and instincts he knows he will have to sacrifice in the end: the encounter with Kosinsky who revives the memory of his own sufferings is followed by the meetings with Amalia and, finally, with his father. Such reckless exposure to the emotions inevitably carries the risk of regression. This tendency is clearly seen in Karl's irresistible longing to go *home*, in his unnerving encounter with the old Daniel (IV. iii) who had known him from his early childhood – we may register, in passing, the close correspondence between the function of this figure here and that of Hanna Kennedy in the closing scenes of *Maria Stuart* – and culminates in the blessing stolen from his father. But does such a sensitization of the whole man necessarily undermine his spiritual resolve? Karl goes manfully to his death. And may we not discern an increase of moral stature in his progression from grandiloquent rantings to the quiet finality of 'dem Mann kann geholfen werden'?

We have noted Marquis Posa's extraordinary equanimity in another chapter. This composure is gravely shaken, when the Marquis, in the most deeply ambivalent action of his career, both saves and all but destroys his friend by arresting him. It is at this moment – on which he will expatiate later to Don Carlos (V. iii) – that he realizes that he must die. Yet following this decision he seeks out first the Queen and then Don Carlos,

in prison, and engineers two emotion-charged scenes in which he exposes
his resolution to every lure that life may offer. These scenes – some of the
loveliest Schiller ever wrote – are a hair's breadth from the sentimental.
Besides, in one important respect at least, they are open to the charge of
redundancy. For the messages which Posa sends to his friend through the
Queen he will presently convey to him in person. Is Schiller here indulging
his own emotional expansiveness or is he giving controlled expression to a
need on the part of his hero?

In both scenes, initial composure gives way to an outburst of feeling.
In IV. xxi the grim stoicism with which Posa announces that he has 'lost
the game' for himself to the overwhelmed cry

<blockquote>
Königin!
– O Gott! das Leben ist doch schön . . .
</blockquote>

In V. iii, the controlled opening gambits to the rapturous acclaim of death
as a source of unsuspected life:

<blockquote>
Und ich – ich drücke dich an meine Brust
Zum erstenmal mit vollem, ganzem Rechte;
Ich hab' es ja mit allem, allem, was
Mir teuer ist, erkauft – O Karl, wie süß,
Wie groß ist dieser Augenblick! . . .
</blockquote>

'How sweet, how great': here, close to death, these two do not exclude
each other. Could Schiller be showing us through this protracted leave-
taking that a man who is fully responsive to the *sweetness* of life is for that
reason no less able to rise to moral *greatness* when the occasion demands
it?[5] And even that Posa, for so long 'der kältere, der spätere Freund',[6] so
practised in aloofness, *needs* the emotional articulacy of those last hours as
part of learning how to live now that he is about to die? And Carlos himself:
in him the oscillation between equanimity and vulnerability is very marked
indeed. After the first stupor into which Posa's murder has plunged him he
rises up and bears witness to their friendship with reckless eloquence. Then
he sinks back into himself, exhausted, knowing that all is over and unwilling to let himself be emotionally roused again. 'Mein Leben ist
verwirkt,' he says at the end of his reckoning with the King:

<blockquote>
. . . Ich weiß. Was ist
Mir jetzt das Leben? Hier entsag' ich allem,
Was mich auf dieser Welt erwartet.
</blockquote>

(V. iv)

To Merkado who comes to announce that the Queen wishes to speak to him on important business, he reiterates:

> Wichtig ist mir nichts mehr
> Auf dieser Welt.
>
> (V. vi)

He will not let Lerma kneel before him, pleading

> Nicht also, Graf – Sie rühren mich – Ich möchte
> Nicht gerne weich sein –
>
> (V. vii)

and he hushes the Queen when she is about openly to avow their love: 'Vollenden Sie nicht, Königin,' he pleads, baldly stating 'es ist vorbei' and virtually repeating what he had said to the King, his father:

> . . . Meine Leidenschaft wohnt in den Gräbern
> Der Toten. Keine sterbliche Begierde
> Teilt diesen Busen mehr.
>
> (V. ii)

It is after these protestations – so like Maria Stuart's – that he takes the Queen into his arms (and now, more honestly and sensitively than before, he reverts to calling her 'Elisabeth' and 'Sie' after a shortlived aberration to 'Mutter' and 'du') and kisses her. And that this experience still is an all but overpowering one is attested by the fact that, boy as he is, he marvels at his own strength in remaining unshaken and true to his resolve:

> Bin ich nicht stark, Elisabeth?

he asks;

> Ich halte
> In meinen Armen Sie und wanke nicht.
>
> (V. xi)

And again:

> . . . Ich hielt Sie in den Armen
> Und wankte nicht . . .
>
> (ibid.)

Now, for the second time and more truly, he can say: 'Das ist vorbei.'

Das ist vorbei. Jetzt trotz' ich jedem Schicksal
Der Sterblichkeit . . .

(ibid.)

By the unfailing delicacy and truthfulness of her own response the Queen
has saved Carlos – as before she had saved Posa – from an all too easy
stoical victory of the spirit over blunted senses, a victory based on the
denial of what has to be renounced. She has forced him to abandon all
heroic attitudes, to expose himself to the live situation, and to abide by the
less pretentious and more exacting vow he himself made at their first
encounter: 'to renounce but never to forget' (I. v). Literally from her
embrace – he catches her in his arms as she faints – he goes to the 'Blut-
gerüste' (this, too, he had foreseen); and there is not only tragic irony in
this entwining of life and death, of vulnerableness and freedom, but a deeper
truth, the one which was to find utterance in Hanna Kennedy's words.

In *Die Jungfrau von Orleans* the confrontation of the heroine with her
own sense-drives is treated subliminally, in a highly stylized fashion.
None the less the tragic rhythm of composure and exposure is apparent
here, too; only it is peripherally enacted on the level of the plot rather
than directly realized by a process of introspection on the part of the
heroine. Johanna, fully resolved to pursue her divine mission, meets
Lionel, and after an initial unwillingness to concede the impact of this
experience – she turns her face away from him – she is momentarily
touched by him. The repercussions of this encounter with what is elemental may be seen in her nocturnal Odyssey through a 'grausam,
mördrisch Ungewitter' in which the elements rage like hell itself let loose.
Yet towards the end of this symbolic episode she once more appears serene,
'gefaßt und sanft', as the stage direction has it, and declares to her companion:

. . . Komme, was da will,
Ich bin mir keiner Schwachheit mehr bewußt!

(V. iv)

But here again such assurance turns out to be premature. Captured and
compelled to see Lionel face to face, she recoils in horror:

Zu Lionel! Ermorde mich
Gleich hier, eh' du zu Lionel mich sendest . . .

(V. v)

she beseeches Isabeau and, conscious of her unconquered weakness, incites the English soldiers to kill her. Finally she does face him and it is here, in the cruellest bondage and from a position of the utmost weakness, that she finds the strength to free herself and to liberate her people.

Nowhere is the rhythm we are tracing more transparent than in Schiller's last finished tragedy. Tormented by jealousy of his sister and also of his mother, Don Cesar has murdered his brother. He is overwhelmed with revulsion at his deed and at the situation of which he finds himself the author and vows never to set eyes on them again. 'Gefaßter', he now resolves to die, alone, withdrawn:

> . . . Wer das erfuhr,
> Was ich erleide und im Busen fühle,
> Gibt keinem Irdischen mehr Rechenschaft.
>
> (IV. viii)

Yet here again such seeming finality turns out to be deceptive. Once more face to face with his mother and Beatrice, his hard-won composure melts like snow in the midday sun. As his sister approaches, he shrinks away and, veiling his face, exlaims:

> O Mutter! Mutter! Was ersannest du?

Then – in words recalling Maria's state when she thought she heard her liberators on the morning of her execution – he gives voice to his agitation at the unbidden and overpowering onslaught of life when he thought he was ready for death.

> Arglist'ge Mutter! Also prüfst du mich!
> In neuen Kampf willst du zurück mich stürzen?
> Das Licht der Sonne mir noch teuer machen
> Auf meinem Wege zu der ew'gen Nacht?
> – Da steht der holde Lebensengel mächtig
> Vor mir, und tausend Blumen schüttet er
> Und tausend goldne Früchte lebenduftend
> Aus reichem Füllhorn strömend vor mir aus,
> Das Herz geht auf im warmen Strahl der Sonne,
> Und neu erwacht in der erstorbnen Brust
> Die Hoffnung wieder und die Lebenslust.
>
> (IV. x)

It is only thus, stirred to his depths and wholly sensitized, that he renounces what he holds in his very arms –

. . . Ich halte
In meinen Armen, was das ird'sche Leben
Zu einem Los der Götter machen kann . . .

– and dies to obey the call of duty.

III

This sustained rhythm of composure and exposure, which is characteristic
of the tragedies themselves, has a surprising counterpart in Schiller's
theoretical writings; not, to be sure, in *Über das Erhabene*, according to
which moral freedom is attained by way of an instantaneous and radical
severance of the spirit from the senses; but in those other major essays
which are concerned with the more central question of the sublime, not in
history and nature, but in art: *Über den Grund des Vergnügens an Tragischen Gegenständen*, *Über die Tragische Kunst* and *Über das Pathetische*.
In these three essays the poet is concerned to explain the fact that plea-
surably painful emotions are called forth in us by the impact of human
suffering upon the imagination, and to define the ways in which such
mixed emotions – *Rührung*, *Mitleid* or *Das Gefühl des Erhabenen* as he
variously calls them – may be aroused and exploited by the tragic artist
whose special province they are. The basis of Schiller's reflections is a
curiously ambivalent conception of man as a being compounded of spirit
and sense. Ambivalent because, on the one hand, this is a dualistic conception of clearly Kantian lineage: our sense portion and our spiritual
portion are envisaged as radically different principles, the one passive and
unfree, the other active and free, so that the arousal of the first will inevitably provoke the other into its own peculiar, and conflicting, activity,
and what causes distress to the one may cause pleasure to the other. On
the other hand, this 'vernünftig empfindendes' or 'sinnlichmoralisches
Wesen'[7] for the tragic artist is a single instrument on which he plays. It
takes the lively awareness of suffering to sound the discordant strains of
the spirit, and the response of the latter would lack its distinctive resonance – a sort of mellow exultance – were it not for the darker notes of
suffering that reverberate in it. Our sense nature is as it were the sounding
board which lends volume and poignancy to the music of the spirit, as the
word 'Weh-Mut', one of Schiller's favourites in the context of tragic
art, readily demonstrates.

This sensuous–spiritual nature then is to be moved in its entirety by the
tragedian whose noblest business it is to draw harmonies from its very

discord. He must alternately assail our senses with the spectacle of suffering and feed the spirit's powers of resistance so that it may stand up to the assault and maintain a modicum of independence. Anyone familiar with Schiller will know that he does not dream of safeguarding the freedom of the spirit by exposing it to moderate doses of sensual distress. Far from it; he has in mind an ever-intensified interplay of opposites, and for two reasons. Firstly, a temperate approach would be foreign to one who cannot but envisage life, and art, in terms of conflict, of whom it has been well observed that at bottom he would not be happy in a world in which all conflict were resolved. Nothing expresses the virile mettle of this man better than his remark in *Über den Grund des Vergnügens an Tragischen Gegenständen*: 'Je furchtbarer die Gegner, desto glorreicher der Sieg; der Widerstand allein kann die Kraft sichtbar machen.'[8] But this temperamental disposition is backed by a specific philosophical argument which is made explicit in the third of these essays, *Über das Pathetische*. The ultimate purpose of tragic art, we read in the opening paragraph of that treatise, is 'die Darstellung des Übersinnlichen'. But the supersensible – i.e. freedom – by definition cannot directly appear to the senses. It can only be inferred, or gauged, by the resistance it offers to a visible force. 'Nur der Widerstand, den es gegen die Gewalt der Gefühle äußert, macht das freie Prinzip in uns kenntlich; der Widerstand aber kann nur nach der Stärke des Angriffs geschätzt werden.'[9] Accordingly Schiller, in *Über das Pathetische*, does not tire of stressing the cardinal importance for the tragedian of the liveliest presentation of suffering. 'Man kann niemals wissen,' he writes, 'ob die Fassung des Gemüts eine Wirkung seiner moralischen Kraft ist, wenn man nicht überzeugt worden ist, daß sie keine Wirkung der Unempfindlichkeit ist.' And, with obvious allusion to Winckelmann's and Lessing's description of Laocoon: 'Es ist keine Kunst, über Gefühle Meister zu werden, die nur die Oberfläche der Seele leicht und flüchtig bestreichen; aber in einem Sturm, der die ganze sinnliche Natur aufregt, seine Gemütsfreiheit zu behalten, dazu gehört ein Vermögen des Widerstandes, das über alle Naturmacht unendlich erhaben ist.' Thus he argues:

Man gelangt also zur Darstellung der moralischen Freiheit nur durch die lebendigste Darstellung der leidenden Natur, und der tragische Held muß sich erst als empfindendes Wesen bei uns legitimiert haben, ehe wir ihm als Vernunftwesen huldigen und an seine Seelenstärke glauben. *Pathos* ist also die erste und unnachlaßliche Forderung

an den tragischen Künstler, und es ist ihm erlaubt, die Darstellung
des Leidens so weit zu treiben, als es, ohne Nachteil für seinen
letzten Zweck, ohne Unterdrückung der moralischen Freiheit,
geschehen kann. Er muß gleichsam seinem Helden oder Leser die
ganze volle Ladung des Leidens geben . . .[10]

We note the entire open-endedness of the formulation 'seinem Helden
oder Leser' – we shall return to it later – and go on to observe the fact that
Schiller's argument here – and the passionate plea that follows for a repudiation of the frosty stoicism of the French classicists and for a return to
the richer humanity of the ancient Greeks, to that 'zarte Empfindlichkeit
für das Leiden', that 'wahr und offen da liegende Natur' which so moves
us in their art – fully corroborates what we have seen the poet do in his
tragedies. For there too he exposes his heroes to the 'full load of suffering',
and it is thus, wholly sensitized and susceptible to the sweetness of life that
they lay it down, and testify to the indomitable freedom of their spirit.

But this poetic assault on the emotions and senses – 'of the hero or
reader' – must not be a sudden and overpowering one. 'Wenn der
Anfänger den ganzen Donnerstrahl des Schreckens und der Furcht auf
einmal und fruchtlos in die Gemüter schleudert, so gelangt jener' –
Schiller refers to the mature artist – 'Schritt vor Schritt durch lauter
kleine Schläge zum Ziel und durchdringt eben dadurch die Seele ganz,
daß er sie nur allmählich und gradweise rührte.'[11] Thus we read in the
slightly earlier essay *Über die Tragische Kunst*, and it is here that the poet
gives us the clearest insight into the complicated and secret strategy of the
tragic artist. The goal for which he strives is to attain, by the narrowest of
margins, the victory of the free mind over the storm of emotions he has
unleashed. Expressing the matter in a more contemporary idiom, he would
aim at attaining, in 'his hero or his reader', the maximal diminution of
psychical distance without its total loss.[12] In Schiller's terms, the poet will
avoid arousing emotions so weak or otherwise ineffectual that they fail to
threaten our mental equipoise. Equally, however, he will avoid arousing
affects so powerful as to paralyse the free play of the mind. He will summon up a spectacle of suffering so vivid, so true, so comprehensive and
sustained as will tax the spirit to the limits of its endurance. Then, by a
hair's breadth, he will ensure its victory. But to guide the action to this
end he has to adopt a highly ingenious if not contrary procedure. He must
forestall the mind's tendency to shake off too soon insufferable strain.
Somehow, to make its eventual triumph the more complete, he must coax

it into bearing 'die ganze volle Ladung des Leidens' for which it is to prove a match. To do this, he cannot proceed, simply, by piling horror upon horror. The mind's answer would only be to withdraw into an unassailable distance. To prevent this, the poet must summon all the resources of his organizing power. To raise the mind's level of tolerance, he must carefully manipulate the affects to which he intends to subject it. He must dose them, that is to say, interrupt them, vary them in themselves and, most of all, grade them. By such a cunning deployment of the forces on the sense side he will *enable* the mind to tolerate a greater degree of disturbance by giving it a breathing space here and there and by arousing its interest in the architecture of passion rather than subjecting it to its blind onslaught. But also he will *require* it to tolerate more, in that the cumulative power of emotions thus organized is greatly enhanced.

Thus, step by step the poet escalates the passionate contest between spirit and sense, between serenity and suffering – each attracting and repelling the other, each checking and challenging the other into an ever more vigorous activity until, by the narrowest of margins, freedom wins.

Each attracting the other? Critics have conditioned us into assuming that sublimity, in an aesthetic context no less than in the more narrow field of moral choice, implies a dichotomous relation of sense and spirit. Even Emil Staiger, in an otherwise masterly exposition of Schiller's classical theory,[13] concludes that the whole artistic generalship Schiller expounds to his readers is geared to only one end: to demonstrate the cherished autonomy of the spirit – his readers' and his own – and mercilessly to demonstrate to the senses who is the master of the house. But this is not the impression we ourselves have gleaned from Schiller's handling of his tragedies, where the interrelation between sense and spirit seems much more subtle, nor indeed from our opening reflections on the sublime at the beginning of this section. Would the sublime still be what it is if our spirit were not vibrant with the suffering that is the price of its triumph in this world? Is not the mixed emotion we call sublime made up of strains that inseparably blend in a single chord drawn from a single instrument? Schiller's own conclusion to his fascinating account, at any rate, reads thus:

Unaufhörlich muß dieses [i.e. das selbsttätige Vermögen] geschäftig sein, gegen den Zwang der Sinnlichkeit seine Freiheit zu behaupten, aber nicht früher als am Ende den Sieg erlangen und noch weit weniger im Kampf unterliegen; sonst ist es im ersten Falle um das *Leiden*,* im zweiten um die *Tätigkeit* * getan, und nur die *Vereinigung* * von beiden erweckt ja die Rührung. In der geschickten Führung dieses Kampfes beruht eben das große Geheimnis der tragischen Kunst; da zeigt sie sich in ihrem glänzendsten Licht.[14]

The operative word, in Schiller's own summing up, is *Vereinigung*. And the statement in which it is embedded sends the mind forward to one of the most crucial sentences in the whole of the *Ästhetische Briefe*. There, in Letter XXV, Schiller concedes the separateness of activity and receptivity, of *Tätigkeit* and *Leiden* in all modes of consciousness. But of the aesthetic mode he writes:

> Da nun aber bei dem Genuß der Schönheit oder der ästhetischen Einheit eine wirkliche *Vereinigung* * und Auswechslung der Materie mit der Form und des *Leidens* * mit der *Tätigkeit* * vor sich geht, so ist eben dadurch die *Vereinbarkeit* beider Naturen, die Ausführbarkeit des Unendlichen in der Endlichkeit, mithin die Möglichkeit der erhabensten Menschheit bewiesen.[15]

Vereinigung des Leidens mit der Tätigkeit – this is the hallmark of the aesthetic mode which Schiller here – it is worth noting – apostrophizes as the mark of the 'erhabenste' humanity; it is also – we have seen – 'the great secret of tragic art', for from this *union of opposites* there issues the sublime in poetry. Are sense and spirit really as dichotomously opposed in 'the hero's or reader's' experience of sublimity as is generally supposed? And is the sublime in art really separated from the realm of beauty by a gulf as deep and unbridgeable as critics would have us believe? Or could it be that the sublime is an ultimate beauty born of the union of enhanced opposites?

IV

The rhythmic alternation between serenity and suffering or, as we have called it, between composure and exposure is thus common to Schiller's theory of tragedy and the tragedies themselves. Some critics, it is true, may regard this statement as an oversimplification. It has recently been emphatically asserted that the poet, in the essays that concern themselves with tragic art, exclusively deals with the readers' or spectators' response to the suffering presented on stage rather than with that of the tragic

* My italics.

characters themselves.[16] But such a neat division, in the case of Schiller, is an untenable one to maintain. We have noted the casualness with which the poet prescribes that the full load of suffering be doled out to 'his hero or reader'. In fact, it does not matter which, because for Schiller it is always both. We have seen elsewhere that it is a cardinal principle of Schiller's aesthetic theory and artistic practice that the aesthetic effects he desires to induce in the recipient of his art be prefigured in the poetic characters themselves.[17] 'Doppelt genäht hält besser', a German proverb runs, or, as Schiller puts it, 'Alle Affekte sind ästhetischer aus der zweiten Hand'.[18] A similar observation occurs in the closing paragraph of *Über das Erhabene*, where we read: '. . . der Mensch ist, wie in andern Fällen, so auch hier, von der zweiten Hand besser bedient als von der ersten und will lieber einen zubereiteten und auserlesenen Stoff von der Kunst empfangen als an der unreinen Quelle der Natur mühsam und dürftig schöpfen.'[19] The same aesthetic principle operates, we have seen, throughout Schiller's dramas themselves. The tragic protagonists – Fiesco, Posa, Wallenstein, Don Manuel or Isabella, to mention only some – through their own aesthetic distance from the onrush of events prefigure the aesthetic distance from the pressures of the tragic action the poet would instil into his spectators or readers; and in Schiller's last tragedy, *Die Braut von Messina*, this underlying principle has become explicit in a preface concerned to explain the introduction of the chorus, and the resultant handling of the dramatic characters, in these very terms. Of the dramatis personae we read: 'Sie stehen gewissermaßen schon auf einem natürlichen Theater, weil sie vor Zuschauern sprechen und handeln, und werden eben deswegen desto tauglicher, von dem Kunst-Theater zu einem Publikum zu reden.'[20] And of the chorus itself we read: 'Dadurch, daß der Chor die Teile aus einander hält und zwischen die Passionen mit seiner beruhigenden Betrachtung tritt, gibt er uns unsre Freiheit zurück, die im Sturm der Affekte verloren gehen würde.'[20] For: 'Wenn die Schläge, womit die Tragödie unser Herz trifft, ohne Unterbrechung auf einander folgten, so würde das Leiden über die Tätigkeit siegen . . .',[21] a formulation in which we may recognize yet another, and the last theoretical statement of that tragic pulse of composure and exposure we have been at pains to demonstrate.

This rhythm is sustained, in the individual tragedies, by a variety of means. Karl Moor's motives for exposing himself to the painful impact of what he loves and must forfeit are vastly different from those of, say, Marquis Posa, Maria Stuart or Don Cesar. Karl is motivated by a kind of perverse moral obduracy, one might almost say a desire to flagellate himself, as becomes evident from such formulations as 'Nein! sehen muß ich sie – muß ich ihn – es soll mich zermalmen!' (IV. i) or, on deciding to see Amalia once again, 'Ich muß den Gifttrank dieser Seligkeit vollends ausschlürfen . . .' (IV. iii). Posa is driven to the Queen and Carlos by his need for 'scenes' – whether we take this to mean that he loves to indulge in heroic poses (as Elisabeth suggests and some critics suspect) or, as I have argued, that he needs these poignant moments to make up for what he has deprived himself of during a lifetime and must at long last learn – articulacy of feeling. Maria Stuart is driven by her irrepressible vitality to expose herself to situations which are painful in themselves and mercilessly show up the flaws in her stoic stance. And Don Cesar: it is rank jealousy which makes him face his mother and his sister, all resolutions never to do so again notwithstanding, and rank jealousy which informs every one of the impassioned pleas for love on the part of one who had seemed so ready to die.

All these, in their own and different ways, are accounted impure motives and all of the characters I have named, above all Maria Stuart and Don Cesar, have come under critical fire for this reason. Maria's sensuality, it has been argued, is a stumbling block on her road to sublimity, and the value of Don Cesar's free death is gravely marred, it is felt, by the impurity of the motive that drives him to it.[22] In fact, his title to sublimity has been disputed on this very ground as also has that of Marquis Posa, for analogous reasons.[23]

These are serious charges and they need rethinking. For one thing, we cannot be so sure that Schiller intended these motives to be as 'impure' as critics, inured with a time-worn conception of what Schiller meant by sublimity, have tended to assume. In these pages this very conception is under review, and from our analysis, in the first section of this chapter, of Maria's 'lapses' from her lofty moral platform in the final scenes of the tragedy it has become patently clear that in her case at least the love of life and the readiness for death, sensuality and sublimity are more intimately bound up with one another than has been suspected. What is more, all these diverse motives – manifestations of sensuality in each case and 'pure' or 'impure' whichever way we are disposed to look at the matter – have been found to contribute to the rhythm we have seen to operate throughout Schiller's tragedies and to constitute the basic 'beat', indeed 'the great secret' of tragic art. Whatever the particular mechanism that propels these characters into situations fraught with pain – masochistic obduracy, emotional exhibitionism, vitality or plain jealousy – it triggers off that repeated exposure to suffering which alternates with periods of composure. It is, we might say, the diastole of a pulse which runs not only through the final phase of their human and moral development but is – so Schiller's theoretical essays tell us – the very life-beat and organizing principle of tragedy as he sees it. Once this is realized and we understand that Maria's excess of sensuality and Don Cesar's excess of jealousy are not there for their own sakes but, like other particular motives of other particular characters, point beyond these individuals and play a strictly functional part in the establishment of the tragic rhythm of Schiller's tragedy – is it not wise to stop making specific psychological and evaluative judgements and instead to ask what the function of this pervasive tragic rhythm might be?

V

Towards the end of the fourth aesthetic letter, the key concept of the whole treatise, *Totalität des Charakters*, is mentioned for the first time. To pinpoint the gulf that separates this ideal from the contemporary reality, Schiller writes:

> Der Mensch kann sich aber auf eine doppelte Weise entgegengesetzt sein: entweder als Wilder, wenn seine Gefühle über seine Grundsätze herrschen; oder als Barbar, wenn seine Grundsätze seine Gefühle zerstören. Der Wilde verachtet die Kunst und erkennt die Natur als seinen unumschränkten Gebieter; der Barbar verspottet und entehrt die Natur, aber verächtlicher als der Wilde fährt er häufig genug fort, der Sklave seines Sklaven zu sein. Der gebildete Mensch macht die Natur zu seinem Freund und ehrt ihre Freiheit, indem er bloß ihre Willkür zügelt.

Of such 'men of culture' who possess wholeness of character, there are but two in the whole of Schiller's dramatic world: the non-tragic figure of Wilhelm Tell and, in the tragedies, the solitary and noble figure of the younger Piccolomini. For the rest, the characters of such tragedies as these which are persistently concerned with fragmentation, the predicament of the modern Western world, may be said to fall into one or the other of the categories identified in this searching analysis. Either they are savages – to use Schiller's nomenclature – in whom nature has run amok and feeling overrules principle. One thinks of Karl Moor, Don

Carlos, Maria Stuart or Don Cesar. Or they are barbarians in whom principle violates feeling – and under this harsh name one is bound to include figures such as Marquis Posa, Wallenstein or Johanna, to name only those amongst the many characters of this mould who may justifiably aspire to the title of sublimity.

In either case, whether they are 'savages' or 'barbarians', they have transgressed against wholeness of character. For either they have flouted conscience and reason in the name of unbridled nature, or they have denied or repressed feeling and instinct in the name of principle and of reason, 'dem tötenden Insekte gerühmter besserer Vernunft', as Marquis Posa, for so long her slave, contemptuously calls her. But in a deeper sense, the denizens of both camps alike have offended against nature. For to fail to cultivate her as does the savage is scarcely better than to deny her as does the barbarian. And in both alike, nature having been dishonoured by excess or by repression, there opens an ugly rift: a rift between the undifferentiated and mistrusted feeling side of these characters on the one hand and their moral consciousness on the other. It is this gulf that the poet, in his *Ästhetische Briefe*, seeks to close through the intervention of art; and this same gulf that the rhythm between composure and exposure, which we have found to pervade Schiller's tragedies, is designed to lessen and finally to bridge.

This steady oscillation between serenity and suffering – and the different motivations which cause the hero to seek out painful situations – is nothing less than the commanding principle of the tragic action, designed to make the hero face his own inner division and surmount it. He must die because, by neglecting or denying his natural heritage, he has transgressed against that ideal of wholeness which, in the universe of discourse of Schiller's poetic work, represents the only morally and psychologically viable model of being. The consciousness of this comes to him readily enough, by way of a sudden illumination such as Maria experiences on the morning of her execution. But even such insight – and in Maria's case it is already a long way from the theoretical knowledge that she is under judicial sentence of death – still falls short of acceptance by the person as a whole. The resolve to expiate transgression by voluntary death – Karl Moor's, Marquis Posa's, Maria Stuart's, Johanna's and Don Cesar's – when it is first conceived, is blurred by feelings of guilt and shame and perhaps even in some small measure occasioned by such promptings. Maria's stance at the beginning of the last act is, as we have seen, not altogether convincing. The image of death covering her degradation with its wings betokens her wish to conceal from herself desires and drives with which she has not yet come to terms. Don Cesar's haste to remove the victim of his crime as well as the criminal from the face of the earth, and his determination not to be faced with the reflection of his 'verhaßtes Antlitz' in his mother's eyes or indeed to show her 'des Mörders gottverhaßten Anblick', are the expression of profound shame. Shame at his ravaged nature prompts Karl Moor's wish to flee from the misdeeds perpetrated in his name and 'mich in irgend eine Kluft der Erde zu verkriechen, wo der Tag vor meiner Schande zurücktritt' (II. iii). Shame makes Johanna avert her face from Lionel and shun not only her King in the hour of his triumph, but also Sorel, her sisters and even the humble charcoal burners in the woods.

In every one of these instances the compulsion to go and seek out the very situation that will bring to light the concealed sore of guilt and shame is – we have seen – motivated differently. But in every case it serves the identical end. Karl Moor's return home to his father and his bride, Posa's visit to Carlos whom he had arrested in a paroxysm of repressiveness, Maria's reliving of her sensuality, Johanna's nocturnal Odyssey through the unleashed elements, Don Cesar's renewed encounter with his mother and his sister – all these are redundant from the point of view of the outward action in that the die has been cast and the resolve to atone has been made. It is on a different level altogether that we must seek their function. These compulsive returns to 'the scene of the crime' signify a confrontation of the person with those aspects in himself or herself which have remained concealed because they are felt to be unworthy. As Schiller's tragic characters relinquish their hard-won composure and willy-nilly, driven by forces that are stronger than their conscious resolve, expose themselves to situations forcing them to relive their guilt and shame, the very feelings, desires or instincts they have repudiated are brought before the forum of their moral consciousness. And by this confrontation – repeated, as we have seen – both parties, the criminal as well as the judge, and the relation between them, become transformed.

On the one hand, the rejected aspect of the characters' sense-being is redeemed, stage by stage. In the first place, what is made conscious receives a measure of recognition by the mere fact of becoming a content of consciousness. Johanna 'owns' instinctual drives of the very existence of which she had taken no cognizance, through her encounter with Lionel. And such appropriation is the first step towards acceptance. For, strangely enough, what is thus faced as her own turns out to be more acceptable than it was while it lacked recognition. What Johanna sees when she looks Lionel in the face is 'die Züge . . . des *edeln**** Angesichts' (IV. i). Yet what does she perceive in her noble enemy if not the reflection of her own instinctuality? As Maria comes to terms with the fatal consequences of her sensuality, she can say:

> Die Krone fühl' ich wieder auf dem Haupt,
> Den *würd'gen* Stolz in meiner *edeln**** Seele.
>
> (V. vi)

Recognition confers dignity and nobility on what was shameful while it went unrecognized. And what is thus raised to the level of consciousness and ennobled by contact with it loses the compulsive character of a grossly physical appetite. It becomes transparent, capable of being experienced symbolically. Karl embracing Amalia and accepting his sullied self in her embrace, Don Cesar accepting himself in that of Beatrice, Posa kneeling before the Queen and Carlos locking her to his breast, Maria's turbulence coming to rest in Leicester's arms – all this has the lightness and the swiftness of a dream and is as long known and awaited and yet as new as the symbolic moment of Faust's and Helena's fulfilment: 'verlebt und doch so neu'. And what is thus lightly held can be lightly renounced, without bitterness or shame. All those of Schiller's characters we have mentioned start by dishonouring their natural legacy, be it as a *Wilder* or as a *Barbar*. All end by avowing and honouring it and by truly giving up what for one brief moment they have truly called their own; and all could bid farewell to what they have thus held, with Goethe's wonderful word: 'mir ward es auch'.

On the other hand, as in the confrontation between criminal and judge the former is redeemed from the deeps, so the latter is brought down to the real. We have observed that the resolve of the protagonists to expiate their transgression in its initial stages is divorced from their emotional reality. Their composure is not free of bravado or of inner dishonesty. Karl Moor knows that he is morally lost and yet continues to indulge in moral posturing. 'Da steht der Knabe, schamrot und ausgehöhnt vor dem Auge des Himmels,' he confesses (II. iii); and yet he continues to preach as though he stood on a pulpit. Posa, when first he meets the Queen, is determined to die yet unaccepting and grim: '. . . alle Ihre Züge wie eines Sterbenden entstellt', the Queen comments as she sees him enter; and even later, much later, when he is more like himself, accuses him of

* My italics.

lusting after heroics. And neither Don Carlos, nor Maria, nor Johanna nor indeed Don Cesar is able to renounce the world when they first profess their readiness to do so.

In the rhythmic alternation between composure and exposure, the hero's resolve, shallow at first, is time and again tested upon the pulse of reality. Time and again it is shown up as premature as he is exposed to situations revealing, as with a searchlight, unpacified desires or instincts tenaciously clamouring to be gratified and compromising his conscious stance. By such repeated confrontations, stroke by stroke, mental claims are measured against emotional realities in all the depth and complexity in which these searching situations reveal this reality to us and the hero himself. And gradually resolve and reality are matched up to one another. As unsanctioned drives are ennobled by recognition, so spiritual pretensions are shed and the hero's moral stature is scaled down to his true size and proportions. The sobriety of Karl Moor's final gesture – 'dem Mann kann geholfen werden' – matches the sobriety of his assessment of what he has done, and done to himself. These final words are shatteringly real. The lack of all bathos in Maria's parting words matches the unheroic situation in which they are spoken. It is a chastened Johanna, stripped of all presumption, who is able to acknowledge the smallness of man and the majesty of nature, and to say: 'Der Mensch braucht wenig, und an Leben reich ist die Natur' (V. iv). She is absolutely true to her existential condition here and now when she laments that she has no more access to the supernatural: 'Die Wunder ruhn, der Himmel ist verschlossen' (V. vi). Like two photographic images, separate and split at the outset, principle and feeling, reason and instinct, what the hero feels he ought to be and what he in fact is, coalesce. *Sollen* is rooted in *Sein*. The gap is closed. At the last, when he puts his resolve into practice, the hero consents to his deed with all he is and has: 'Befriedigt ist mein Herz, ich folge dir' are Don Cesar's dying words; and they significantly echo, and transpose into a new key, Isabella's earlier protestation that she may look into 'der Zeiten Unermeßlichkeit' 'mit zufriednem Geist' (II. v). Don Cesar is no longer making an intellectual statement. In reiterating his resolve to follow his brother into death, he is giving expression to a need endorsed by the whole person, the heart as well as the head.[24] And it is he who gives expression to the awareness – more or less pronounced in every Schillerian character – that in coming to terms with the other, his antagonist, he is coming to terms with the 'other' in himself – with those aspects of himself he had previously fought and dishonoured.[25] When he exclaims:

. . . das verhüte
Der allgerechte Lenker unsrer Tage,
Daß solche Teilung sei in seiner Welt . . .

(IV. x)

he is giving voice, not only to his sense of justice which forbids him to enjoy what he himself has denied to his brother, but, more deeply, to his ideal of wholeness which he has violated in giving free rein to unbridled instincts and which he restores in learning to die for it.

VI

Of all the figures peopling the universe of Schiller's tragedies, Max alone is whole. How whole has scarcely been appreciated. True, it is a commonplace to say that Max is what the author of *Über Anmut und Würde* called 'eine schöne Seele', and what a few years later the author of the *Ästhetische Briefe* was to call 'eine edle Seele'; by which he means one in whom spirit and sense, reason and feeling are so completely at one that he does by free and unprompted inclination what his moral conscience would in any case prescribe.

Wallenstein himself, so sensitive to the beauty of the *Venuskind* he loves and will nevertheless destroy, admirably sums up the aesthetic totality, harmony and freedom of the youth:

Sanft wiegte dich bis heute dein Geschick,
Du konntest spielend deine Pflichten üben,
Jedwedem schönen Trieb Genüge tun,
Mit ungeteiltem Herzen immer handeln . . .

he says to him, and ominously adds:

So kann's nicht ferner bleiben.

(*Tod*, II. ii)

These are ambiguous words. Wallenstein has, at one stroke, drawn a sketch of a rare felicitousness of being and of the fleeting charm of youth. *Sanft, wiegen, spielend, üben, Trieb* – words such as these denote not only the lightness of moral grace whenever and wherever we see it but also the playful freedom of the child who exercises his growing faculties, cradled by a maternal destiny. And in a way the older man is right (though little does he suspect how his words will boomerang against him): 'So kann's

nicht ferner bleiben.' Max himself had said – and this had been his answer
to Friedland's declaring his political hand –

> Mein General! – Du machst mich heute mündig.
>
>   (ibid.)

The hour has come for Max to grow up. He *had* been spoilt by nature (but
then, nature chooses the children on whom she lavishes her affection) in
that he could at all times revere what he loved and love what he revered;
Wallenstein and his own father as much as Thekla. Those to whom his
being spontaneously inclined had been the cherished repositories of his
values. The cloud of a conflict had nowhere even remotely crossed the
horizon of his consciousness.

But now Max has come of age; and that means, precisely, that he is
ready and compelled to excise the spiritual values by which he lives from
those loved figures who had first implanted their seed in his soul; ready
and compelled to abstract them from the concrete emotional bonds in
which they are embedded. To do so hurts; so much so indeed that Max
involuntarily exclaims, a moment later in the same conversation:

> O! welchen Riß erregst du mir im Herzen!

From this operation in which spirit and soul are severed from the senses,
the soul is retrieved bleeding and wounded – but whole. It is different
with Thekla. For whilst his loving reverence towards the male figures in
his world testifies to his own magnanimity rather than to their integrity
of spirit, she is in truth as he experiences her. As he loves her and, in her,
loves the good, so too Thekla loves the good she reveres in Max. In each,
spirit and sense are indissolubly united; and so too, in their loving, spirit and
sense intercommunicate.

Max and Thekla are not only 'beautiful' or 'noble souls' taken separately. Their love itself is an aesthetic phenomenon in that it involves, and
harmoniously activates, the whole of their humanity. Schiller himself is at
pains to stress this, its aesthetic character: '. . . die Einrichtung des
Ganzen erforderte es,' he writes to Goethe, 'daß sich die Liebe nicht sowohl
durch Handlung, als vielmehr durch ihr ruhiges Bestehen auf sich und
ihre Freiheit von allen Zwecken der übrigen Handlung, welche ein
unruhiges planvolles Streben nach einem Zwecke ist, entgegensetzt und
dadurch einen gewissen menschlichen Kreis vollendet.'[26] This – and not
any unconquered tendency towards the subjective and the sentimental –
is why Schiller set such store by it in a drama which is for the most part –

as he explains to his friend Körner[27] – a 'Staatsaktion' in which all characters are geared to purposes which in the nature of things are more or less ignoble.

> Ich sah es gleich,
> Sie haben einen Zweck . . .
>
> (*Pic.*, III. v)

Thekla astutely observes as soon as she sets foot in this political world. Placed in such a context, their loving, in its harmonious totality, does not only reflect and confirm the inner totality of each. It creates a world.

> . . . Es schufen sich einst die Einsamen liebend,
> Nur von Göttern gekannt, ihre geheimere Welt . . .

Hölderlin writes of himself and Diotima. Like those later lovers, Max and Thekla have by their secret communion created a world within a world, an inner cosmos, a refuge of flesh and blood for their disembodied humanity. As Max has it:

> Der einzig reine Ort ist unsre Liebe,
> Der unentweihte in der Menschlichkeit.
>
> (*Tod*, V. vii)

And as Thekla responds, tragically, when Max lies dead:

> . . . Es ist nur *ein* Ort in der Welt!
> Wo er bestattet liegt . . .
> Der einz'ge Fleck ist mir die ganze Erde.
>
> (*Tod*, IV. xi)

Theirs is a sacramental bond. To destroy it is to destroy the wholeness within each of which it is the outward and visible sign, to separate in each that indivisible union of sense and spirit by which severally and jointly they live, and which is the mark of their nobility.[28]

This inviolate wholeness, forfeited in advance by every other one of Schiller's tragic characters, Wallenstein attacks when he asks Max to follow him in defecting from the Emperor. Wallenstein himself knows it. Up to now you were always able to act 'mit *ungeteiltem** Herzen', he had said to him: 'So kann's nicht ferner bleiben.' And, already earlier on in the same conversation he had argued: there are situations, and this is one of them

* My italics.

. . . wo sich das Herz
Nicht *ganz* zurückbringt aus dem Streit der Pflichten . . .

(*Tod*, II. ii)

Wallenstein clearly knows that the conflict of duties he is about to un-
leash is not going to be waged in the mental outskirts of Max's being, that,
committed as he is, whatever choice he will eventually make is going to
tear at his heart. What he cannot foresee is the deadliness of the dilemma
into which he plunges the youth. For in Max duty is so deeply rooted in
the heart that no one can pluck it out without plucking out that heart
itself. The first intimation of this comes when Max, confronted with
Wallenstein's high treason, tells him that he is forced

. . . eine Wahl
Zu treffen zwischen Dir und meinem Herzen.

(ibid.)

Looked at closely these are strange words. They reverse all our normal
expectations. It is Wallenstein who is close to Max's heart (quite apart from
being the father of Thekla); it is to him that Max inclines, far more
spontaneously than to his own father's legalistic temper and the conventional order he represents. There if anywhere, in relation to Octavio and
the Emperor rather than to Wallenstein, we would expect Max to speak of
his duty; and yet he speaks of his heart. He does so because duty, for him,
is rooted in the heart. Duty *is* his inclination, a total Inclination to the
good; and from that all-embracing unity he is now forced to dissect the
inclination to Wallenstein, and brand it as private, amoral or even
opposed to the good. A similar situation is revealed later on when Max
turns to Thekla for counsel, saying

. . . deine Liebe will ich fragen,
Die nur den Glücklichen beglücken kann,
Vom unglückselig Schuldigen sich wendet.

(*Tod*, III. xxi)

'Den Glücklichen'? It is quite clear that the word here means neither 'the
fortunate' nor 'the happy one', in the simple sense in which he would be
both were Thekla to give him her hand in marriage. Max is neither and
Thekla's love, as she will presently prove, is entirely independent of any
consideration of his happiness or indeed her own, in the conventional
sense of the word. The only meaning we can give to 'the happy one' here
is the obverse of the 'unglückselig Schuldigen': that is to say, he who is at

peace in the knowledge of his integrity. As duty is Inclination, so duty too
is Happiness, a Happiness to be distinguished, now, from happiness in any
ordinary sense in that it embraces the most acute consciousness of pain. It
is Happiness in that tenuous and esoteric sense of the word for which
Thekla is willing to stake everything, this to which she refers a little later
in the same scene when she says:

> . . . aber Reue soll
> Nicht deiner Seele schönen Frieden stören . . .
>
> (ibid.)

– words which, from afar, hold out the possibility that even in the
extremity of conflict harmony and wholeness need perhaps not in every
case be sacrificed.

And yet a third time the same mental pattern is confirmed when Max,
in the very next line, asks of Thekla:

> Kannst du mich dann noch lieben, wenn ich bleibe?
>
> (ibid.)

The question Max is really asking is whether, should he stay, Thekla will
continue to honour and respect him. There is no trace of an opposition
between respect and love, *Achtung* and *Liebe*, not even implicitly. It is
resolved in a higher synthesis in which to respect *is* to love, with a Love
embracing and transcending both the opposites into which not even this
foul situation can force Max to break it down again. In every one of the
instances we have been examining the sphere of feeling, designated
variously by *heart*, *happiness* and *love*, appears both as a term within an
opposition – between feeling and conscience, happiness and misery, inclination and duty – and as a higher concept in which that opposition is
embraced and transcended, in what has lately been called a 'binary
synthesis'.[29]

Through Wallenstein's defection, Max, a character of luminous integrity, is caught in an inescapable dilemma. If he sides with Wallenstein,
he degrades that total Inclination towards the good by which he lives to a
morally indifferent or even immoral inclination. He will love without
revering and that, for him, is not Love. If, on the other hand, he sides with
his father and the Emperor, he reduces that total Inclination towards the
good to a dutiful act bereft of all nobility; he will revere without loving
and that, for him, is no longer Reverence. He will have trodden underfoot
those

> . . . schönen freien Regungen
> Der Gastlichkeit, der frommen Freundestreue . . .
> (ibid.)

those 'unvollkommene Pflichten' (as Schiller calls them elsewhere)[30] which nevertheless constitute 'eine heilige Religion dem Herzen'; he will be 'ein Hassenswerter, ein roh Unmenschlicher', worse still, *ein Barbar*: and we know from the *Ästhetische Briefe* that Schiller thought even less of the barbarian who sacrifices feeling to principle and reason than he thought of the savage who allows his feelings to dominate his reason. Worst of all, he will lose Thekla, and in her he will not only lose happiness in the ordinary sense of the word, but that all-embracing Happiness which lies in the inviolate wholeness of spirit and sense: for of that their love is the sacramental embodiment.

Thus, whichever choice he makes, he will be 'Verbrecher, wohin ich mich neige'. A criminal, basically, not in that he is forced to betray either Octavio and the Emperor or Wallenstein and Thekla: but because he is forced, 'ein unglückselig Schuldiger', to betray the ideal of wholeness of character to which he is pledged; because, whichever way he turns, that total Inclination of his being towards his Duty, which is the hallmark of his nobility, will be wrenched asunder and broken down into its baser elements – into a duty that is shorn of humanity and grace, or else into an inclination that is anarchic. Max's plight is like that of Tell when he is brought *vis à vis* the forces of evil: here, too, a highly differentiated whole is threatened with regression to a more rudimentary stage. Tell, in an untragic world, resists the murderous onslaught on his personality and survives whole to avenge wholeness. Max, to preserve wholeness, has no option but to die: and, dying, testifies to that wholeness of being of which he, and his love, are the embodiment.

VII

But for all that his dilemma is inescapable and his fate is sealed, Max knows that he has something to lose; and he comes to claim it when for the last time he storms into Wallenstein's hall, loudly crying 'Ja! Ja! da ist er!' (*Tod*, III. xviii). What he has come to claim in those last anguished moments is something immeasurably precious: it is Thekla's compassion.

He had told his father that this is what he must do, when Octavio had ordered his son to follow him in the Emperor's name.

Kein Kaiser hat dem Herzen vorzuschreiben . . .

he had replied; and then he had gone on to plead:

> Und willst du mir das Einzige noch rauben,
> Was mir mein Unglück übrig ließ, ihr Mitleid?
> Muß grausam auch das Grausame geschehn?
> Das Unabänderliche soll ich noch
> Unedel tun, mit heimlich feiger Flucht,
> Wie ein Unwürdiger mich von ihr stehlen?
> Sie soll mein Leiden sehen, meinen Schmerz,
> Die Klagen hören der zerrißnen Seele
> Und Tränen um mich weinen – O! die Menschen
> Sind grausam, aber sie ist wie ein Engel.
> Sie wird von gräßlich wütender Verzweiflung
> Die Seele retten, diesen Schmerz des Todes
> Mit sanften Trostesworten klagend lösen.
>
> (*Tod*, II. vii)

'Du reißest dich nicht los,' his father had replied, little suspecting the deadly truth of his words. But Max had gone to Thekla, cutting off all hope in a hopeless situation, and saying:

> . . . Ich komme nicht, zu bleiben.
> Abschied zu nehmen, komm' ich – Es ist aus.
>
> (*Tod*, III. xviii)

And then he had turned to Thekla and pleaded exactly as he had said he would:

> Ich muß, muß dich verlassen, Thekla – muß!
> Doch deinen Haß kann ich nicht mit mir nehmen.
> Nur einen Blick des Mitleids gönne mir,
> Sag', daß du mich nicht hassest. Sag' mirs, Thekla.
> (*Indem er ihre Hand faßt, heftig bewegt*).
> O Gott! – Gott! Ich kann nicht von dieser Stelle.
> Ich kann es nicht – Kann diese Hand nicht lassen.
> Sag', Thekla, daß du Mitleid mit mir hast,
> Dich selber überzeugst, ich kann nicht anders.
>
> (ibid.)

Here and in the speeches that follow in which he clarifies before her every aspect of his dilemma, Max is asking of Thekla to identify herself with his perception of it, to approve the course he senses he is about to take and, by showing him her pity, to help him endure his own inhuman plight.[31] His turning to Thekla to receive illumination from her is of course a last sacramental communion between the lovers. Both the words they exchange – that wonderful 'Wie du dir selbst getreu bleibst, bist du's mir' – and their speechless embrace are the tokens of that indivisible oneness of each and both which is denied to them by the world.[32]

But Max's quest signifies more than that. It is his last attempt to salvage humanity from despair, his last bid to find a tolerable answer to the question he himself had earlier on posed to his father – the crucial question of the whole action of the trilogy in so far as it is rooted in Max:

> Muß grausam auch das Grausame geschehn?

In his ultimate extremity, Max is invoking 'das Mitleid', daughter of love, 'die, mit dem finstern Schmerz vertrauter, . . . alle Zugänge meiner Seele den Eindrücken der Zärtlichkeit wiederum öffnet', as Lessing's Tellheim has it.[33] In the first place, Thekla's compassion for him. She will weep for him –

> Sie wird von gräßlich wütender Verzweiflung
> Die Seele retten, diesen Schmerz des Todes
> Mit sanften Trostesworten klagend lösen.

Her pity will soothe the pain of their parting; but also it will enable him to expose himself to the bitterness of Wallenstein's betrayal.

Unlike the other characters of whom we have spoken earlier, Max has no untended desires to conceal. There is no rift in him between moral understanding and emotional reality. He is luminous and whole. His duty is his total Inclination, and he does not know other than that 'the whole man must move at once'. His resolve, once he sees it to be inevitable, stands, and however odious it is, all his being endorses it. It could not be otherwise with him. Because he is so completely of a piece and so incapable of moral poses, he can beg of Thekla with a modesty which is infinitely touching from his lips:

> . . . Nicht
> Das Große, nur das Menschliche geschehe.
> (*Tod*, III. xxi)

But then, as we have seen, *das Menschliche* is more difficult to achieve than the great act. And even Max has to learn to endure it.

When Wallenstein had first confirmed Max's fear that he is bent on treason, Max had exclaimed:

> Nein! wende nicht dein Angesicht zu mir!
> Es war mir immer eines Gottes Antlitz,
> Kann über mich nicht gleich die Macht verlieren;
> Die Sinne sind in deinen Banden noch,
> Hat gleich die Seele blutend sich befreit!
>
> (*Tod*, II. ii)

Later, when he comes for the last time to take his leave, he sees the Duke[34] and grimly asks:

> Du hier? – Nicht du bist's, den ich hier gesucht.
> Dich sollten meine Augen nicht mehr schauen.
> Ich hab' es nur mit ihr allein. Hier will ich,
> Von diesem Herzen freigesprochen sein,
> An allem andern ist nichts mehr gelegen.
>
> (*Tod*, III. xviii)

We know these words and this mental gesture. They are the words, and the gesture, of one who thinks that he has done with life and is not willing to risk his resolve by courting more pain and confusion than he can bear. The Countess Terzky had used Thekla as a bait to hold Max in Wallenstein's camp ('. . . und wohl seh' ich den Angel, womit man dich zu fangen denkt,' Octavio had shrewdly warned his son). The *poet* uses Thekla's compassion as the magnet that will draw Max into Wallenstein's orbit once again, and ease him into that tragic rhythm in which, in an ultimate exposure to suffering, the last resistances melt and a wholly sensitized person can go to meet his death with total acceptance. As he permits himself to respond to Wallenstein's pathetic plight, he yields, saying:

> Das ertrag' ich nicht.
> Ich kam hieher mit fest entschiedner Seele,
> Ich glaubte, recht und tadellos zu tun, . . .
> Das Herz in mir empört sich, es erheben
> Zwei Stimmen streitend sich in meiner Brust . . .
> Ich stehe wankend, weiß nicht, was ich soll.
>
> (*Tod*, III. xxi)

It is only then when he has dared give himself up to this conflict – an existential conflict surely, if any[35] – that his strength, through such uncalculating exposure to suffering, has grown to the point where he can beg of Wallenstein:

> . . . O wende deine Augen
> Nicht von mir weg! Noch einmal zeige mir
> Dein ewig teures und verehrtes Antlitz.
> (*Tod*, III. xxiii)

But Thekla's compassion achieves something more crucial still, for Max's inner development as well as for the poetic quality of the play as a whole. It empowers the youth temporarily to make good the rift which threatens to tear him asunder, that inner division to which time and again he refers to as 'den Riß' – and to restore his desecrated humanity. And this Thekla does by sanctioning him, through the completeness of her empathy, to feel compassionate towards himself. In the last resort it is for this that he has sought her out; this which for a few fleeting moments empowers him to transcend the gruesomeness of his actual fate; and this which restores to him a transient wholeness of being even as, in a murderous conflict, he is being torn apart, and to us the ability to bear it.

VIII

For compassion, like love, is an aesthetic emotion. In fact, since Aristotle, Mendelssohn, Lessing and the Schiller of *Über die Tragische Kunst*, it has been hailed as *the* aesthetic emotion *per se*. In the first instance it is the emotion which the spectacle of tragedy is to arouse, and catharize, in the spectator. But as we have seen it is one of the cardinal principles of Schiller's tragic art that he prefigures the effects he intends his plays to have on the spectator or reader within the economy of the tragedy itself.[36] So with the aesthetic distance the poet wants his spectators to maintain in the midst of the tragic action and so – these two are more closely related than might appear at a first glance – with the pity he wants to arouse in them. 'Alle Affekte sind ästhetischer aus der zweiten Hand,' Schiller writes in *Über das Pathetische* and significantly adds: 'und keine Sympathie ist stärker, als die wir mit der Sympathie empfinden.' We can at once see that through her compassion for Max, Thekla calls forth our sympathy. More importantly, however, she calls forth Max's sympathy with himself, and it is through this emotion, kindled in the midst of deadly inner strife, that the poet prefigures in his spectators a response which combines, in an almost unique fashion, distance and immediacy.

For compassion turned inward upon the suffering self – Max's own compassion – is the aesthetic emotion raised to its highest power; not only because in it all the registers of responsiveness are opened, the feelings and mental energies engaged in the primary conflict as well as the pity which encompasses them: it is aesthetic, precisely, because whilst it is a total response of the greatest immediacy it nevertheless involves a modicum of psychical distance.

'Mit-Leid' is not only, as a recent critic and aesthetician has emphatically stated, 'ein Affekt der Annäherung';[37] nor is it true to maintain that Schiller '. . . will "Mitleid" immer als "Miterleiden" verstanden wissen', as 'eine unserer Autonomie abträgliche Passivität', so that, like all other forms of suffering, it argues 'im Grunde also wieder die Übermacht unserer sinnlichen Existenz'.[38] As the very word implies, and as Schiller himself is at pains to stress, it is a weakened, distanced affect, suffering at one remove; most of all so when the object of such suffering is the self. 'Mit-Leid' turned in upon the suffering self presupposes a curious doubling, or even tripling, of consciousness. There is the part of the self that suffers with every conceivable immediacy – Max torn by a deadly rift; there is the part of the self which looks on, pleading for compassion and compassionate with itself, embracing its own suffering with tenderness – Tell in the sunken lane; and lastly, there is a new self: a self born of the interaction of pity and pain, of exposure and composure, passionately involved and yet curiously detached from itself – the self which first announces itself in Max's 'Ja! Ja! da ist er!' – and, most important, whole.

To make this difficult conception clearer, I cannot forbear quoting once more at length one of the most illuminating passages in any work dealing with aesthetic problems that I have ever come across. In a series of lectures entitled *The Modern Conception of Aesthetics*, Edward Bullough writes:

> There are many who are 'actors', not in the sense that they *pretend* to do and think before others what they would neither do nor think in the privacy of their own chamber . . . , but in the sense that they perform perfectly natural and spontaneous acts with so clear a perception of their nature, their value and their sensuous, concrete effectiveness that these acts assume for them an intrinsic importance (quite apart from ultimate aims and results), an importance such as acts, done un-

consciously or only with some definite purpose in view, can never assume. In the doing of them they experience a kind of separation within themselves, a doubling of consciousness, as if they were two individuals, of which one acts while the other looks on, criticizes and enjoys, with the free and impartial interest and the satisfaction which the artist feels in the production of his own handiwork. Thus they combine in themselves the threefold aspect of artist, work of art and spectator, an exceedingly complex mental state, common enough in the actor, but realized in actual life, too, more often than we are inclined to think. The result is a curious enhancement of the acts, of the most trivial as of the most sublime. They are invested with a value as ends in themselves, done for their own sake, with a devotion and detachment impossible in acts performed for the sake of further ends or ulterior reasons. Perhaps such acts represent, in their freedom from personal motives and the perfect abandonment to their performance, the highest kind of behaviour of which a human being is capable: deeds of heroism as well as the simplest acts of kindness, always done with the full intensity of the whole personality behind them. To realize this is the ideal of aesthetic culture.[39]

The Max who storms into Wallenstein's hall, exclaiming 'Ja! Ja! da ist er' is such an 'actor' – the harmonious interplay between sense and spirit, throughout his life, has prepared him for that role; and we must not forget that he is in fact an actor on the stage, conceived by his creator so that he may draw harmonies from sense and spirit of those that hear him and see him 'act' his tragic part. Thekla's sympathy has released an answering capacity in himself. And now, encompassing and transmuting his own conflict – as deadly a conflict as any – by his perception of it, he is momentarily transported into a different dimension of awareness. From the rhythmic alternation of suffering and resolve, of exposure and composure, of *Leiden* and *Fassung*, following each other in an ever swifter and sharper succession – like the trumpet blasts that accompany the closing stages of the action – there is born a third thing, 'ein Drittes, Neues, Höheres, Unerwartetes':[40] com-passion of the self with the self, and with it, pathos. Suffering, in Greek *pathos*, by all accounts the basest and most sensuous component of the sublime, is not just the foil of the spirit's triumph. Not even its sounding-board or its groundbass as I have suggested before. Refined into *Mit-Leid*, the com-passion of the self with the self, it becomes pathos,[41] and as such it is nothing less than the sensuous body of the sublime, its carrying-medium, empowered to transmute the agony of death into a mighty torrent of mellifluous lament. 'Das Pathos des Schmerzes scheint ohnmächtig', writes the same critic who is so anxious to prove that suffering, for Schiller, is always a resistance to be overcome, a passive affection which detracts from the autonomy of the spirit. Yet he continues, inconsistently but aptly: 'Doch was hier sein soll, ist die Anerkennung des ungeheuren Leids, im Helden selbst und in allen, die ihm nahen, die Höhe des Bewußtseins, das der Schmerz erfahren muß'.[42] Released into the aesthetic dimension of pathos where perfect abandon is matched with perfect disinterestedness, Max resolves his 'gräßlich wütende Verzweiflung' into 'Melodie und Rede' and achieves what Thomas Mann, in a lovely phrase, once called 'Anmut in der Qual'.[43] This abandon and this inner freedom find expression in his leavetaking from Wallenstein. While he yet shunned more pain than his resolve could bear, he had twice refused to look the author of his misery in the face. Now he not only begs him to look upon him for the last time; in a gesture of incomparable tenderness he encompasses him in his grief and, parting, longs to protect him, to surround him with his own all-seeing love:

> Des Kaisers Acht hängt über ihm und gibt
> Sein fürstlich Haupt jedwedem Mordknecht preis,
> Der sich den Lohn der Bluttat will verdienen;
> Jetzt tät' ihm eines Freundes fromme Sorge,
> Der Liebe treues Auge not – und die
> Ich scheidend um ihn seh'. . .
>
> (*Tod*, III. xxiii)

This surely is the realized 'ideal of aesthetic culture' of which Bullough speaks: that blend of 'devotion and detachment', of total exposure to the human situation and some ultimate composure through the power of form, which permits one torn to pieces to stand back from the war within and to perceive it, and even its author, with dispassionate compassion, as if he were not the victim but an onlooker of a situation which costs him life and limb. What is such serenity in the midst of pain but sublimity in its purest form? Max has momentarily succeeded in achieving the seemingly impossible of which Schiller speaks in his last essay on these matters, *Über das Erhabene*: 'das wirkliche Leiden in eine erhabene Rührung aufzulösen'.[44] He has been liberated to do so through the power of compassion, the aesthetic emotion *per se*. For, as Schiller has it in *Über die tragische Kunst*: 'Sie, die allein fähig sind, sich von sich selbst zu trennen, genießen allein das Vorrecht, an sich selbst teilzunehmen und eigenes Leiden in dem milden Widerschein der Sympathie zu empfinden.'[45]

IX

Everywhere in Schiller's tragedies, the tragic rhythm of *Leiden* alternating with *Tätigkeit*, of exposure with composure, flowers in the twin-phenomena of pathos and compassion; compassion called forth by others, turned inward upon itself and flowing out again in an ultimate act of forgiveness. And everywhere such compassion is token of the fact that richness of response and aesthetic totality of being can be preserved or regained, miraculously if tenuously, even in situations of moral choice and the extremest conflict.

Such a miraculous flowering is granted to Karl Moor as, weeping, Amalia embraces the weeping man who is over and over sullied and whom she loves. It is then that, 'aufblühend und in ekstatischer Wonne', Karl speaks some of the deepest words that ever flowed from Schiller's pen: 'Sieh, o sieh, die Kinder des Lichts weinen am Hals der weinenden Teufel' (V. ii). Accepted, he accepts himself in compassion; and is ready compassionately to flow out to a fellow man in need.[46] Maria Stuart, so impatient of her ladies' pity in the beginning, is transformed by the experience of divine mercy and forgivenesss. Now she is able to look at her own life with tenderness, seeing it completed, its end contained in its beginning, almost as if it were someone else's. It is now that she can make that touching request that her old nurse who carried her into life might lead her, gently, out of it; now that she can forgive her enemy and, in Elisabeth, herself; and now that she can take her final farewell with a swift and simple grace from which the last traces of conflict or even strain have disappeared. And Don Cesar: he argues and pleads for his sister's compassion almost more impetuously than does Max for Thekla's.

> Nicht den Geliebten hab' ich dir getötet!
> Den *Bruder* hab' ich dir und hab' ihn *mir*
> Gemordet – dir gehört der Abgeschiedne jetzt
> Nicht näher an als *ich*, der Lebende,
> Und *ich* bin mitleidswürdiger als er,
> Denn *er* schied rein hinweg, und ich bin schuldig. . . .
> Weine um den Bruder, ich will mit dir weinen,
> Und mehr noch – rächen will ich ihn! Doch nicht
> Um den Geliebten weine! . . .

In *einen* Fall verstrickt, drei liebende
Geschwister, gehen wir vereinigt unter
Und teilen gleich der Tränen traurig Recht. . . .
– Jetzt bist du meine Schwester, und dein Mitleid
Fordr' ich von dir als einen heil'gen Zoll.

(IV. vii)

It is jealousy that drives him to seek her pity. But when that pity is granted to him, when Beatrice gently leans against his breast and almost fulfils his vision –

. . . das schöne Mitleid
Neigt sich, ein weinend Schwesterbild, mit sanft
Anschmiegender Umarmung auf die Urne . . .

(IV. ix)

– what a transformation it effects in him! It enables him to stop thinking dichotomously in terms of *him* and *me*,[47] to comfort his mother in words of quiet pathos and to embrace, in one perception which is objective at once and compassionate, the truth that his own and his brother's life are one and indivisible as that of the Dioscuri, as though he himself stood clear of the relation he perceives. At the end, it empowers him to say:

– Die Tränen sah ich, die auch mir geflossen,
Befriedigt ist mein Herz, ich folge dir . . .

(IV. x)

and to attest by dying to the wholeness he has perceived.

X

A critic has recently advanced the thesis, with great powers of persuasion and authority, that Schiller entertained the notion of an 'aesthetic modality of the sublime'.

Moral harmony, however perfect, and however self-renewing, is bound . . . to involve a one-sided retrenchment of potential whenever it issues as determinate action. And it is on such determinate actions that Schiller envisages the aesthetic . . . exercising an influence . . . which affects their modality without altering their structure; which lends to their performance a grace which, though superfluous as regards their strictly moral value, allows them to partake of the harmony of beauty.[48]

The whole argument I have advanced in this chapter and indeed throughout this book confirms, largely on the evidence of the tragedies themselves, the thesis that sublime conduct too, so carefully distinguished by the author of the *Ästhetische Briefe* from nobility of character and bearing,[49] is capable of taking on an overall aesthetic 'tone'. But I would go further than that and suggest firstly that, for the *poet* Schiller at least, no act born of moral conflict deserves to be called sublime unless it transcends divisiveness and attains such 'superfluous' grace – if this were not so, Verrina in *Fiesco* or the Grand Inquisitor in *Don Carlos* would by their actions qualify for the title; and, secondly, that sublimity thus understood as a legitimate manifestation of the aesthetic mode does evince a structure which is basically at odds with that which characterizes moral conduct.[50]

In moral conduct – and even more obviously in an act born of moral conflict – the agent is wholly determined by the dictate of the moral law, executed in total disregard of the demands of feeling and instinct. The structure of such an action is characterized by a rift running between the 'intelligible' aspect of our psyche, between reason and the will determined by the moral law on the one hand, and the 'sensible' sphere of feeling, impulse and instinct on the other; and the more purely 'moral' the action, the more marked the rift. In the sublime mode as we have got to know it, this rift is not only considerably narrowed – we have seen the reciprocal process by which feeling and instinct become ennobled and principle becomes anchored in reality; more importantly, it has shifted in its entirety. The basic stratification of the psyche has changed. What subtle rift remains no longer splits the spiritual and the sensible strata of the psyche into two halves, but runs between the whole complex of the sensuous–spiritual conflict on the one hand and, on the other, the compassionate perception by which this conflict is embraced. The dramas as a whole, including *Wilhelm Tell*,[51] support this view, and so does much of Schiller's theory. True, there are a good many statements, notably in *Vom Erhabenen*, which assert of the sublime the essentially dualistic structure which we associate with the moral domain. There we may read statements such as this:

[Beim Praktischerhabenen] . . . muß uns völlig gleichgültig sein, wie wir als Sinnenwesen dabei fahren, und bloß darin muß unsre Freiheit bestehen, daß wir unsern physischen Zustand, der durch die Natur bestimmt werden kann, gar nicht zu unserm *Selbst* rechnen, sondern als etwas *Auswärtiges und Fremdes** betrachten, was auf unsre moralische Person keinen Einfluß hat.[52]

Or:

Praktischerhaben ist also jedweder Gegenstand, der uns zwar unsre Ohnmacht als Naturwesen zu bemerken gibt, zugleich aber ein Widerstehungsvermögen von ganz andrer Art in uns aufdeckt, welches zwar von unsrer physischen Existenz die Gefahr *nicht* entfernt, aber (welches unendlich mehr ist) *unsre physische Existenz selbst von unsrer Persönlichkeit absondert.** . . . Dieses [das Erhabene] gründet sich also ganz und gar nicht auf Ueberwindung oder Aufhebung einer uns drohenden Gefahr, sondern auf Wegräumung der letzten Bedingung, unter der es allein Gefahr für uns geben kann, indem es uns den sinnlichen Teil unsres Wesens, der allein der Gefahr unterworfen ist, *als ein auswärtiges Naturding** betrachten lehrt, das unsre wahre Person, unser moralisches Selbst, gar nichts angeht.[53]

'Groß! Groß und abscheulich!' we might say with Lessing's Nathan and comfort ourselves with the thought that in this particular essay Schiller was rehearsing Kantian thoughts rather than exploring his own. For indeed, it is not the poet who speaks here. How could definitions such as these, which so radically divorce the spirit, the 'real' self, from its embodiment, hope to account for the sad exultance of our spirit and for the pleasurable shudders that tingle down our spine at the sight of the sublime – painful thrills this poet was so expert at evoking?

Not that an element of separation is missing in Schiller's more mature statements about the sublime. 'Daher der hohe Wert einer Lebensphilosophie,' we read in *Über die Tragische Kunst*, 'welche durch stete Hinweisung auf allgemeine Gesetze das Gefühl für unsere Individualität entkräftet . . . und uns dadurch in den Stand setzt, *mit uns selbst wie mit Fremdlingen umzugehen.'** [54] Or: 'Sie, die allein fähig sind, *sich von sich selbst zu trennen,** genießen allein das Vorrecht, an sich selbst teilzunehmen und eigenes Leiden in dem milden Widerschein der Sympathie zu empfinden.' But then this is not the dissociation between our mental and our physical selves of which Schiller speaks in *Vom Erhabenen*; it is a separation between 'uns selbst' – that is to say, the whole area of our

* My italics.

spiritual–sensible conflict – and the 'devotion and detachment' of the 'actor' who compassionately perceives what he suffers and, in doing so, transcends his divided self. It is in fact that psychical distance which intervenes between the subject and its own affections in any and all aesthetic states, a distance which Edward Bullough has aptly described as a 'curiously dualistic, yet unified psychosis';[55] and it is surely not accidental that Schiller should have arrived at a formulation closely reminiscent of the ones I have alluded to just now in a discussion which is specifically focused upon the processes of *artistic* creation. The poet must learn '*sich selbst fremd zu werden*, den Gegenstand seiner Begeisterung von seiner Individualität los zu wickeln, seine Leidenschaft *aus einer mildernden Ferne anzuschauen*.'*[56]

Sublimity, then, is the furthest extension of the aesthetic mode in situations of extreme conflict. But an aesthetic mode it is, nevertheless, evincing the structure peculiar to all aesthetic experience. It rests, not on feelings repressed or retrenched, but on currents of passion flowing swift and strong and being transformed, together with the intellectual elements that enter the psychical configuration, into a response that is different in kind from any that went into its making. It is not the negation of moral grace, nor does it borrow grace as a desirable but superfluous adjunct: the sublime is the miraculous and transient flowering of grace in the face of the gruesome: 'Anmut in der Qual'. Schiller has demonstrated the birth of sublimity from grace, and the final rebirth of grace from pain and strain time and time again, and nowhere more movingly than in the figure of Max Piccolomini. He has unequivocally traced the aesthetic lineage of the sublime, even in that least aesthetically orientated and most nearly metaphysical of his essays, in *Über das Erhabene*. There we plainly read:

Das Schöne macht sich bloß verdient um den *Menschen*, das Erhabene um den *reinen Dämon* in ihm; und weil es einmal unsre Bestimmung ist, auch bei allen sinnlichen Schranken uns nach dem Gesetzbuch reiner Geister zu richten, so muß das Erhabene zu dem Schönen hinzukommen, um die *ästhetische Erziehung* zu einem vollständigen Ganzen zu machen und die Empfindungsfähigkeit des menschlichen Herzens nach dem ganzen Umfang seiner Bestimmung, und also auch über die Sinnenwelt hinaus, zu erweitern.[57]

* My italics.

XI

'Nach dem ganzen Umfang seiner Bestimmung': these words hold good, in full force, for the domain of sublimity. True, the sublime cultivates our sensibilities beyond their normal range in that it enables us to respond to things beyond the visible world, as it brings us face to face with the majesty of the moral law. But never by blunting the senses. We have seen how Schiller, in his theory, insists on 'die lebendigste Darstellung der leidenden Natur' if only so that we may be able to gauge the power of a spirit which can prove a match to such suffering. We have seen him follow a finer hunch in the tragedies themselves: revealing, step by step, the hero's 'wahr und offen da liegende Natur', developing to the utmost his 'zarte Empfindlichkeit für das Leiden', and by no means only so that, by contrast, the spirit's triumph shall shine the more brightly. But because that adept of death knew that the lines of life and death intersect and mingle and that the richest sensuality and the purest sublimity mysteriously go hand in hand. Perhaps this was because death, to him, was the supreme feast; certainly because he knew – and we have seen this, too – that what is not recognized and lived through can never be truly renounced. This is the deeper reason for that extravagant influx of life just before death which is experienced by, among others, Marquis Posa, Wallenstein, Maria Stuart and Don Cesar; an experience which found its most memorable expression in the words of Hanna Kennedy quoted at the outset of this chapter:

> O Sir! Wir litten Mangel, da wir lebten,
> Erst mit dem Tode kommt der Überfluß zurück.

We have also seen – though we did not put it in these words – that Kennedy's lines could equally well be reversed. Superfluity only returns as the great liberator, death, is knocking at the door. In the universe of discourse of Schiller's tragedies it would be no less true to say that death can only enter when there is such bounty. Certainly a sublime death, freely chosen. For such a death is not extraneous to the person, enforced from the outside, as is the end of Fiesco, Luise Millerin or Demetrius. It is an organic and deeply personal event, endorsed and desired by the whole person. For it to become thus wholly desired, Schiller – as we have seen – deploys the tragic rhythm of composure alternating with exposure, moral resolve with emotional upheaval, until by and by the moral consciousness coincides with the existential condition of the hero and he wants to be what he ought to be and what he in fact is. It is in such a state of utter sensitivity and honesty that Don Cesar can say:

> Befriedigt ist mein Herz, ich folge dir.

This is what every one of Schiller's characters that has occupied our attention in substance does say. And to be able to say it, and act on it, he must be whole.

We have become unhappily inured with the critical cliché, too often repeated to be recounted, that for Schiller sublimity is the abnegation by the spirit of the senses or, as one critic puts it, 'the victory of the spirit over the flesh'.[58] Perhaps certain formulatons in essays such as *Vom Erhabenen* or *Über das Erhabene* have helped to create such an impression; perhaps even that magnificent passage from *Über Anmut und Würde*, which I have quoted before in another context, has had its share in crystallizing such a wrongheaded notion. 'Wäre die sinnliche Natur im Sittlichen immer nur die unterdrückte und nie die mitwirkende Partei,' the author argues there, 'wie könnte sie das ganze Feuer ihrer Gefühle zu einem Triumph hergeben, der über sie selbst gefeiert wird?'[59] A triumph of the spirit, yes. But a triumph in which the senses share as equal partners, an all-consuming sacrificial flame for which they provide the fuel. And how could it be otherwise? The energy of our vital drives is needed to give reality to any principle or decision of our reason. Schiller says this un-equivocally in the *Ästhetische Briefe*, at a crucial turn of the argument when he has shown that our reason knows what is amiss with Western civilization and looks for the drives which can implement what reason knows, the very energies which are to be reached, and refined, by aesthetic education. There, in Letter VIII, we read:

> Die Vernunft hat geleistet, was sie leisten kann, wenn sie das Gesetz findet und aufstellt; vollstrecken muß es der mutige Wille und das lebendige Gefühl. Wenn die Wahrheit im Streit mit Kräften den Sieg erhalten soll, so muß sie selbst erst zur *Kraft* werden und zu ihrem Sachführer im Reich der Erscheinungen einen *Trieb* aufstel-len; denn Triebe sind die einzigen bewegenden Kräfte in der emp-findenden Welt.[60]

We have seen the rhythm between composure and exposure, between principle and feeling pervading Schiller's tragedies and culminating in the emergence of pathos and compassion, manifestations, both, of the aesthetic mode. We might go further and venture to say that the ultimate function

of this tragic rhythm is to accomplish the aesthetic education of those
feelings and instincts which are constantly exercised, more deeply known
and more truly accepted so that, at the last, ennobled and transparent to
will and reason, they can fire the moral resolve and translate it into action;
an action which is sublime in the measure in which it is true and springs
from the person as a whole. It is sublimity in this more liberal and comprehensive sense which is, I believe, at the back of Schiller's mind when
in fact he speaks of nobility; when he writes, in the second paragraph of
the footnote appended to Letter XXIII, that actions performed aesthetically
'exceed duty', in that duty can merely prescribe 'daß der *Wille* heilig sei,
nicht daß auch schon die *Natur* sich geheiligt habe . . .'; and adds:
'. . . ein solches Betragen heißt edel'.[61] Nature herself taking on a sacral
character: this is a notion that is absolutely central to Schiller's tragedies;
one need only think of Karl Moor's experience of redemption in Amalia's
arms – 'Rein bin ich wie der Äther des Himmels, sie liebt mich! – Weinenden Dank dir, Erbarmer im Himmel!' (V. ii) – or of Maria's or Johanna's
manifest transfiguration. But it is a notion that is utterly foreign, and
repugnant, to Schiller's teacher Kant who rejects it as sheer and sacrilegious
presumption. From the vantage point of Kant's metaphysical and methodological premisses, the moral law alone is sacred – 'das *heilige* Gesetz' we
read time and time again – whilst feelings and instincts are anarchic and
blind; and to him virtue is at all times 'moralische Gesinnung *im Kampfe*,
und nicht *Heiligkeit* im vermeinten Besitze einer völligen *Reinheit* der
Gesinnungen des Willens'.[62]

But how are we to reconcile our reading of Schiller – of his tragedies
and even of the first two paragraphs of this footnote – with the express
statement which follows in the third section of that same footnote, namely
that noble conduct is to be rated less highly than sublime conduct? That
for all that the former transcends moral obligation, '. . . wir es [i.e.
erhabenes Betragen] ungleich höher als jenes achten'? Is here not Schiller
revoking, at one blow, all that the tragedies have told us? Is he not revers-
ing his earlier position and giving unconditional precedence to the sublime
over the noble? Before we concede this vital point and charge him, as has
so often been done, with a logical volte-face or an ambivalent oscillation
between an aesthetic and a moral ideal of freedom for which it is impossible
to give any rational explanation, we ought to take note of the signification
the word *achten* is likely to have for him in the context in which he is here
using it, that is to say in the discussion of the sublime, this being the
concept he evolved – as we have seen – in the closest dependence on Kant.

Achtung is the key concept of the section of the *Kritik der praktischen Vernunft* which is entitled *Von den Triebfedern der reinen praktischen Vernunft*. A mere count of the number of times this word is used in the twenty-odd pages of this chapter will indicate something of its importance: it occurs no less than 58 times! In this packed section Kant is asking the crucial question (picked up – as we have seen – by Schiller in the eighth aesthetic letter) how it is that a law or principle of reason can, unaided by feeling, become a determinant of our volition. This, he frankly admits, 'ist ein für die menschliche Vernunft unauflösliches Problem', coinciding with the problem of how there can be a free will.[63] Yet solve it he must, since only the will which is directly determined by the moral law, that is to say, in the absence of all sensuous or 'pathological' motive-springs arising from its content, is considered morally pure. He solves his problem by introducing the concept of an emotion that has a numerically and qualitatively unique status. Unlike all other emotions, it neither springs from the senses nor is it to be accounted as pleasurable or painful. A 'moral emotion', it is nothing but our entirely 'non-pathological' apperception of the pure form of the moral law. This unique emotion Kant terms *Achtung*. It is nothing but the subjective correlative of the moral law itself: '. . . die Achtung fürs Gesetz', Kant states, '. . . ist die Sittlichkeit selbst, subjektiv als Triebfeder betrachtet . . .',[64] just as the moral law, in turn, is the objective correlative of *Achtung* which has no other object besides the generalized maxim of the will. The two are geared to one another in a logical one-to-one relation, as two quotations chosen from amongst many others clearly demonstrate. 'Achtung fürs moralische Gesetz', Kant writes, 'ist also die einzige und zugleich unbezweifelte moralische Triebfeder, so wie dieses Gefühl auch auf kein Objekt anders, als lediglich aus diesem Grunde gerichtet ist.'[65] Or: 'Der Begriff der Pflicht fodert also an der Handlung, *objektiv*, Übereinstimmung mit dem Gesetze, an der Maxime derselben aber, *subjektiv*, Achtung fürs Gesetz, als die alleinige Bestimmungsart des Willens durch dasselbe.'[66] Both the moral law and its subjective correlative, *Achtung*, are defined the way they are for methodological reasons.[67] For were the principle of morality furnished by any extraneous object of the will rather than by the pure generalized form of the volition itself, the result would be the heteronomy of the will, and *a priori* moral judgements would be impossible. Similarly, were the motive-spring of morality any 'pathological' – i.e. accidental – determinants of our volition rather than pure *Achtung* at the apperception of the lawfulness of the will *per se*, there could be no motive-spring of the will which is *a priori* ascertainable. This methodological origin and function explains a certain emptiness attaching to both concepts. As morality is the determination of the will by a purely formal criterion, i.e. by the idea of its own maxim envisaged as a universal law in disregard of any specific object it enjoins, so our apperception of this law, *Achtung*, is stripped of any emotive content such as might be called forth by any specific object given to the will. This is not to say, of course, that these majestically vacuous twin-concepts, the pure lawfulness of the will and the pure respect it evokes in us, are not in themselves objects of Kant's highest regard. Indeed they are the object of his 'grenzenlosen Hochschätzung'[68] and humanity, to him, only has worth in so far as it signifies the respect paid by finite rational beings to the autonomy of the will. But *Achtung, within* this tightly organized argument, is not so much an evaluative term as a philosophical concept answering to that of the pure will, methodologically motivated and furnishing the only link between our cognitive and volitional faculties on the one hand and the conative sphere on the other which is capable of being ascertainable *a priori*.

I would suggest that when Schiller states that however much we value noble conduct, we 'achten' sublime conduct 'ungleich höher', he is not primarily making a value judgement, but echoing Kant in his highly specialized and almost technical use of the term. Echoing him loosely, it is true, because, morality being the sole object of our respect, it is impossible to respect its manifestation, sublime conduct, *more* than any other mode of conduct. For respect has no application to anything beyond this unique object. Nevertheless, what Schiller is echoing in substance is Kant's nomenclature in which *Achtung* and sublimity, that is to say the determination of the will by the universalized form of its own maxim, in total disregard of all 'pathological' motives or inclinations, are coupled together as *logical* correlatives.

Thus I do not think that we need consider Schiller's statement that we 'respect' sublime conduct incomparably more than noble conduct as constituting a serious counter-indication to our main argument regarding Schiller's priority of values. Nor indeed can it be said that in his theoretical writings as a whole Schiller accords to the sublime a higher rank than to the noble. Far from it. The noble is clearly regarded as the consummation of the sublime in a passage such as the following which – this is significant to note – follows immediately upon his unstinted eulogy of Kant's rigoristic, that is to say, methodologically systematic thinking 'im Felde der reinen Vernunft und bei der moralischen Gesetzgebung'; '. . . im Feld der

Erscheinung und bei der wirklichen Ausübung der Sittenpflicht', Schiller argues, the priorities are at once reversed.

> So gewiß ich nämlich überzeugt bin, . . . daß der Anteil der Neigung an einer freien Handlung für die reine Pflichtmäßigkeit dieser Handlung nichts beweist, so glaube ich eben daraus folgern zu können, daß die sittliche Vollkommenheit des Menschen gerade nur aus diesem Anteil seiner Neigung an seinem moralischen Handeln erhellen kann. Der Mensch ist nämlich nicht dazu bestimmt, einzelne sittliche Handlungen zu verrichten, sondern ein sittliches Wesen zu sein. Nicht Tugenden, sondern *die* Tugend ist seine Vorschrift, und Tugend ist nichts anders 'als eine Neigung zu der Pflicht'.[69]

This shift from the single act to the total disposition, from conduct to character, which has already been perceptible in the footnote to the twenty-third aesthetic letter, is further developed here, in his subsequent exposition of his conception of the beautiful – or noble – soul: '. . . bei einer schönen Seele [sind] die einzelnen Handlungen eigentlich nicht sittlich, sondern der ganze Charakter ist es.'[70] And that Schiller is not here thinking in terms of a static and ultimately sterile ideal of harmony but in terms of vigorous choice and conflict such as are the stuff of the sublime, becomes apparent a few lines later:

> Die schöne Seele hat kein andres Verdienst, als daß sie ist. Mit einer Leichtigkeit, als wenn bloß der Instinkt aus ihr handelte, übt sie der Menschheit *peinlichste Pflichten** aus, und *das heldenmütigste Opfer, das sie dem Naturtriebe abgewinnt,** fällt wie eine freiwillige Wirkung eben dieses Triebes in die Augen.[71]

The consummation of the sublime in the noble is most clearly the gist of the essay *Über den moralischen Nutzen ästhetischer Sitten*, which culminates in an even more radical repudiation of the single moral action, indeed of 'morality' itself, in favour of the 'größern Kongruenz der ganzen Naturanlage mit dem moralischen Gesetz';[72] a repudiation of doing in favour of a being in which nature itself has taken on a sacral character. In this essay, Schiller recalls the case of a certain Duke of Brunswick who risked his life to save others, 'einzig aus Bewußtsein dieser Pflicht'. Supposing now, Schiller continues, that he who thus obeyed the dictate of reason to perform an action against which his very nature rebelled, possessed

* My italics.

. . . einen so reizbaren Schönheitssinn, den alles, was groß und
vollkommen ist, entzückt, so wird in demselbem Augenblick, als die
Vernunft ihren Ausspruch tut, auch die Sinnlichkeit zu ihr übertreten,
und er wird das *mit* Neigung tun, was er ohne diese zarte Empfindlichkeit für das Schöne *gegen* die Neigung hätte tun müssen.
Werden wir ihn aber deswegen für minder vollkommen halten?[73]

Schiller's answer, here and in his tragedies, is unequivocal. Feelings
ennobled through that aesthetic education which is vouchsafed by the
tragic rhythm of composure and exposure are the crown and consummation of sublimity. Ennobled feelings and instincts are the mainspring of
the sublime resolve if it is to be put into action without loss of quality.
They fire the will; they are as it were the wings of a resolve that is to come
from the whole man. In one of the boldest formulations in the whole of
the *Ästhetische Briefe*, Schiller declares that man 'muß lernen *edler*
begehren, damit er nicht nötig habe, *erhaben* zu wollen.'[74] This is the key
to the problem. These words sum up the difference between a Verrina or a
Grand Inquisitor on the one hand and a Maria or Don Cesar on the other.
The Grand Inquisitor's decision, for all that it testifies to the indomitable
strength of man's will and spirit (for he obeys his duty as he sees it), is not
sublime but inhuman. He executes his sensibilities – actually he has already lost them: he is blind and there is no channel from the world to his
heart – as he executes Don Carlos. And *mutatis mutandis*, the same holds
good for Verrina. Maria and Don Cesar, Karl Moor, Carlos, Posa and
Johanna, on the other hand, carry out a no less unnatural decision backed,
nevertheless, by the intensity of desires and instincts that are fully
aroused. Sustained by such a carrying-medium, these figures, at the end,
are empowered to say in all simplicity 'I want to die' and to act on this
desire. In this simplicity, in this wholeness of motivation resides the true
sublimity of an act that is rooted in the nobility of its agent and inseparable
from it. Having learnt to *desire* more nobly, those of Schiller's characters
that are nearest to our heart do not need to *will* sublimely.

In life as in death, wholeness, for Schiller, is all. Even the ultimate sublimity of self-sacrifice, born of regard for wholeness and aimed at restoring
or avenging wholeness, is realized by the total resources of the personality
acting in unison.[75] 'The whole man must move at once', even into extinction.

Notes

Chapter 1

This chapter is based on part of my thesis for the Ph.D., *Schiller's View of Tragedy in the Light of his General Aesthetics* (University of London, 1951), shortly to be published under the title *Schiller: A Master of the Tragic Form: His Theory in his Practice* (New York, 1974).

1 Cf. L. Bellermann, *Schiller's Dramen: Beiträge zu ihrem Verständnis* (Berlin, 1898), Vol. I, pp. 128 ff.; E. Kühnemann, *Schiller* (Munich, 1905), p. 182; H. Cysarz, *Schiller* (Halle/Saale, 1934), pp. 94 ff.; K. Cunningham, *Schiller und die französische Klassik* (Bonn, 1930), p. 29; G. Storz, *Der Dichter Friedrich Schiller* (Stuttgart, 1959), pp. 65 ff.; and B. v. Wiese II, pp. 175 and 181.

2 L. Bellermann has very pertinently raised all the objections which may properly suggest themselves to a critic primarily concerned with the poet's handling of the plot (op. cit. pp. 133 ff.).

3 Cf. pp. 41 ff. and note 42 of this chapter.

4 For a diametrically different reading cf. K. Berger, who holds that the subaction centred on Fiesco's relation with Julia serves to animate 'die kalte Staatsaktion durch die Leidenschaften des Herzens . . .'

(*Schiller: Sein Leben und seine Werke* (Munich, 1914), Vol. I, p. 287). I hope to dispose of this view in the following pages.

5 This possibility has been recently explored by F. Fowler in 'Schiller's Fiesco Re-Examined', *PEGS*, New Series, Vol. XL (1969–70), pp. 1 ff. For the rest, critics have been content to ascribe Fiesco's playfulness to the delight, on the part of his creator, in dissimulation and artistic play. This convenient inference – so readily resorted to by adherents of the biographical method – has absolved them all too easily from discovering the unifying thread that runs through the drama and gives it its coherence. In this connection, see Cysarz, op. cit. pp. 98 ff., v. Wiese II, pp. 181 f., and Staiger who writes: 'Wir haben den Eindruck, er [Schiller] treibe das Spiel viel weiter, als unbedingt nötig wäre – offenbar deshalb, weil den Dichter die Virtuosität des

Betrugs entzückt' (*Friedrich Schiller*
(Zürich, 1967), p. 135). Cf. note 13.

6 J. Minor is not unrepresentative of
critical opinion as a whole when he
writes: 'Wie der Räuber Moor
bewährt auch Fiesco seine ganze
Größe in der That: darin unter-
scheidet er sich zugleich bedeutsam
von seinem geschichtlichen Vor-
bilde' (*Schiller, sein Leben und
seine Werke*, Vol. II (Berlin, 1890),
p. 31). Those critics who regard
Fiesco as, first and foremost, a poli-
tician motivated by ambition implicitly assume that he is, first and
foremost, a man of action. And they
are the overwhelming majority.

7 Staiger remarks on the fact that
Fiesco is more difficult to decipher
without his mask than the others are
with theirs on: 'gerade er, mit dem
freien Gesicht, ist aber am schwer-
sten zu entziffern' (op. cit. p. 135).
Staiger sees Fiesco as one in a long
row of frauds and stresses the intimate relationship, in Schiller's universe of discourse, between the
fraud – i.e. the character that consciously controls his every manifestation – and the morally autonomous
person. 'Der Betrüger ist sozusagen
der illegitime Bruder der autono-
men Person' (ibid. p. 138). This is
an interesting thought, well developed throughout Staiger's book, and
it touches in many points upon the
correlation I myself trace, here and
elsewhere, between the motif of
political usurpation and the morality
of merit. (Cf. Chapters 8 and 10 and
I. Appelbaum-Graham, 'The Structure of the Personality in Schiller's
Tragic Poetry', in *Schiller*, Bicentenary Lectures, ed. F. Norman
(London, 1960), pp. 134 ff.) I differ
from Staiger in that I am not prepared to extrapolate from the configurations found within the dramas
themselves to the psychology of the
poet. Most radically I differ from
him in my interpretation of Schil-

ler's experience of freedom. (Cf.
Chapter 4, especially note 30, and
the Introduction to this book.)

8 For similar images characterizing
the rationalistic and mechanistic
psychology of Schiller's figures,
especially in his early work, cf.
Die Räuber, II. i; *Kabale und
Liebe*, V, letzte Szene; *Don Carlos*,
V. viii and *Wallensteins Tod*, IV.
viii. In this connection, see the very
interesting and detailed investiga-
tion of P. Böckmann, 'Die innere
Form in Schillers Jugenddramen',
DuV, 35 (1934), pp. 442 ff., and
also *Kabale und Liebe*, ed. E. M.
Wilkinson and L. A. Willoughby
(Oxford, 1944), pp. xxvi ff.

9 Cf. *Die Räuber*, IV. iv; *Kabale und
Liebe*, I. iii and V. viii and *Don
Carlos*, III. x.

10 Bellermann draws attention to the
similarity of Fiesco's words here to
those of the *Ästhetische Briefe*, but
dismisses it as of no relevance (op.
cit. p. 151). J. G. Robertson, more
pertinently, argues that Fiesco 'is
by no means a mere replica of Karl
Moor . . .', in that he shows a
'development in the direction of a
"beautiful humanity"' (*Schiller
after a Century* (Edinburgh and
London, 1905), p. 35).

11 In a letter to Körner dated 18
February 1793.

12 In the *Ästhetische Briefe*, Schiller
repeatedly stresses lightness as the
mark of the aesthetic object or response, e.g. 'Indem es mit der
Empfindung zusammentrifft, legt
das Notwendige den seinigen [Ernst]
ab, weil es *leicht* wird'. (Letter XV,
5, Schiller's italics.) Or: 'der ern-
steste Stoff muß so behandelt werden, daß wir die Fähigkeit haben,
ihn unmittelbar mit dem leich-
testen Spiele zu vertauschen'. (Letter XXII, 5.) Cf. also *Das Ideal und
das Leben*: 'Nicht der Masse qualvoll
abgerungen, / Schlank und leicht,
wie aus dem Nichts entsprungen, /

Steht das Bild vor dem entzücktem Blick.'

13 The histrionic element in Fiesco's make-up has, of course, been widely remarked, notably by H. B. Garland (I, pp. 56 ff., II, pp. 44 f. and 57 f.), v. Wiese (II, pp. 177 f.), Cysarz (op. cit. p. 101), Staiger (op. cit. p. 135), Fowler (op. cit.). But cf. note 5.

14 J. Minor, op. cit. p. 55.

15 This 'act' recalls Sartre's famous description of the waiter who is playing at *being* a waiter in a café, i.e. pretending to be what he in fact is (*Being and Nothingness* (London, 1969), pp. 59 f.), and the brilliant use made of this narrative passage by R. D. Laing in a discussion of the mechanism of psychological elusion (in *The Self and Others* (London, 1961), pp. 27 ff.). Fiesco's 'acts', by their exaggerated 'rightness', have an air of insincerity and inauthenticity about them; they are a series of impersonations rather than actions in the ordinary sense of the word. Clearly they are acts of 'bad faith' in Sartre's sense of the word, and subtle 'elusions' of reality in that of Laing. Such a manœuvre is, as Laing points out, motivated by fear of reality. The application to Fiesco will become clear later in this chapter, for the findings of which Laing's book, written ten years later, furnishes most welcome corroboration. Cf. also Chapters 6 and 10, especially the section dealing with *Warbeck*.

16 Benno v. Wiese lists three instances in which Fiesco's showmanship is to the fore; the revelation of his plot in front of Romano's tableau, his revenge on Julia and his warning to Andreas where Fiesco is 'gleichsam der Zuschauer seiner selbst' (II, pp. 177 f.). Of the tableau scene v. Wiese writes that the conspirators appear, all of a sudden, 'als bloße Marionetten in der Hand eines Helden, der den Schein der Kunst noch zu übertrumpfen weiß und die Majestät des Bildes durch die Majestät der revolutionären Tat überbietet' (ibid. p. 187). This, he argues, is not Schiller's ultimate intention. 'Ganz gewiß hat es Schiller so gemeint, daß *sein* Fiesco nicht ein bloßes "Gaukelwerk", nicht ein "markloses Marionettenspiel" vorführt, sondern mit durchaus "tatenerwärmender Kraft" vor uns steht' (p. 188). Yet v. Wiese does not feel comfortable at this identification of the hero. 'Dennoch' – he continues – 'läuft das Pathetische der hier von der künstlerischen Einbildungskraft vorgestellten "Tat" wieder eigentümlich leer . . . Es wird gleichsam ein Pathos um seiner selbst willen, noch unabhängig von jedem "Zweck"' (p. 189). Transfer these reflections on the *poet* and the disinterestedness of *his* pathos back to his creation – Fiesco himself – and an ostensibly hybrid character will be seen to be homogeneous in his motivation and all appearance of the poet vacillating in the definition of his poetic theme will become obviated. Witte is similarly dogged by Fiesco's inherent lability. He puts it down to his ambivalence as between his 'overweening ambition' and 'his moral self'; and this in turn he explains in terms of the poet's own ambivalence which then, according to him, finds expression in the 'straining for merely theatrical effects . . .', that is to say, in Fiesco's own histrionic behaviour (W. Witte, *Schiller*, Mod. Lang. Studies IV, (Oxford, 1949), pp. 121 f.). It would be simpler to approach Fiesco's lability directly, as a controlled phenomenon in its own right, without resorting to devious hypotheses regarding the poet; these stave off the problem rather than solve it. Cf. also H.

Nohl who writes: 'So kommt in das Drama selbst ein jünglingshaftes Schwanken hinein, das bis zuletzt nicht klar werden läßt, was Fiesco aus sich machen wird, den Bürger oder den Herrn.' (In *Friedrich Schiller* (Frankfurt am Main, 1954), p. 34.)

17 Goethe has shown, in the figure of his Tasso, the relaxation of practical tensions and the interpolation of psychical distance between the experiencing subject and the immediacy of his experiencing through the exercise of his virtuos¹ty in contact with his – verbal – medium. In this connection, see E. M. Wilkinson, 'Goethe's *Torquato Tasso*. The Tragedy of the Poet', in Wilkinson and Willoughby, *Goethe Poet and Thinker* (London, 1962), pp. 86 ff. For a theoretical formulation of these aspects of creativity and receptivity in art, cf. S. Alexander's distinction between 'material' and 'formal' passions, in *Beauty and other Forms of Value* (London, 1933), pp. 54 f., and E. Bullough, '"Psychical Distance" as a Factor in Art and an Aesthetic Principle', in *Æsthetics, Lectures and Essays*, ed. Wilkinson (London, 1957), pp. 93 ff.

18 This would be the argument to advance against those critics who, despite all indications to the contrary, maintain that Fiesco's dominant response is a practical, political one.

19 *Ästhetische Briefe*, Letter XXI. For a similar statement cf. also the essay *Über das Pathetische*: 'Die Dichtkunst führt bei dem Menschen nie ein besondres Geschäft aus, und man könnte kein ungeschickteres Werkzeug erwählen, um einen einzelnen Auftrag, ein Detail, gut besorgt zu sehen. . . . Sie kann ihm weder raten, noch mit ihm schlagen, noch sonst eine Arbeit für ihn tun . . .' (*SA*, 11, p. 272).

20 S. Alexander, op. cit. p. 22.

21 E. Bullough, op. cit. p. 95. Cf. also Ernst Cassirer, *An Essay on Man* (New Haven, 1944), p. 164: 'Play and Art . . . are non-utilitarian and unrelated to any practical end. In play as in art we leave behind us our immediate needs in order to give our world a new shape.'

22 In 'The Modern Conception of Aesthetics' in *Aesthetics, Lectures and Essays*, pp. 66 f. In this connection, see chapters 2, 3, 9 and 12.

23 This is where I differ from critics who, while stressing Fiesco's delight in play, find that this is subordinated to a pragmatic mode of responding. Cf. Staiger who characterizes the showmanship in and of Fiesco as 'zweckbestimmter Trug des Intriganten, der hinter dem Schimmer seine weitgesteckten Ziele verbirgt . . .' (op. cit. p. 264) or Garland who speaks of 'the consummate skill of Fiesco in pretending to be absorbed only in his own pleasure, while in reality ruthlessly preparing a plot' (I, p. 56). Cf. also E. L. Stahl, *Friedrich Schiller's Drama: Theory and Practice* (Oxford, 1954), p. 19, for a similar reading. In my view the pragmatic impulse, time and again, is subordinated to the aesthetic impulse and terminates in it.

24 I, p. 60.

25 Cf. Minor, op. cit. p. 70; O. Harnack, *Schiller* (Berlin, 1905), p. 93; Bellermann, op. cit. p. 136; and Berger, op. cit. p. 293.

26 The influence of Lessing's diction on Schiller's dialogue in *Fiesco* is discussed by Minor (op. cit. pp. 66 f.).

27 Garland notes the prevalence of imagery 'linked with acting, make-belief, concealment' (II, pp. 57 f.). But in his enumerations he will lump together statements made by Leonore with those made by Fiesco; thus he robs his linguistic observations of their true structural significance.

28 This connection is denied by Storz (op. cit. pp. 73 f.).

29 Garland points out the frequency of these basic words; but so far from noting that their deployment is controlled and that they help to articulate the counterpoint of the principal theme, he is content to conclude that they underpin 'an elemental quality in Schiller . . .' (II, p. 62).

30 By Berger (op. cit. p. 283), Bellermann (op. cit. p. 133) and Storz (op. cit. p. 65), amongst others.

31 It is to be noted that the word 'Anbeter' as used here by Fiesco himself ironically echoes Verrina's earlier use of it to describe Fiesco's dominant trait: 'Fiesco ist ein Anbeter der Kunst' (I, iii). Read together as they should be, the two statements suggest a great deal about the theme of the play. The 'Anbeter der Kunst', in the sense in which Fiesco is one, ends by turning away from life, towards death. It remains to be seen how this indication on the level of form is borne out on the plane of character and action.

32 This analysis of the linguistic materials of which Verrina and the action centred on him are made up should suffice to disprove M. Gerhard's hypothesis that Verrina's republic is the forerunner of Schiller's aesthetic state. (In *Schiller* (Berne, 1950), p. 62.)

33 Storz objects to the personal motivation of Verrina's and Bourgognino's deed (op. cit. pp. 65 f.). We shall encounter the question of the legitimacy of a personal motive in a moral act again, notably in chapters 8 and 9. It is a crucial question for determining Schiller's conception of morality and indeed sublimity.

34 Cf. Kühnemann (op. cit. p. 189); Berger (op. cit. pp. 289 f.); Minor (op. cit. p. 70); Bellermann (op. cit. p. 136) and Witte (op. cit. p. 123).

Garland, on the other hand, is well aware of the schizoid quality of Fiesco's reaction: 'For three short minutes her death by his own sword produces in Fiesco all the symptoms of frenzied grief, but the love of display immediately reasserts itself and he consoles himself with the idea that her funeral rites shall dazzle all beholders with their pomp.' (I, p. 59.)

35 Cf. III. iv; III. v and IV. xv.

36 Cf. Graham, *Schiller: A Master of the Tragic Form*, Epilogue and Apologia. In this connection, Wilkinson's observation is relevant: 'There is in him' – she writes, referring to Schiller himself – 'an almost pathological attachment to wholes, a fear of letting them go, of breaking them down, lest they never return – a fear of disorganization, dissimilation, decomposition, perhaps even at the sheer bodily level.' In *Schiller: Poet or Philosopher?*, Special Taylorian Lecture (Oxford, 1961), p. 33.

37 Fiesco's dismissal of the Moor is one of the things responsible for the widely held opinion that Schiller, in his first historical panorama, neglected psychological truth in the interest of episode and action. Cysarz writes of this incident: 'Wir erblassen. Ist Fiesco von Irrsinn befallen? Schiller zeigt Fiescos angeborenen Leichtsinn, die augenblickliche Verblendung, nicht mehr. Doch was ist Schillern die Psychologie?' (Op. cit. p. 102.) Cysarz fails to distinguish between the psychological insight of Fiesco, i.e. a character within the play, and the psychological insight of the playwright. This is a particular form of the general critical fallacy of reading any dramatic statement as though it directly expressed the view of the author. This fallacy has done incalculable harm to Schiller scholarship, especially in Germany. It is

directly responsible for the two-dimensional picture of Schiller as a poet of high moral ideals but lacking in all psychological *finesse*. The principal means of safeguarding the poet against such over-simplification is to approach his works, as has been done here, by the method of close textual analysis, i.e. by seeing characters as made up of and embedded in verbal structures which in their entirety determine the full meaning of any given statement.

38 III. x and IV. xii are especially important in this context, and many examples could be cited from these scenes.

39 Garland has drawn attention to the frequent occurrence of imagery drawn from the animal kingdom, but has failed to spot to what extent such images are centred in the relation between Fiesco and the Moor (II, p. 59).

40 For a further discussion of the same technique and its conceptual implications, cf. chapters 3, 7, 9 and Appelbaum-Graham, 'The Structure of the Personality, etc.', pp. 122 ff.

41 This has been clearly seen, and formulated, by Böckmann who writes: 'Indem der Wille zur Macht blind wird, richtet er sich gegen das eigenste Leben . . . In Leonore trifft Fiesco seine eigene Menschlichkeit . . .' (op. cit. p. 464).

42 A closely similar view of Schiller's conception of wholeness has been put forward by Wilkinson, in *Schiller: Poet or Philosopher?* (p. 14) and more latterly by the same author and Willoughby in their edition and translation of the *Ästhetische Briefe* (Oxford, 1967), pp. xxxix, lxxix f., lxxxiv and cxcii. Even at this early point in Schiller's career, the authors urge, Schiller has an essentially dynamic conception of wholeness as 'a pattern of changing responses in time: responses involving the subordination of the rest of the psyche to the dominance of that force or faculty which is appropriate to the demands of the particular situation' (ibid. p. cxcii). This is a welcome corroboration of my thesis from the theoretical angle. I hope to have demonstrated by close textual analysis and from within, as it were, that this is precisely the conception of wholeness that is in fact operative in this early play. Cf. also Chapters 2 and 8.

43 H. Broch in *The Death of Vergil*.

Chapter 2

This chapter is a modified version of a lecture addressed to the English Goethe Society on 19 October, 1955 and printed in *PEGS*, New Series, Vol. XXIV (1955).

1 31 Aug. 1794.

2 Since the publication of this chapter, the obverse of my contention – that Schiller's reflective bent was turned to good account in his poetry-making – has been powerfully and repeatedly argued by E. M. Wilkinson, who demonstrates how fruitfully Schiller's poetic gifts were employed in the 'strategy' of presenting his *Ästhetische Briefe*. Cf. 'Reflections after translating Schiller's *Letters on the Aesthetic Education of Man*', in *Schiller*, Bicentenary Lectures, ed. F. Norman (London, 1960), pp. 68 f. and 76 f.; also *Schiller: Poet or Philosopher?* (esp. pp. 20 f.) and Friedrich Schiller, *On the Aesthetic Education of Man*, ed. and trans. by Wilkinson and Willoughby (Oxford, 1967), esp. p. lvii, p. lxx f. and pp. xcvii ff.

3 For a sound discussion of this point, cf. R. Wellek and A. Warren, *Theory of Literature* (New York, 1949), Chapter X (Literature and Ideas). The authors conclude, correctly in my view, that the value of ideas in art depends, not on their intrinsic merit, but on the measure in which they 'are actually incorporated into the very texture of the work of art, when they become "constitutive", in short, when they cease to be ideas in the ordinary sense of concepts and become symbols, or even myths' (p. 121). But they add the important rider that philosophical poetry of even the most integrated kind 'is only one type of poetry, and that its position is not necessarily central in literature unless one holds to a theory of poetry which is revelatory, essentially mystical' (pp. 122 f.). Cf. also Wilkinson, *Schiller: Poet or Philosopher?* (p. 25).

4 For the gradual recognition that the analytical and the synthetic mode need not conflict with one another as long as each is kept within its own sphere of competence, cf. Schiller's letter to Goethe of 7 Jan. 1795; and for a description of the confusion that ensues when one is made to do duty for the other, cf. the letter to Goethe of 9 Feb. 1798. Goethe's encouraging words about 'diese sonderbare Mischung von Anschauung and Abstraktion, die in Ihrer Natur ist . . .' (letter to Schiller, 6 Oct. 1795) lead Schiller to believe that he is capable of a kind of productivity holding the two heterogeneous elements, poetry and philosophy, together 'in einer Art von Solution . . .' (letter to Goethe, 16 Oct. 1795), an intimation which is certainly confirmed by his best achievements in either mode.

5 This is the avowed purpose of Stahl's book on *Friedrich Schiller's Drama: Theory and Practice*. In a number of considered statements, Stahl raises the question of applying extraneous criteria to a work of art and concludes that, because of 'the simultaneous operation of reflective and imaginative processes' in Schiller, he is methodologically justified in treating his dramas in the light of his theory. 'His philosophy . . . is intrinsic to his creative artistic activity' (p. 156). For a different approach to the same complex problem, cf. I. Graham, *Schiller: A Master of the Tragic Form: His Theory in His Practice*, Chapter III, Section 1.

6 By Fricke in 'Die Problematik des Tragischen im Drama Schillers', *JFDH* (1930).

7 By Witte and Stahl, both of whom rightly stress the centrality of Schiller's belief in harmony (Stahl, op. cit. p. 45) and 'in the civilizing world mission of art . . .' (Witte, op. cit. p. xv). Similarly Cysarz (op. cit. p. 202) and Buchwald (*Schiller* (Leipzig, 1937), Vol. I, p. 221).

8 By Udo Gaede, *Schiller und Nietzsche als Verkünder einer tragischen Kultur* (Berlin, 1908), Cysarz, *Von Schiller zu Nietzsche* (Halle, 1928), H. Gumbel, 'Die realistische Wendung des späten Schiller', *JFDH* (1932–3), W. Deubel, 'Umrisse eines neuen Schillerbildes', in *JbdDGG*, 20 (1934) and K. May, *Friedrich Schiller: Idee und Wirklichkeit im Drama* (Göttingen, 1948).

9 By Kommerell, *Der Dichter als Führer in der deutschen Klassik* (Berlin, 1928) and M. Gerhard, op. cit.

10 In this connection the more recent book by H. B. Garland (II) should be mentioned. But although Garland's discussion of the images used in the dramas is detailed and sometimes illuminating, it fails, on the whole, to throw light upon the structure of the plays in their en-

tirety. Among other departures from the traditional pattern of Schiller scholarship are the chapters devoted to him by O. Seidlin in 'Wallenstein: Sein und Zeit', in *Von Goethe zu Thomas Mann* (Göttingen, 1963), Willoughby's and Wilkinson's introduction to *Kabale und Liebe*, Blackwell's German Texts (Oxford, 1944), May, op. cit. Chapter VI: 'Die Sprachanalyse im Beitrag zur Sinnauslegung des "Wallenstein"', and M. Jolles, 'Das Bild des Weges und die Sprache des Herzens', in *Deutsche Beiträge zur geistigen Überlieferung*, V (1965) and 'Die Sprache des "Spiels" und "Antispiels" in den frühen Dramen Schillers', in *M.Ph.*, 58, No. 4 (1961).

11 It is not insignificant, surely, that *Dichtung* and *dicht* are cognate words. R. Wellek and A. Warren conclude their comments on this problem with the words: 'Poetry of ideas is like other poetry, not to be judged by the value of the material but by its degree of integration and artistic intensity' (op. cit. p. 123). Similarly A. C. Bradley writes that ideas gain poetic worth 'only when, passing through the unity of the poet's being, they reappear as qualities of the imagination and then are indeed mighty powers in the world of poetry' (*Oxford Lectures on Poetry* (London, 1926), p. 7).

12 Cf. J. G. Robertson's devastating entry under the heading 'Schiller' in the *Encyclopedia Brittanica* (ed. 1963, vol. xx): 'He was the exponent of ideas which belonged essentially to the Europe of the period before the French Revolution'. In a subtler fashion, Stephen Spender made the charge that Schiller lacks poetic resonance by reason of the fact that he is 'totally unambiguous' (*The New Statesman*, 4 Oct. 1958).

13 Letter to Goethe, 2 Feb. 1798.
14 Letter to Goethe, 27 Feb. 1798.
15 Letter to Goethe, 31 May 1799.
16 Cf. v. Wiese (II, p. 260), Minor (op. cit. pp. 569 f.).
17 Minor (op. cit.).
18 Gerhard (op. cit. p. 105).
19 The most vicious exponent of the charge of excessive subjectivism – and reflectiveness – which is so frequently levelled against Schiller is undoubtedly Otto Ludwig. In connection with Posa, he writes: '. . . bei [Schiller], da die Reflexionen sich unverhüllt als seine eignen zeigen, sehen wir ihn selbst über seinem Helden stehen, der darüber seine individuelle Existenz einbüßt, und die Wirkung ist mehr die Bewunderung der Hoheit des Dichters, also seines Werkes und seiner Kunst.' (In *Shakespeare-Studien, Ludwigs Werke*, ed. A. Eloesser, Goldene Klassiker-Bibliothek (Berlin, Leipzig, Vienna and Stuttgart), Pt 4, p. 185.) Also, under the heading *Don Carlos*, and with unmistakable reference to the *Audienzszene*, we read: 'Bei Schiller kollidieren die Gesichtspunkte, nicht die Charaktere; jene sind die eigentlichen Helden, die Personen nur die Träger derselben.' (Ibid. p. 206.) Cf. also Robertson (op. cit.) who traces the disruption of the total economy of the drama and the confusion in its motivation to the supposed incursion of Schiller's own ideas into Posa's plea (pp. 48 f.).

20 Most of these are noted and discussed by Bellermann, op. cit. vol. I. pp. 260 ff. and 318.

21 Cf. Bellermann (op. cit. Vol. I, pp. 267 f.) and Storz who comments on the 'alarmierende Gewaltsamkeit, mit der Posa seine Selbstaufopferung betreibt', which annuls his influence over the King and defeats his own and Carlos's mission. ('Die Struktur des Don Carlos', in

JbdDSG, 4 (1960), p. 135.) Storz argues that Schiller had to avoid a 'happy end' to the encounter between Posa and the King in order to remain true to his dramatic plan and that, having once elevated the Maltese to a stature to match that of the King, his main concern was 'den Posa auf eine ihm angemessene Weise zu Tode zu bringen' (ibid.). Stahl judges that Posa, in the latter part of the drama, acts both opportunistically and frantically and that ' . . . except for the Prince, the drama does not end on a note of moral triumph' (op. cit. p. 40).

22 Bellermann has noted this episode and the discrepancy between its psychological implications and the popular picture of the hero which he, in common with other critics, has helped to create. The tone of moral censure, so evident in his words, is a measure of his perplexity and of the *naïveté* of a critical procedure based on criteria that are extraneous to the work of art itself. For both reasons it is worth while quoting his disarming observation: 'Und das hätte sich der Knabe Roderich gefallen lassen?' Bellermann asks: 'Er hätte es mit ansehen können, wie Karl für seinen Leichtsinn oder Ungeschicklichkeit büßte? Ein ordentlicher, braver, deutscher Junge, der gar nicht im mindesten ein zukünftiger Marquis Posa zu sein braucht, läßt sich das jedenfalls nicht gefallen, sondern wenn er den Federball so schlecht geworfen hat, und es muß wirklich für das kleine Vergehen einer bluten, so hat er auch das Herz, sich dazu zu bekennen, und steht nicht "zitternd in der Ferne", während sein Freund die Streiche bekommt.' (Op. cit. Vol. I, pp. 283 f.)

23 A. von Gronicka has interestingly dealt with some of the above-mentioned points from a predominantly psychological angle in 'Friedrich Schiller's Marquis Posa', *GR*, XXVI (1951), pp. 197 ff.

24 Cf. note 18 of this chapter.

25 Schiller gives illustration upon illustration of this concept in the so-called 'Kalliasbriefe'. I quote one of many which culminates in a statement to which the author of the *Ästhetische Briefe* would still have fully subscribed. 'Wann sagt man wohl,' Schiller asks, 'daß eine Person schön gekleidet sei? Wenn weder das Kleid durch den Körper, noch der Körper durch das Kleid an seiner Freiheit etwas leidet; wenn dieses aussieht, als wenn es mit dem Körper nichts zu verkehren hätte, und doch auf's Vollkommenste seinen Zweck erfüllt. Die Schönheit oder vielmehr der Geschmack betrachtet alle Dinge als *Selbstzwecke*, und duldet schlechterdings nicht, daß eines dem andern als Mittel dient, oder das Joch trägt. In der ästhetischen Welt ist jedes Naturwesen ein freier Bürger, der mit dem edelsten gleiche Rechte hat, und *nicht einmal um des Ganzen willen darf gezwungen werden*, sondern zu allem schlechterdings consentieren muß.' (Letter to Körner, 23 Feb. 1793.) This 'democracy of the aesthetic' is taken up in Letter IV of the *Ästhetische Briefe*, with significant modifications (§4); it culminates on the one hand in the formulation of the noble – or aesthetic – soul (Letter XXIII, footnote §1): 'Edel heißt jede Form, welche dem, was seiner Natur nach bloß *dient* (bloßes Mittel ist), das Gepräge der Selbständigkeit aufdrückt. Ein edler Geist begnügt sich nicht damit, selbst frei zu sein; er muß alles andere um sich her, auch das Leblose in Freiheit setzen.' On the other hand, in the conception of the aesthetic state of which we read: '*Freiheit zu geben durch Freiheit* ist das Grundgesetz dieses Reichs' (Letter XXVII).

26 This is, of course, the position adopted in the central section, dealing with the *schöne Seele*, of *Über Anmut und Würde*. 'Mit einer Leichtigkeit, als wenn bloß der Instinkt aus ihr handelte, übt sie [die schöne Seele] der Menschheit peinlichste Pflichten aus, und das heldenmütigste Opfer, das sie dem Naturtriebe abgewinnt, fällt wie eine freiwillige Wirkung eben dieses Triebes in die Augen.' (*SA*, 11, p. 221.) That same harmony is once again invoked in the concluding sentence of the *Ästhetische Briefe* (Letter XXVII).

27 Schiller himself forcibly distinguishes between the 'schöne Künstler' and the 'pädagogischen und politischen Künstler' as regards their different relation to their respective media (*Ästhetische Briefe*, Letter IV). In this connection, however, cf. Friedrich Schiller, *On the Aesthetic Education of Man*, ed. cit., note to IV. iv, p. 228. Ironically, Posa's attitude, at first that proper to the *pädagogische Künstler*, in the course of the drama, and even within this scene, deteriorates to that of the *mechanische Künstler* manipulating his material – the King here, and later Carlos and the Queen – without regard for its own life and law. Cf. Jolles 'Die Sprache des "Spiels" und "Antispiels" in den frühen Dramen Schillers' (p. 253) and R. D. Miller, *The Drama of Schiller* (Harrogate, 1966), p. 70.

28 This social ideal is given expression in the letter to Körner of 23 Feb. 1793, where we read: 'Das erste Gesetz des guten Tons ist's: *Schone fremde Freiheit*; das zweite: *Zeige selbst Freiheit*.' It is followed up in Letters IV and XXVII of the *Ästhetische Briefe*.

29 This question has in fact been asked, most pertinently, by Bellermann, who marvels at Posa's declaration 'Meine Wünsche / Verwesen hier' and comments: 'Ein Mann, der in der eifrigsten und tätigsten Weise für Flanderns Befreiung wirkt, kann nicht behaupten, daß seine Wünsche in seiner Brust enden, er will ihnen im Gegenteil eine möglichste Gestaltung in der Wirklichkeit verschaffen. Mag es auch seine Überzeugung sein, daß "das Jahrhundert seinem Ideal nicht reif" sei . . . und daß er insofern ein Bürger der Jahrhunderte ist, "welche kommen werden", aber darum kann er sich doch nicht als jemand bezeichnen, der ohne jeden Wunsch nach Verwirklichung bloß theoretisch seine Gedanken hegt.' (Op. cit. Vol. I, p. 318.)

30 Schiller makes this point in Letters XX and XXI of the *Ästhetische Briefe*, where we read: 'Freilich besitzt er diese Menschheit der Anlage nach schon vor jedem bestimmten Zustand, in den er kommen kann; *aber der Tat nach verliert er sie mit jedem bestimmten Zustand, in den er kommt . . .*' (XXI, 5, my italics.) Wilkinson and Willoughby write: 'Moral harmony, however perfect, and however self-renewing, is bound . . . to involve a one-sided retrenchment of potential whenever it issues as determinate action.' (*On the Aesthetic Education of Man*, ed. cit. p. lxxxvii.)

31 Cf. one of the most crucial statements of the *Ästhetische Briefe*: '. . . der Mensch spielt nur, wo er in voller Bedeutung des Worts Mensch ist, und *er ist nur da ganz Mensch, wo er spielt*' (Letter XV). For a representative modern statement cf. E. Cassirer: 'Play and art . . . are non-utilitarian and unrelated to any practical end. In play as in art we leave behind us our immediate needs in order to give our world a new shape.' (In *An Essay on Man* (New Haven, 1944), p. 164.)

32 Schiller does not, of course, accord the ideal of aesthetic freedom such absolute and static superiority. Cf. note 42 below, and *On the Aesthetic Education of Man* (ed. cit. p. lix).

33 This has, of course, been widely noted. Cf. Bellermann (op. cit. Vol. I, pp. 267 ff.), Stahl (op. cit. p. 40), Witte (op. cit. p. 143), and v. Wiese (II, p. 268).

34 Cf. Chapters 1 and 6.

35 Cf. Garland (II, p. 103) and Miller (op. cit. p. 66) for similar readings.

36 Cf. Chapters 1 and 3.

37 Cf. Kant's characterization of the aesthetic judgement as involving the awareness of a 'Zweckmäßigkeit ohne Zweck' (*Kritik der Urteilskraft*, Pt 1, Erster Abschnitt, Erstes Buch, Drittes Moment, Para. 15). The meaning of the word 'Zweck' here is echoed by the concluding words of the soliloquy: 'So könnte, / Was erst so grillenhaft mir schien, sehr zweckvoll / Und sehr besonnen sein. Sein oder nicht sein − / Gleichviel! In diesem Glauben will ich handeln.' Posa himself ends on a note of doubt about the purposiveness of what he is about to do. We share this doubt, partly because the word 'besonnen', which here appears in conjunction with 'zweckvoll', on the lips of Schiller's dramatic characters always signifies a pre-eminently contemplative response, and partly because by echoing Hamlet's famous soliloquy the poet subtly queries the impression of resoluteness his hero is busy creating.

38 Cf. such formulations as 'Ich habe solch einen Menschen nie gesehen' and 'Ihr sollet unter meinen Augen fortfahren dürfen, Mensch zu sein'. The word 'Mensch' here has the specific and rich meaning it will assume in key passages of the *Ästhetische Briefe* such as Letter XV

(cf. note 31 of this chapter) and Letter XXI where we read that we must regard 'das Vermögen, welches ihm in der ästhetischen Stimmung zurückgegeben wird, als die höchste aller Schenkungen, als die Schenkung der Menschheit . . .'

39 And yet, on closer inspection, the Marquis's words are not altogether harmless. The famous 'Meine Wünsche verwesen hier' which has exercised Bellermann, and rightly so (cf. note 29 of this chapter), has an ominous ring in one seemingly so vital and on the side of life as is Posa. The image of decomposition is taken up again later in the same scene when Posa makes his apologia for the freedom in Creation ('Er, der große Schöpfer, wirft / In einen Tropfen Tau den Wurm und läßt / Noch in den toten Räumen der Verwesung / Die Willkür sich ergetzen . . .'); and both passages become perplexing and sinister in that they presage the Grand Inquisitor's final words which signify Carlos's death: 'Der Verwesung lieber als / Der Freiheit!' (V. x). Here is one of those telling links − there are many − which give substance to Schiller's own explanation of the play, in his *Briefe über Don Carlos*. There he not only charges the Marquis with the ruthlessness of one pledged to an abstract ideal, but, more specifically, with wielding a 'despotische Willkür' *vis à vis* his friend (11. Brief); and presently such excessive idealism is shown to lead to a lack of human care and concern comparable to that of the 'most selfish of despots'. Thus, implicitly, Schiller himself confirms the existence of a secret and paradoxical link between the champion of freedom and his repressive antagonist and, indeed, between their methods; for as Alba takes with him, to the Netherlands, 'einen Vorrat Blutsentenzen, im voraus

unterzeichnet' (II. vi), so Posa requests a secret warrant for Don Carlos's arrest from the King, also 'just in case'. Such links lend substance to Stahl's contention that there is a 'profound affinity' between idealist and despot and that 'in their characters and their methods Posa and Philip are at times barely distinguishable' (op. cit. p. 36); also to Storz's contention that Posa's request to the King to subjugate the world in the name of freedom (III. x) is the exact parallel of the terror of the Counter-Reformation: 'Posa postuliert für das Heil der Zukunft, was der Großinquisitor für die Erhaltung des Bestehenden praktiziert' (op. cit. p. 146).

For a detailed discussion of the deterioration of an initially pure aesthetic mode into a repressive stance, cf. Chapter 1.

40 Garland describes Posa as 'leaning towards statuesque posture' (II, p. 103).

41 Cf. Schiller's description of Juno Ludovisi at the end of the fifteenth letter of the *Ästhetische Briefe*, as being in space, but not of space, and in time, but not of time.

42 A static conception, leaving out of account the fact that whereas the internal relations governing a work of art are stable, those governing a living organism are not, and that whereas the work of art can be meaningfully said, in some sense, to exist out of a time, a living being cannot. Posa conceives of the psyche as a stable structure, rather than as a hierarchy of functions flexibly changing in response to an ever-changing internal and external situation. This conception is well reflected in the imagery he uses. When he hears of the Prince's desperate reaction to his own ostensible withdrawal, he comments: 'Mein *Gebäude* / Stürzt zusam-

men – ich vergaß dein Herz'; and a little later, continuing in terms of the same static metaphor: 'Meine Zuversicht . . . sie war / Auf deiner Freundschaft *Ewigkeit gegründet*' (V. i, my italics).

43 Cf. especially Chapter 6.

44 As so often in Schiller, this normal development of a situation and the human agents in it towards imbalance – and the corresponding falseness of Posa's unchanging equipoise – is beautifully expressed in terms of the symbolism of the picture. Carlos had sent his picture to his bride-to-be, Elisabeth (conversely, in Marquis Posa's covert report to the Queen, Fernando possesses, and loves, a picture of his bride-to-be (I. iv)). Marquis Posa, we have seen, conceives of himself and others as if they were a work of art. The gulf between reality – always tending towards asymmetry – and the unchanging symmetry of art becomes apparent in IV. ix, when the little Princess plays with Carlos's picture (which had already caused so much havoc in III. i), exclaiming 'das *schöne* Bild': within a moment the King insults his wife, the child cries 'meine *schöne* Mutter weint' (IV. ix), and the Queen is reported to be '. . . in Tränen, und auf ihrem Gesichte Blut' (IV. x). (My italics.) For all that art inspires man and the aesthetic state is the richest human condition, the analogy between art and life is limited and the very susceptibility to the beautiful which art may feed in us may, in reality, lead to suffering and stress which are far from beautiful. Posa makes the proper distinction between art and life in IV. xxi when he asks: 'Was geht es König Philipp an, wenn seine / Verklärung in Escurial den Maler, / Der vor ihr steht, mit Ewigkeit entzündet?' For a similar use of the symbol of the picture, cf.

its role in the relation of Mortimer and Leicester to Maria Stuart.

45 Letter XXI, footnote.

46 The other two being Letter VI of the *Ästhetische Briefe* in which he states as a fact the radical onesidedness and indeed fragmentation of the modern individual and thus provides the rationale for the main structural device of his tragedies, the externalization of the undeveloped or repressed part of the psyche of one character in the separate being of his counterpart. (Cf. Chapters 1, pp 34 ff., Chapter 7, pp. 152 ff., and 9, pp. 202 f. and 208). The other is the essay *Über das Pathetische* in which he adduces purely aesthetic grounds for having the dramatist concentrate on the morally neutral state of pure determinability rather than on the actual moral conduct of his character. Cf. I, Graham, *Schiller*, etc., Chapter III, and I. Appelbaum-Graham, 'The Structure of the Personality, etc.'.

47 Schiller shows himself fully aware of this problem facing the tragedian in *Über die Tragische Kunst*. It is one of the key questions discussed between him and Goethe in the letters of 1797 which Goethe eventually worked up into the essay *Über epische und dramatische Dichtung*. Schiller, in his response to the essay, emphasizes the necessity for the dramatist to interpolate a measure of aesthetic distance between the spectator and 'die individuell auf uns eindringende Wirklichkeit . . .', in order to ensure that the mind retains 'eine poetische Freiheit gegen den Stoff . . .' (Letter to Goethe, 26 Dec. 1797). Hence, he argued, the dramatist is compelled to approximate to the character of the epic, i.e. to employ some of the *retrogradierende* motifs which had earlier on in the exchange of letters been established as being characteristic of the epic.

The principle of psychical distance is reaffirmed throughout the *Ästhetische Briefe* and receives its final articulation, in conjunction with tragedy, in the essay *Über den Gebrauch des Chors in der Tragödie*. (Cf. Chapter 3, esp. pp. 82 ff.) It is worthy of note that both Schiller and Goethe themselves experienced the *writing* of tragedy as a pathological state threatening to rob them of their 'poetische Freiheit gegen den Stoff'. Cf. Schiller to Goethe, 8 Dec. 1797, and Goethe's reply of 9 Dec. In this connection, cf. also Goethe's own letter to Zelter, 31 Oct. 1831.

48 Cf. Schiller to Goethe, 24 August 1798.

49 He labours under a threefold illusion: first, that it is possible to perpetuate indefinitely the stance of pure determinability; second, that his non-action will have no consequences; and third, that he is not accountable for any such consequences as do unexpectedly spring from his conduct. This book is designed to show up this illusion on the part of Schiller's characters, to adduce reasons, aesthetic as well as psychological, for their deludedness and to clearly distinguish between the content of the characters' consciousness and the poet's own awareness, a distinction which has all too often been blurred by critics accustomed to read utterances in a drama out of context.

50 Cf. Chapter 3.

51 Cf. I. Graham, *Schiller: A Master of the Tragic Form*, Chapter III.

52 It is tempting to lift a remark concerning man's moral conduct out of its context and transpose it to the battle between *Stoff* and *Form* that goes on in the making of tragedy: the artist no less than the practical man 'muß . . . den Krieg gegen die Materie in ihre eigene Grenze spielen, damit er es überhoben sei,

auf dem heiligen Boden der Freiheit gegen diesen furchtbaren
Feind zu fechten . . .' (*Ästhetische
Briefe*, Letter XXIII). Cf. Chapter
12.

53 *SA*, Vol. 11, p. 262. Cf. also the
statement towards the end of *Über
das Erhabene*: '. . . der Mensch ist,
wie in andern Fällen, so auch hier
[i.e. regarding his susceptibility towards the Beautiful and the Sub-
lime] von der zweiten Hand besser
bedient als von der ersten und will
lieber einen zubereiteten und auserlesenen Stoff von der Kunst empfangen, als an der unreinen Quelle
der Natur mühsam und dürftig
schöpfen.' The principle of the

artistic prefiguration of effects is of
cardinal importance, both in Schiller's dramatic theory and in his
creative writing, and will be further
explored in Chapter 12.

54 As has indeed been done in Wilkinson's searching lecture, *Schiller:
Poet or Philosopher?* But in her
estimate the philosopher comes off
better than the poet, and to this
extent the present reading (as well
as Chapters 1 and 3 of this book)
may serve as a corrective.

55 As one glance at Goethe's *Werther*
will show. Cf. I. Graham, *Goethe
and Lessing: The Wellsprings of
Creation* (London, 1973), Chapter
V and footnote 588, and Chapter VI.

Chapter 3

This chapter is a modified version of an article published in *Deutsche Beiträge zur
geistigen Überlieferung* (Friedrich Schiller 1759–1959), IV (1961).

1 For an excellent discussion of
Schiller's use of antithesis, both as a
structural and linguistic device, cf.
Kabale und Liebe (ed. cit.), pp.
xxiv ff.

2 The discrepancy between the violence of the subject and the formalizing treatment Schiller has
accorded it has been stressed by v.
Wiese (II, p. 753) and Storz (op.
cit. p. 382).

3 Garland notes the prevalence of
images of fire. But he does not show
the manner in which they function
in the structure of the play as a
whole (II, p. 254). In this connection, cf. Appelbaum-Graham,
'The Structure of the Personality in
Schiller's Tragic Poetry', pp. 116 f.

4 Cf. Chapter 2, note 42. Schiller frequently expresses the desire for control and permanence on the part of
his characters through the imagery
of edifices. The most palpable example occurs in *Wilhelm Tell*, where
Geßler's fortress, called 'Zwing Uri',

symbol of his repressive power over
the Swiss people, is first seen being
built (I. iii) and finally demolished
(V. i). Both in *Die Braut von Messina* and elsewhere, notably in
Wallenstein, he also exploits the
equivocation of 'house' meaning an
actual building and a dynasty.

5 Nor indeed is the obverse poetic
statement missing in the tragedy.
Beatrice, this elemental force, cannot be restrained, let alone repressed. There is no stronghold of
nature's or of man's devising firm
enough to contain this force. This is
the burden of Beatrice's own statement: 'Eindringt der Gott auch zu
verschloßnen Toren, / Zu Perseus'
Turm hat er den Weg gefunden, /
Dem Dämon ist sein Opfer un-
verloren. / Wär' es an öde Klippen
angebunden / Und an des Atlas
himmeltragende Säulen, / So wird
ein Flügelroß es dort ereilen.' (II. i.)
Cf. also Paulet's lament at the in-
sufficiency of any man-made prison

to contain Maria Stuart, another embodiment of elemental drives. (*Maria Stuart*, I. i. Cf. pp. 149 f.)

6 Cf. Schiller to Goethe, 21 April 1797 and 26 December 1797, and *Ästhetische Briefe*, Letter XXII, 5.

7 Cf. Chapter 10, pp. 229 f.

8 Benno v. Wiese suggests that the external issue of enmity and reconciliation is indicative of an internal event when he writes of Don Cesar's death that, through it, '. . . der Sterbende und durch sein Sterben Entsühnte sich wieder vereinigt' (II, p. 757).

9 For the significance of this symbol cf. Chapter 7, pp. 169 f.

10 Cf. Chapter 10. For Schiller's call for a 'second nature', cf. *Ästhetische Briefe*, Letters VI, 15 and VIII, 4. In this connection, cf. Staiger, op. cit. p. 80, and Wilkinson, 'Reflections After Translating Schiller's *Letters on the Aesthetic Education of Man*', pp. 70 f.

11 Cf. also IV. v, where Isabella once again looks back upon her shattered hopes and recapitulates them in terms which are consistently aesthetic: 'Schöne Früchte', 'schöne Bande', 'schöne Liebe'.

12 Oskar Walzel has rightly quoted this passage – and Don Cesar's ignoring of Beatrice's reaction to him – as evidence of Schiller's occasional neglect of psychological motivation, not because he was not capable of it, but because he ruthlessly pursued his own artistic ends (*SA*, 7, pp. xvii and xi ff.).

13 It is significant that Don Cesar does not resort to images of stable structures to give expression to his own vision of fulfilment. A fiery and elemental character, he is closer to his sister than the others; which may account for his own sense of taboo in the earlier part of the drama and for the crucial part she plays after the recognition in the final stages of his development. (Cf.

Chapter 12.) The poet has articulated this kinship through the similarity of the verbal materials associated with these two figures.

14 For a full discussion of Schiller's ambivalent attitude towards effort and merit versus grace, cf. Chapter 10.

   An excellent treatment of this, especially in his relation to Goethe, is to be found in Schiller, *On the Aesthetic Education of Man* (ed. cit.), pp. xxxvii ff., and in Wilkinson, *Schiller: Poet or Philosopher?*

15 B. v. Wiese stresses the arrogance of Don Cesar's attitude towards Beatrice (II, p. 751).

16 Bellermann quite consistently objects to Isabella's tardiness in revealing Beatrice's existence (op. cit. Vol. II, pp. 369 f.).

17 Cysarz makes the point that the Sicily Schiller depicts is not 'das Natur-Sizilien der "Italienischen Reise"', sondern der weltgeschichtliche Nordmänner-Traum, der einst die Staufer im Süden verzehrt und vergeudet hat, während jenseits der Alpen die deutsche Einheit unheilbar verfiel . . .' (*Schiller*, p. 359). It is right to see Schiller's Sicily as he does, not as an idyllic but as a tragic symbol of the South as viewed from the North.

18 As it is indeed in Thomas Mann's *Die Buddenbrooks, Tod in Venedig, Tristan* and *Doktor Faustus*, and in Wilde's *The Picture of Dorian Gray*. 'Öde' frequently recurs in this tragedy, significantly always in conjunction with such structures as are destroyed by Beatrice's coming.

19 R. Buchwald regards the tragedy as due to the workings of an 'unsinnigen Weltordnung', an 'ungeheuerliche Weltmacht' (op. cit. Vol. II, p. 462). I would urge that this drama can at no level be interpreted realistically, i.e. as embodying a discursively definable ideology, but

that its content as much as its form must be regarded as determined by the exigencies of an artistic experiment. Cf. pp. 89 f. below and note 24 of this chapter.

20 W. Silz argues that Schiller shifted his ground in elucidating the poet's predicament by reference to the visual arts. First, he argues, Schiller urges that it is the poet's business to reveal the basic human form, and in this context he uses the analogy of the sculptor. But Schiller tries surreptitiously to accommodate reflection in his account of the poet's task. Accordingly he changes the analogy from the sculptor to the painter, who uses drapery as the poet uses the *lyrische Prachtgewebe* of reflection. ('Chorus and Choral Function in Schiller', in *Schiller 1759–1959. Commemorative American Studies*, ed. J. R. Frey (Urbana, 1959).) But Schiller urges that the sculptor dispense, not with all clothes, but merely with 'moderne Gewänder'; and his subsequent elaboration of the analogy between the poet's treatment of intellectual matter and the artist's use of drapery is not limited to the painter but is perfectly consistent with his earlier observations about the sculptor.

21 Critical opinion on Schiller's intentions regarding the chorus and on his success vary enormously. Silz mounts a vicious and uncomprehending attack on the experiment, condemning it from the vantage point of the very naturalism Schiller is out to transcend, and calling it by turns artificial, undramatic and anti-dramatic, magniloquent and unnecessary (op. cit. pp. 151 ff.). At the other extreme are Cysarz and v. Wiese, both of whom accord it an essentially religious significance. Cf. Cysarz (*Schiller*, p. 363) and v. Wiese who writes that this 'Kunstorgan' attains 'den Rang eines religiösen

Organs der Phantasie' (II, p. 761). Most balanced is Storz's view that the chorus is a forerunner of Brecht's 'Verfremdungseffekt' (op. cit. p. 369) and that Schiller's lyrical tendency found its consummation in the 'szenische Chorlied. . . . erst die erhabene Tragödienmaske des Chors ist für seine Lyrik die gemäße *persona*' (p. 384); '. . . durch das Chorlied erlangt die szenische Situation diejenige Unmittelbarkeit, die alles Fragen nach Grund und Wahrscheinlichkeit vergessen läßt' (p. 386). The correctness of Storz's aesthetic judgement may be in doubt. There can be no doubt but that he is assessing Schiller's *intentions* correctly. Cf. note 24 below. Contrary to the universal condemnation of the chorus's twofold function, as contemplative bystander and participant in the action, Storz defends this device on the grounds that Schiller thereby deliberately destroys any 'Wirklichkeitsillusion' (p. 380). Again, this argument seems to me to be correct in itself and entirely consonant with Schiller's avowed intentions as expressed in the preface to the drama.

22 And, indeed, what scholar has paused to consider the daring nature of Schiller's materials and appreciated the connection between such content and the unusually formalizing treatment accorded to it by the poet? Did he need the excessive psychical distance he interpolated between his matter and his recipients (including himself) in order to 'cope' with such content? Or did he need the challenge of such content in order to explore to the full the possibilities of style and form? The latter is the rationale Schiller himself puts forward in *Über naive und sentimentalische Dichtung* where we read: 'In der Tragödie muß . . . die Gemüthsfreiheit künstlicherweise und als

Experiment aufgehoben werden, weil sie in Herstellung derselben ihre poetische Kraft beweist . . .' (*S A*, Vol. 12, p. 198.)

23 Silz comments that Don Manuel's description of Beatrice's attire is 'altogether unnecessary, since he is himself going to the bazaar . . .' (op. cit. p. 153). A more well-meaning critic, defending the poet against repeated charges of lengthiness, explains: 'Die wunderbare Wandlung, die mit Manuel geschehen ist, konnte gar nicht glücklicher gezeichnet werden als durch die Sorgfalt, mit der er, der rasche Krieger von einst, die Toilettenfrage behandelt.' (H. Gaudig, *Schillers Dramen* II, p. 276, *Aus Deutscher Dichtung*, Vol. XIII (Leipzig and Berlin, 1914).)

24 For a similar approach to the drama as a whole – though not to this particular aspect of it – cf. Storz (op. cit. pp. 370 ff.): 'der "Gewalt der Affekte" muß in der Perspektive und in der Struktur des Dramas gleichsam als bestimmendes Vorzeichen die Wirklichkeitsferne zugeordnet sein' (p. 370). Figures and actions are 'bedeutsame, aber bloße Formen, die gewissen Wirkungen zu dienen haben' (p. 380). 'Zustände, Reden, Taten, weisen höchst bedeutsam auf das Menschenleben hin, jedoch auf seine Urbilder, nicht auf faktische, individuelle Verwirklichungen' (p. 380).

25 For the approximation of the arts to one another cf. *Ästhetische Briefe*, Letter XXII, 4, and the comment on this by Wilkinson and Willoughby in *On the Aesthetic Education of Man*, ed. cit. p. 265. Schiller writes: 'die Poesie in ihrer vollkommensten Ausbildung muß uns, wie die Tonkunst, mächtig fassen, zugleich aber, wie die Plastik, mit ruhiger Klarheit umgeben.'

26 Silz condemns I. viii as a 'mere "time-filler" and lyrical embroidery

of generalities . . .' It is 'utterly superfluous for the action' (op. cit. p. 153).

27 Cf. Chapter 1, note 22, and Chapter 12 pp. 322 ff. It is easy to apply E. Bullough's description of the actor to the present scene. Don Manuel combines within himself the three-fold aspect as defined by Bullough: he is the 'actor', his verbal evocation of Beatrice and his relationship with her is his work of art, whilst the chorus – here, as throughout the tragedy – might be described as the embodiment or externalization of that part of himself which looks on in the role of spectator.

28 The principle that art is able to prefigure, and thus to refine, the response of the recipient is formulated both in *Über das Pathetische* and *Über das Erhabene*. Cf. Chapter 12.

29 26 December 1797.

30 The charge of being contrived has frequently been made, e.g. by F. Prader, 'Schiller und Sophokles', in *Zürcher Beiträge zur deutschen Literatur und Geistesgeschichte*, ed. Staiger, No. 7 (1954), pp. 94 f., and v. Wiese, II, p. 750.

31 Letter to Goethe, 31 August 1794.

32 'Was ich indessen wünschte, wäre, daß Sie bald wieder einen in sich mächtigen, schon durch seinen Umfang mühsam zu bändigenden Stoff . . . behandelten. Der unkünstlerische Teil des Publikums wird zwischen der Braut und diesen Stücken [*Wallenstein* and *Die Jungfrau von Orleans*] . . . Vergleichungen anstellen und den letzteren in jeder Hinsicht den Vorzug geben, schon darum, weil sie neben der künstlerischen Wirkung auch einer anderen durch ihren bloßen Stoff fähig sind. Eine gewisse Wahrheit liegt aber diesen Urteilen . . . zu Grunde . . . Alles in diesem Werk besteht nur durch die dichterische Form.' (Letter to Schiller, 22 October 1803.)

Chapter 4

1 The parable certainly is central to Schubart's 'Geschichte des Menschlichen Herzens' which was Schiller's most important literary source. It is generally assumed that 'Der Verlorene Sohn' originally was to be the title of Schiller's play; but this assumption has become dubious in the light of Stubenrauch's investigations (*NA*, 3, pp. 313 f.).

2 This point has been noted by Hans Schwerte ('Schillers "Räuber"', in *Interpretationen* 2. *Deutsche Dramen von Gryphius bis Brecht* (Frankfurt, 1965)), who, however, reads the drama as the tragedy of the 'prodigal father' rather than that of the Prodigal Son.

3 The 'Prodigal Son' in Schubart's story, also Karl by name, is the younger one of the brothers (cf. R. Buchwald, *Schiller* (Leipzig, 1937), Vol. I, p. 295). Schiller freely made Karl the older brother, to what end remains to be seen.

4 The story of Jacob wresting the birthright from Esau is mentioned in a general discussion of the theme of the hostile brothers in the literature of the *Sturm und Drang* (in *Die Räuber*, ed. C. P. Magill and L. A. Willoughby, Blackwell's German Texts (Oxford, 1949), p. xlvi). More deviously, P. Böckmann associates Franz's deception of Der alte Moor with Jacob's deception of Abraham (in 'Die innere Form in Schillers Jugenddramen', p. 455).

5 Cf. Chapter 10. For similar readings, cf. v. Wiese (II, p. 147), Storz (op. cit. p. 48), H. Stubenrauch (*NA*, 3 (Weimar, 1953), pp. xviii f.).

6 Cf. Schiller's own characterization of Karl in the *Selbstrezension*: 'Der Mordbrenner liebt und wird wieder geliebt . . .' (*SA*, 16, p. 26). The words *Liebe* and *lieben* are used of Karl time and again.

7 For the symbolic significance of Franz's ugliness, cf. Stubenrauch, *NA*, 3, pp. xviii f. Magill and Willoughby advance a psychological explanation suggesting that 'his cold wooden exterior' is 'the result rather than the cause of the lack of love he received' (*Die Räuber*, ed. cit. p. lvii). This argument may be correct but it obscures the fact that, from the first, Schiller speaks a symbolic language in which ugliness, illegitimacy and their obverse have a fixed connotation that is prior to any individual antecedents. Cf. Chapter 10.

8 Cf. Chapter 10. Here, then, is the deeper reason why Schubart's younger son Karl, in the poetic universe of discourse of Schiller, had to become the first-born.

9 This crowning metaphor in the life of a robber militates against v. Wiese's statement: 'Bezeichnenderweise wird er zum Mörder, ohne etwa ein Dieb zu sein' (II, p. 147). This is a distinction which Karl himself is at pains to maintain through the major part of the drama; but he himself repudiates it at the end. To ascribe it objective validity and attribute it to the poet himself is to impute to him an 'idealistic' position he does not in fact hold and to rob both the figure of Karl and the drama as a whole of the quality of devastating honesty which is their distinguishing mark.

10 Text according to the (anonymous) first edition: *Die Räuber: Ein Schauspiel* (Frankfurt and Leipzig, 1781), quoted in *NA*, 3, p. 357.

11 Scholars have taken up diametrically opposed attitudes to the separateness of the actions centred in Karl and Franz respectively. The connection between them is criticized as being fortuitous by W.

Witte (op. cit. p. 115) and Stubenrauch (*NA*, 3, p. xiii). B. v. Wiese (II, p. 145) and Storz (op. cit. pp. 46 ff.) analyse the deeper reasons underlying such ostensible separateness. Storz rightly stresses, side by side with it, the likeness of the brothers. The most searching formulation of the nature of their connectedness and the level on which it must be sought is to be found in Schwerte who writes: 'Die Tiefe dieses Dramas enthüllt sich im antagonistischen Wort, im Wortfeld, mehr als in den Bühnenvorgängen selbst' (*Die Räuber*, ed. cit. pp. 153 ff. Cf. also ibid. pp. 161 f.).

12 This immature dependence of Karl's spiritual values on the actual figure of his father is noted by v. Wiese, II, pp. 148 f., and A. Beck in 'Die Krisis des Menschen im Drama des jungen Schiller', *Schiller in unserer Zeit* (Weimar, 1955), p. 129. B. v. Wiese and Schwerte (op. cit. p. 157) stress, in a more general fashion, the representative function of the father figure for the world of spiritual values and the divine.

13 For a different reading of Spiegelberg's pantomime as a diversion or juxtaposition with comic intent cf. Storz (op. cit. p. 29) and Magill and Willoughby, *Die Räuber* (ed. cit. p. lii).

14 Cf. Chapter 11.

15 A number of critics regard this dissociative tendency in Karl as being endorsed by the poet. Staiger asserts that 'Schiller . . . verfolgt sein Tun mit kaum bemeisterter Sympathie' (*Friedrich Schiller* (Zürich, 1967), p. 125); v. Wiese takes the contrast between Karl's own intentions and the performance of his accomplices at its face value and attributes a positive significance to Karl's repudiation of them (II, pp. 151 ff.). Similarly, Erich Schmidt argues that Schiller intended to idealize his robber hero by letting

him strike nobler poses than the members of his band; i.e. by showing him as a protector of the weak and suppressed, a patron of the talented young and a self-appointed judge (*SA*, 3, p. xvii). Accordingly he regards Karl's association with Schufterle and Spiegelberg as poetically inconsistent (ibid. p. xviii). Underlying such readings is the – tacit – assumption that Schiller operates with the Kantian concept of the pure motive being the decisive constituent of moral action and indeed the only one that has intrinsic moral value. My analysis of *Die Räuber* is designed to challenge this assumption. Much closer to the mark is H. Cysarz in the following observation: 'Jeder Versuch, das Gute vom Bösen zu trennen, . . . das ritterliche Räubertum von spitzbübischer Niedertracht, flicht den Knäuel nur noch dichter. Karl handelt aus falscher Voraussetzung, aber auch falsch in sich selbst.' (In *Schiller*, p. 62.)

16 This alternating rhythm of recognition and recoil is well brought out by Stubenrauch (*NA*, 3, pp. xxii ff.). But no attempt is made to trace this movement to its logical end, the acceptance of the consequences of an act as part of that act, which is the hallmark of Schiller's notion of moral accountability.

17 For a similar reading, cf. Kurt May, op. cit., who writes: 'Ja-sagen auf alles was notwendig bisher geschehen, . . . Aufnehmen alles Vergangenen als eines schicksalhaft Notwendigen in den eigenen Willen . . .' (p. 25). It is precisely this concrete involvement of Karl Moor, and the Schillerian hero in general, in his existential condition which is vigorously denied by G. Fricke in his brilliant and influential but wrong-headed article on 'Die Problematik des Tragischen im Drama Schillers'. Fricke argues that the un-

conditional validity of Karl's ethos –
which is Schiller's ethos – detracts
from the 'unbedingten Ernst des
Individuums, der Person, des Ich
. . .' (p. 9). According to Fricke,
the Schillerian hero is always free
to retreat into the 'heilige Freiheit
der Geister', an unquestioned domain of spiritual values; thus he
concludes that 'Die Tiefendimen-
sion des Ich, der Abgrund des Kon-
kreten, individuellen Existenzer-
lebnisses . . . bleibt bei Schiller
. . . notwendig unsichtbar' (ibid.).
In thus proclaiming the uncommittedness of the Schillerian protagonist to his sense-being, Fricke is at
best articulating a tragic illusion on
the part of the hero himself, rather
than the view of the poet. A close
textual analysis (rather than the
discussion of Schiller's tragedies
within an *a priori* metaphysical
frame of reference) would have
revealed to Fricke that the Schillerian protagonist, for all that he
consciously rejects his sense-being,
is in fact inescapably involved in its
fate, if only through his relation to
his antagonist in whom that ignored part of his self is separately
embodied, and with whom he must
come to terms. Fricke's theory in its
entirety rests on the assumption
that Schiller's characters are divided into two heterogeneous halves
such that what befalls the one does
not vitally affect the other. This
assumption, based no doubt on
Schiller's theory of the sublime, is
not only highly questionable in
view of the position adopted in
Anmut und Würde and the *Ästhetische Briefe*. It is proven to be untenable by the textual evidence of
the tragedies themselves. Fricke is
like a person asserting that only
half the moon exists because only
half of it is illuminated. My interpretations seek to demonstrate a
commitment of the Schillerian hero

to their selves and their condition
in their existential depth which is
nowhere more marked than in *Die
Räuber*. Cf. Chapter 12, note 35.

From a different standpoint,
Staiger comes to similar conclusions. According to him, Schiller
himself maintains a slightly cynical
artistic distance from his figures and
we are permitted 'die Sache nicht
ganz ernst zu nehmen' (op. cit. p.
121). A drama more deadly serious
that *Die Räuber* would be difficult
to conceive, as this reading is at
pains to demonstrate. In connection
with both, Fricke and Staiger, see
my Introduction.

18 This transference of his moral
values to an immoral community is
stressed by v. Wiese (II, p. 149).
19 Stubenrauch, similarly, speaks of
the 'tragische Passion' of Karl's
career. (*NA*, 3, pp. xxii ff.)
20 Käthe Hamburger argues in a com-
parative study of Schiller and Sartre
that it was left to the latter to coin
'den Begriff der extremsten "*Verantwortung*", der, wie das Wort
selbst, in der idealistischen Ethik,
und auch der Schillerschen, noch
fehlt.' ('Schiller und Sartre',
JbdDSG, 3, (1959), p. 58.) I
would argue that, as the word is
there, so is the concept, and that by
this token we may infer that even
the very young Schiller has transcended the idealist position.
21 Heidegger defines existence as
'Möglichkeit seines Selbst, es selbst
oder nicht es selbst zu sein' (*Sein und
Zeit*, 'Erste Hälfte', 5th ed. (Halle/
Saale, 1941), p. 12.) Existentialist
readings of Karl's words along these
lines have been essayed by Schwerte
(op. cit. p. 149) and Hamburger
('Zum Problem des Idealismus bei
Schiller', *JbdDSG*, 4 (1960), p. 69).
22 *SA*, 16, p. 28.
23 Ibid. p. 16.
24 This is how R. Petsch, in a still very
readable book, sees the process

(*Freiheit und Notwendigkeit in Schillers Dramen* (Munich, 1905)). Starting from the concept of totality and wholeness, which I too regard as central to Schiller's thought, he argues that the tragic guilt of the Schillerian hero lies in his onesidedness, and that this onesidedness, once it has been allowed to disrupt the balance of the psychic household, gains momentum from the inside and is confirmed from the outside until the energy of the overweening drive has spent itself. Petsch, however, sees the therapeutic function of the repressed drive in its periodic reassertion at moments when the dominant drive is temporarily exhausted. As against this, I seek to demonstrate in this and subsequent readings that the repressed drive 'avenges' itself by attaching itself to the dominant function, increasing its excess, vitiating its quality and thereby bringing about its eventual collapse.

More importantly, Petsch's theory of onesidedness, however right in itself, is gravely impaired in its value by having reference only to the empirical half of the personality. In his view, the tragedy of onesidedness in Schiller is always the victory of the passional drives over the intellectual ones, 'die Tragik der leidenschaftlichen Einseitigkeit . . .' (p. 35), and Schiller's tragedies are 'vorwiegende Leidenschaftstragödien'. This evaluative singling out of any one part of the personality as being *a priori* inferior to the other runs counter to Schiller's notion of totality with its strong organicistic slant. It also makes havoc of the tragedies themselves in that it overrides the fact that the protagonists are at all times conceived as complementary opposites to one another, in such a fashion that a predominantly intellectual protagonist will

be matched against a predominantly instinctual antagonist. In this way every tragedy embodies the two principal possibilities of onesidedness (as well as the infinite *nuances* between them) and enables us to cull from these aberrations in both directions the ideal image of the integrated and whole personality. The uniformity of Petsch's scheme robs the tragedies of their dramatic life which lies precisely in the confrontation, within each tragedy, of characters who are opposed yet inescapably related. (Cf. my *Structure of the Personality*, etc., and Chapter 1.)

25　*SA*, 16, p. 26.
26　Cf. Chapters 1 and 10.
27　Cf. Chapter 11.
28　Cf. Chapter 9.
29　The resemblance between Franz and Kirillov in Dostoevsky's *The Possessed* is striking. E. K. Kosta notes that Kirillov 'bears considerable resemblance to the young Schiller . . .' (*Schiller and Russian Literature* (Philadelphia, 1965)), but asserts that Schiller had not drawn the full conclusions from his 'God-defying anthropocentric philosophy'. Dostoevsky does so in Kirillov's suicide 'which, in the eyes of the atheist, is the supreme proof that . . . he has triumphed over his instinctive fear of the unknown' (p. 230). Clearly, the figure of Franz and the manner of his death have escaped the author's attention.
30　Staiger is as far off the mark as Fricke when he characterizes the ultimate uncommittedness of Karl and the young Schiller as follows: '"Möglichkeit" – das ist das Wort, das diese Größe, dieses Ich-Selbst am genauesten trifft. Als Möglichkeit erdreistet sich Karl, der ganzen Welt gegenüberzutreten' (op. cit. p. 55). Far from it: Karl's way, like that of Wallenstein, is precisely

that from supposed freedom of potentiality to the absolute definition of reality.

31 Maria's husband, Darnley, was murdered on 9 February 1567 and Maria herself was executed on 8 February 1587. Schiller opens the action on 9 February 1587, that is to say, on the anniversary of her husband's murder. This change of dates (noted by Stahl, op. cit. p. 109) surely signifies that Schiller intensifies the connection which Maria herself perceives between two apparently separate events: her real guilt and her wrongful accusation and sentence. By the coalescence of the dates he makes her old guilt 'hers' here and now, and establishes a causal nexus. (For the opposite view, cf. Hamburger, 'Schiller und Sartre', p. 64.)

32 Not even the famous end of the play argues an acceptance, on the poet's part, of Kantian categories, as is usually stated or implied. Cf. Fricke, who writes 'Im Schlusse der "Räuber" hat Schiller um der Reinheit des Ethischen willen den Ausgang trivialisiert' (op. cit. p. 11); R. D. Miller who notes that 'Karl's last decision is a Kantian decision' (op. cit. p. 26); and Schwerte by implication (op. cit. p. 168). It is true that Karl, at the end, voluntarily abrogates his freedom and bows to the moral law. But in what form does he embrace the moral law? 'Ich geh, mich selbst in die Hände der Justiz zu überliefern,' he says. The forensic law is the most public manifestation of the moral conscience, in which unacted intention or motive count for nothing and the act itself and its palpable consequences have become the relevant data of the judgement. (The fact that Kant himself, in his *Metaphysik der Sitten*, written some twenty years later, came to distinguish between

pure morality and morality in a forensic context, need not concern us here.) Karl's voluntary surrender to 'the law' in this forensic sense demonstrates not, as Böckmann argues, his return 'in die Innerlichkeit des Gewissens' ('Die innere Form in Schillers Jugenddramen', p. 452); quite on the contrary, it demonstrates his development from his initial inwardness and preoccupation with intention (which is the distinguishing feature of Kant's system of morality) to his recognition of the public aspect of his act, i.e. the consequences of those intentions for which he feels fully accountable, and to a future- and outward-orientated reality. This new realism is once again echoed in the final 'dem Mann kann geholfen werden'.

33 This secret interaction of self and world has been beautifully formulated by Max Kommerell: 'Dem Handeln steht der Stoff gegenüber — der Begriff dessen, *worauf,* aber auch *womit* gewirkt wird. . . . Durch die feinsten Rückwirkungen des täuschenden Getäuschtwerdens, des glaubenden Geglaubtwerdens, des stärkenden Gestärktwerdens hängt die einsame Seele des Handelnden unprüfbar mit diesem Stoff, der wiederum nichts ist als Menschen-Inneres, zusammen.' (*Geist und Buchstabe der Dichtung* (Frankfurt am Main, 1939), p. 242.)

34 *L'Existentialisme est un humanisme* (Paris, 1946), p. 55. Many other statements of Sartre's could be cited as evidence of the existentialist position that 'man is his acts'. In *L'Existentialisme est un humanisme* Sartre writes: 'L'homme . . . n'est rien d'autre que ce qu'il se fait' (ed. cit. p. 22). In *L'Être et le néant* we read: 'Ce qui m'arrive m'arrive par moi . . . D'ailleurs, tout ce qui m'arrive est mien . . .'

((Paris, 1943), p. 639). In this reading of the existentialist position, I find myself at variance with Wilkinson's and Willoughby's account in *On the Aesthetic Education of Man* (ed. cit. p. clxxxv). The authors stress the existentialist emphasis 'on the view from within, on . . . the "invisible thought", as opposed to the "visible work", on the unseen "purity" of will, or "authenticity" of conviction, rather than on the articulation of these as they become manifest to others.' Thus, Wilkinson and Willoughby argue, the Kantians and the existentialists, however far removed from one another in other respects, are united in this essential inwardness and by that token equally distinguished from Schiller. While I agree with their emphasis on Schiller's concern for the manifest action, I cannot accept their reading of Sartre or indeed any other major existentialist. The whole of *Being and Nothingness*, especially Part Four, III, 'Freedom and Responsibility', points in the opposite direction. In support of my reading I quote the following passage from a monograph on Sartre: 'An "essentialist" can speak of a man who has a good nature but who behaves badly. An existentialist cannot. The goodness of a man's "nature" is the goodness of his behaviour in existentialist eyes, what a man *is* is the sum total of what he *does*. It would be an absurdity for the existentialist to say that a man who acts badly is "essentially" good. There is no invisible essence to *be* good.' (M. Cranston, *Sartre*, Writers and Critics (Edinburgh, 1962, 1965 and 1970), p. 40.) Professor Cranston and Professor J. Cocking of King's College, London, have confirmed in personal communication my view that in their regard for the overt manifestations of the self in action

and indeed in the consequences of action the existentialists hold a position which is diametrically opposed to that of Kant. Professor Cocking has most kindly permitted me to quote extracts from his letter. 'The intention is identical with the action itself and cannot be separated from it as an intention or motivation. . . . Sartre recognizes that we cannot foresee all the consequences of our actions; his view is that we must nevertheless accept full responsibility for those consequences. . . . We must be prepared to have our essence assessed by other people as the sum of our manifest actions.' As for Wilkinson's and Willoughby's assertion that existentialists in their inwardness are indifferent to 'the manifest manner of the performance itself: all those overt bodily signs and symptoms whose significance an observer may indeed interpret so promptly and unconsciously that he could never give an account of them, but which are nevertheless there to be observed . . .' (ibid.), it is contrary to Sartre's position as formulated in *Being and Nothingness*, Chapter Two, pp. 346 f.: '. . . these emotional manifestations' – Sartre writes – 'or, more generally, the phenomena erroneously called the phenomena of *expression*, by no means *indicate* to us a hidden affection lived by some psychism which would be the immaterial object of the research of the psychologist. These frowns, this redness, this stammering, this slight trembling of the hands, these downcast looks which seem at once timid and threatening – these do not *express* anger; they *are* the anger.'

These points need to be clarified. For the contention that Schiller, from *Die Räuber* onwards, was a forerunner of the contemporary existentialist position, in precisely that sense in which the latter is incompatible with Kant's premium on the purity of the moral intention, to the best of my knowledge has not been hitherto advanced and is basic to my view of Schiller as a whole.

Other aspects of the relation between Schiller and existentialism have been investigated by Hamburger in 'Schiller und Sartre', pp. 34–70, by the same author in 'Zum Problem des Idealismus bei Schil-

ler'; L. W. Kahn in 'Freedom: An Existentialist and an Idealist', *PMLA*, LXVI, No. 1, Part 1 (1949), and H. Jaeger, 'Schillers Philosophie der Existenz', *Schiller 1759–1959, Commemorative American Studies*, ed. J. R. Frey (Urbana, Ill., 1959). A comprehensive review of existentially oriented studies on Schiller is to be found in W. Paulsen, 'Friedrich Schiller 1955–1959, Ein Literaturbericht', *JbdDSG*, 6 (1962), pp. 421 ff.

Chapter 5

This chapter is a modified version of an article which appeared in *GLL*, New Series, Vol. VI (1952).

1 Cf. *Kabale und Liebe*, ed. E. M. Wilkinson and L. A. Willoughby (ed. cit.).

2 Critical opinion is sharply divided in the assessment of Luise. There are two camps: those who consider that Luise is caught in an objective conflict in which she proves herself true to her own – and the poet's – conception of sacrificial love; and those who argue that, for one reason or another, Luise is not in fact free absolutely to love Ferdinand. The most eminent exponents of the first view are v. Wiese (II, pp. 199 and 213), Storz (op. cit. pp. 98 f.), Martini ('Schillers "Kabale und Liebe": Bemerkungen zur Interpretation des "Bürgerlichen Trauerspiels"', *DdU*, 5 (1952), p. 32), Böckmann ('Die innere Form in Schillers Jugenddramen', pp. 469 and 477), W. Binder ('Schiller: Kabale und Liebe', in *Das Deutsche Drama*, ed. B. v. Wiese (Düsseldorf, 1960), Vol. I, p. 260, and *NA*, 5, ed. H. O. Burger and W. Höllerer, p. 183). More critical interpretations are offered by J. Minor (op. cit. Vol. II, pp. 139 and 152), Wilkinson and Willoughby (ed. cit. pp. xiv ff.), H. A. Korff

(*Geist der Goethezeit* (Leipzig, 1954), Vol. I, p. 207), Witte, (op. cit. p. 129), J. Müller (*Das Edle in der Freiheit: Schillerstudien* (Leipzig, 1959), p. 107), Fricke, ('Die Problematik des Tragischen im Drama Schillers', p. 16) and Jolles ('Die Sprache des "Spiels" und "Antispiels" in den frühen Dramen Schillers', pp. 250 f.).

3 The lyrical beauty of this passage has been noted by Wilkinson and Willoughby (ed. cit. p. xxxii). As against this, Binder deplores it as a 'Stilbruch' (op. cit. p. 265).

4 As in the case of Luise, critical opinion about Ferdinand is sharply divided. Some consider Ferdinand to be true to the ideal of love which informs the tragedy; notably v. Wiese who considers that for him love has become 'Religion schlechthin' (II, p. 199), Müller (op. cit. p. 107) and, with certain reservations, Wilkinson and Willoughby, who argue that, if anything, he fails by 'clinging too stubbornly to the absolute of love' (ed. cit. p. xvii), or, for that matter, to any one absolute to the exclusion of any other (ibid. p. xviii). More critical views are expressed by K. Berger (op. cit.

Vol. I, p. 371), Garland (II, p. 75), Binder (op. cit. pp. 257 ff.), K. Hamburger ('Schiller und Sartre', p. 42), whilst Stahl (op. cit. pp. 11 and 26), Böckmann ('Die innere Form, etc.', pp. 473 f.), Beck (op. cit. p. 139) and Martini (op. cit. p. 38) all expound the more specific thesis that Ferdinand is a reflection both of his father and of the corrupt values current in his class.

5 This point has been convincingly argued, with regard to Ferdinand, by Beck (op. cit. pp. 136 ff.). His article is a welcome corroboration and complementation of my own approach. I have, however, concentrated on the imagery of monetary possessions in so far as it helps to articulate the relationship between Miller and Luise for the simple reason that this relation emerges as the crucial one in the course of the tragedy.

6 For details of these sordid transactions cf. *NA*, 5, p. 221, note to 28, 20.

7 For details of casting cf. *NA*, 5, pp. 231 and 238. After the unofficial performance by the Grossmann troupe Schiller insisted on having the scene restored and, at his instigation, it was played by Iffland himself (letter to Dahlberg, 1 May 1784).

8 Cf. O. Harnack, op. cit. p. 107: the lackey scene is 'noch kühner und von unmittelbarerer realistischer Wahrheit' than the extortion scene between Wurm and Luise; L. Bellermann, op. cit. p. 98: 'Solche Szenen waren *nicht erfunden*, sie waren schreckliche Wirklichkeit' (my italics); Buchwald, op. cit. Vol. II, p. 462 (my italics): 'Immer wieder *lodert* aus der Zeichnung die Anklage, am *grellsten* in der berühmten Kammerdienerszene, die man zuerst in Mannheim gar nicht zu spielen wagte; wirkt sie doch auch heute, wo alle Zeitnähe

vorbei ist, noch ebensosehr aufpeitschend . . .'; H. Kindermann, in *Theatergeschichte der Goethezeit* (Vienna, 1948), p. 250, calls the scene 'die sozial wirksamste Szene des ganzen Stücks'; H. J. Geerdts, in *Deutsche Literaturgeschichte in einem Band* (Berlin, 1967), p. 226, writes: 'Die Schärfe einer *direkten politischen* Anklage erhält die Tragödie in der Kammerdienerszene, die zwar dramaturgisch nur eine Episode darstellt, dem Drama aber erst . . . seinen *unmittelbaren Gegenwartscharakter* verleiht' (my italics); H. Koopmann, in *Schiller Kommentar, zu den Dichtungen*, Vol. I (Munich, 1969), p. 120, argues that, in revising the play for the stage in 1784, Schiller made many cuts: 'Die Kammerdienerszene aber beließ er und nahm damit bewußt dem Stück nicht jegliche politische Aktualität'. In *Friedrich Schiller 1759–1959*, ed. Deutscher Kulturbund (Berlin, 1959), the scene is printed verbatim in its entirety as documentary proof of the poet's political and social convictions (p. 62); and in a preceding statement by the Schiller-Komitee der Deutschen Demokratischen Republik we read: 'Indem er den Soldatenhandel der deutschen Fürsten vor aller Welt entlarvte, identifizierte er sich zugleich mit dem Protest der leidenden Massen des Volkes' (p. 14).

9 The irrelevance of the social or political tendencies of a playwright to the artistic merit of his play has, however, been forcefully stressed by Willoughby and Wilkinson who write: 'Strictly speaking such questions should never have been asked by the literary critic, even when the play came red-hot from the poet's social conscience; for, while important in themselves, these questions belong to the ethical or political sphere and are out of place in an

artistic context.' (*Kabale und Liebe*, ed. cit. p. xii.)

10 This is by no means universally accepted. For primarily sociological readings, cf. Korff, op. cit. Vol. I; Garland, I, p. 74, M. Gerhard, op. cit. pp. 63 ff., and E. Auerbach, *Mimesis* (Berne, 1946).

11 This scene was severely criticized by early critics such as Minor (op. cit. Vol. II, p. 144) and Bellermann (op. cit. Vol. I, p. 200). Cf. also Martini (op. cit. p. 38).

12 Later, of course, Miller will return the money to Ferdinand saying: 'Wolltest du mir mein Kind damit abkaufen?' (V, letzte Szene). Beck comments: '. . . soll mit den Worten des Alten nicht nochmals zum Ausdruck gebracht werden, daß kein Mensch in dem despotischen Sinne, wie ihn Ferdinand wahrgemacht hat, *des andern sein* und von diesem als Eigentum behandelt werden kann . . .' (op. cit. p. 139).

13 The fact that Luise's social ethos inclines her towards an attitude of resignation has been stressed by Erich Schmidt (*SA*, 3, p. xlvii) and by Böckmann ('Die innere Form, etc.', pp. 476 ff.).

14 This kind of image – culminating in Ferdinand's 'das Mädchen ist mein' – is a pointer to the possessiveness of Ferdinand's love and to his place in the thematic structure of the play. Here my interpretation is complemented by that of Beck (op. cit.) and is in tacit agreement with those critics who argue that, for all his idealism, Ferdinand is his father's son (cf. note 4 of this chapter). Only I would argue more specifically that the proprietary attitude towards human beings which has found its most palpable expression in the Duke's sale of his subjects is the central theme of the tragedy, and that in view of its crucial importance the poet has articulated it triply, in the rela-

tionship between Miller and Luise, in that between the President and Ferdinand, and finally, by an extension of this filial pattern, in the possessiveness Ferdinand evinces towards the girl he loves.

15 B. v. Wiese argues that Ferdinand's loyalty to his father has become conditional because the President is a 'Zerrbild' of what a father should be (II, pp. 200 f.). This assessment of the President is of course correct; but Ferdinand's employment of the symbolism of possession to characterize both his father's attitude to human beings and his own attitude to his father – 'es ist erlaubt, einen Räuber zu plündern' – suggests that, exonerating circumstances apart, he *is* his father's son: like his father, and indeed like Luise's father, and the *Landesvater*, he becomes associated, through his use of the dominant imagery, with a deeply irreligious attitude which degrades a loved person into a thing. Cf. Beck (op. cit. p. 138). B. v. Wiese regards Ferdinand's love for Luise as expressive of a truly religious attitude (II, p. 199).

16 The unusual degree of realistic detail in this play, psychological and verbal, has been repeatedly observed. Cf. Garland (I, p. 77), Böckmann ('Die innere Form, etc.', p. 478), and Stahl who notes the differentiated use of language 'to suit the station and mentality of the different characters' and concludes that 'the employment of such subtly varied and characteristic forms of expression is peculiar to this play' (op. cit. p. 28). This observation is of course quite true; but it serves to enhance the status of the imagery of monetary possessions which overrides all individual differences of character and directly contributes to the central theme of the play.

17 Beck speaks of this exclamation as being a 'schauerliche Satz, der die freie Person zur Sache entwürdigt' (op. cit. p. 136). He is right. There is not much to choose between the attitudes of the rivals.

18 Cf. note 2 of this chapter.

19 Wilkinson and Willoughby rightly note the string of rationalizations covering up, step by step, the unconscious motives for Luise's withdrawal (ed. cit. p. xvi) and observe that, in the end, she is not even willing to die for love (ibid.). But the primary cause they assign to her inertia is fear of the unknown (p.xv).

20 This point is forcefully made by Witte (op. cit. p. 129). Cf. also Wilkinson and Willoughby (ed. cit. pp. xxviii f.) who subtly link Miller's possessive love with the inhibitions implanted in Luise's conscience, which is itself dominated by the 'father' figure (p. xvi).

21 Cf. note 11 of this chapter.

22 This change of stance has been adversely noted by Bellermann (op. cit. Vol. I, p. 200).

23 This filial dependence is interpreted by some as testifying to Luise's moral, emotional and religious stature, in a poetic universe of discourse where the figure of the father plays a decisive role. This is the view of v. Wiese (II, pp. 199 and 213), Storz (op. cit. p. 99), Burger and Höllerer (NA, 5, p. 183) and Martini (op. cit. p. 37). The absolute fidelity to the father is critically viewed by Stahl (op. cit. p. 24), Korff (op. cit. Vol. I, p. 207), Wilkinson and Willoughby (ed. cit. p. xvi) and Müller (op. cit. p. 107).

24 Korff argues that the real theme of the play is 'die Freiheit der Gattenwahl' (op. cit. Vol. I, p. 205). Similarly Witte states that the tragic issue is 'the right to love, the right to choose a mate' (op. cit. p. 127).

Chapter 6

1 Storz has noted that this song foreshadows Wallenstein's problem — 'die vorbehaltlose Entscheidung, die ebenso sehr verzichtet wie wagt' (op. cit. p. 272).

2 The 'Problematik des Handelns' has, of course, been stressed by many critics. Cf. v. Wiese, III, p. 251; Kommerell, Geist und Buchstabe, etc., pp. 147 ff.; Böckmann, 'Politik und Dichtung im Werk Fr. Schillers', p. 201; O. Seidlin, 'Wallenstein: Sein und Zeit', pp. 41 ff.; Böckmann, 'Gedanke, Wort und Tat in Schillers Dramen', JbdDSG, 4 (1960); Thomas Mann, Versuch über Schiller, Stockholmer Gesamtausgabe, Nachlese (Prosa, 1951–5), p. 87; Hamburger, 'Schiller und Sartre', p. 69; Storz, op. cit. p. 284; and Garland, I, p. 204.

3 May has observed that Gordon's comments serve to illuminate Wallenstein's 'Fallhöhe' (op. cit. p.151).

4 Cf. Seidlin who points out that Buttler's comparison of Wallenstein with Archimedes pinpoints Wallenstein's presumption 'die Welt aus ihren Angeln heben zu können, vorausgesetzt daß ein fester Punkt außerhalb des Universums zu finden sei . . .' (op. cit. p. 132).

5 Rather oddly and ineptly, May compares Wallenstein's vision with Faust's words invoking the Erdgeist (op. cit. p. 118). Seidlin is more to the point when he asks how it is possible that a man of such vision could be labelled, during more than a century of Schiller criticism, as 'the realist' pure and simple (op. cit. p. 123).

6 For similar readings cf. especially R. Buchwald, op. cit. Vol. II, p. 379; Seidlin, op. cit. p. 124;

Storz, op. cit. p. 284; and W. Binder, 'Die Begriffe "Naiv" und "Sentimentalisch" in Schillers Drama', *JbdDSG*, 4 (1960), p. 155.

7 Böckmann has demonstrated convincingly 'die handelnde Kraft des Wortes' ('Gedanke, Wort und Tat, etc.', pp. 5 f.).

8 Seidlin (op. cit. p. 42) and Böckmann ('Gedanke, Wort und Tat, etc.', p. 19) have noted the consequential nature of non-action.

9 Wallenstein's innocence has been argued at length by R. N. Linn ('Wallenstein's Innocence', *The Germanic Review: J. F. Schiller*, Vol. XXXIV, No. 3 (October 1959), p. 205).

10 M. Jolles observes: 'In der Schrift ist die Sprache gleichsam festgelegt und gebunden', in 'Die Sprache des "Spiels" und des "Antispiels" in den frühen Dramen Schillers', pp. 251 f. However, he rightly distinguishes Max's unwillingness to sign the officer's pledge from Wallenstein's disinclination to commit himself in writing, arguing that Max's refusal is an instance of his inner maturity (ibid.).

11 Cf. Thomas Mann, op. cit. p. 92.

12 This aspect of Wallenstein's character has been repeatedly noted. Cf. v. Wiese, II, p. 650; Kommerell, *Geist und Buchstabe*, etc., pp. 157, 210 and 215; May, op. cit. pp. 106 f. and 122.

13 Cf. Thomas Mann, op. cit. p. 92, Kommerell, *Geist und Buchstabe*, etc., p. 210, Storz, op. cit. p. 285.

14 Cf. Chapter 11, pp. 263 ff., 269.

15 Cf. Chapter 11, pp. 274 ff.

16 Storz makes the point that Wallenstein is both more vulnerable than and, by that token, superior to the true realists in the play (op. cit. p. 298). Staiger's intriguing characterization of Wallenstein as 'ein in der Basis gefährdeter, angeschlagener Realist' points in the same direction (op. cit. p. 306).

17 Cf. Staiger, op. cit. pp. 37 ff.

18 Illo is customarily presented as a coarse and brutal figure. The fact that he is the only character in the play that fully appreciates the 'Problematik des Handelns' and counters it by a coherent philosophy of action has been ignored in such estimates. This reading emphasizes Illo's Iago-like intelligence. That the poet himself thought more highly of this character than is generally assumed may be inferred from the fact that he made him into the mouthpiece of his own reflections on time in life and, by implication, in art.

Once a more considerable intellectual stature is conceded to this figure, the style of some of his speeches appears less out of keeping with his character than has been assumed. (By May, op. cit. pp. 176 f., and Witte, op. cit. p. 156.)

19 This inconsistency has been noted by Böckmann (in 'Gedanke, Wort und Tat in Schillers Dramen', p. 17).

20 R. Schneider writes: 'Wallenstein – und das ist die Schwäche der Figur – möchte Freiheit gar nicht ausüben; er möchte nur das Gefühl ihres Genusses haben, mit ihr spielen, und darüber wird es zu spät für ihn . . .' ('Tragik und Erlösung im Weltbild Schillers', *Schiller. Reden im Gedenkjahr 1955*, p. 291).

21 Cf. Chapter 11.

22 In this connection, cf. Jolles, 'Das Bild des Weges und die Sprache des Herzens. Zur strukturellen Funktion der sprachlichen Bilder in Schillers *Wallenstein*', *Deutsche Beiträge zur geistigen Überlieferung*, IV (1961). This article gives an impression of the extensiveness of this image pattern rather than of the ambiguity it assumes at the hands of the diverse characters, notably with Wallenstein himself.

23 The more obvious correspondence

between Max's fate and Wallenstein's dream prior to the battle of Lützen (*Tod*, II. iii) has been pointed out by myself. Cf. I. Appelbaum, *Schiller's Tragedies in the Light of his General Aesthetics*, Ph.D thesis (London, 1951), p. 170 (I. Graham, *Schiller: A Master of the Tragic Form*, Chapter II), and by Seidlin (op. cit. p. 128).

24 Storz has noted the consonance between Max's and Thekla's end. But he compares Thekla's words in IV. xi with the words Max speaks at his parting rather than with the claustrophobic circumstances of his actual death as reported by the Swedish Officer in *Tod*, IV. x.

25 For a very different reading cf. Stahl who writes: '. . . he is deeply moved by Gräfin Terzky's forebodings and mournfully recalls the scene of Henri Quatre's premonition of death.' (Op. cit. p. 99.) I fail to see any trace of mournfulness about Wallenstein's demeanour here.

26 In various degrees and formulations this would seem to be the position adopted by Petsch (op. cit. pp. 192 f.), May (op. cit. pp. 160 f.), Witte (op. cit. p. 161), Witte (ed.) (*Wallenstein*, Blackwell's German Texts (Oxford, 1952), pp. xxxiv f.), v. Wiese (II, pp. 671 ff. and 678), Jolles ('Das Bild des Weges, etc.', p. 128), and Staiger (op. cit. p. 310). In fact, however, Wallenstein is not blind to portentous signs. He ignores them because he has accepted what they signify – what he himself emphatically calls 'das Unvermeidliche' (V. iii). He accepts change and death: he no longer expects to spellbind 'das flücht'ge Glück' permanently; and it is not by accident that he chooses the image of the tides – paradigm of change – to express his own sense of 'being on top of the world'. In this connection, cf. Chapter 11, p. 273.

27 This is the position adopted by

Schneider and Blumenthal in *NA*, 8, pp. 392 f.), who maintain that the dying Wallenstein has attained to 'das Erhabene der Fassung', and has 'sich moralisch entleibt'. 'Erdenfurcht reicht nicht mehr an ihn heran' (392 f.). This position is contested by v. Wiese (II, p. 650) and Stahl (op. cit. pp. 93 ff.). Stahl, however, does not concede to Wallenstein any sublimity whatever, a position which is not likely to be found acceptable by many.

28 This is the argument of Seidlin (op. cit. p. 43).

29 This 'positiveness' on the part of Wallenstein has been noted time and again. It has been interpreted realistically by Stahl who sees in Wallenstein's attitude 'the conquest of uncertainty through resolute self-assertion' (op. cit. p. 105). Similarly Linn argues that Wallenstein's rejuvenation, at the end, is due to the fact that instead of wanting to retain power, he is now poised to regain it. 'The dying Wallenstein is . . . a calm optimist, because his second goal is a possible one, whereas his first goal was doomed to failure' (op. cit. p. 207). Less practical motivations are adduced to explain Wallenstein's youthful vigour by v. Wiese (II, p. 673) and May (op. cit. p. 150), both of whom regard this as the consequence of his new self-acceptance. (B. v. Wiese writes: 'identisch mit sich selbst und seinem großem Schicksal, so wie er es deutet'; May observes: 'Entscheidend . . . ist, daß Wallenstein sich zu sich selbst bekennt, zu seiner Tat, die einmal geschehen, . . . daß er eine verjüngte Kraft zum Herrschen aufweist.') Cf. also Schneider and Blumenthal (*NA*, 8, p. 391); Witte (ed. cit. pp. xxxvii, note 9, and xxxv) concedes a change of mood but no more. My reading explains Wallenstein's sense of rejuvenation and

enrichment with greater precision than has been done hitherto.

30 For a similar conception of Wallenstein and 'his' world as being part of one another, cf. Kommerell, *Geist und Buchstabe*, etc., p. 242 (quoted in Chapter 4, note 3); v. Wiese, who writes: 'Ein privater, isolierter, gleichsam seiner Seele überantworteter Wallenstein ist undenkbar' (II, p. 651) and: 'Wer Wallenstein eigentlich ist, erfahren wir im Grunde nur durch die Fabel seines Geschicks' (ibid.). May too emphasizes: '[Er] steht am Ende ganz zu sich selbst, wie er bis dahin geworden' (op. cit. p. 160).

Indeed in this context of Wallenstein's existential experience of himself in the world, the following reflection of Heidegger assumes relevance: 'Der Mensch "ist" nicht und hat überdies noch ein Seinsverhältnis zur "Welt", die er sich gelegentlich zulegt . . . Solches Aufnehmen von Beziehungen zur Welt ist nur möglich, weil Dasein als In-der-Welt-Sein ist, wie es ist.' (*Sein und Zeit*, 5th ed. (Halle/Saale, 1941), p. 57.) Seidlin comes closest to my approach here (op. cit. pp. 133 f.). It is not accidental that Seidlin's title should be borrowed from Heidegger.

Chapter 7

1 The symbolic significance of Maria's incarceration has, of course, been recognized. B. v. Wiese formulates it most radically, but also misleadingly, as a symbol of the 'Gefangenschaft des Irdischen' *per se* (*NA*, 9, ed. v. Wiese and L. Blumenthal, pp. 327 and 337 f.).

2 Adolf Beck describes the two Queens as 'einander zugewandt und aneinander schicksalsmäßig gebunden' ('Maria Stuart', in *Das Deutsche Drama*, p. 308).

3 B. v. Wiese is alive to the transpersonal significance of this statement. '[Es] bezeichnet genau die Kontrastsituation zum physischen Untergang der Maria,' he writes, 'mit dem und in dem zugleich eben jener "edlere Teil" des Menschen gerettet wird' (II, p. 724).

4 For a functional analysis of the imagery of fire here and elsewhere in Schiller's dramas, cf. Chapter 1, pp. 35 ff., and Chapter 3, pp. 68 ff.

5 Witte notes Schiller's emphasis on 'the vanity and coquetry' Elisabeth had inherited from her mother (op. cit. p. 174). Julius Petersen contrasts the 'offen eingestandenen Liebessünden Marias' with the 'geheimen Laster der Elisabeth' and convincingly argues that Schiller underpinned this opposition through the Queens' opposed response to Mortimer. 'Elisabeth stellt für einen Meuchelmord den Preis in Aussicht, um den Maria ihr eigenes Leben nicht erkaufen will.' (*SA*, 6, ed. Petersen, p. xv.)

6 B. v. Wiese stresses the role assigned in the early stages of German classicism to the woman as the preserver and guardian of civilization (II, p. 474).

7 The significance of this scene is universally regarded as lying in the fact that it is a stepping-stone on Maria's way to sublimity. Some critics argue – untenably, in my opinion – that Maria attains to sublimity even during this hostile encounter. Cf. notably v. Wiese (III, pp. 295 ff., and II, pp. 38, 297 and 715 ff.), also Beck ('Maria Stuart' in *Das Deutsche Drama*, pp. 313 f.). Beck emphasizes, however, that this encounter not only demonstrates Maria's incapacity to suffer violence, but also betrays 'die Maria von einst . . . , die leidenschaftlich Lebensgierige' (ibid. p.

315). Other critics regard Maria's response as an indubitable if necessary setback on the road to sublimity. Cf. Stahl, op. cit. p. 112, K. Hamburger, 'Schiller und Sartre', p. 64. But whatever the direction of critical opinion, positive or negative, it is oriented, in an especial measure, to the notion of the sublime as put forth in Schiller's theory. Even a critic like Staiger who specifically warns against any easy inference from Schiller's theory of tragedy to his actual practice (op. cit. pp. 66 and 407 f.) at this point operates with the category offered by Schiller's theory and unquestioningly applies it to the poetic material in hand (ibid. p. 320). My own reading offers a radical change of perspective. Leaving aside the theory and all evaluative judgements based upon it, I am concerned, solely, to show the scene as making a crucial and organic contribution to the statement of the theme of the drama, i.e. the correlation and equivalence between the visible and the invisible which finds its climactic articulation in the communion scene in Act V.

8 Cf. Don Carlos: 'Die ewige / Beglaubigung der Menschheit sind ja Tränen.' (II. ii.) Cf. also v. Wiese who writes: 'Wer sich außerhalb der Menschheit stellt, hat mit der Natur auch die Träne verloren' (II, p. 255).

9 B. v. Wiese makes this point, which is valid for Schiller in his entirety, in connection with the figure of Elisabeth in *Don Carlos*. 'Die Königin verkörpert . . . den Bund des fühlenden Herzens mit der Schönheit. Sie verkörpert genau das, was Schiller später "Anmut" nennt.' (II, p. 269.) He rightly emphasizes the essentially religious character of this union (ibid. p. 472). Storz, by contrast, implicitly denies the crucial correlation between natural and moral beauty when he speaks of 'das dämonische Leuchten schuldloser und zugleich seelenloser Frauenschönheit' and – in a formulation curiously reminiscent of Thomas Mann – stresses 'das unpersönliche, elementar-sylphidische Wesen dieser Schönheit . . .' ('Maria Stuart', in *Interpretationen* 2, pp. 333 f.).

Not dissimilarly, Beck describes Maria as 'edelste Natur' ('Maria Stuart', p. 311). Beck's reading excels in that he stresses the intimate interlacing, to the very last, between Maria's sense-drives and her sublimity. (Oddly enough, however, he does not mention the crowning paradox which drives home this interlacing – Maria's lapse into Leicester's arms, on her way to the scaffold.) But Beck does not go far enough: he concedes to Maria 'Echtheit natürlichen Wesens . . . , und dazuhin *trotz alledem* . . . Selbstständigkeit des Geistes.' (Ibid. p. 320, my italics.) This argues an ultimately dualistic view and hence a dualistic conception of sublimity such as might be culled from portions of Schiller's theoretical writings. And indeed, Beck unquestioningly operates with categories derived from Schiller's theory in his interpretation of the drama itself. Thus he misses its unique message. Maria is not sublime *despite the fact* that she is, and remains, sensuously receptive and alive, any more than she is morally beautiful *despite the fact* that she is physically lovely. Schiller's import, here and elsewhere, is the deep correlation between spiritual and physical reality, between the visible and the invisible. This equivalence is the hallmark of his monism. For a further elaboration of this point, cf. Chapter 12, pp. 294, 306, 331 f. and 336 and n. 12 of this chapter.

10 Storz defines the tragic in Elisabeth

as being the 'Mißverhältnis von Aufgabe und Kraft' and in turn defines this as 'Tragik des verfehlten Berufes': 'Sie hat den Rechtstitel für die Krone, der sie nicht gewachsen ist.' ('Maria Stuart', p. 177.) Storz does not see, however, that in the case of Elisabeth (as indeed in that of *Warbeck* and *Demetrius* which he himself cites as the obverse) the whole question of kingship and legitimacy is a metaphor for the ultimate problem of moral endeavour and the cruel limits set to such conscious effort by natural endowment. Cf. Chapter 10, pp. 231 ff. and 239 ff.

11 To say this is also to safeguard the figure of Mortimer against the severe condemnation which he has received at the hands of almost all critics. Amongst the exceptions are F. Schultz in *Epochen der deutschen Literatur*, Band IV, 2. Teil, Klassik und Romantik der Deutschen, II. Teil (Stuttgart, 1952), who argues that Mortimer's account of his conversion cannot be dismissed, simply, as that of a *Schwärmer*. 'Es fehlt ihr in ihrer Gehobenheit und werbenden Kraft nicht der persönliche Anteil des Dichters' (p. 168). Witte, in his edition of *Maria Stuart*, characterizes Mortimer as a 'mentally and morally unstable youth', but concedes that in this passage Schiller has projected himself, 'with a poet's imagination, into the state of mind of an impressionable young man to whom his first contact with the Church of Rome comes as an overwhelmingly glorious revelation.' (*Maria Stuart*, ed. Witte, Macmillan's Modern Language Texts (London, Melbourne, Toronto, 1965), p. 147.) The majority of readings, however, are unremittingly critical. (Cf. especially Garland, I, p. 49; Staiger, op. cit. p. 318; Wiese, II, p. 720 and R. Ay-

rault, 'La figure de Mortimer dans Marie Stuart et la conception du drame historique chez Schiller', *Études Germaniques*, 4 (1959).) Mortimer's detailed account of his art-experience in Rome is not, as Storz suggests, a digression from the economy of the drama and disruptive of its inner unity. On the contrary, it is vitally important because of the contribution it makes to the central theme of the play: the – sacramental – relation between the visible and the invisible. To this relation the phenomenon of art, whose physical symbols are the 'objective correlatives' of its imports, testifies in a special measure. Both Storz and v. Wiese show some awareness of the connection between the aesthetic and the religious spheres which lies at the centre of the drama. But Storz's argument (in common with that of many other critics) that Schiller's handling of the religious motif is to be regarded as proof of his 'lediglich ästhetischen Verhaltens zu den religiösen Phänomenen' ('Maria Stuart', p. 183) is superficial and illustrates the dangers to which Storz's own excessive preoccupation with technical problems occasionally gives rise, notably in his reading of this play and of *Die Jungfrau von Orleans* where the significance of the religious theme is seen in the fact that it adds colour and creates atmospheric effects. B. v. Wiese's observations are bold and come much closer to the heart of the issue. 'Die auf die Bühne gebrachte sakrale Handlung', he writes, 'sollte durch das Sakramentale des Theaters noch überboten werden. Nicht der christliche Glaube wird durch das Theater profaniert, sondern das für Schiller bereits Profane dieses Glaubens durch das Theater erneut geheiligt.' (II, p. 722.) (For a similar approach, cf. also Cysarz, *Schil-*

ler, p. 346.) B. v. Wiese has put his finger on the life-nerve of Schiller's thinking when he speaks of 'seine geheime Theologie des Ästhetischen' (ibid. p. 758). Schiller's writings – the *Ästhetische Briefe* and his poems no less than his dramas – suggest that, like his puritanical Mortimer, he himself experienced the marriage of mind and medium in the art-process, and the incarnation of spiritual imports in material symbols in the art-product, as an essentially religious revelation. I would agree with v. Wiese that the artistic experience may have remained for him the radiant centre of such a religious illumination, his own personal channel of access to it. But to make this metaphysical reality ancillary to the aesthetic experience and to say that '. . . die Mittlerstelle, die bisher Christus und die Kirche innehatten, übernimmt nunmehr die . . . zur Kultstätte erhobene Bühne . . .' and 'Der Dichter selbst wird zum stellvertretenden Erlöser . . .' (ibid. p. 758) seems to me to overshoot the mark and to reverse the ascending order of values which Schiller himself, in the context of this drama at least, has indicated through its very form: for the aesthetic revelation vouchsafed to Mortimer is the *prolegomenon* to the encompassing religious illumination granted to Maria. His quick exchange of the transitory for the eternal is the *anticipation* of Maria's swift rise to sublimity – 'Man löst sich nicht allmählich von dem Leben!' (V. i). His blurring of the heavenly and the earthly Mary *foreshadows and reflects* Maria's own temporary confusion between the arms of Christ and those of her lover, Leicester, on her way to the scaffold (V. ix). To deny such parallels and to regard them as a series of oppositions as Ayrault does, is unfeasible. If

Maria's last-minute mistaking of one pair of arms for another does not detract from her moral stature, neither does Mortimer's last-minute confusion of the two Queens. If we condemn him for being unable to distinguish, 'dans son délire, entre les plus images que recouvre le nom de Marie . . .' (op. cit. p. 324), we are constrained to condemn Maria too for ending up in Leicester's arms after beseeching Christ to spread his arms to receive her in them (V. ix). To argue that 'Tandis que la figure de Marie Stuart se purifie au Ve acte, . . . la figure de Mortimer subit une dégradation continue . . .' (ibid. p. 321) is to ignore the clearly defined pattern of parallel responses and events in the drama itself. Such parallels need to be duly stressed, both to safeguard Mortimer from uncritical condemnation and to assign to him his proper subordinate place in the thematic structure of a drama in which his aesthetic credo forms no more than part of an encompassing religious statement: the articulation, through the cognate symbol of an incarnational doctrine, of a monistic position.

12 Mortimer's confusion is almost universally condemned. Cf. note 11. Only v. Wiese and Blumenthal see that it argues a fusion as much as a confusion (*NA*, 9, p. 331). Similarly, Maria's 'lapse' is critically noted. Petersen can only explain it by a lapse on the part of the poet who, by his own confession, momentarily lost sight of his poetic conception and was led astray by the historical figure of Maria (*SA*, 6, p. xiv). L. A. Willoughby and E. M. Wilkinson argue that 'nothing could bring home more vividly the attachment to life and power which has been the driving force of this woman's nature' (*Kabale und Liebe*, ed. cit. p. xli). The word 'power'

vitiates what might otherwise be a valuable observation. Schiller is concerned to show, not at all a lapse or regression on Maria's part, but the ineluctable rootedness of sublimity in the undiminished life of the senses, even in the very act of their immolation. To establish, from the evidence of Schiller's tragedies themselves, this conception of sublimity over the one that is traditionally held, whatever the notion of sublimity which emerges from his theoretical writings, is one of the major objectives of this book. Cf. Chapter 12.

13 The reading of this scene which Schiller himself regarded as 'den unentbehrlichen Schlußstein des Ganzen' is the acid test of every interpretation of *Maria Stuart*. Storz reveals his own formalistic tendency when he judges that this scene, like Mortimer's earlier account of Rome, 'zielt ebenfalls auf Stimmung ab'. 'Der Reiz des Historischen ist entdeckt.' ('Maria Stuart', p. 182.) The Duke Karl August, Storz observes, complained about the communion scene because he '. . . nahm sie naiv und geradezu, deutlicher gesagt, er nahm sie ernst. Dem Dichter kam dies vermöge seines Begriffes von dichterischer Form und Wirkung nicht in den Sinn.' (Ibid. p. 183.) It is true that Storz's unremitting emphasis on artistic perspectives has provided a welcome and valuable corrective to the ideological approach of German Schiller scholarship as represented, say, by Fricke. But here, as in his readings of the later dramas in their entirety, an excessive emphasis on technical problems leads to a perceptible impoverishment of his interpretations, and the 'wirklichkeitsflüchtige Streben' he perceives in the later Schiller would seem to reflect the formalism in his own approach rather than any insubstantiality in the poet himself (*Der Dichter F. Schiller*, p. 323). The secular reading of Joachim Müller who asserts that Schiller, in this scene, 'meint den Himmel des freien Willens, die Seligkeit der sittlichen Autonomie . . .' misses the centre by as much in the ethical direction as does Storz in the aesthetic one (*Das Edle in der Freiheit* (Leipzig, 1959), p. 127).

Blumenthal and v. Wiese come much closer to the reading attempted here when they write: 'Die Sterbeszene der "Maria Stuart" ist für Schiller der Höhepunkt einer Tragödie, die in der Vermählung des Menschen mit dem Göttlichen gipfelt. Es ist eine zugleich schöne und erhabene Seele, die hier ihren Abschied von der Welt nimmt.' (*NA*, 9, p. 337). But when, in the same context, the editors speak of the 'Gefangenschaft des Lebens' (ibid.), of the 'grausamsten Verfallenheit an die Welt als Gefängnis' (p. 327) or of the 'Unzulänglichkeit des Irdisch-Geschichtlichen' (p. 328), they deny the parity of the earthly and visible with the spiritual and invisible which the metaphor of the 'marriage' appears to affirm. They lapse into a basically dualistic stance where on every level of the drama I see the expression of a monistic faith. 'Das Unzulängliche, hier wird's Ereignis.'

Storz, v. Wiese, Staiger, Petersen, Ayrault and others are all anxious to point out that from the communion scene no 'katholisierende Neigungen' on the part of Schiller himself may be inferred. Such a view does not, I think, do full justice to the monistic implications of the sacramental doctrine of Catholicism and the germaneness of this to the monistic faith mediated to Schiller through the experience of art-making. It hardly needs saying that Schiller did not write this scene or indeed the drama of which it forms the centre-piece as a Catholic. It has, however, been argued, correctly in my opinion, that Schiller did indeed write this drama with the inside knowledge of a Catholic. Cf. O. Walzel in *Schiller und die Romantik: Vom Geistesleben des 18. und 19. Jahrhunderts* (Leipzig, 1911), p. 83: '*Maria Stuart*', Walzel writes, is 'katholisch gedacht, so katholisch, wie damals nur irgendein Romantiker denken konnte. Similarly F. Schultz (op. cit. p. 169): 'Diese universalistische und vereinigende Idee des Katholizismus hätte schärfer nicht von dem späteren Friedrich Schlegel, von Adam Müller, Görres und anderen gefaßt werden können.' The internal evidence of the drama itself suggests that Schiller wrote it fully cognizant of the fact that Christianity, by reason of its incarnational basis, and more especially Catholicism, through its sacramental doctrine, offered him *the* symbol of symbolism as such, that is to say, a religious and metaphysical anchorage for his own monistic faith in the equivalence of the spiritual and the material in the sphere of art. To say this is to posit a more far-reaching and complex relation between poetic and religious experience than critics anxious to acquit Schiller of 'katholisierende Neigungen' are willing to concede. The example, in our day, of W. H. Auden, H. v. Hofmannsthal and T. S. Eliot may throw some light on the close connection between a dedication to symbolism in art and

sacramental doctrine. For a searching discussion of the interrelation between art and Catholicism, cf. Evelyn Underhill, *Worship*, Fontana Library (London, 1962).

The ultimate test of an interpretation of a work of art is the amount of coherence it reveals. I submit that the central place my reading accords to the imagery of seeing and being seen enables me to demonstrate greater coherence between the main action, Mortimer's account of Rome and the communion scene than has hitherto been perceived. Inevitably from such a reading the communion scene, being more fully integrated with the main action, emerges as crucially important to the drama as a whole, indeed as the 'unentbehrliche Schlußstein' Schiller himself regarded it to be: and this central position in the total statement of the drama makes it less easy to assume that Schiller took up as airy and non-committal an attitude to its ostensible import as is generally supposed.

14 B. v. Wiese speaks of Don Cesar's 'festlichen Tod, . . . mit dem der Sterbende und durch sein Sterben Entsühnte sich wieder vereinigt' (II, p. 757). I maintain that such an inner reconciliation of the warring parts of the personality – which may be reflected in an external reconciliation with the antagonist – is the ideal centre of this and every other tragedy by Schiller, and that 'catharsis', in Schiller's sense of the word, means nothing other than the act of self-acceptance which ensues from such a reconciliation. Cf. Chapter 12.

Chapter 8

1 This criticism has in fact been levelled at the play by Garland (I, p. 220) and B. von Heiseler, who

writes that Schiller turned 'the life of the young saint into a gaily beribboned fairytale about the age of chivalry, which ends with Johanna's glorious death on the battlefield, draped in banners' (*Schiller*, transl. J. Bednall (London, 1962), p. 167).

2 Stahl considers that Schiller actually 'had to invent a flaw in the heroine's character before he was able to dramatise her story' (op. cit. p. 117).

3 Goethe himself made this point in a diary entry dated 27 May 1807.

4 Cf. Goethe to Schiller, 18 March 1795. This link has been noted by Böckmann who argues that Johanna's vow rests on an 'eigentümliche Vertauschung von subjektiver Entschlossenheit und objektivem Gebot . . .' ('Gedanke, Wort und Tat in Schillers Dramen', pp. 32 f.). Böckmann, however, does not follow out the implications of his own recognition that Johanna's initial identification with the divine rests upon an illusion.

5 It is here that I part company with other scholars. With two notable exceptions, Schiller critics have traditionally regarded Johanna's sense of unconditional identification with her mission as warranted and laudable. The one exception is R. Petsch who notes the 'pathologische Unterdrückung des empirischen Charakters' in Johanna and urges, not radically enough in my opinion, that the seed of Johanna's guilt is to be found, long before her encounter with Lionel, in the estrangement from her own mission which she confesses to Montgomery. 'Mit ihrem "Fall" bricht das böse Geschwür nur auf.' (Op. cit. p. 241.) Similarly, H. Cysarz states: 'Lionel also läßt Johanna nicht ihrer Aufgabe untreu, vielmehr ihrer wahren Aufgabe inne werden' (*Schiller*, p. 355). Of this task he writes somewhat cryptically yet excitingly: 'Vielmehr erweist die Liebe, und nicht erst die zum

Feind, das Heilige als uneigentliche, unvollständige Erfüllung, ja als Umgehung der Aufgabe.' (Ibid.) A textual analysis makes it evident that, from the Prologue onwards, Johanna represses a side of herself which is in fact not identified with her mission – i.e. the natural, ininstinctual side on which she turns her back on leaving home – and that consequently her own identification with the divine, and her interpretation of the terms of her mission are questionable. Cf. Chapter 10, pp. 239 f.

By not approaching this play with the tools of textual analysis, critics have fallen into the pitfall of taking Johanna's statements at their prima facie level, thus remaining unaware of strata of her being of which she herself is unconscious and accepting her account of her mission and of her response to it as representing the poet's intention. The consequences of such readings are particularly disastrous in a play the heroine of which is afflicted with a unique degree of blindness, notwithstanding the fact that she possesses prophetic powers. This paradoxical concatenation runs through Schiller's tragedies in their entirety and I have analysed it in full elsewhere. (Cf. I. Graham, *Schiller: A Master of the Tragic Form*, Chapter II.) To note this is particularly important, since Johanna's delusion is singular, being as complete as the repression of her natural self, and her own statements afford no guidance whatsoever as to her true condition and the underlying intention of the poet.

Thus critics taking Johanna's subjective sense of identification with the divine as objective fact are faced with insoluble problems arising from her actual state of dividedness, i.e. the lack of feeling she evinces towards her fellow human beings and the disastrous consequences of this when eventually feeling breaks through. Scholars here sought to deal with this problem in a variety of ways, all of which do violence to the vision of totality which lies at the heart of Schiller's drama and theory. Storz has articulated the critical dilemma most perspicaciously. If her call is genuine – and Storz argues that it is – then 'die Pflicht besteht für Johanna gerade in der vollkommenen Unnatur' ('Die Jungfrau von Orleans', *Das Deutsche Drama*, I, p. 327). Storz notes the incompatibility of this position with that of the *Ästhetische Briefe* which aim at the 'Wiederherstellung des gespaltenen Menschen' (p. 327), and the implications of accepting the terms of her mission as she herself interprets it. If so, the drama would sanction not only 'die übermenschliche Leistung der Heldin . . . , sondern zugleich die unmenschliche' (p. 328). Storz evades the problem he has himself raised by accounting for the monstrosities, into which the 'berserkerische Amazone' is driven, as springing from the stylizing tendencies of a poet who endeavoured to achieve a 'Synthese des Edlen mit dem Barbarischen' (p. 333), as Goethe did in the contemporaneous Helena sequences of *Faust* II. B. v. Wiese similarly asserts that 'Johanna wird nicht etwa idealisiert, wohl aber auf mythisch verfremdende Weise stilisiert' (II, p. 730). But he does not choose such an easy way out as Storz; he insists both on Johanna's inhumanity (pp. 732 ff.) and on the inhumanity of a mission which is incompatible with natural, human let alone beautiful promptings (ibid. p. 738; III, p. 305; *NA*, 9, ed. v. Wiese and L. Blumenthal, pp. 395 f.). Thus he is driven to the conclusion that hers is 'keine sittliche,

sondern eine metaphysische Schuld' (ibid.; also III, p. 304, and II, p. 738). It is no accident that v. Wiese, in this portion of his interpretation, heavily leans on Hebbel's criticism of the play. The category of a metaphysical guilt which he has to invoke is as alien to Schiller as it is natural to Hebbel.

Staiger deals with Johanna's cruel plight and active cruelty in a manner that is entirely characteristic of this book. Darting from work to author and back again, he simply gleans from it that uncommitted and luciferic quality of greatness which to him, *a priori*, constitutes the hallmark of Schiller's own character, and writes: 'Welche seltsame Zimperlichkeit, ihm eine solche Bewunderung heroischer Grausamkeit und Rührung über ihr schwaches Gefäß nicht zuzutrauen!' (op. cit. p. 402). Indeed, he goes so far as to assert that Johanna's leniency towards Lionel is 'Schwäche und Schuld, Schwäche, die einmal sichtbar sein muß, damit wir das Maß ihrer Größe besitzen' (p. 403). Witte goes furthest in facing the ugly implications of a reading based on the acceptance of Johanna's own interpretation of her divine mission. He takes exception to the caprice of divinity 'degrading Joan after having exalted her, and restoring her just as arbitrarily' (op. cit. p. 179). Kommerell operates with a radically dualistic antimony between idea and world (applicable, he concedes, within the world of Schiller's tragedies but not to his aesthetic thought) and concludes that Johanna symbolizes 'das Mißverhältnis von Idee und Menschheit überhaupt . . .' (*Geist und Buchstabe*, etc., pp. 162 ff.).

If we sum up and reconsider the explanations that have been advanced on the hypothesis that the awareness of the dramatic character is identical with the intentions of the poet, i.e. that Johanna is in fact identified with the divine because she feels herself to be so identified, we come upon evasions of the problems raised by such readings (Storz and Staiger) or find that the answers raise more problems than they solve (Wiese – metaphysical guilt; Witte – divinity become diabolical; Kommerell – a dualistic scheme which is not valid for some areas of Schiller's thinking).

What unites these divergent readings is the almost universal rejection of a commonsense psychological approach which is considered ill fitting or even indecent. My own reading makes unashamed use of psychological tools, subject at all times to the method appropriate to my discipline, i.e. textual analysis and the evidence furnished by it.

6 Schiller wrote of Gustav Adolf, his favourite historical hero: 'Gern verwechselt er *seine* Sache mit der Sache des Himmels' (*SA*, 15, p. 207). Clearly an argumentation along such lines would not be psychologically subtler than was Schiller himself; nor would it militate against the poet's profound sympathy for his heroine.

7 A number of critics have stressed the unconscious and involuntary nature of Johanna's obedience. Cf. v. Wiese (II, p. 732) who argues that this compulsiveness is a token of the fact that she has not reached sublimity – rightly in my opinion; Witte who perceptively writes that 'Joan has no will of her own; in a kind of emotional trance she carries out the commandments of a higher power. Her encounter with Lionel finally breaks the spell' (op. cit. p. 178), but who does not see that this compulsiveness is a symptom of her guilt; Fricke, who rightly emphasizes that in her unquestioning obedience the early Johanna 'war . . . noch nicht –

sie selber. . . . Sie wird gleichsam erst wahrhaft Mensch, indem sie zu lieben beginnt' (op. cit. p. 41), but who denies that this discovery of herself has deeper existential reverberations (ibid. p. 44); and Stahl who surmises that, in *Die Jungfrau von Orleans*, 'Schiller struck out on a new line in his conception of tragic guilt by giving more weight to involuntary transgression than he had done hitherto' (op. cit. p. 124).

8 This point is clearly made by Stahl who writes that 'Johanna's guilt lies in her transgression of the limits of her mission', and rightly adds that her love of Lionel is a consequence of this (op. cit. pp. 121 f.). On the other hand, R. Miller argues that 'her idealism triumphs' in her refusal to spare Montgomery's life (op. cit. p. 118).

9 The Black Knight has long been recognized as a personification of Johanna's own doubts (by Petsch, op. cit. pp. 241 f.), as 'eine Abspaltung ihres eigenen Ichs', and by Eduard Castle in 'Der falsche Demetrius in der Auffassung Schillers und Hebbels' (*JFDH* (1930), p. 239). Such arguments are important in that they concede by implication that for all that she herself is entirely unaware of the fact, there is a concealed part of her being which is so dissociated from her that she encounters it as if it were an extraneous reality.

10 This parallel has been observed by v. Wiese, II, p. 740; cf. also *NA*, 9, pp. 397 f.

11 Cf. Chapter 1 (esp. p. 59), Chapter 7 (pp. 153 ff.), Chapter 3 (pp. 68 ff.) and Graham 'The Structure of the Personality in Schiller's Tragic Poetry' (pp. 109 ff.).

12 It is striking but perhaps not altogether surprising that the jarring note struck by Johanna in the reconciliation scene has not been

noted. Not surprising because, once Johanna's mission is accepted as divinely ordained and she is regarded as embodying 'die Fremdheit des Transzendenten inmitten einer eitlen, unreinen, herabziehenden Welt . . .' (v. Wiese, II, p. 735), any strangeness of her behaviour is accounted for in advance. In fact, her response here, to the best of my knowledge, has been commented upon only a few times and always favourably: by Bellermann who writes that it is clearly perceptible 'wie sie in all diesem friedebringenden Thun sich dem natürlichen Triebe ihres Herzens überläßt' (op. cit. Vol. II, p. 263), by Böckmann who regards the marriage suit of La Hire and Dunois as objective temptations to which her indignant response is justified ('Gedanke, Wort und Tat, etc.', p. 32) and by Miller who regards Johanna's rejection of a husband as yet another triumph of her idealism (op. cit. p. 118).

13 Bellermann regards these words as the appropriate reaction to an embarrassing and humiliating conversation. He, as much as any other critic, fails to see that Schiller's view of integration is a dynamic one, revealed in a hierarchy of responses that is ever flexible and ever attuned to the changing demand of the hour. This concern, here and elsewhere, is invariably brought out by the repeated emphatic and formalized use of the antitheses 'jetzt' and 'jetzt nicht', or 'jetzt' and 'immer'. (Cf. also *Maria Stuart*, III. iii.)

14 *Die Jungfrau von Orleans* continues to probe into the theme of the tragic limitations of moral endeavour which had first presented itself to Schiller in the subordinate figure of Buttler, then had engaged his attention in the figure of Elisabeth in *Maria Stuart*, to be

fully explored in *Warbeck* and *Demetrius*. B. v. Wiese explicitly denies that *Die Jungfrau von Orleans* is an 'Existenzanalyse' on the pattern of the two fragments (II, p. 731). In defence of my reading I would point out that Schiller himself described *Demetrius* as 'das Gegenstück' of *Die Jungfrau von Orleans*. (Quoted by Stahl, op. cit. p. 150.)

15 Kommerell has noted this fact but, in keeping with his premiss that there exists an objective and absolute antinomy between the idea and human life, has accorded it a metaphysical rather than psychological interpretation: 'Die gestellte Frage ist: Wie erlebt das Göttliche sein Leben in einem menschlichen Leib? . . . Wiederum erlebt der Träger der Idee das höchste menschliche Gefühl als Verrat. Das Gefühl ist der Feind: Die dramatische Anschaulichkeit dieser allgemeinsten Feindschaft ist es, daß die Jungfrau gerade ihren Feind lieben muß . . . Die Idee hat sich an ihr, für das Ungeziemende jeder Verkörperung, gerächt.' (*Geist und Buchstabe*, etc., pp. 162 ff.) For a similar reading, cf. v. Wiese, II, p. 743, and I, p. 305.

16 It will by now be clear that my reading is diametrically opposed to all those which regard Johanna's initial identification with the divine as objectively valid, and the dichotomy between idea and person as absolute.

17 Cf. Chapter 1, pp. 42 f.

18 H. Ide sees a conflict between Johanna's free moral allegiance to her mission and her moral obligation towards Lionel as a fellow human being. ('Zur Problematik der Schiller-Interpretation, Überlegungen zur Jungfrau von Orleans', *Jahrbuch der Wittheit zu Bremen*, Vol. VIII (1964), p. 83.) Ide misses the point that Johanna is only capable

of being free when she comes face to face with Lionel and, through him, with the ignored part of herself which had exercised the concealed motive-force of all her actions.

19 Cf. Chapter 7, pp. 161 ff.
20 Cf. Stahl, op. cit. p. 128.
21 Cf. Chapter 10, pp. 283 ff.
22 Miller exhibits this popular critical fallacy in its crudest form, when he writes: 'The proof of her sublimity is the sacrifice she makes in suppressing her natural self' (op. cit. p. 113). Cysarz, on the other hand, comes closest to my own view when he writes: '. . . als leidender Mensch, nicht als Heilige, macht sie den Geist zum Beweger der irdischen Dinge' (*Schiller*, p. 356). For a further discussion of this concept, cf. Chapter 12.

Chapter 9

This chapter is a modified version of an article which appeared in German in *Neophilologus* (1960). For its translation I am profoundly indebted to my friend Tom Eason without whose unsparing help it would have remained piecework.

1 H. Voß der Jüngere, *Schillers Gespräche*, ed. Frh. von Biedermann (Munich, n.d.), p. 368.
2 B. v. Wiese stresses the 'Naturverbundenheit' of the characters and the inseparable oneness of 'Menschenwelt und Natur' (II, pp. 768 f.). Similarly, Storz writes that the drama projects a 'Bild des Einklangs von Menschentum und Natur' (*Der Dichter F. Schiller*, p. 406). G. W. McKay stresses the 'mythical solidarity' between the Swiss and their land, in 'Three Scenes from *Wilhelm Tell*', in *The Discontinuous Tradition*, Studies in German Literature in Honour of E. L. Stahl, ed. P. F. Ganz (Oxford, 1971), p. 105.
3 In fact, Witte regards the play as being centrally concerned with political freedom: 'Instead of an individual protagonist caught in the coils of a tragic fate . . . it depicts a national community successfully rebelling against repression; instead of the hero's inward freedom, the political freedom of the people is the issue' (op. cit. p. 187). This leads Witte to conclude that 'a community, not a person, is the hero of the play' (ibid. p. 191). The priority of the public cause or the personal action centred in Tell and the relation between the two is of course the most widely debated issue of the play. Critical opinion on this point is discussed in note 26. My own interpretation of the interaction between the political and the personal spheres of the drama, here as always, is governed by the perception of verbal links mediating between the two and, in particular, by the awareness of Schiller's steady employment of the technique of externalization. Cf. Chapter 1 and my 'Structure of the Personality, etc.'
4 B. v. Wiese stresses '. . . die urtümlichen, naturhaften und so gar nicht künstlichen Ordnungen des politischen Lebens . . .' (II, p. 769).
5 In the dedicatory lines that Schiller wrote in a copy of Tell for his patron, the Kurfürst of Mainz, K. T. von Dalberg, he describes the Swiss as '. . . ein Volk, das fromm die Herden weidet'.
6 B. v. Wiese, similarly, holds that nature, in this drama, is 'ein Gleichnis für die Idee der Freiheit' (II, p. 769). Gerhard expatiates on this idea when she writes: 'Als Sinnbild naturhaft freien und *harmonisch schönen* Lebens erscheint

die Schweizer Umwelt in Schillers Werk' (op. cit. p. 414, my italics). But this description ignores the element of constriction which characterizes both the mountain world and the experience of freedom which is fostered, and reflected, by such surroundings (cf. III. i; III. iii and V. ii). W. Mainland has pointed out the 'sublime and even terrifying, character of the landscape which Tell describes to Parricida (*Wilhelm Tell*, ed. W. Mainland, Macmillan's Modern Language Texts (London, Melbourne, Toronto, 1968), p. lxv), and linked its forbidding aspect with Tell's own longing for expiation. But in fact the Swiss landscape as evoked in this drama is 'sublime' throughout – eloquent reflection of the constricting character of commitment, which is true freedom. This correlation comes out most clearly in Tell's conversation with his son in III. iii.

7 B. v. Wiese quotes the fisherman's description of the storm as proof that 'Geßlers Tat als Ursünde des Bösen gegen die Natur und die aus ihr hervorgegangenen Ordnungen verstanden werden muß . . .' (II, p. 773). Similarly Buchwald writes: 'Die Natur selbst, die wir in der Rütliszene so großartig mithandeln sahen, empört sich in wildem Grimm über den Frevel, der durch Geßler geschehen ist (op. cit. Vol. II, p. 472).

8 For similar readings, cf. Garland who quotes Tell's words and observes: '. . . his whole nature is subjected to stresses so severe that it emerges changed and warped' (*Wilhelm Tell*, ed. H. B. Garland, Harrap's German Classics (London, 1957), p. xviii). Cf. also Mainland who argues that the murder Tell is forced to commit is a reversion to the 'alter Urstand der Natur . . .' (ed. cit. p. lix).

9 This – deceptive – simplicity, a simplicity which is at the far end of complexity, has been well characterized by Staiger who hails it as 'eine Errungenschaft . . . , [die] alle Abenteuer eines im Höchsten und Tiefsten bewanderten Geistes verschweigt und als geheime Kraft in ihrer schlichten Hülle bewahrt' (op. cit. p. 396).

10 A structural analysis, as is put forward here, furnishes an answer to critics who regard the figures of Berta, Rudenz and Melchthal and the action centred in them as being extraneous to the main concern of the play. Cf. Storz (*Der Dichter F. Schiller*, pp. 417 f.) and Garland who considers that the lovers owe their regrettable existence to the same 'enthusiastic participation' on the part of the poet which gave rise to Max and Thekla (ed. cit. p. xxii).

11 Cf. *Ästhetische Briefe*, Letter XXVI, 6: 'In dem Auge und dem Ohr ist die andringende Materie schon hinweggewälzt von den Sinnen, und das Objekt entfernt sich von uns, das wir in den tierischen Sinnen unmittelbar berühren. . . . Der Gegenstand des Taktes ist eine Gewalt, die wir erleiden; der Gegenstand des Auges und des Ohrs ist eine Form, die wir erzeugen. . . . Sobald er [der Mensch] anfängt, mit dem Auge zu genießen, und das Sehen für ihn einen selbstständigen Wert erlangt, so ist er auch schon ästhetisch frei, und der Spieltrieb hat sich entfaltet.' Perhaps influenced by this passage, Goethe states a very similar view: 'Das Gesicht', we read in *Maximen und Reflexionen*, 'ist der edelste Sinn. Die andern vier belehren uns nur durch die Organe des Takts: wir hören, wir fühlen, riechen und betasten alles durch Berührung; das Gesicht aber steht unendlich höher, verfeint sich über die Materie und nähert sich den

Fähigkeiten des Geistes.' (*Wilhelm Meisters Wanderjahre, AGA,* 9, p. 600).

12 Melchthal's effusions have often been harshly criticised as intrusions of the poet's own reflective and rhetorical vein into a character and context ill fitted to accommodate such flights of the imagination. (Cf. Gerhard, op. cit. p. 490, and Storz, *Der Dichter F. Schiller,* pp. 418 f.) Such criticisms are grounded in the failure to perceive the central role played in this drama by the symbol of the eye, as the point of intersection between spirit and sense. I have no doubt but that Kleist, in whose work perception plays a decisive role, was profoundly influenced by Schiller's drama and Melchthal's speeches in particular. In the face of such objections it is useful to remember Mainland's wise admonition: 'If we do not accept artifice, Schiller's mature art will remain entirely alien to us.' (Ed. cit. p. xlii.)

13 The diabolical unnaturalness of Geßler's command has been stressed by v. Wiese (II, pp. 772 and 775), Storz who writes that this scene represents 'die schrecklichste Überwältigung der Natur durch die Unnatur' (*Der Dichter F. Schiller,* p. 420), Garland (I, p. 234), and, especially, by Mainland who rightly stresses the tragic potentialities of the drama throughout his reading (ed. cit.).

14 Bellermann has taken exception to Rudenz's words, writing: 'Rudenz hat dies noch niemals getan, sein Herz ist noch nie empört oder überschwellend gewesen, sondern er hat mit kühler Weisheit seine Landsleute . . . über die thörichte Verkennung ihres wahren Nutzens belehrt.' (Op. cit. Vol. II, p. 505.) We may leave out of account Bellermann's euphoric view of Rudenz's 'wisdom'. More interest-

ing is his criticism of Rudenz's words. It rests on the failure to perceive the close-knit verbal texture of the play and the imports accruing to it through its rigorous formal structuring. Rudenz is about to discover what Fürst will later call 'sein wiederkehrend Herz . . .' (IV. ii). But, having suppressed its promptings, he now is at its mercy, just as Tell, who has never denied his heart, at this precise moment shows himself to be master of his feelings.

15 This silence has been variously interpreted. Garland and Böckmann come nearest to the reading advanced here. Garland writes that 'the silent resolve and swift action entirely fits Tell's character' (I, p. 242); Böckmann stresses that 'für ihn hat das entschlossne Tun immer den Vorrang vor dem Gedanken und dem Wort' ('Gedanke, Wort und Tat in Schillers Dramen', p. 36). Staiger adduces a somewhat indifferent explanation not uncharacteristic of the peremptory fashion in which he tends to deal with a poet whom he himself charges with peremptoriness. The laconic treatment Tell receives in the 'Apfelschußszene', he argues, is due to the fact that 'in der Apfelschußszene so viel geschieht, daß schon die Ereignisse selber leidenschaftliche Anteilnahme verbürgen und aller Redeprunk sich erübrigt' (op. cit. p. 385).

16 Garland makes many just points in a comparison of *Don Carlos* and *Wilhelm Tell,* both of which are concerned with the theme of oppression. He opposes Marquis Posa's width of vision to the limited outlook of the farmers' characters of the later play who 'see no farther than the oppression under which they themselves suffer. Yet what they lose in breadth and distance of vision they gain in balance and solidity' (I, p. 248). This com-

parison has some justice. Yet characters such as Attinghausen, Rudenz and Hedwig no less than the passages under discussion show that as a general statement about the figures of *Wilhelm Tell* Garland's formulation is untenable. It is applicable to Tell alone in a fashion which will become apparent. It is true, Schiller has relegated to the periphery of this non-tragic drama traits which we associate not only with Posa but with his tragic protagonists in general. But they are none the less there, and fulfil their specific function in serving as a foil for Tell's own close-knit integration or what Garland calls 'solidity'.

17 Precisely this contemplative character is attributed to Tell by F. Martini ('Wilhelm Tell, der ästhetische Staat und der ästhetische Mensch', *DdU*, 12 (1960)). Martini rightly concludes that Tell is an 'ästhetisch gestimmter Mensch' (*Ästhetische Briefe*, Letter XXIII, 5) (cf. below pp. 211 ff.); but by this he understands a person persisting in a frozen harmonious totality and indeterminacy and refusing to accept the retrenchment of potential which is inseparable from choice, commitment and action (pp. 103 ff.). Such a protracted contemplative indeterminacy or pure disponibility is far from describing Tell – who, on the contrary, tends towards the determinacy of 'bestimmter Tat'; it is equally far from Schiller's dominant conception of 'the Whole Man', as it emerges from his theoretical writings. Schiller is at pains to point out that the aesthetic state is no more than a brief transitional state mediating between one determination and another (*Ästhetische Briefe*, Letter XXI, 5). In support of his reading of Tell's character, Martini quotes the important footnote to that paragraph. However,

he significantly omits its opening sentence which expatiates on the fleeting character of aesthetic wholeness which has already been established in the text. This footnote in fact describes, to a nicety, the spurious contemplative equipoise of Schiller's tragic protagonists who labour under the poetically fruitful but psychologically fatal illusion that they may persist in a state of aesthetic totality resisting all onesided determination. The one major figure this footnote assuredly does not describe is Wilhelm Tell, who is a whole, free and aesthetic personality in the more basic sense that he is able to respond appropriately and flexibly to the demands of different situations, subordinating his psychic faculties to whichever one is needed to master the present challenge. His delight in playful, physical prowess, his charitable forbearance when he encounters the defenceless Geßler (III. i), his self-mastery in the 'Apfelschußszene' and his unshakeable resolve to destroy the tyrant – all these testify to a dynamic and flexible totality *in time* rather than to an unchanging persistence in a sterile harmony. Because Tell is thus able to respond appropriately and flexibly, he does not fall into the trap of Schiller's tragic protagonists. He is free, the true 'Meister seines Schicksals', and the only inevitable destiny, for him, is death. It is interesting to note that Martini specifically ascribes 'Besonnenheit' to Tell, notwithstanding the fact that Tell says of himself 'Wär' ich besonnen, hieß' ich nicht der Tell'. For a discussion of the spurious contemplative equilibrium of Schiller's tragic protagonists, cf. Chapters 1, 2, 6 and 11.

For a full discussion of the psychological implications and aesthetic function of the protagonists' illusion, cf. I. Graham, *Schiller: A Master of the Tragic Form.*

18 Bellermann takes exception to Geßler's exhortation in the face of an undertaking 'bei dem im eigentlichen Sinn alles andere eher möglich ist als ein Zudrücken der Augen' (op. cit. Vol. II, p. 505). Any sharpshooter would tell him differently. More important, such objections demonstrate the failings of any reading which is not governed by regard for the verbal texture and the meanings created by it.

19 Cf. Böckmann, 'Gedanke, Wort und Tat, etc.', p. 36. Martini dubs this remark as signifying a streak of 'Quietismus' in Tell ('Wilhelm Tell, etc.', p. 102).

20 In this connection, see *Ästhetische Briefe*, Letter XIII, 6. Schiller describes the corrective and supportive interaction of sensuous drive and formal drive as follows: '. . . Jene Abspannung des sinnlichen Triebes darf aber keineswegs die Wirkung eines physichen Unvermögens und einer Stumpfheit der Empfindungen sein, welche überall nur Verachtung verdient; sie muß eine Handlung der Freiheit, eine Tätigkeit der Person sein, die durch ihre moralische Intensität jene sinnliche mäßigt und durch Beherrschung der Eindrücke ihnen an Tiefe nimmt, um ihnen an Fläche zu geben. Der Charakter muß dem Temperament seine Grenzen bestimmen, denn *nur an den Geist* darf der Sinn verlieren. Jene Abspannung des Formtriebs darf ebensowenig die Wirkung eines geistigen Unvermögens und einer Schlaffheit der Denk- oder Willenskräfte sein, welche die Menschheit erniedrigen würde. Fülle der Empfindungen muß ihre rühmliche Quelle sein . . .'

21 I must here distinguish my position from that of Martini ('Wilhelm Tell, etc.', pp. 99 f.), Gerhard (op. cit. pp.

396 ff.) and H. Reiß 'The Concept of the Aesthetic State in the work of Schiller and Novalis', *PEGS*, XXVI (1956/7), p. 26), who regard Tell's Swiss community as the realization, in dramatic form, of the theoretical concept of the Aesthetic State as developed towards the end of the *Ästhetische Briefe*. This is a position mistakenly attributed to me by Wilkinson and Willoughby in their edition of the Aesthetic Letters (p. cxcv and note 1). I am concerned to demonstrate the organic wholeness and the aesthetic modality of the central figure of the drama, Wilhelm Tell. That the community he represents does not itself possess this character of organic wholeness should be clear from the fact that its constituents – Rudenz and Melchthal, Stauffacher and Hedwig – are dramatic embodiments of part-aspects of Tell's psyche, rather than autonomous entities 'die [sich] zur Idee des Ganzen hinauf gestimmt haben' (Letter IV, 5).

22 *Ästhetische Briefe*, Letters XIV, 1 and XXV, 6.

23 Both these strands are combined in Martini's reading ('Wilhelm Tell, etc.', pp. 99, 103 f., 111, and 105, 109 f.).

24 Goethe, *Polarität, AGA*, 16, p. 864.

25 *Ästhetische Briefe*, Letter XV, 9. In this connection, see Chapter 12.

26 Tell's self-sufficiency has received a wide variety of interpretations and evaluations. Storz (*Der Dichter F. Schiller*, pp. 410 ff.) and Witte (op. cit. p. 187) stress the collective character of Tell, as a representative of the common people; hence his separateness is not, for them, a factor to be reckoned with. B. v. Wiese (II, p. 770), Böckmann ('Gedanke, Wort und Tat, etc.', pp. 35 ff.), W. Muschg (*Die Tragödie der Freiheit* (Berne and Munich, 1959)), M. Jolles ('Die Sprache des

"Spiels" und "Antispiels", etc.', p. 252) and Buchwald (op. cit. Vol. II, pp. 475 f.) stress Tell's isolated and autonomous position, but on varying grounds argue that his personal cause coincides with that of the Confederates. Most convincing is Buchwald's formulation: 'Tell ist nicht ein allenfalls entschuldbarer Einzelgänger, und die Tellhandlung nicht eine Sonderaktion neben dem historischen Hauptvorgang. Die Rettung geschieht im ganzen Schauspiel wie in der Eingangsszene des ersten Aktes durch die Tat des Einzelnen. Und *seine* Not ist die Not *seines* Nächsten und Heiligsten, nämlich von Frau und Kind; *diese* Not gibt ihm Kraft und Entschluß und macht ihn auch schuldlos gegenüber der Gesamtheit, . . . und noch mehr gegenüber dem Sittengesetz . . . die Tat des großen Einzelnen, aus eigenster Not geboren, [dient] dennoch dem Ganzen . . .' (Op. cit. Vol. II, pp. 437 f.) For a discussion of the place of personal motivation in moral conduct, cf. Chapter 1, pp. 32 f. Stahl takes a critical view of the interlacing of the two strands of action, the private and the public cause, arguing that they do not coincide and that 'the closing tableau . . . is . . . Schiller's belated attempt to establish a unity which the play, in effect, does not possess' (op. cit. pp. 142 and 144 f.). The more problematic aspects of the relation between the hero and his people and their cause are elaborated by Martini ('Wilhelm Tell, etc.', p. 103), by W. Kohlschmidt who argues that Tell matures from an initial and questionable aloofness to an acceptance of his involvement in historicity ('Tells Entscheidung', *Gedenkjahr 59* (Stuttgart, 1961), pp. 90 ff.) and by W. G. Moore ('A new reading of "Wilhelm Tell"', *German Studies*

presented to H. G. Fiedler (Oxford, 1938)) who stresses the tragic possibilities inherent in the play. Most impressively, the relation between the solitary man and the popular myth, of which he is the centre and victim, has been developed by Mainland (ed. cit. pp. lv ff.).

27 The crossbow has repeatedly figured in readings of the play. R. Schneider, who finds the non-tragic issue of the drama unconvincing, objects to the fact that Tell, incredibly, sacrifices nothing but his bow. 'Es ist schwer zu begreifen,' he writes, 'daß in diesem einen und einzigen Falle die Realisierung der Freiheit in der Geschichte ohne Tragik abgehen soll.' ('Tragik und Erlösung im Weltbild Schillers', *Schiller. Reden im Gedenkjahr 1955* (Stuttgart, 1955), p. 297.) As against that, Mainland urges that the sacrifice of Tell's bow and, with it, of his native vocation, signifies hidden depths of tragedy which form the undercurrent to the popular legend. 'The bow has been used to carry out a cruel order and then to kill a man.' Were Tell to use it, it would be 'the constant reminder of an ordeal and a murder' (ed. cit. pp. lxviii f.). Perhaps this reading is tinged by associations with Kleist's *Penthesilea*. In any case it represents a challenging and welcome change from the cheerful trivialities that have been written about this play. Although I take the crossbow as being pre-eminently a symbol of an inner-psychological state, Mainland's reading and mine are perfectly compatible and, indeed, complementary. What is common to both is the awareness that Tell, for all that he survives and is celebrated as 'a model of propriety' (Stahl, op. cit. p. 145), will never again be the man he was before his inhuman ordeal. His murder of another is a form of death, not

unlike that which, on the imaginative plane, Iphigenie endures when she realizes that she may have to kill her brother.

28 This inwardness has been repeatedly stressed, both as the dominant feature of this monologue and, more problematically, as a trait inherent in Tell's make-up. Cf. Mainland (ed. cit. pp. lii f. and lv ff.) and Kohlschmidt who argues that the crux of the monologue is 'ein ganz individueller sittlicher Konflikt', designed 'die Schmerzhaftigkeit dieses Überganges aus der unbefleckten, in sich ruhenden sittlichen Sphäre in die der Politik sinnfällig zu machen' (op. cit. pp. 96 ff.). Martini sees in it an immersion in a dream-like state of inwardness and contemplation ('Wilhelm Tell, etc.', p. 109).

29 And of course, of his solidarity with his family and the community at large. The connection between his concern for his family and the public cause has often been observed. Cf. Storz who writes: 'Allein um seine eigene Sache geht es ihm auch jetzt, aber diese ist in ihrer Eigenheit zugleich der große Gegenstand der verletzten und nun wiederherzustellenden Ur-Ordnung' (*Der Dichter F. Schiller*, pp. 420 f.); or v. Wiese who reiterates at this point a theme which is crucial to his book as a whole. Political murder, he argues, is justified to safeguard 'die Familie, die Urzelle alles gemeinschaftlichen Lebens . . .' (II, p. 772). In avenging 'die "holde Unschuld" seiner "lieben Kinder" und das eigene Eheweib', Tell avenges 'die beleidigte "heilige Natur" . . .' (p. 773). But it is important to see that for Schiller the integrity of the individual psychic organism is the nucleus of that natural – and moral – order which pervades larger structures such as family and state.

30 In *Geschichte des dreißigjährigen Kriegs* Schiller writes: 'Es bleibt eine ewige Wahrheit, daß eine Gewalttätigkeit, wenn die Weisheit sie gebietet, nie dem Gewalttätigen darf aufgetragen werden, daß nur demjenigen aufgetragen werden darf, die Ordnung zu verletzen, dem sie heilig ist.' (*SA*, 15, p. 56.) Tell's deed and the motives leading up to it have been variously assessed. Stahl somewhat surprisingly denies that there is, in Tell, 'any conflict between duty and inclination . . .' Tell performs no more than 'an arduous task' and thereby achieves 'an untragic form of sublimity' (op. cit. p. 144). Martini, Moore and Mainland, among others, rightly stress the agonizing nature of Tell's choice and ensuing action. Martini, however, is more preoccupied with Tell's supposed reluctance to exchange 'die spontane, unbeschränkte Aktivität der ganzen Person in der Fülle ihrer Kräfte, also die Freiheit zu dem höchsten "Spiel"' ('Wilhelm Tell, etc.', p. 104) in favour of any determinate action whatever than with the fact that the action Tell is faced with happens to be a murder. Moore and Mainland rightly stress this fact and its tragic and ironic implications. Mainland forcefully drives home the paradox that 'to become, incidentally, the hero of his people, Tell has to relinquish all principles of conduct but those of the hunter' (ed. cit. p. lix).

31 For the function of compassion as a factor inducing psychical distance, cf. Chapter 12. Martini has rightly stressed the aesthetic nature and function of this monologue. It is regrettable that this conclusion, correct in itself, should have been based on such radically false premisses (cf. note 17). Contrary to the thesis advanced here, Mainland is at pains to emphasize the unmiti-

gated agony which finds utterance in the obsessional language of a soliloquy which is 'the frenzied articulation of a resolve to destroy a fellow-man . . .' (ed. cit. p. lviii). 'What we witness in the monologue' – Mainland writes – 'is the terrifying caesura or hiatus of self-judgement in a man forced by circumstance beyond reach of the injunction: "Nichts von Klagen über die Erschwerung des Lebens . . . über Unterdrückung, Verfolgung; allen *Uebeln* der Kultur mußt du mit freier Resignation dich unterwerfen." Tell has tried resignation, and his son's life has been threatened. . . . Tell experiences the turmoil of sudden involvement; the frenzy of the monologue springs from a violence of compulsion he has never known before.' (Ed. cit., p. lix.) Mainland is here urging tragic potentialities no doubt inherent in the drama at the expense of those aesthetic considerations which must surely have been in the mind of the author of the essay *Über den Gebrauch des Chors in der Tragödie*. Frenzy is not likely to be the mood in which Schiller wished to portray a balanced man at this climactic moment of his career, or which he wished to whip up in his spectators. Besides, Tell's vociferous lapse from that stoic acceptance which the passage from *Über naive und sentimentalische Dichtung* commends, may be prompted by reasons other than his despair; it may be dictated by ultimate aesthetic considerations on the part of the poet. In this connection, see Chapter 12, pp. 321 ff.

Such criticisms, however, are not meant to detract from the overall merit of a reading which refuses to gloss over the gravity of the deed exacted from Tell; a reading moreover which is strongly supported by Schiller's startling in-timation to W. v. Wolzogen, early on in his work on the play, that he envisaged working up his material into 'eine große Tragödie' (4 Sept. 1803).

32 H. Nohl aptly describes the end of the play as '. . . eine restlose Auflösung aller Trennung, eine vollständige Umarmung' (*Friedrich Schiller* (Frankfurt am Main, 1954), p. 105).

33 F. Schnapp, 'Schiller über seinen "Wilhelm Tell", mit unbekannten Dokumenten', *Deutsche Rundschau*, 206 (1926), p. 107. The history of this important statement is an interesting one and not easy to piece together from studies that are readily accessible. Iffland, the director of the Royal National Theatre in Berlin, wrote to Schiller on 7 April 1804, saying that he had some misgivings concerning several passages in *Wilhelm Tell*. He suggested that his secretary, H. Pauly, should personally discuss the problematic passages with Schiller when he came to Weimar. Pauly duly arrived and met Schiller in the second week of April, probably on 10 April. He had brought along with him a questionnaire prepared by Iffland, and Schiller straight away entered his replies in the column adjoining the questions. As regards the monologue in the sunken lane, Iffland complained that during his reading of it his initial tension got dissipated: '. . . aber ich weiß nicht, was sich inwendig regte und mir zuflüsterte: So lange sollte *Tell* vor dem Morde nicht da stehen und mit sich allein dabei reden.' (Schnapp, op. cit. pp. 107 f.) The crux of Schiller's reply is the statement quoted in the text. The questionnaire, with Schiller's comments, was discovered by Schnapp in the Iffland files of the Berlin Staatstheater where it is still kept.

Chapter 10

This chapter has appeared in *MLR*, Vol. 66 (July 1971). Some references to Schiller's fragments which are not in *SA*, are according to the text of *Werke*, Bibliographisches Institut, ed. L. Bellermann (Leipzig and Vienna). The edition is referred to as *BI*.

1 In *Glückliches Ereignis*, *AGA*, 16, p. 866.
2 Ibid. p. 876.
3 *SA*, 11, pp. 208 f. It is now generally assumed that the passage was aimed at Bürger or Heinse rather than at Goethe himself. But it is thought equally certain that Goethe understood it as referring to himself. Cf. *SA*, 11, p. 330; *NA*, 21, p. 226 and v. Wiese, II, p. 470.
4 *SA*, 11, p. 209, footnote.
5 *AGA*, 16, p. 866.
6 In a letter to Zelter, 30 Oct. 1808.
7 *SA*, 11, p. 185.
8 Ibid. p. 213.
9 Ibid. p. 229.
10 *Italienische Reise*, III, Rome, 6 Sept. 1787.
11 *SA*, 11, pp. 214 f.
12 Ibid. p. 184. I note with delight that Thomas Mann advances the identical argument supported by the same illustrations ('Goethe und Tolstoi, Fragmente zum Problem der Humanität', *Adel des Geistes* (Stockholm, 1955), p. 200). Altogether Mann's argument, in so far as it bears on Schiller, is in close accord with my own approach and conclusions here.
13 *SA*, 11, p. 196.
14 Ibid. p. 195.
15 Ibid. p. 208, footnote.
16 Letter II.
17 Letter VIII.
18 Cf. Schiller to Goethe, 23 Aug. 1794, in which Schiller makes just this point, and Goethe's enthusiastic reply of 27 Aug. 1794.
19 *SA*, 11, p. 217.
20 *SA*, 18, p. 65.
21 *SA*, 11, p. 208, footnote.
22 Ibid.; for an opposite view cf.

Cysarz who categorically denies that biological and natural qualities have any part in Schiller's conception of moral aristocracy (*Schiller*, pp. 202 f.).
23 The term has been used generically by F. Prader and v. Wiese in an attempt to isolate a certain type of character recurring throughout Schiller's dramas. Prader describes such figures as predominantly lyrical, possessed of that inner harmony between conscious and unconscious which Schiller designates by the term 'schöne Seele', and deriving from the age of sensibility. Their function in the total economy of Schiller's plays, according to him, is the aesthetic one of balancing the tragic emotions of fear and terror by those of pity and 'Rührung' ('Schiller und Sophokles', pp. 49 ff.). B. v. Wiese adopts Prader's nomenclature but develops his thesis in another, less formalistic direction. According to him, '"die Kinder des Hauses" sind die Gotteskinder, die reinen schönen Seelen, die das Haus Gottes niemals verlassen, mag Schiller diese ewige Heimat auch verschieden benennen, sei es als "Natur" oder als "das Heilige", als "Herz" oder als "Wahrheit", als "Ideal" oder als "Schönheit"' (II, p. 788). 'Sie sind zwar nicht die letzten Christen, aber dennoch die letzten, die reinen Herzens sind' (ibid.). This is perceptive, but it is also loose and positively misleading. The meaning of the term 'Die Kinder des Hauses' cannot be explicated in terms of vaguely moral and religious categories taken from the stock of German idealism. The

exciting and indeed revolutionary thing about this conception is that it designates a cluster of basically amoral qualities – those natural excellences Schiller characterizes when he says that Maria Stuart outshines her rival '. . . durch Gestalt nicht minder als Geburt'. Investing as he does a morally indifferent natural aristocracy with moral and indeed religious significance, Schiller is much more the precursor of Nietzsche than the heir of the age of sensibility.

B. v. Wiese interprets the exile of the 'Kinder des Hauses' factually, in close connection with his basic thesis that relationships within the family are representative of the various ways in which a person is at home ('zu Hause') in society, the world and with God: '. . . Die Kategorie von Haus und Familie steht seit Schillers Jugend im engsten Zusammenhang mit der des Tragischen, weil eben dieses Tragische mit der Zerstörung des Hauses und der Familie beginnt' (p. 787). Thus, being exiled, they are 'schutzlos der Willkür und Gemeinheit einer brutal realen, unbehausten Welt preisgegeben . . . im schuldhaft befleckten Dasein wie Fremdlinge, deren heimlicher höherer Ursprung nicht mehr erkannt wird . . .' (p. 788). This is correct as far as it goes, but it does not go nearly far enough. The 'home', besides being a symbol of oneness with family, society or God, for Schiller is also always a symbol of inner oneness, of being at home with oneself. 'Die Kinder des Hauses' are those who, trusting their natural endowment, feel at home as it were in their own skin, and tragedy begins where this at-home-ness is disrupted. This inner-psychological meaning, which is the centre of the interpretation advanced by me here and elsewhere, is nowhere touched upon by v. Wiese.

Conversely, I would argue that the exile of the 'Kinder des Hauses' signifies much more than the victimization of creatures that are uncomplicated in themselves, at the hands of a vulgar and deceitful world. It is rather the condition of being divided within themselves and disturbed in their naïve and unreflecting relation to themselves which Schiller, in love with innocence yet unable to resist teasing and tormenting it, could not help invoking in drama upon drama. Here I find myself in accord with critics like Thomas Mann, Fricke, and Storz who have stressed that the later Schiller adumbrates problems of consciousness and identity which altogether threaten to disrupt the ideological framework of Schiller's classicism and point forward to the Romantic age and to Kleist in particular. Cf. note 68.

24 *Wallensteins Tod*, II. iii.
25 Cf. Schiller's letter to Goethe, 31 Aug. 1794.
26 *SA*, 11, p. 213.
27 Ibid. p. 215.
28 Ibid. p. 219.
29 Ibid.
30 Ibid.
31 I am choosing this rendering for 'der uneigennützige Affekt in der edelsten Brust' rather than, say, 'innate nobility', because 'nobility', with its associations of idealistic uplift, would obscure Schiller's basic position. Besides, the strong physical overtones both of 'Affekt' and 'Brust' would seem to warrant such an emphasis.
32 Ibid.
33 Ibid. p. 220.
34 Römer VIII, 14–17. I have quoted this passage in Luther's translation to bring out the verbal parallels with Schiller's text. Cf. also Galater IV, 1–7.
35 Romans 8: 7–8.
36 Romans 9: 15–17.

37 *SA*, 11, p. 220.
38 This correlation between inner and outer rank is vehemently denied by Cysarz who writes: 'Es ist nicht Menschenrecht, es ist Theater-Moral, daß der Wuchs einen Anspruch auch auf das Kleid gebe, daß einer, weil Prinz von Beschaffenheit, den Prinzen von Abstammung spielen dürfe' (*Schiller*, p. 403).
39 Cf. Chapter 3.
40 In 'The Structure of the Personality in Schiller's Tragic Poetry'. Cf. also Chapter 1.
41 Cf. pp. 11 ff.
42 III. ii.
43 *SA*, 8, p. 233.
44 Ibid. p. 230.
45 Ibid. p. 233.
46 Ibid. p. 135.
47 *BI*, 10, pp. 140 f.
48 Ibid. pp. 137 f.
49 Especially in IV. ix.
50 For a detailed discussion of this point cf. Chapter 3.
51 Schiller to Goethe, 20 Aug 1799.
52 *SA*, 8, p. 96.
53 Ibid. p. 118.
54 Ibid. pp. 86 f.
55 Ibid. p. 118.
56 *BI*, 10, p. 466.
57 Ibid. p. 319.
58 20 Aug. 1799.
59 *BI*, 10, pp. 146 f.
60 *SA*, 8, p. 119.
61 Ibid. p. 120.
62 Ibid.
63 Ibid. p. 121.
64 Ibid. p. 132, footnote.
65 Ibid.
66 Ibid. p. 137, footnote.
67 *BI*, 10, p. 150.
68 I am aware of the fact that these words might equally describe Kleist's experience of consciousness. In perceiving, in the late work of Schiller, strong Kleistian overtones, I find myself at one with Fricke, 'Die Problematik des Tragischen im Drama Schillers', pp. 59 and 63, and Storz, *Der Dichter F. Schiller*,

pp. 487 and 490. W. Binder, on the other hand, expressly denies the presence of Kleistian traits (in 'Schillers Demetrius', *Euphorion*, Dritte Folge, 53. Band (1959), p. 266), a position which cannot, in my opinion, be consistently maintained together with an essentially Kleistian statement such as this one: '. . . dem Sündenfall des Bewußtseins folgt die Vertreibung aus dem Paradies des Seins . . .' (ibid. p. 278), or indeed with the tenor of Binder's argument as a whole.
69 Cf. Staiger, *Friedrich Schiller*, pp. 136 and 409.
70 To Körner, 25 May 1792.
71 In this connection, cf. Thomas Mann, *Versuch über Schiller*, p. 70; Staiger, *Friedrich Schiller*, p. 80; and Schiller, *On the Aesthetic Education of Man*, ed. cit., pp. xxxv and 326 (Glossary).
72 In his treatment of *Warbeck*, v. Wiese comes close to the position maintained here. 'In seiner Konsequenz würde das bedeuten,' he writes: 'es gibt einen Adel der Natur, des Geschlechts, der bereits angeboren und von den Vorfahren ererbt ist . . .' (II, p. 785). He considers, however, that for Schiller to have adopted this conception in earnest would have meant the disruption of his total ideological framework and that, for this reason, he could not finish *Warbeck*. In the immediately adjoining discussion of 'Die Kinder des Hauses', v. Wiese has already dropped this conception like a red-hot brick and proceeds to interpret the fragment and the term derived from it along conventional lines (cf. note 23). But what if the dramatist Schiller had thought this revolutionary conception of an aristocracy of nature through to the end and had come to conclusions that consistently disrupt the framework of transcendental idealism in which

he is supposedly moving? This chapter, tracing as it does the motif of inborn aristocracy through the length and breadth of Schiller's work and culminating in *Demetrius*, suggests that a review of Schiller's moral categories is perhaps timely. Cf. also Appelbaum-Graham: 'The Structure of the Personality in Schiller's Tragic Poetry', pp. 134 ff.

73 Cf. v. Wiese, II, p. 802; Cysarz, *Schiller*, p. 394; and Fricke, op. cit. pp. 64 ff. On the other hand, Wolfgang Wittkowski cogently argues the case that Demetrius is from the beginning motivated by a lust for power which organically issues in despotism at the perepeteia, in an article which at many points supports my own position: 'Demetrius – Schiller und Hebbel', *JbdDSG*, 3 (1959), pp. 142 ff. F. M. Fowler, although critical of Wittkowski, tentatively comes to a similar conclusion: 'The crisis may then be seen as bringing out his full weakness, altering his behaviour rather than his essential character.' ('The Riddle of Schiller's "Demetrius"', *MLR*, LXI, No. 3 (July 1966), p. 454.)

74 *BI*, 10, p. 304.
75 Ibid. p. 309.
76 Ibid. pp. 304, 327, 340, 465 and 469.
77 *SA*, 11, p. 240.
78 Ibid. p. 87.
79 Ibid. p. 68.
80 Schiller expatiates on this motif in his notes for Act IV. Cf. *SA*, 8, p. 79.
81 To Eckermann, 23 March 1829.
82 *SA*, 8, p. 73.
83 Ibid. p. 73.
84 Ibid. p. 74.
85 Ibid. p. 75.
86 Ibid. p. 147.
87 *BI*, 10, p. 167.

88 *SA*, 8, p. 71.
89 This interpretation is diametrically opposed to that of Binder who sees in Demetrius a genuinely naïve character, saying: 'Die Person des Demetrius ist in sich eins und ganz, nicht, weil sie *nicht mehr* gespalten wäre, sondern weil sie *noch nicht* gespalten ist' ('Schillers Demetrius', p. 266). Staiger follows Binder in formulations such as this: 'Die Schuld des Demetrius ist gerade durch das [motiviert], was seinen Zauber ausmacht, sein zu naiv-begnadetem Dasein geeignetes Wesen . . .' (*Friedrich Schiller*, p. 327). With this it is difficult to reconcile his later statement that Demetrius's demand that Marfa *pretend* to be his mother is 'ein Schiller selbst vermutlich unbewußtes und doch abgründiges Gleichnis für sein Verhältnis zur Natur' (p. 409). As against this, Thomas Mann's reading furnishes welcome corroboration of my thesis: 'Man sieht, das ist die psychologische Skizze von etwas Ungeheuerlichem. Erwägt man, was für einen Künstler, einen Dichter, der Glaube an sich selbst, seine Echtheit und Reinheit, seinen Adel, seine Menschheitssendung bedeutet, so hat die Intensität etwas Furchtbares, mit der ein solcher . . . den Gedanken der Falschheit durchlebt und durchwühlt, den Gedanken der Täuschung und des Blendwerks . . .' (*Versuch über Schiller*, p. 116.)
90 Goethe to Eckermann, 18 Jan. 1827. Similarly Thomas Mann in *Adel des Geistes* (pp. 178 f. and 202 f.).
91 *SA*, 8, p. 12.
92 Ibid. p. 99.
93 *BI*, 10, p. 343.
94 Cf. note 1.
95 *AGA*, 23, p. 807.

Chapter 11

1 On 5 July 1797.

2 B. v. Wiese quotes from Schiller's 'thank you' letter to Goethe, without mention of *Laokoon* but comments: 'Das Drama "Wallenstein" ist nicht zuletzt auch ein überdauerndes Zeugnis dafür, wie sehr Schiller im Umgang mit Goethe noch über sich selbst hinausgelangt und doch dabei sich selber treu geblieben ist' (II, p. 630).

3 Of course, Schiller had already shown his preoccupation with the Laocoon debate as early as 1793 when he illustrated his conception of the *Pathetische* in the essay *Über das Pathetische*, quoting at length from Winckelmann's description of the statue (*NA*, 20, pp. 205 f.) and operating with Lessing's notion of the pregnant moment (ibid. p. 201).

4 *Friedrich Schiller*, p. 339.

5 *Der Briefwechsel zwischen Schiller und Goethe*, ed. E. Staiger (Frankfurt, 1966), p. 468 n.

6 *Die Symbolik von Faust II* (Frankfurt, 1964), p. 241.

7 *Die Zeit als Einbildungskraft des Dichters* (Zürich, 1963), p. 130. Cf. also Wolfgang Schadewaldt in Ernst Grumach, *Goethe und die Antike* (Berlin, 1949), Vol. II, p. 1004.

8 *Propyläen*, ed. W. Frhr. v. Löhneysen (Stuttgart, 1965), p. 1104.

9 *AGA*, 13, p. 192.

10 On 14 July 1797.

11 For an excellent discussion of Lessing's position, cf. F. Nolte, *Lessing's Laokoon* (Lancaster, Pa., 1940), Chapter XI, pp. 94 ff.

12 Underlying this essay, and indeed the extensive preoccupation during this period with the formative arts, is the conviction that the laws informing poetry and the visual arts are identical. Goethe states

this conviction apodictically in Letter VI of *Der Sammler und die Seinigen*, where the speaker asserts: 'Die alten Tragödienschreiber verfuhren mit dem Stoff, den sie bearbeiteten völlig wie die bildenden Künstler . . .' (*AGA*, 13, p. 292). In the paralipomenon to Letter VI we also read: 'Doch ist mir erlaubt, aus der Analogie beyder Künste . . . zu behaupten, daß der bildende Künstler eben so wie der Dichter verfuhr' (quoted in Grumach, op. cit. II, p. 557).

13 For a similar reading of Goethe's conception of *Anmut*, cf. H. Althaus, *Laokoon Stoff und Form* (Berne and Munich, 1968), p. 89. Althaus points out that Goethe's conception is nourished by Winckelmann's 'akademisches Maßbewußtsein' which was in turn based on A. R. Mengs's investigations into the proportions of the human figure (op. cit. pp. 88 and 136, footnote 23).

14 Althaus writes: 'Die Dialektik von Ruhe in der Bewegung und von Bewegung in der Ruhe schafft dem Künstler den entscheidenden Moment, der zwischen einem Noch-Nicht und Nicht-Mehr liegt, alle darin liegende Spannung in sich aufgenommen hat und damit erkennbar macht, daß die organische Disposition der Gestalten vor Beginn des Moments eine andere war und unmittelbar danach wiederum eine andere sein wird.' (Op. cit. p. 91.)

15 To Goethe, 2 Oct. 1797.

16 Althaus considers that Goethe himself does not commit himself to any of the views voiced in *Der Sammler und die Seinigen* (op. cit. p. 97). He may not do so explicitly within the work, but his statements elsewhere leave no doubt as to where his own sympathies lay.

17 Letter VI, *AGA*, 13, p. 292.
18 Ibid. p. 293.
19 Cf. note 11 of this chapter.
20 Letter V, *AGA*, 13, pp. 288 f.
21 Ibid. p. 298.
22 And in this regard his position is much closer to that of Herder than to Lessing's. In the *Kritische Wälder*, Herder attacks Lessing's strictures on the transient moment and asks: '. . . aber was ist denn eigentlich, was in der Natur nicht transitorisch, was in ihr völlig permanent wäre? Wir leben in einer Welt von Erscheinungen, wo eine auf die andre folgt und ein Augenblick den andern vernichtet . . .' (*Werke*, ed. Th. Mattias (Leipzig and Vienna, n.d.), Bibliographisches Institut, I, Erstes Wäldchen 9, p. 230.) In answer to the objection that bodies are, after all, permanent, Herder argues that in so far as they are expressive they are also transitory (ibid. p. 231). Lessing's emphasis on the stasis of art alienates it from the transitoriness of the 'ewig wandelbaren endlichen Natur' (ibid. p. 232). Goethe arrives at a similar position from the vantage point of his morphological insights. Cf. pp. 255 ff. of this Chapter.
23 Althaus notes: 'mit Lessings Transitorischem kann er [Goethe] sich nicht befreunden', but argues that the difference in their positions was after all not so great. Both fought the distorted and the unnatural in art; but whereas Lessing chastised those 'im Transitorischen enthaltenen Übergänge vom plötzlichen Auftreten zum plötzlichen Verschwinden', Goethe did not (op. cit. p. 50). Summing up, Althaus writes: 'Die unausschöpfliche Wirklichkeit des im Laokoon konkret gewordenen ''Kunstwerks'' gestattet es, die Bewegung zum Prinzip des fruchtbaren Augenblicks zu machen, wie Herder und Goethe es tun; sie läßt es aber ebenso zu, die Prägnanz

des Moments in einem gegen die Bewegung gerichteten Verharren zu erkennen.' (Op. cit. p. 51.) The sculpture itself may accommodate these two readings. But this must not lead us to minimize the basic differences of artistic temper and intellectual conviction revealed by Lessing's, Herder's and Goethe's approach to the statue.
24 *Maximen und Reflexionen, AGA*, 9, p. 538.
25 Letter to Zelter, 30 Oct. 1808.
26 *Die Zeit als Einbildungskraft des Dichters*, p. 137.
27 *Bildung und Umbildung Organischer Naturen*, Die Absicht eingeleitet, *AGA*, 17, pp. 13 f.
28 *Werke, WA*, II, 6, p. 446.
29 *Propyläen, Einleitung, AGA*, 13, pp. 141 f.
30 Cf. notes 22 and 23 of this chapter.
31 *Goethe and Lessing: The Wellsprings of Creation*, Chapter XI.
32 Cf. Clarence Ellis, *The Pebbles on the Beach*, Faber paper-covered editions (London, 1969), p. 15.
33 Even in Goethe's most sturdy affirmations of the present, the dialectic between permanence and transience remains perceptible: only transience is projected outward, as it were, into the consciousness of the spectator. Cf. Wilhelm Meister's reflections upon the perennial present of the scenes depicted in the 'Saal der Vergangenheit' (*Lehrjahre*, VIII, 5; *AGA*, p. 580); and Goethe's description of Pompeian murals: the impression of health these convey – 'die Gesundheit . . . des Moments und was diese wert ist' – is inseparable from the knowledge of the cataclysm which overtook those whose lives they represent. Under the influence of this impression, Goethe gives one of the most telling formulations of the pregnant moment: '. . . diese Gestalten geben uns das Gefühl: der Augenblick müsse prägnant und

sich selbst genug sein um ein würdiger Einschnitt in Zeit und Ewigkeit zu werden.' (Letter to Zelter, 19 Oct. 1829.)

34 Cf. v. Wiese (II, pp. 650 and 652 f.). The aesthetic and, more especially, histrionic aspect of Wallenstein has been variously noted. Cf. May (op. cit. pp. 106 f.), Binder ('Die Begriffe "Naiv" und "Sentimentalisch" in Schillers Drama', p. 155), Kommerell (*Geist und Buchstabe*, etc., pp. 210 and 215), Buchwald (op. cit. II, p. 379), Miller (op. cit. pp. 95 ff.) and Storz (*Der Dichter F. Schiller*, p. 284).

35 *AGA*, 14, p. 56.

36 By v. Wiese (II, p. 638) and Staiger (in *Friedrich Schiller*, pp. 339 f.).

37 This unreal quality of Wallenstein's freedom has often been noted. It is powerfully formulated by R. Schneider and Storz. Schneider writes: 'Wallenstein – und das ist die Schwäche der Figur – möchte die Freiheit gar nicht ausüben; er möchte nur das Gefühl ihres Genusses haben, mit ihr spielen . . .' ('Tragik und Erlösung im Weltbild Schillers', p. 291). Storz defines Wallenstein's aim as being 'frei zu sein ohne jede Grenze, aber auch ohne den Preis dafür zu erlegen . . .' (*Der Dichter F. Schiller*, p. 284) and adds: '. . . die völlige Unbegrenztheit [ist] so absurd wie unmöglich . . .' (ibid.).

38 This ambivalence in Wallenstein, who is at once *planvoll* and *planlos*, was first stressed in Goethe's review which was written with Schiller's connivance (*AGA*, 14, p. 51). It has since been noted time and again, notably by Thomas Mann (*Versuch über Schiller*, pp. 42, 49 and 55), Storz (*Der Dichter F. Schiller*, p. 281), v. Wiese (II, p. 637, and III, I, p. 263), Garland (I, p. 204), and Witte (ed. cit. p. xxxii). It is interesting that Storz

and v. Wiese (III) use the identical image: 'Wallenstein will den Lauf der Dinge anhalten und in eine unhaltbare Schwebe bannen', writes Storz, whilst v. Wiese speaks of 'ein Charakter in der Schwebe einer Situation'.

39 Letter to Goethe, 28 Nov. 1796.

40 Letter to Goethe, 2 Oct. 1797.

41 This connection between character and artistic function has been clearly seen by Seidlin (op. cit. p. 122).

42 Cf. Chapter 3. For a formulation of the same principle, i.e. one genre serving as the corrective to another, cf. letter to Goethe, 26 Dec. 1797. For a more inclusive statement of one art serving as a corrective to the other, cf. *Ästhetische Briefe*, Letter XXII.

43 Cf. especially the letter to Goethe of 28 Nov. 1796 and the letter to Körner of the same date.

44 Cf. Storz (ed.), *Wallensteins Lager, Die Piccolomini, Wallensteins Tod, Dokumente*, Rowohlts Klassiker der Literatur und Wissenschaft (Leck/Schleswig, 1967), pp. 277 f.

45 Garland notes 'the simultaneous diversity and unity of the army' as represented in *Wallensteins Lager* (II, p. 147).

46 Critical opinion on the whole inclines towards questioning the genuineness of Wallenstein's concern for *das Ganze*: cf. May, op. cit. pp. 112 f., Staiger, *Friedrich Schiller*, p. 305, Garland, II, pp. 157 f., and Schneider and Blumenthal, *NA*, 8, p. 388. As against that, Minor considers this concern to be one of Wallenstein's ennobling features (*SA*, 5, p. xxxvi).

47 Garland notes the realism of the images given over to the Wachtmeister but does not indicate their more specific nature or significance (II, p. 145).

48 Cf. note 10 of this chapter.

49 May (op. cit. pp. 176 f.) critically

notes the idealistic idiom of Illo which reflects the 'idealistische Weltansicht' to which the poet still adheres. Witte makes a similar criticism, explaining Illo's two speeches as prompted by Schiller's 'desire to maintain a uniformly elevated style', and arguing that their poetic quality 'rather blurs the portrait of Wallenstein's coarse and brutal henchman' (op. cit. p. 156). For a more detailed assessment of the figure of Illo, cf. Chapter 6.

50 Müller is aware of the close connection between Wallenstein and the Piccolomini. Expressly he states that the intrapersonal conflicts which dominate the second part of the trilogy are continued and resolved in the figure of Wallenstein himself, 'so daß seine Gestalt wahrhaft die Spitze der Pyramide wird' (op. cit. p. 130).

51 Critical opinion differs about the 'status' to be assigned to the astrological motif. Stahl is most emphatic in rejecting it as '. . . a ludicrous superstition, a *Fratze* . . .' (op. cit. pp. 101 ff.); Staiger, interpreting Wallenstein as a realist in the meaning of the term established in *Über naive und sentimentalische Dichtung*, argues that he 'sucht das Ewige im Vergänglichen. Er "verwechselt die Sphären" als . . . phantastischer Realist' (*Friedrich Schiller*, p. 35). Less negatively, v. Wiese defines Wallenstein's 'Sternenglauben' as lying in between 'Glauben und Aberglauben' (II, p. 654). At the other end of the spectrum, there are such positive readings as those of May and A. Beck. May stresses Wallenstein's astrological faith as being one of his truly humanizing features. 'Es gehört zum "Menschen",' he writes, 'daß er in der frommen Bindung stehe' (op. cit. p. 101). Similarly Beck reads Wallenstein's

'Religion ist in der Tiere Trieb' as an indication of his trust, 'religio' ('Die Krisis des Menschen im Drama des jungen Schiller', pp. 149 f.). It seems to me that v. Wiese comes closest to the meaning of Goethe's letter to Schiller of 8 Dec. 1798 in which we read: 'Diesen und ähnlichen Wahn möchte ich nicht einmal Aberglauben nennen, er liegt unserer Natur so nahe, ist so leidlich und läßlich als irgendein Glaube.' Before passing a negative verdict, it is also important to consider Goethe's reaction to the total work – with which he was so intimately familiar both in its intention and execution – in the letter to Schiller of 18 March 1799. There he stresses the 'Reinmenschliche' which, in the last part of the trilogy, gradually emerges from the veils of the political and even the historical in which it had been shrouded. In view of such an informed judgement it is difficult to regard Wallenstein's faith as no more than a *Fratze*.

52 This is a point already made by Petsch, op. cit. p. 180.

53 Witte strongly stresses the opportunistic lack of regard for others in Wallenstein's make-up (op. cit. pp. 159 f.).

54 This passage has been cited as an instance of that poetic carelessness or even ruthlessness which the old Goethe sometimes criticized in Schiller. How can one more step on the part of Wallenstein cause him to reach and touch vengeance when vengeance is envisaged as following him from behind? In fact, this is an image of great precision, in that it articulates the secret compulsiveness with which Wallenstein pursues Octavio who is, after all, his *böses Schicksal*. This unconscious reversal of the conscious configuration is perfectly expressed in *Pic.*, I. iii, when Octavio tells Questenberg

of the events preceding the battle of Lützen and concludes:

Seit jenem Tag verfolgt mich sein Vertrauen
In gleichem Maß, als ihn das meine flieht.

55 This secret, partial identity between Wallenstein and Max has been variously noted. Cf. Kommerell (*Geist und Buchstabe*, etc., pp. 148 f.), W. Binder who plainly states that Max is 'ein Teil Wallensteins' ('Die Begriffe "Naiv" und "Sentimentalisch"', etc.', p. 147), Müller (op. cit. p. 130), Storz (*Der Dichter F. Schiller*, p. 286) and Seidlin (op. cit. p. 128). Seidlin supports this claim by pointing to the interlacing of Wallenstein's dream (recounted in *Tod*, II. iii) and the reality of Max's death to which I have drawn attention as early as 1951, in my thesis for the Ph.D., pp. 128 f.

56 Cf. Chapter 6, pp. 142 ff., and Chapter 12.

57 This passage has been interpreted as variously as Wallenstein's end: as testifying to his hubris, his tragic deludedness or an inexplicable rejuvenation. As far as I know, no critic has taken into account the significance of the imagery Wallenstein uses here – i.e. the imagery of water – and placed it into the context of the meaning which has accrued to this imagery throughout the tragedy as a whole.

58 Cf. note 22 of this chapter.

59 The spectrum of critical opinion on the ideological basis of the *Wallenstein* trilogy is extremely wide. There are those who deny that any ultimate meaningfulness of destiny can be discerned in it and read the drama as testimony of a growing and radical metaphysical pessimism. Cf. H. Gumbel, op. cit., p. 147; H. Nohl, op. cit. p. 26; May, op. cit. pp. 164 f.; and Storz who apodictically

states: 'Die Weltgeschichte ist nunmehr ganz und gar ohne Weltgericht', but denies that this amounts to a personal poetic confession (*Der Dichter F. Schiller*, p. 293). Of late, the strongest case in this direction has been put forward by Staiger who characteristically entitles the opening chapter of his Schiller book 'Fremde des Lebens' and stresses the 'unwillkürliches Grauen' which pervades the *Wallenstein* trilogy, thus marking the poet's inner connectedness with the world view of the baroque (*Friedrich Schiller*, pp. 41 f.). Staiger repeatedly, and convincingly, regards 'einen nie überwundenen Ekel vor der Wirklichkeit' as Schiller's primary experience (ibid. pp. 27, 68 f. and 418). Storz pursues similar paths, both in 'Schiller's Dichtertum', *Schiller. Reden im Gedenkjahr 1955* (Stuttgart, 1955), pp. 126 ff., and in *Friedrich Schiller*, Athenäum Schriften 2 (Frankfurt and Bonn, 1960), pp. 14 ff. B. v. Wiese steers a middle course in reading the play as 'eine Tragödie der Nemesis' (II, p. 675). 'Nemesis dient Schiller sozusagen als poetische Chiffre für eine rätselhafte, rational nicht mehr begriffene, aber nichtsdestoweniger teleologisch in der Geschichte und über die Geschichte hinaus wirkende Macht' (ibid. p. 676).

The other extreme is represented by Fricke who writes: 'Auch das Schicksal ist kein bloßes Ungefähr, kein im Gewande der Notwendigkeit auftretender sinnleerer Zufall. . . . Es befindet sich in einem unsichtbaren, geheimen Bunde mit dem Sittlichen. Seine Notwendigkeit steht gleichsam als Urteilsvollstrecker im Dienste des Sittlichen.' (Op. cit. p. 12.) I believe that it is possible to concede the initial distrust and even disgust of life stressed by both Staiger and Storz and yet to maintain Schiller's belief in the ultimate meaningfulness of a monistic universe. The connecting link between the initial psychological response and the mature ideological position is to be found in the insights Schiller gained in his capacity as an artist. In this connection, cf. my Introduction.

60 Garland has noted the frequency of images of plants, 'and especially their seed, growth and bloom'. He draws the conclusion that 'Wallenstein's imagery serves to underline the element of mystic fatalism in his character, for it is a growth which is unamenable to control' (II, p. 187). Garland overlooks the fact that such insight is the result of a far-reaching development. Wallenstein's image here unequivocally suggests a belief in the possibility of prediction and control. Stahl notes the contrast between the tenor of the two speeches quoted on pp. 275–6 and the one in *Tod*, II. iii (quoted on p. 274), but in implicit contrast to Garland concludes that all but this last-named speech are tragic deviations from the determinism and fatalism appropriate to a realist (op. cit. pp. 97 f.).

61 In the face of a critic like Staiger who persistently denies these strata of Goethe's experiencing, it should suffice to bear in mind *Die natürliche Tochter* and, especially, the profound dread of disintegration evinced in III. ii and III. iv. In this connection, cf. Graham, *Goethe and Lessing*, etc., Chapters VII and XI.

62 This reading is diametrically opposed to that of Fricke who is concerned to deny Schiller's drama existential depth. Of Wallenstein he argues that he becomes guilty '. . . weil er sich des moralischen Majestätsrechtes jedes Menschen begeben hat' (op. cit. pp. 25 f.). This being a guilt which is in a higher sense

moral, we have the consolation 'daß es so nur dem Realisten gehen kann' (ibid. p. 26). It seems that whether Schiller articulates the tragedy of the idealist or the realist, he cannot measure up to Fricke's expectations. In the one case the 'Idea', and in the other Fate 'consumes' 'das Menschlich-Individuelle . . .' (ibid. p. 28).

63 Garland takes the maternal imagery as revealing Wallenstein's 'impurity of motive' (II, p. 159). Similarly, May considers Wallenstein's reminiscences of Max's youth to be 'stark sentimental aufgeschwemmt . . .' (op. cit. p. 144).

64 Cf. Chapter 12.

65 In this connection cf. Graham, *Goethe and Lessing*, etc., Chapters VII and XI. In general it may be said that Goethe, on the whole, confidently accepts the metamorphosis of any given 'Gestalt' which the pregnant moment illuminates. The imagery drawn from the organic sphere which is used to articulate such life process is overwhelmingly positive in its connotation. One need only think of *Hermann und Dorothea* to appreciate the gulf between Goethe and Schiller for all that they operate with the same aesthetic tool: the pregnant moment. Nevertheless one should not gloss over the fact that Goethe too, for all his life-acceptingness and flexibility, deeply mourns transience. *Die natürliche Tochter* permits of no doubt of this fact, and indeed the many glimpses we gain into his response to death, in his life as well as in his works, confirm this.

66 Letter to Körner, 27 Dec. 1796.

67 *Werke, J.A.*, VIII, pp. 121 and 246 ff.

68 *AGA*, 13, pp. 421 f.

69 Ibid. p. 29.

70 Cf. Graham, *Goethe and Lessing*, etc., Chapters VII and XI.

71 Letter to Goethe, 19 March 1799.

Chapter 12

1 *SA*, 12, pp. 272 f.

2 Cf. Elisabeth's '. . . Mit hohen Tugenden / Muß ich die Blöße meines Rechts bedecken . . .' (IV. x). The image is closely linked with that of the *Mantel* which is an *Ehrenmantel* but stained (cf. the last speech of I. vii). This imagery is closely interwoven with the plot. The attempt on Elisabeth fails because 'Der Stoß ging fehl, der Mantel fing ihn auf / Und Shrewsbury entwaffnete den Mörder' (III. viii). Elisabeth has not yet shown her hand, and her pretended virtue has once more been her saving.

3 Cf. Chapter 7, pp. 153 ff., and Appelbaum-Graham, 'The Structure of the Personality in Schiller's Tragic Poetry', pp. 112 ff.

4 Cf. Chapter 7.

5 For the same conclusion reached on the evidence of Schiller's theory, cf. Schiller, *On the Aesthetic Education of Man*, ed. cit. pp. lx and lxxxix.

6 *Briefe über Don Carlos*, Dritter Brief, *SA*, 16, p. 58.

7 *Über das Pathetische*, *SA*, 11, p. 249, and *Über die Tragische Kunst*, ibid. p. 177.

8 *SA*, 11, p. 146.

9 Ibid. p. 246.

10 Ibid. pp. 246 f.

11 Ibid. p. 173.

12 Cf. E. Bullough (*Aesthetics*, ed E. M. Wilkinson), who has coinded the concept of the *Antinomy of Distance* with which I am here operating (pp. 98 ff.).

13 In *Friedrich Schiller*, pp. 280 ff.

14 *SA*, 11, p. 172.

15 *SA*, 12, pp. 102 f.

16 By Staiger, in *Friedrich Schiller*, p. 283.

17 Cf. Chapters 1, 2, 3 and 11.

18 *Über das Pathetische*, *SA*, 11, p. 262.

19 *SA*, 12, p. 281.

20 *SA*, 16, p. 127.

21 Ibid.

22 In this connection, cf. *Die Braut von Messina*, ed. E. F. George, Nelson's German Texts (London and Edinburgh, 1956). After a careful analysis of Don Cesar's motivation in the final scenes, George concludes that his 'desire for purification . . . is mingled with considerations of envy and as such to a great extent vitiated' (p. xxv). Staiger stresses the presence of jealousy and envy and roundly denies Don Cesar's title to sublimity (*Friedrich Schiller*, pp. 407 f.). Similarly, Stahl emphasizes the impurity of the motive – 'a passionate urge' – which drives him into suicide. According to him, Schiller 'portrayed the defeat of that ideal' [i.e. of sublimity] 'through the supremacy of passion' (op. cit. pp. 132 f.).

23 This would seem to be the position of Stahl (op. cit. p. 40) and of Storz (*Der Dichter F. Schiller*, pp. 143 ff.).

24 The most sensitive appraisal of Don Cesar's development comes from Walzel (ed. *SA*, 7, pp. xvii f.). He writes: '. . . Schiller hat dafür gesorgt, daß er unter dem Druck der Verhältnisse des Besten bewußt wird, das in ihm liegt. In meisterhafter Steigerung läutert Schiller dem Todesentschluß, bis Cesar in voller Freiheit, nicht um selbstischer Motive willen, sondern um dem Recht seinen Lauf zu lassen, die Strafe an sich vollstreckt.'

25 This inner-psychological aspect of Don Cesar's development is stressed by v. Wiese who speaks of his 'festlichen Tod . . . mit dem der Sterbende und durch sein Sterben Entsühnte sich wieder vereinigt' (II, p. 757).

26 On 12 December 1797.

27 On 28 November 1796. This poetic

function has been missed by Garland who criticizes Schiller's 'failure to link their beauty [i.e. that of the love scenes] with the harsh realism of the baser world around them' and considers this to be a significant flaw in a remarkable play (I, p. 208). Stahl, too, argues that the love-idyll remains extraneous to the economy of the play as a whole (op. cit. p. 96). Jolles, on the other hand, emphasizes the connection between the lovers and their love with the aesthetic mode. (Cf. 'Das Bild des Weges und die Sprache des Herzens. Zur strukturellen Funktion der sprachlichen Bilder in Schiller's *Wallenstein*', pp. 137 f.)

28 Witte finds it 'irritating to see both Max and Thekla so priggishly conscious of their own (and each other's) "moral grace"' (*Wallenstein*, ed. cit. p. xxxvi). Storz takes a positive view more akin to my own (*Der Dichter F. Schiller*, pp. 289 and 296).

29 By E. M. Wilkinson and L. A. Willoughby, to whose elucidation of this pattern of Schiller's thinking and its diagrammatic presentation I am indebted. (Schiller, *On the Aesthetic Education of Man*, ed. cit. pp. lxxxv ff. and 350.)

30 In *Über die notwendigen Grenzen beim Gebrauch schöner Formen*, *SA*, 12, p. 146.

31 Storz takes strong exception to Max's appeal to Thekla for compassion and understanding. He finds it inconsistent with Max's clear perception of the situation as a whole and dismisses the very idea that Thekla could misunderstand his motives as 'ungereint' (*Der Dichter F. Schiller*, p. 304).

32 This scene has come under critical fire from H. Schneider and L. Blumenthal who take exception to the fact that 'der junge Offizier aus der Geliebten Mund die Richtlinie seines Handels empfangen muß

. . .' (*NA*, 8, pp. 383 and 395). This is the editors' chief reason for denying to Max the 'Höhe des tragischen Heldentums' (ibid. p. 395). For a similar judgement cf. Minor (in *SA*, 5, p. xxxvi).

33 *Minna von Barnhelm* (V. v).

34 Storz considers Max's belated discovery of Wallenstein's presence as improbable in the extreme (*Der Dichter F. Schiller*, p. 304).

35 This is strenuously denied by Fricke for whom Max is a 'Jüngling' – 'liebenswürdig, unreif, Phraseur, Pathetiker und Held aus Mangel an Wirklichkeit, wie es Jünglinge wohl sind' (op. cit. p. 28). Fricke's judgement here is quite consistent with his general thesis that Schiller's idealistic anthropology with its dichotomous partition of the personality into a moral and a sense-being makes an absolute, existential tragedy all but impossible. The hero, however threatened in his sensuous self, is always free to dissociate himself from that truly existential stratum of his being by a timely escape into the 'heilige Freiheit der Geister'. To disprove this slick and dangerous thesis is one of the major purposes of this book. Cf. Chapter 4, note 17.

36 Cf. p. 305 of this chapter.

37 Staiger, in *Stilwandel: Studien zur Vorgeschichte der Goethezeit* (Zürich and Freiburg, 1963), p. 44.

38 Staiger, *Friedrich Schiller*, pp. 288 ff.

39 E. Bullough, *Aesthetics*, ed. E. M. Wilkinson (London, 1957), pp. 66 f.

40 Goethe, *Polarität* (*AGA*, 16, p. 864).

41 For a diametrically opposed view, cf. *NA*, 21 (ed. H. Koopmann and B. v. Wiese, p. 189, note to 196, 14).

42 Staiger, *Grundbegriffe der Poetik*, 3rd ed. (Zürich, 1956), p. 151.

43 In *Der Tod in Venedig* (Berlin, 1921), p. 24.

44 *SA*, 12, p. 279. As against that,

Stahl argues that Max attains to moral rather than aesthetic greatness (op. cit. p. 95).

45 *SA*, 11, p. 159.

46 The ethos of helpfulness implicit in Karl's last words is stressed by Schwerte, 'Schillers "Räuber"', pp. 164 ff.

47 George stresses the healing function of Beatrice's love (ed. cit. pp. xxiv f.).

48 *On the Aesthetic Education of Man* (ed. cit. p. lxxxvii).

49 Letter XXIII, footnote § 3. In this connection, cf. Wilkinson, *Schiller: Poet or Philosopher?* (p. 11) and *On the Aesthetic Education of Man* (ed. cit. and 272).

50 The difference between my account and the view expressed by Wilkinson and Willoughby (ed. cit. pp. lxxxvii–lxxxix) may not be as absolute as it appears. I base my conclusions upon the analysis of Schiller's poetic work in the first instance, whilst they are exclusively concerned with his theory. This divergence may serve as a reminder that a poet may not be his own best theoretician, and that inferences from theory to practice should be drawn with the greatest caution, if at all, an insight which is gradually becoming more widespread.

51 Cf. Chapter 9, pp. 214 f.

52 *SA*, 12, p. 308.

53 Ibid. pp. 308 f.

54 *SA*, 11, p. 158.

55 In 'Mind and Medium in Art', *Aesthetics*, p. 150.

56 *Über Bürgers Gedichte*, *SA*, 16, pp. 239 f.

57 *SA*, 12, pp. 280 f.

58 Witte, op. cit. p. 166.

59 *SA*, 11, p. 220.

60 *SA*, 12, p. 27.

61 *SA*, 12, p. 91.

62 *Kritik der Praktischen Vernunft*, *Werke*, ed. Wilhelm Weischedel, Insel-Verlag (Wiesbaden, 1960), Vol. IV, p. 207. Cf. also Kant's emphatic and repeated denial that, as 'Menschen und . . . erschaffene vernünftige Wesen . . . wir . . . jemals in den Besitz einer *Heiligkeit* des Willens kommen könnten' (ibid. pp. 203 f.).

63 Ibid. p. 192.

64 Ibid. p. 196.

65 Ibid. p. 199.

66 Ibid. p. 203.

67 This point is emphatically and repeatedly made by Ernst Cassirer (*Kants Leben und Lehre* (Berlin, 1921)). Throughout the book he argues that Kant's assumption of a dualistic position – and the resultant moral rigorism – are due, not (as Schiller and others at times suspected) to a monkish and ascetic disposition, but to his epistemological intent to expound systematically, in the cognitive sphere, the possibility of *a priori* synthetic judgements and, in the practical sphere, of universal, i.e. objective moral judgements. In this connection, cf. Schiller's letters to Goethe of 22 [21] Dec. 1798 and 2 Aug. 1799.

68 *Kritik der Praktischen Vernunft* (ed. cit. p. 201).

69 *Über Anmut und Würde*, *SA*, 11, p. 217.

70 Ibid. p. 221.

71 Ibid.

72 *SA*, 12, p. 157.

73 Ibid.

74 Letter XXIII, *SA*, 12, p. 92.

75 Accordingly, the association of the sublime act with self-abnegation which is all but universally maintained by Schiller scholars, in my view rests on a misunderstanding. Even Wilkinson, by far the subtlest commentator on this aspect of Schiller's thought, writes that the sublime '. . . exceeds all our expectations of the heights of self-abnegation to which a man might attain' (*Schiller: Poet or Philosopher?* p. 11). The notion is misleading on two counts: psychologi-

cally, because our vital drives are needed as the energies that will implement any principle perceived by reason; and morally, because only in so far as they freely endorse that principle will the ensuing action be noble or, in Schiller's own sense, sublime.

Bibliography

ALEXANDER, S. *Beauty and other Forms of Value*. London, 1933.

ALTHAUS, H. *Laokoon Stoff und Form*. Berne and Munich, 1968.

APPELBAUM-GRAHAM, I. 'The Structure of the Personality in Schiller's Tragic Poetry'. In F. Norman (ed.), *Schiller*. Bicentenary Lectures. London, 1960.

AUERBACH, E. *Mimesis*. Berne, 1946.

AYRAULT, R. 'La figure de Mortimer dans Marie Stuart et la conception du drame historique chez Schiller'. *Études Germaniques*, 4 (1959).

BECK, A. 'Die Krisis des Menschen im Drama des jungen Schiller'. In *Schiller in unserer Zeit. Beiträge zum Schillerjahr 1955*. Ed. Schiller-Komitee 55. Weimar, 1955.

——'Maria Stuart'. In *Das Deutsche Drama*. Ed. B. von Wiese. Vol. I. Düsseldorf, 1960.

BELLERMANN, L. *Schillers Dramen. Beiträge zu ihrem Verständnis*. Berlin, 1898.

BERGER, K. *Schiller: Sein Leben und seine Werke*. Munich, 1914.

BINDER, W. 'Die Begriffe "Naiv" und "Sentimentalisch" in Schillers Drama'. *JbdDSG*, 4 (1960).

——'Schiller: Kabale und Liebe'. *Das Deutsche Drama*. Ed. B. von Wiese. Vol. I. Düsseldorf, 1960.

——'Schillers Demetrius'. *Euphorion*, Dritte Folge, 53. Band (1959).

BÖCKMANN, P. 'Die innere Form in Schillers Jugenddramen'. *DuV*, 35 (1934).

——'Politik und Dichtung im Werk Fr. Schillers'. *Schiller. Reden im Gedenkjahr 1955*. Stuttgart, 1955.

——'Gedanke, Wort und Tat in Schillers Dramen'. *JbdDSG*, 4 (1960).

BRADLEY, A. C. *Oxford Lectures on Poetry*. London, 1926.

BUCHWALD, R. *Schiller*. Leipzig, 1937.

BULLOUGH, E. *Aesthetics, Lectures and Essays*. Ed. E. M. Wilkinson. London, 1957.

CASSIRER, E. *An Essay on Man*. New Haven, 1944.

——*Kants Leben und Lehre*. Berlin, 1921.

CASTLE, E. 'Der falsche Demetrius in der Auffassung Schillers und Hebbels'. *JFDH* (1930).

CRANSTON, M. *Sartre*. Writers and Critics. Edinburgh, 1962, 1965 and 1970.

CUNNINGHAM, K. *Schiller und die französische Klassik*. Bonn, 1930.

CYSARZ, H. *Schiller*. Halle/Saale. 1934.

DEUBEL, W. 'Umrisse eines neuen Schillerbildes'. *JbdGG*, 20 (1934).

DEUTSCHER KULTURBUND (ed.) *Schiller: 1759–1959*. Berlin, 1959.

ELLIS, C. *The Pebbles on the Beach*. London, 1969.

EMRICH, W. *Die Symbolik von Faust II*. Frankfurt, 1964.

FOWLER, F. 'Schiller's Fiesco Re-examined'. *PEGS*, New Series, Vol. XL (1969–70).

———'The Riddle of Schiller's "Demetrius"'. *MLR*, LXI, No. 3 (July 1966).

FRICKE, G. 'Die Problematik des Tragischen im Drama Schillers'. *JFDH* (1930).

GAEDE, U. *Schiller und Nietzsche als Verkünder einer tragischen Kultur*. Berlin, 1908.

GARLAND, H. B. *Schiller*. London, 1949.

———*Schiller the Dramatic Writer: A Study of Style in the Plays*. Oxford, 1969.

GAUDIG, H. *Schillers Dramen II. Aus Deutscher Dichtung*. Vol. XIII. Leipzig and Berlin, 1914.

GEERDTS, H. J. *Deutsche Literaturgeschichte in einem Band*. Berlin, 1967.

GERHARD, M. *Schiller*. Berne, 1950.

GRAHAM, I. *Schiller: A Master of the Tragic Form: His Theory in his Practice*. Pittsburgh, 1974.

———*Goethe and Lessing: The Wellsprings of Creation*. London and New York, 1973.

GRONICKA, A. von. 'Friedrich Schiller's Marquis Posa'. *GR*, XXVI (1951).

GRUMACH, E. *Goethe und die Antike: Eine Sammlung*. 2 vols. Berlin, 1949.

GUMBEL, H. 'Die realistische Wendung des späten Schiller'. *JFDH* (1932–3).

HAMBURGER, K. 'Schiller und Sartre'. *JbdDSG*, 3 (1959).

———'Zum Problem des Idealismus bei Schiller'. *JbdDSG*, 4 (1960).

HARNACK, O. *Schiller*. Berlin, 1905.

HEIDEGGER, M. *Sein und Zeit*. 5th ed. Halle/Saale, 1941.

HEISELER, B. von. *Schiller*. Trans. Bednall. London, 1962.

IDE, H. 'Zur Problematik der Schiller-Interpretation, Überlegungen zur Jungfrau von Orleans'. *Jahrbuch der Wittheit zu Bremen*, Vol. VIII (1964).

JAEGER, H. 'Schillers Philosophie der Existenz'. In J. R. Frey (ed.), *Schiller 1759–1959. Commemorative American Studies*. Urbana, Ill., 1959.

JOLLES, M. 'Das Bild des Weges und die Sprache des Herzens. Zur strukturellen Funktion der sprachlichen Bilder in Schillers *Wallenstein*'. *Deutsche Beiträge zur geistigen Überlieferung*, V (1965).

———'Die Sprache des "Spiels" und "Antispiels" in den frühen Dramen Schillers'. *M.Ph.*, 58, No. 4 (1961).

KAHN, L. W. 'Freedom: An Existentialist and an Idealist'. *PMLA*, LXIV, No. 1, Part 1 (1949).

KINDERMANN, H. *Theatergeschichte der Goethezeit*. Vienna, 1948.

KOHLSCHMIDT, W. 'Tells Entscheidung'. *Gedenkjahr 59*. Stuttgart, 1961.

KOMMERELL, M. *Der Dichter als Führer in der deutschen Klassik*. Berlin, 1928.

———*Geist und Buchstabe der Dichtung*. Frankfurt am Main. 1939.

KOOPMAN, H. *Schiller Kommentar*. Munich, 1969.

KORFF, H. A. *Geist der Goethezeit*. Leipzig, 1954.

KOSTA, E. K. *Schiller and Russian Literature*. Philadelphia, 1965.

KÜHNEMANN, E. *Schiller*. Munich, 1905.

LAING, R. D. *The Self and Others*. London, 1961.

LINN, R. M. 'Wallenstein's Innocence'. *The Germanic Review: J. F. Schiller*, Vol. XXXIV, No. 3 (October 1959).

LÖHNEYSEN, W. Frh. von (ed). *Goethe Propyläen*. Stuttgart, 1965.

LUDWIG, O. *Shakespeare-Studien, Ludwigs Werke*. Ed. A. Eloesser. Goldene Klassiker-Bibliothek. Berlin, Leipzig, Vienna and Stuttgart, n.d.

MANN, T. *Versuch über Schiller*. Stockholmer Gesamtausgabe. Nachlese. Prosa, 1956.

——'Goethe und Tolstoi, Fragmente zum Problem der Humanität'. In *Adel des Geistes*. Stockholm, 1955.

MARTINI, F. 'Schillers "Kabale und Liebe". Bemerkungen zur Interpretation des "Bürgerlichen Trauerspiels"'. *DdU*, 5 (1952).

——'Wilhelm Tell, der ästhetische Staat und der ästhetische Mensch'. *DdU*, 12 (1960).

MAY, K. *Friedrich Schiller: Idee und Wirklichkeit im Drama*. Göttingen, 1948.

MCKAY, G. W. 'Three Scenes fron Wilhelm Tell'. In P. F. Ganz (ed.), *The Discontinuous Tradition*. Studies in German Literature in Honour of E. L. Stahl. Oxford, 1971.

MILLER, R. D. *The Drama of Schiller*. Harrogate, 1966.

MINOR, J. *Schiller, sein Leben und seine Werke*. Berlin, 1890.

MOORE, W. G. 'A New Reading of "Wilhelm Tell"'. *German Studies Presented to H. G. Fiedler*. Oxford, 1938.

MÜLLER, J. *Das Edle in der Freiheit: Schillerstudien*. Leipzig, 1959.

MUSCHG, W. *Die Tragödie der Freiheit*. Berne and Munich, 1959.

NOHL, H. *Friedrich Schiller*. Frankfurt am Main, 1954.

NOLTE, F. *Lessings Laokoon*. Lancaster, Pa., 1940.

PAULSEN, W. 'Friedrich Schiller 1955–1959. Ein Literaturbericht'. *JbdDSG*, 6 (1962).

PETSCH, R. *Freiheit und Notwendigkeit in Schillers Dramen*. Munich, 1905.

PRADER, F. 'Schiller und Sophokles'. *Zürcher Beiträge zur deutschen Literatur und Geistesgeschichte*. Ed. Staiger. No. 7 (1954).

REISS, H. 'The Concept of the Aesthetic State in the work of Schiller and Novalis'. *PEGS*, XXVI (1956–7).

ROBERTSON, J. G. *Schiller after a Century*. Edinburgh and London, 1905.

SARTRE, J.-P. *L'Existentialisme est un humanisme*. Paris, 1946.

——*L'Être et le néant*. Paris, 1943.

——*Being and Nothingness*. Trans. H. E. Barnes. London, 1969.

SCHNAPP, F. 'Schiller über seinen "Wilhelm Tell", mit unbekannten Dokumenten'. *Deutsche Rundschau*, 206 (1926).

SCHNEIDER, R. 'Tragik und Erlösung im Weltbild Schillers'. *Schiller. Reden im Gedenkjahr 1955*. Stuttgart, 1955.

SCHULTZ, F. *Epochen der deutschen Literatur*. Stuttgart, 1952.

SCHWERTE, H. 'Schiller's "Räuber"'. In *Interpretationen 2. Deutsche Dramen von Gryphius bis Brecht*. Frankfurt, 1965.

SEIDLIN, O. 'Wallenstein: Sein und Zeit'. *Von Goethe zu Thomas Mann. Zwölf Versuche*. Göttingen, 1963.

SILZ, W. 'Chorus and Choral Function in Schiller'. In J. R. Frey (ed.), *Schiller 1759–1959. Commemorative American Studies*. Urbana, Ill., 1959.

STAHL, E. L. *Friedrich Schiller's Drama: Theory and Practice*. Oxford, 1954.

STAIGER, E. *Friedrich Schiller*. Zürich, 1967.

——*Die Zeit als Einbildungskraft des Dichters*. Zürich, 1963.

——*Stilwandel: Studien zur Vorgeschichte der Goethezeit*. Zürich and Freiburg, 1963.

———*Grundbegriffe der Poetik.* 3rd ed. Zürich, 1956.
STORZ, G. *Der Dichter Friedrich Schiller.* Stuttgart, 1959.
———*Friedrich Schiller.* Athenäum Schriften 2. Frankfurt and Bonn, 1960.
———*Wallensteins Lager, Die Piccolomini, Wallensteins Tod.* Dokumente, Rowohlts Klassiker der Literatur und Wissenschaft. Leck/Schleswig, 1967.
———'Die Struktur des Don Carlos'. *JbdDSG,* 4 (1960).
———'Maria Stuart'. *Interpretationen 2. Deutsche Dramen von Gryphius bis Brecht.* Frankfurt, 1965.
———'Die Jungfrau von Orleans', *Das Deutsche Drama.* Ed. B. von Wiese. Vol. I. Düsseldorf, 1960.
———'Schillers Dichtertum'. *Schiller. Reden im Gedenkjahr 1955.* Stuttgart, 1955.
VOSS DER JÜNGERE, H. *Schillers Gespräche.* Ed. Frh. von Biedermann. Munich, n.d.
WALZEL, O. *Schiller und die Romantik: Vom Geistesleben des 18. und 19. Jahrhunderts.* Leipzig, 1911.
WELLEK, R., and WARREN, A. *Theory of Literature.* New York, 1949.
WIESE, B. von. *Die Dramen Schillers. Politik und Tragödie.* Leipzig, 1937.
———*Schiller.* Stuttgart, 1959–63.
———*Die deutsche Tragödie von Lessing bis Hebbel.* Hamburg, 1948.
———(ed.) *Das Deutsche Drama.* 2 vols. Düsseldorf, 1960.
WILKINSON, E. M. *Schiller: Poet or Philosopher?* Special Taylorian Lecture. Oxford, 1961.
———'Reflections after translating Schiller's *Letters on the Aesthetic Education of Man'.* In F. Norman (ed.), *Schiller.* Bicentenary Lectures. London, 1960.
———and WILLOUGHBY, L. A. *Goethe Poet and Thinker.* London, 1962.
WITTE, W. *Schiller.* Oxford, 1949.
WITTKOWSKI, W. 'Demetrius – Schiller und Hebbel'. *JbdDSG,* 3 1959.
UNDERHILL, E. *Worship.* Fontana Library. London, 1962.

Schiller Texts

Die Braut von Messina. Ed. E. F. George. Nelson's German Texts. London and Edinburgh, 1956.
Kabale und Liebe. Ed. E. M. Wilkinson and L. A. Willoughby. Blackwell's German Texts. Oxford, 1944.
Maria Stuart. Ed. W. Witte. Macmillan's Modern Language Texts. London, Melbourne, Toronto, 1965.
Die Räuber. Ed. C. P. Magill and L. A. Willoughby. Blackwell's German Texts. Oxford, 1949.
Wilhelm Tell. Ed. H. B. Garland. Harrap's German Classics. London, 1957.
Wilhelm Tell. Ed. W. Mainland. Macmillan's Modern Language Texts. London, Melbourne, Toronto, 1968.
Wallenstein. Ed. W. Witte. Blackwell's German Texts. Oxford, 1952.
On the Aesthetic Education of Man. In a Series of Letters. Ed. and trans. E. M. Wilkinson and L. A. Willoughby. Oxford, 1967.
Der Briefwechsel zwischen Schiller und Goethe. Ed. E. Staiger. Frankfurt, 1966.

Index